FOR ORGANS, PIANOS & ELECTRONIC KEYBOARDS

E-Z PLAY® TODAY

360

More 100 Years of Song
1900-1999

ISBN 0-634-00992-3

HAL•LEONARD®
CORPORATION

7777 W. BLUEMOUND RD. P.O. BOX 13819 MILWAUKEE, WI 53213

Visit Hal Leonard Online at
www.halleonard.com

More 100 Years of Song

More 100 Years of Song

Alphabetical Listing

Note: In many cases a song's popularity hit its peak in a year (or years, occasionally) after it was written.

A BIRD IN A GILDED CAGE

1900

Words by Arthur J. Lamb, Music by Harry Von Tilzer. This was one of the most successful of the sentimental ballads that were tremendously popular in the early 1900s. Von Tilzer agreed to set Lamb's lyric to music, but only if it was altered to make it clear that the unhappy woman the lyric described was a rich man's wife and not his mistress. Following its introduction – in a brothel, of all places (ironic, considering Von Tilzer's puritanical concerns) – the song sold more than two million copies of sheet music.

THE AMERICAN PATROL

1901

Music by F.W. Meacham. Although this march was written in the 1880s, it did not become a national favorite until John Philip Sousa's band recorded it in 1901. Sousa recorded it again during World War I, as did Charles Adam Prince's orchestra. Glenn Miller and his orchestra recorded their famous march/swing arrangement of the tune in 1942. It was also heard in the 1954 film *The Glenn Miller Story*.

ON A SUNDAY AFTERNOON

1902

Words by Andrew B. Sterling, Music by Harry Von Tilzer. Von Tilzer was on the beach one day when he heard someone say, "People work hard on Monday, but one day that's fun is Sunday." He talked Sterling into working the line into a song lyric. The result was one of Von Tilzer's most successful ballads, selling more than two million copies of sheet music in its first year alone. Von Tilzer and Sterling's song is not to be confused with the 1935 song of the same name by Arthur Freed and Nacio Herb Brown.

IN THE GOOD OLD SUMMERTIME

1903

Words by Ren Shields, Music by George Evans. One summer day in 1902, George Evans was dining with a few show business friends, when he made a remark in passing, saying that some people might like the winter, but he himself preferred the good old summertime. Singer Blanche Ring suggested that he write a song on the topic. She introduced it later that year in the musical *The Defender*. Publishers shied away from the tune, believing that seasonal songs would only sell during the three-month window of the season they described. "In the Good Old Summertime" broke that stereotype, keeping strong sales throughout the year.

GIVE MY REGARDS TO BROADWAY

1904

Words and Music by George M. Cohan. "Give My Regards to Broadway" was introduced by Cohan playing the title role in the 1904 musical *Little Johnny Jones*. It served as the title song in the 1948 film *Give My Regards to Broadway* and was heard in such films as *Yankee Doodle Dandy* (1942), *Jolson Sings Again* (1949), and *With a Song in My Heart* (1952). Cohan's famous tune remains the unofficial anthem of The Great White Way.

IN MY MERRY OLDSMOBILE

1905

Words by Vincent P. Bryan, Music by Gus Edwards. Just as bicycle songs had been popular in the heyday of the bike, automobile songs took over as cars appeared on American roads. "In My Merry Oldsmobile" was inspired by a cross country trip, from Detroit to Portland, Oregon, designed to publicize the Oldsmobile. The song became part of the commercial campaign. It was heard in the 1944 film *The Merry Monahans*, and was also used at various times in radio and television advertising for Oldsmobile.

I LOVE YOU TRULY

1906

Words and Music by Carrie Jacobs-Bond. "I Love You Truly" appeared in 1901 in a collection of art songs entitled *Seven Songs*. It did not become a hit until it was published as a single song in 1906, and crossed from art song to popular song. Bing Crosby recorded "I Love You Truly" in 1934 on the first disc released by the new Decca label. For decades the song was a standard at weddings. Beyond the wedding service, many brides and grooms throughout the country danced their first dance as a married couple to this song.

MY GAL SAL

1907

Words and Music by Paul Dresser. Also known as "They Called Her Frivolous Sal," this was Paul Dresser's last hit song. Dresser's career was in a shambles when he wrote it. His sentimental ballads were no longer in fashion, his fortunes had been frivolously spent, and he was discovering that his good friends were of the fair-weather variety. Dresser was certain he could still produce a hit, which he did. Unfortunately "My Gal Sal" sold more than two million copies, but only just after Dresser died.

CUDDLE UP A LITTLE CLOSER, LOVEY MINE

1908

Words by Otto Hauerbach, Music by Karl Hoschna. This was Otto Hauerbach's first hit. Not long after its success he altered his last name to the more American sounding "Harbach." Hauerbach and Hoschna intended the song for a vaudeville revue, but placed it in the operetta *The Three Twins* (1908) instead. The song was heard in several films, including *Birth of the Blues* (1941), *Coney Island* (1943), *Is Everybody Happy?* (1943), *The Story of Vernon and Irene Castle* (1939), and *On Moonlight Bay* (1951). It is heard as background music in the 1960 film *Tall Story*. Harbach went on to have a major songwriting career writing with several composers, producing hits such as "Smoke Gets in Your Eyes," "Indian Love Call," "Who?," and "Yesterdays."

BY THE LIGHT OF THE SILVERY MOON

1909

Words by Edward Madden, Music by Gus Edwards. Little Georgie Price, a child star in one of Gus Edwards' vaudeville revues, introduced this song in *School Boys and Girls*. Following a gimmick of the time, Price sang it while seated in the audience, under the pretense of an innocent cherub who expectedly bursts into song. That same year vaudeville star Lillian Lorraine sang in the *Ziegfeld Follies of 1909*. In 1933, after Ziegfeld's death, the Ziegfeld Theater was reopened. On opening night Gus Edwards brought Lillian Lorraine onto the stage and invited her to sing "By the Light of the Silvery Moon." She began the song, but broke into tears, overcome by nostalgia, and was unable to finish. This tune was one of the most featured songs in musical films of the 1940s and early '50s, when nostalgia for the early years of the century was in fashion. It was heard in the movies *The Story of Vernon and Irene Castle* (sung by Fred Astaire), *Birth of the Blues* (performed by Guy Lombardo), *Babes on Broadway* (sung by Judy Garland), *Hello, Frisco, Hello* (sung by Alice Faye), *The Jolson Story* (sung by Al Jolson), and *Two Weeks in Love* (sung by Jane Powell). The hit song became a hit movie in 1952's *By the Light of the Silvery Moon*, starring Doris Day.

MEET ME TONIGHT IN DREAMLAND

1910

Words by Beth Slater Whitson, Music by Leo Friedman. Whitson and Friedman made almost nothing from the two million copies of sheet music sold of this song. Their publisher, Leo Rossiter, had bought the song's rights outright and thus owed the songwriters nothing. Rossiter's brother Will opened a rival publishing house in 1910, promising to pay royalties to songwriters. Whitson and Friedman took their next ballad to him and made a fortune from that song, entitled "Let Me Call You Sweetheart." "Meet Me Tonight in Dreamland" was revived in the 1949 film *In the Good Old Summertime*, sung by Judy Garland.

PUT YOUR ARMS AROUND ME, HONEY

1911

Words by Junie McCree, Music by Albert Von Tilzer. It was introduced to vaudeville audiences in 1910 by singer/dancer Blossom Seeley. The song was heard in the 1944 film *Louisiana Hayride* (performed by the queen of the B musical, Judy Canova), and sung by Judy Garland in the 1949 film *In the Good Old Summertime*. "Put Your Arms Around Me, Honey" was given an unlikely revival in 1961 by "Fats" Domino.

MY MELANCHOLY BABY

1912

Words by George A. Norton, Music by Ernie Burnett. Burnett turned out to be a one-hit wonder with this tune. In fact, he may not have written the song at all. Heard in such films as *The Birth of the Blues* (1941) and *A Star Is Born* (1953), the song has been in legal dispute several times. In 1940 Burnett's former wife, Maybelle E. Watson, went to court alleging that she had written the song's lyric. She won damages on back royalties. In 1965 the song was back in court as Alan Light, son of songwriter Ben Light, alleged that his father had written this song but never taken credit for it.

PEG O' MY HEART

1913

Words by Alfred Bryan, Music by Fred Fisher. It first appeared in the *Ziegfeld Follies of 1913*. It was inspired by a successful Broadway comedy of the same name that had opened a year earlier. The song was dedicated to legendary actress Laurette Taylor, who had starred in the Broadway production. "Peg O' My Heart" served as the title song for a 1933 film, and was heard in the 1949 film *Oh, You Beautiful Doll*. The Harmonicats recorded it in 1947, selling over a million records.

BALLIN' THE JACK

1914

Words by Jim Burris, Music by Chris Smith. This ragtime dance piece was introduced in vaudeville by Billy Kent and Jeanette Warner in 1913. The lyric offers no clue as to the meaning of the phrase "ballin' the jack." Eddie Cantor sang it in vaudeville, making it a staple of his repertoire. When "Ballin' the Jack" was heard in the 1942 film *For Me and My Gal*, sung by Judy Garland, it landed on the Hit Parade. Danny Kaye sang the song for years and included it in the film *On the Riviera* (1951). Chubby Checker popularized a twist-styled version of the song.

THEY DIDN'T BELIEVE ME

1915

Words by Michael E. Rourke (Herbert Reynolds), Music by Jerome Kern. "They Didn't Believe Me" appeared in Jerome Kern's first successful musical, *The Girl from Utah* (1914). This was also the first Kern song to become a pop standard. According to legend, when Kern played this song for Victor Herbert, the elder songwriter is said to have commented, "This man will inherit my mantle." More than one historian has cited "They Didn't Believe Me" as the first song in the backbeat, fox trot ballad style. Because of this fresh American musical style, Kern was the model for many songwriters growing up at the time, including George Gershwin and Richard Rodgers.

I LOVE A PIANO

1916

Words and Music by Irving Berlin. Composer Irving Berlin really did love a piano – the one that allowed him to play in various keys. Berlin, an incomparable songwriter, was an extremely limited pianist who could not put his own music on paper. He used a transposing piano, which shifted keys via a large lever that actually moved the keyboard. Berlin referred to the piano as "the Buick." "I Love a Piano" was heard on stage in *Stop! Look! Listen!* (1915), and became popular around the country the next year. Judy Garland and Fred Astaire revived it memorably in *Easter Parade* (1948). The original lyric included the phrase "when Padarewski comes this way." Later, when that piano virtuoso was no longer as well-known, Berlin revised the line to "not only music from Broadway."

FOR ME AND MY GAL
1917

Words by Edgar Leslie and E. Ray Goetz, Music by George W. Meyer. One of the biggest sheet music sellers of 1917, topping three million copies, this song was just another day at work for composer George W. Meyer. "I sat down to and went to work," he said when talking about the song years later. "There was nothing remarkable about it. I was writing songs for a living and I needed the money so I wrote the ballad." Such famous performers as Sophie Tucker, Eddie Cantor, George Jessel and Al Jolson all put the song in their repertoires. Gene Kelly made his movie debut in *For Me and My Gal* (1942), and sweetly crooned the title song with Judy Garland. Their duet became a hit record.

THE CAISSONS GO ROLLING ALONG
1918

Words and Music by Edmund L. Gruber. The songwriter was a West Point graduate, class of 1904. Gruber wrote the song in 1908, while serving in the Artillery Corps of the U.S. Army. It remained fairly obscure until John Philip Sousa arranged it for band in 1918, calling it "U.S. Field Artillery March." The spirit of patriotism engendered by World War I helped launch Sousa's recording of the song that year. After he introduced his arrangement at a Liberty Loan concert at the Hippodrome in 1918, he was incorrectly credited as its composer for several years.

AFTER YOU'VE GONE
1919

Words by Henry Creamer, Music by Turner Layton. "After You've Gone" was popularized by Al Jolson on Broadway and by Sophie Tucker in vaudeville. After its first success in 1919, the song surfaced again in 1929 as the first New York hit for jazz great Louis Armstrong. It became a specialty of Benny Goodman, who played it on the soundtrack of the 1946 film *Make Mine Music*. The song has appeared in several other films, including *Unholy Partners* (1941), *For Me and My Gal* (1942), *Atlantic City* (1944), and the 1958, Frank Sinatra, Dean Martin and Shirley MacLaine film *Some Came Running*. Judy Garland's highly stylized arrangement, featured on her landmark Carnegie Hall album, is the performance that keeps the song alive.

WHISPERING
1920

Words and Music by Richard Coburn, Vincent Rose and John Schonberger. "Whispering" was popularized by Paul Whiteman and his orchestra, in a recording that sold more than a million copies. Now a pop standard, the song was heard in such films as *Ziegfeld Girl* (1941), *Greenwich Village* (1944), *Give My Regards to Broadway* (1948), *Belles on Their Toes* (1952), and *The Eddie Duchin Story* (1956).

LOOK FOR THE SILVER LINING
1921

Words by B.G. DeSylva, Music by Jerome Kern. It was written for a musical, *Brewster's Millions*, that never made it to Broadway. The song was salvaged and recycled in the musical *Good Morning Dearie* (1919). But it wasn't until it was sung by Marilyn Miller, the biggest theater star of her day, in the musical *Sally* (1920) that the song became popular. By 1921 it was a hit across the country. It later appeared in the film version of *Savoy* (1929), and in the film biography of Jerome Kern, *Till the Clouds Roll By* (1946). "Look for the Silver Lining" was also the title song for the 1949 film biography of Marilyn Miller.

APRIL SHOWERS
1922

Words by B.G. DeSylva, Music by Louis Silvers. Al Jolson was one of the greatest entertainers of the twentieth century. His individual style and sound, and his desperate need to please an audience created legendary performances. Jolson introduced "April Showers" in the stage musical *Bombo*. The song was an instant hit. He made "April Showers" a fixture of his act for many years, scoring a hit record with it as late as 1946 during his "come-back" period. He sang it on the soundtracks of the films *The Jolson Story* (1946) and *Jolson Sings Again* (1949).

TOOT, TOOT, TOOTSIE! (GOODBYE!)
1923

Words and Music by Ted Fiorito, Robert A. King, Gus Kahn, and Ernie Erdman. In 1922 Al Jolson was appearing on Broadway in the musical *Bombo*. When he came across a new song, "Toot, Toot, Tootsie, Goodbye," he decided to try it out by interpolating it into the show. The new song stopped the show. He recorded it almost immediately. When sound was added to what was previously only silent film, this was the first song ever heard in the movies, the first number sung by Jolson in *The Jazz Singer* (1927). He sang it again in *Rose of Washington Square* (1939). Doris Day performed it in the film biography of Gus Kahn, *I'll See You in My Dreams* (1951).

CALIFORNIA, HERE I COME
1924

Words by Al Jolson and B.G. DeSylva, Music by Joseph Meyer. By 1924 Al Jolson was on the road with the musical extravaganza *Bombo*. He interpolated "California, Here I Come" into the show while touring, and as he had done with other songs in this period, he launched another hit. He later sang it in the film musical *Rose of Washington Square* (1939). Jolson re-recorded the song in 1946, selling a million records. He also sang the number on the soundtracks of *The Jolson Story* (1946), and *Jolson Sings Again* (1949). The song has been heard in several other films, including *Lucky Boy* (1929) and *With a Song in My Heart* (1952). It was even heard in an episode of "I Love Lucy," sung by Lucy, Ricky, Fred and Ethel as they drive across the country to Los Angeles.

MANHATTAN
1925

Words by Lorenz Hart, Music by Richard Rodgers. "Manhattan" was the first hit for the legendary song-writing team of Rodgers and Hart, though they had been writing together for seven years by this time. It was the song that saved them. Rodgers was just about to give up on songwriting as a career when *The Garrick Gaieties* was an unexpected hit. The revue was originally just a two-performance benefit, but was so successful that a commercial Broadway run was quickly launched. The sophisticated "Manhattan," the hit from the show, took New York and the rest of the country by storm, encouraging Rodgers and Hart in an amazing career that would continue until Hart's death in 1943. The song was interpolated into several films, including the 1948 film biography (ridiculously fictionalized) of Rodgers and Hart entitled *Words and Music*. The song was also heard in other films such as *All About Eve* (1950), *With a Song in My Heart* (1952), *Don't Bother to Knock* (1953), and *The Eddie Duchin Story* (1956).

FIVE FOOT TWO, EYES OF BLUE
1926

Words by Sam M. Lewis and Joe Young, Music by Ray Henderson. This song is the epitome of a flapper era hit. It is so closely associated with the Roaring Twenties that it often appears in television and movie scenes depicting the era. "Five Foot Two, Eyes of Blue" was one of the early successes of Ray Henderson, before he began writing songs with Buddy DeSylva and Lew Brown. The tune has had a life long past its original success in 1926. Art Mooney and his Band made a successful recording of it in 1948. It turned up again in such films as *Has Anybody Seen My Girl* (1952), and *Love Me Or Leave Me* (1955).

BLUE SKIES
1927

Words and Music by Irving Berlin. Belle Baker introduced "Blue Skies" as an interpolation into the show *Betsy* (1927). The show's score had been written by Rodgers and Hart. Without telling the young songwriting team, the day before the opening she persuaded Irving Berlin she needed a hit to make a success of the musical. Her idea paid off, though it miffed Rodgers and Hart at the time. "Blue Skies" became the hit of the show. Al Jolson sang it in *The Jazz Singer* (1927) and dubbed it for Larry Parks in the 1946 film *The Jolson Story*. Eddie Cantor sang it in *Glorifying the American Girl* (1929); Ethel Merman and Alice Faye took a turn at it in *Alexander's Ragtime Band* (1938). Bing Crosby sang it in *Blue Skies* (1946) and *White Christmas* (1954). In 1978 the song was revived by country singer Willie Nelson.

I CAN'T GIVE YOU ANYTHING BUT LOVE
1928

Words by Dorothy Fields, Music by Jimmy McHugh. One day Fields and McHugh paused while walking past Tiffany's in New York. They overheard a young man tell his sweetheart, "Gee, honey, I can't give you nothin' but love." The resulting song, "I Can't Give You Anything But Love" was written for the 1927 Broadway revue *Delmar's Revels*. Although the show closed after just two weeks, the song turned up again in the revue *Blackbirds of 1928*. Cliff "Ukelele Ike" Edwards had the first hit record of this song, followed years later by jazz greats Louis Armstrong and Benny Goodman. The lyrics took on a new meaning during the Great Depression. Katherine Hepburn sang a bit of it in *Bringing Up Baby* (1938) and it served as the title song for a 1940 film. The song appeared in *True to the Army* (1942), *Stormy Weather* (1943), and *Jam Session* (1944). Gloria De Haven sang it in French in *So This Is Paris* (1955). By 1965 this song had been recorded nearly 450 times, Judy Garland's breathlessly slow rendition being one of the most memorable. Dorothy Fields was one of the only women able to break into the male dominated world of Tin Pan Alley as a songwriter.

MORE THAN YOU KNOW
1929

Words by Edward Eliscu and William (Billy) Rose, Music by Vincent Youmans. It would be easier to list the major vocalists of the 1930s-1950s who did not record this song than those who did. Although "More Than You Know" first appeared in the Broadway musical *Great Day* (1929), which ran only 36 performances, it found a second life in the hands of singer Jane Forman, who made the song one of her specialties. It appeared in such films as *Hit the Deck* (both the 1930 and 1955 versions), *The Helen Morgan Story* (1957), and in *Funny Lady* (1975), sung by Barbra Streisand.

PUTTIN' ON THE RITZ
1930

Words and Music by Irving Berlin. It was introduced by Harry Richman, in his screen debut, in the 1930 film *Puttin' on the Ritz*. Clark Gable uncharacteristically sang and danced to this song in the 1939 movie *Idiot's Delight*, a performance excerpted into the 1974 compilation film *That's Entertainment*. "Puttin' on the Ritz" was sung by Fred Astaire, with a revised lyric, in the 1946 film *Blue Skies*, a complex scene that showed him dancing in front of an eight-man chorus of Fred Astaires. Many other artists recorded the song. "Puttin' on the Ritz" was featured in the 1974 film *Young Frankenstein*, with Gene Wilder and Frankenstein singing and dancing in top hats and tails. The Dutch-Indonesian singer Taco had a disco-styled hit with it in 1983.

JUST A GIGOLO
1931

Words by Irving Caesar (English), Julius Brammer (German), Music by Leonello Casucci. "Just a Gigolo" was a hit in Vienna as "Schöner Gigolo" before Vincent Lopez and his orchestra popularized it in the U.S. with an English lyric. Bing Crosby recorded it soon after it became popular. The song was heard in the 1946 film *Lover, Come Back*. Some twenty years later Louis Prima and his band re-popularized it in a recording, coupling it with "I Ain't Got Nobody." David Lee Roth revived it in 1985.

HOW DEEP IS THE OCEAN
(HOW HIGH IS THE SKY)
1932

Words and Music by Irving Berlin. After he finished work on this song Berlin set it aside, thinking it was not one of his best efforts. It was several years before it was published. When the public finally heard it, it became one of the top hits of 1932. Among the many artists to record the song were Ethel Merman, Paul Whiteman and his orchestra, Joan Edwards, Coleman Hawkins, Dick Haymes, Benny Goodman, Margaret Whiting and Artie Shaw. Bing Crosby sang it in the 1946 film *Blue Skies* and Frank Sinatra performed it in *Meet Danny Wilson* (1952). In recent decades it's become a jazz standard.

DID YOU EVER SEE A DREAM WALKING?

1933

Words by Mack Gordon, Music by Harry Revel. One of the most characteristic of Depression era movie songs, it was introduced by Jack Haley in the 1933 film *Sitting Pretty*. Eddy Duchin, with vocal by Lew Sherwood, scored a number 1 hit record with the song. Other notable recordings include Guy and Carmen Lombardo, Bing Crosby, Meyer Davis and his orchestra, and The Pickens Sisters. It was prominently heard in the stylized Steve Martin 1981 film *Pennies from Heaven*, set in the 1930s.

SMOKE GETS IN YOUR EYES

1934

Words by Otto Harbach, Music by Jerome Kern. "Smoke Gets in Your Eyes" was a regular showstopper in the musical *Roberta* (1933), where it was introduced by Tamara. Two years later Fred Astaire and Ginger Rogers danced to it in the 1935 film adaptation of the show. Many years later Astaire recalled that the number had always been one of his favorites. Kern actually wrote this melody as a march, intending to use it as the theme song for a radio show. The radio show never made it to the air, but when the musical *Roberta* needed a new tune for the second act, Kern resurrected this song and slowed it down. He referred to "Smoke Gets in Your Eyes" as one of his favorite compositions, just as Harbach thought of it as some of his best work. The Platters' distinctive arrangement went to number 1 in 1959.

MY ROMANCE

1935

Music by Lorenz Hart, Music by Richard Rodgers. It was first heard in the 1935 musical *Jumbo*, a spectacle combining musical comedy and the circus. Rodgers and Hart had been on contract in Hollywood and hated it. *Jumbo* was their return to Broadway. The show, with actual circus acts, was such an elaborate spectacle that it took months of rehearsal. It always irked Rodgers that the producer, Billy Rose, wouldn't allow the songs from the show to be played on the radio during the rehearsal period or run. The song was heard in the 1963 film *Jumbo* (Rose had insisted on the title *Billy Rose's Jumbo*), and *Brotherly Love* (1970). The song is firmly in the jazz repertoire.

THE WAY YOU LOOK TONIGHT

1936

Words by Dorothy Fields, Music by Jerome Kern. It could be argued that more great songs were written for Fred Astaire by the top songwriters than any other performer. *Swing Time* (1936) was one of the nine great Astaire-Rogers musicals of the 1930s, and his best solo in it is "The Way You Look Tonight." Dorothy Fields had an urbane, casual way with a lyric that loosened up the usually more highbrow Kern. The song won an Academy Award. It has never left the repertoire, with hundreds of recordings. The classic was prominently featured in the 1997 Julia Roberts romantic comedy *My Best Friend's Wedding*.

CARAVAN

1937

Words by Irving Mills, Music by Juan Tizol and Edward Kennedy "Duke" Ellington. "Caravan" was introduced by Duke Ellington and his orchestra, in a performance that featured co-composer Juan Tizol on valve trombone. Billy Eckstine had a hit record with this song in 1949. It hit the charts again in 1953 in a recording by Ralph Marterie.

THANKS FOR THE MEMORY

1938

Words by Leo Robin, Music by Ralph Rainger. "Thanks for the Memory" will always be remembered as Bob Hope's theme song. He introduced it in his screen debut in the 1938 film *The Big Broadcast*. It's a bittersweet, witty duet, sung at the rail of the ocean liner Gigantic with Shirley Ross (playing his ex-wife). Years later he recalled in his autobiography, "[It] was the only number that kept me in pictures when I finished work on my first film. For that matter, it was only the most important song in my life." The song won an Academy Award in 1938 and was a hit record. It's a great example of the sophisticated, self-deprecating wit of the best of the songs of the 1930s. Songs like this were rarely written for the movies, which demanded a more populist approach. Hope's success with the song inspired Paramount to star him in the 1938 film *Thanks for the Memory*. "Thanks for the Memory" is such a well-crafted, intriguing song that it deserves a life of its own, and not just as Hope's theme song.

BEER BARREL POLKA

1939

Words by Lew Brown (English), Vasek Zeman and Wladimir A. Timm (Czech), Music by Jaromir Vejvoda. This most famous of polkas, one of the sheet music and record hits of 1939, is based on the Czech song "Skoda Lasky." It was first heard in the U.S. in the hands of Will Glahe and his Musette Orchestra. The Andrews Sisters soon had a hit record with it. The song was heard on stage in *Yokel Boy* (1939) and in the film *A Night in Casablanca* (1946). "Beer Barrel Polka" owed a good deal of its popularity to the new, streamlined version of the nickelodeon, known as the "juke box." An unusual, interesting use of the song is at every seventh-inning stretch for many years at the Milwaukee Brewers home games – Milwaukee being the unofficial polka capital of the U.S.

TUXEDO JUNCTION

1940

Words by Buddy Feyne, Music by Erskine Hawkins, William Johnson and Julian Dash. Erskine Hawkins and his band introduced this song as an instrumental at the Savoy Ballroom in New York City in 1939, recording it that same year. Named for an Alabama railroad junction, the song became a huge hit for Glenn Miller, and is one of the top Big Band numbers. The Andrews Sisters recorded it after lyrics were added. The song has been in the repertoire of The Manhattan Transfer since their 1973 debut album.

AQUELLOS OJOS VERDES (GREEN EYES)

1941

Words by E. Rivera and Eddie Woods (English), Adolfo Utrero (Spanish), Music by Nilo Menendez. This Cuban song was first heard in the U.S. in a performance by Don Azpiazu and his Havana Casino Orchestra. Jimmy Dorsey and his orchestra recorded it in 1941, with vocals by Bob Eberly and Helen O'Connell, scoring a number 1 hit and selling more than a million records. Dorsey, Eberly and O'Connell can be heard performing "Green Eyes" in the 1946 film *The Fabulous Dorseys*. With its Spanish lyric, the song has a completely different life as a standard of the Latin repertoire.

DON'T SIT UNDER THE APPLE TREE
1942

Words by Lew Brown and Charles Tobias, Music by Sam H. Stept. The familiar melody of "Don't Sit Under the Apple Tree" was originally attached to a lyric entitled "Anywhere the Bluebird Goes." It was introduced in the 1939 stage musical *Yokel Boy* with its "Apple Tree" lyric. The song soon became relevant after the U.S. entered World War II. It summed up the feelings of countless couples, who were separated by the war for several years, and was a particular favorite of service men and women. The Andrews Sisters sang it in the 1942 film *Private Buckaroo* and had a hit record with it that same year. Other best-selling recordings were made of "Don't Sit Under the Apple Tree" by Glenn Miller, Tex Beneke, and Kay Kyser.

THAT OLD BLACK MAGIC
1943

Words by Johnny Mercer, Music by Harold Arlen. The composer once explained this song's success, giving all the credit to Mercer's lyrics. "The words sustain your interest, make sense, contain memorable phrases and tell a story," he said. "Without the lyric, the song would be just another song." "That Old Black Magic" was a number 1 hit for Glenn Miller. It appeared in the films *Star Spangled Rhythm* (1942), *Here Come the Waves* (1944), *Radio Stars on Parade* (1945), *When You're Smiling* (1950), *Meet Danny Wilson* (1952), *Bus Stop* (1956), and *Senior Prom* (1958). Although such stars as Frank Sinatra, Sammy Davis, Jr., Bobby Rydell, and Louis Prima recorded the song, it was associated with Billy Daniels.

MAIRZY DOATS
1944

Words and Music by Milton Drake, Al Hoffman and Jerry Livingston. How successful was this nonsense song? For several weeks in a row after its release it sold some 30,000 copies of sheet music per day! When Milton Drake's little daughter came home from kindergarten one day saying "Cowzy tweet and sowzy tweet and liddle sharsky doisters," Milton had the idea for a song. He turned "Mares eat oats and does eat oats and little lambs eat ivy," into a runaway hit.

CANDY
1945

Words and Music by Mack David, Joan Whitney and Alex Kramer. This song went to number 1 on the charts in a recording by Johnny Mercer, Jo Stafford, and The Pied Pipers. It also did well in recordings by Dinah Shore, Johnny Long, and the Four King sisters performing with Buddy Cole's Orchestra. The Manhattan Transfer's tight vocal arrangement has been the version most often heard in recent decades.

ROUTE 66
1946

Words and Music by Bobby Troup. This hip road song was a hit for the King Cole Trio. Bing Crosby recorded it with the Andrews Sisters and had a success as well. Since that time the song has been part of the jazz standard repertoire. There's always been some bit of confusion about the "Route 66" song. The theme song for the 1962 television series is not the Troup song, but an instrumental by Nelson Riddle.

BEYOND THE SEA
1947

Words by Jack Lawrence (English), Music by Charles Trenet. The song first became popular in France in a recording by Trenet, entitled "La Mer." He also introduced it in the U.S. with the English lyric. Harry James, Benny Goodman, and Mantovani all made popular instrumental recordings of this piece. Tex Beneke and his band recorded it with a vocal by Garry Stevens. Bobby Darin took a swingin' version of "Beyond the Sea" into the Top 10 in 1960.

BUTTONS AND BOWS
1948

Words and Music by Jay Livingston and Ray Evans. Bob Hope and Jane Russell introduced "Buttons and Bows" in the 1948 western comedy film *Paleface*. The song won an Academy Award, and was a best seller in a recording by Hope. Dinah Shore also recorded the song, selling more than a million records. A choral rendition was heard in the 1950 film *Sunset Boulevard*. Other hit versions were by The Happy Valley Boys, The Dinning Sisters, and Betty Garrett.

RIDERS IN THE SKY
1949

Words and Music by Stan Jones. Burl Ives introduced and recorded this song, but it was Vaughn Monroe and his Orchestra that popularized it with a million-selling recording. Peggy Lee had a hit recording, as did Bing Crosby. The song was revived by the Ramrods in 1961, The Baja Marimba Band in 1966, and The Outlaws in 1981. Also known as "A Cowboy Legend" or "Ghost Riders in the Sky," the song was sung by Gene Autry in the 1949 film *Riders in the Sky*.

MONA LISA
1950

Words and Music by Jay Livingston and Ray Evans. Although this was one of Nat King Cole's biggest hits, selling more than three million copies, he recorded it only after much persuasion. At first he thought a song on Leonardo da Vinci's masterpiece was a little too offbeat. The song was introduced in the 1949 film *Captain Carey, U.S.A.*, but only part of it was heard in the film and at that only in Italian. Still, it won an Academy Award. "Mona Lisa" was revived in 1959 by both rockabilly singer Carl Mann and country singer Conway Twitty.

CRY
1951

Words and Music by Churchill Kohlman. Johnnie Ray was one of the more stylized and over-the-top emotional singers of the early 1950s. Not only did Ray hit the charts with "Cry," he went to number 1, stayed there for almost three months, sold more than two million records and started a fashion for wailing ballads. The song was later revived by The Knightsbridge Strings (1959), Ray Charles (1965), Ronnie Dove (1966), Lynn Anderson (1972), and Crystal Gayle (1986).

YOUR CHEATIN' HEART
1952

Words and Music by Hank Williams. The songwriter had a hit record with this song, as did Joni James and Frankie Laine. "Your Cheatin' Heart" was one of the first country hits to have crossover appeal to a wider audience. Hank Williams Jr. performed "Your Cheatin' Heart" in the 1965 film biography of his dad. Such artists as Elvis Presley, Nat King Cole, Patsy Cline, Fats Domino, Jerry Lee Lewis, Petula Clark, and Leon Redbone also recorded the song.

I LOVE PARIS
1953

Words and Music by Cole Porter. Porter spent a significant amount of time in Paris in his life, and at least four of his musicals are set there. "I Love Paris" was inspired by the sumptuous sets created by Jo Mielziner for the stage musical *Can-Can* (1953). It was introduced in the show by Lilo. Frank Sinatra and Maurice Chevalier sang it in the film version of *Can-Can* (1960). The most popular recording of the song was made by Les Baxter and his Orchestra.

SHAKE, RATTLE AND ROLL
1954

Words and Music by Charles Calhoun. This was one of the earliest hits of the fledgling rock era. "Shake Rattle and Roll" was introduced by Joe Turner, who took it to number 22 on the charts in August of 1954. Bill Haley and his Comets had a million-selling record with it, taking it to number 7 that same month. The song was revived by Arthur Conley in 1967.

AUTUMN LEAVES
1955

Words by Johnny Mercer (English) and Jacques Prevert (French), Music by Joseph Kosma. After French singer Juliette Greco popularized "Les Portes de la Nuit" in Paris, Capitol Records contacted Johnny Mercer to write an English lyric for the song. Roger Williams' instrumental version of the song went to number 1 on the charts in 1955, selling more than a million records. Steve Allen, performing with the George Cates Orchestra, took it to number 35 on the charts. Jo Stafford, Monica Lewis, Stan Getz, and Tommy Mercer recorded the song as well. It was the title song for a nonmusical film starring Joan Crawford in 1956, sung on the soundtrack by Nat King Cole.

THE GREAT PRETENDER
1956

Words and Music by Buck Ram. The Platters were the most popular vocal group of the late 1950s, thanks in part to a string of enormously successful recordings that crossed over from the R&B/soul charts to the mainstream. "The Great Pretender" was one of the top ten songs of 1956, and a number 1 hit for the group. The Platters sang it in the 1957 film *The Girl Can't Help It*. The Platters were inducted into the Rock and Roll Hall of Fame in 1990.

ALL SHOOK UP
1957

Words and Music by Otis Blackwell and Elvis Presley. Elvis Presley was the first superstar of the rock era. His bedroom eyes, outlaw hips and swaggering mannerisms made him a sure hit with teens. Elvis' eclectic blues/country/gospel/rock style won him a crossover audience that came from every corner of the country. Nothing like Elvis had ever hit pop culture before. By the time "All Shook Up" hit number 1, where it stayed for eight weeks, Presley had already purchased Graceland with his hit record money. His huge stardom was a sure indication that rock was going to be around for awhile.

I CAN'T STOP LOVING YOU
1958

Words and Music by Don Gibson. When "I Can't Stop Loving You" first appeared, it charted as a crossover hit, starting on the country charts and then hitting the mainstream, recorded by Don Gibson. In 1962 Ray Charles recorded it in a soulful style, selling a million records and taking it to number 1. His version won a Grammy for Rhythm and Blues Song of the Year. Count Basie and his Orchestra recorded the song in 1963. Conway Twitty revived it in 1972.

KANSAS CITY
1959

Words and Music by Jerry Leiber and Mike Stoller. The up-tempo blues tune "Kansas City" first appeared in 1952 under the title "K. C. Lovin'." William Harrison took the "Kansas City" version to number 1 in 1959. Trini Lopez recorded the song in 1963, followed by James Brown in 1967.

IF EVER I WOULD LEAVE YOU
1960

Words by Alan Jay Lerner, Music by Frederick Loewe. The Broadway musical *Camelot* was based on the legends of King Arthur. Guenevere arrives at Camelot in an arranged marriage to Arthur, something she wants to run away from, until she meets the king and falls in love. Lancelot is a Frenchman who crosses the channel, lured by the tales of the high-minded Arthur and his knights of the round table. After a time, Lancelot and Guenevere fall in love. Guilty over their adulterous affair, Lancelot has grappled with thoughts of going away and ending it. But his real feelings are revealed in the song "If Ever I Would Leave You." Robert Goulet played Lancelot on Broadway, to Richard Burton's Arthur and Julie Andrews' Guenevere. The 1967 film version starred Richard Harris, Vanessa Redgrave, and Franco Nero.

RUNAWAY
1961

Words by Del Shannon, Music by Max Crook and Del Shannon. "Runaway" was Shannon's first hit, rocketing to number 1. He sang it again 25 years later, with an altered lyric, as the theme of the T.V. series *Crime Stories*. Bonnie Raitt took a revival of the song to the charts in 1977. The song contains one of the most famous instrumental interludes of the rock era.

I LEFT MY HEART IN SAN FRANCISCO
1962

Words by Douglass Cross, Music by George Cory. This song first appeared in 1952, introduced by Claramae Turner. It didn't make much of an impression. A decade later, sporting a new lyric, Tony Bennett and his musical director Ralph Sharon ran across the song, which had been submitted to them by the songwriters. "I Left My Heart in San Francisco" by Tony Bennett became one of the biggest hits of the year, selling about three million copies and winning a Grammy for Record of the Year. The song became his theme song, and the turning point in a career that he once said had been "all but ruined" by rock.

OUR DAY WILL COME
1963

Words by Bob Hilliard, Music by Mort Garson. This song was the only number 1 hit for an Akron rhythm & blues quintet known as Ruby and the Romantics. The group charted seven more times in the next two years, never again breaking into the top ten. Frankie Valli revived the song in 1975.

THE GIRL FROM IPANEMA
1964

Words by Norman Gimbel (English), Vinicius De Moraes (Portuguese), Music by Antonio Carlos Jobim. This Brazilian song, originally in Portuguese, was a hit record for saxophonist Stan Getz, with cool vocal styling by Astrud Gilberto (English) and Joao Gilberto (Portuguese). The Stan Getz Quartet gave the piece its U.S. introduction at the Café au Go Go in New York. When Jobim performed the song on Andy Williams' television show, it became a national hit. For a time in the mid-1960s, bossa novas were all the rage, and this is the song that started that craze. Ipanema is the name of a Brazilian beach.

YESTERDAY
1965

Words and Music by John Lennon and Paul McCartney. No one who ever saw Paul McCartney sing "Yesterday" on "The Ed Sullivan Show" will ever forget it. He tuned out all the screaming fans and sincerely, with a tear in his eye, sang this tender ballad of regret. It was one of The Beatles' biggest hits. It hit number 1 on the pop charts, winning the Ivor Novello Award in both 1965 and 1966. In the years since it became a hit, this song has been recorded more than 2500 times, making it one of the most recorded songs of all time.

MONDAY, MONDAY
1966

Words and Music by John Phillips. "Monday, Monday" was a number 1 hit for those lovable hippies the Mamas and the Papas. Although the group's lush vocal sound was California folk-pop and its members were connected with the Los Angeles psychedelic scene, their roots were in the Greenwich Village folk music community. The Mamas and the Papas had two years of great success, with six Top 5 hits in 1966 and '67. By '68 things had gone bad and the group disbanded, but not before becoming an icon of the flower-power era. They reunited briefly in 1971. "Mama" Cass Elliot went on to a solo career, but died in 1974. John Phillips, formerly of the Journeymen, was married to Michelle Phillips until 1970. She went on to an acting career, as did her daughter, MacKenzie Phillips.

HAPPY TOGETHER
1967

Words and Music by Garry Bonner and Alan Gordon. "Happy Together" was the biggest hit scored by the short-lived group The Turtles. The song was one of 1967's Top Ten records. The Turtles started out as The Nightriders, then changed their name to The Crossfires. The name changed to The Turtles in 1965 (in the wake of The Beatles, many groups adopted animal names). The band's personnel were never very stable, except for the core duo of Mark Volman and Howard Kaylan. The Turtles disbanded in 1970. Besides "Happy Together," their other hits were "Elenore," "It Ain't Me Babe," "She'd Rather Be with Me," "You Know What I Mean," and "You Showed Me." In 1987 the Nylons, a Canadian a cappella quartet, revived "Happy Together."

HEY JUDE
1968

Words and Music by John Lennon and Paul McCartney. Of all the hit singles The Beatles produced, this was the biggest. It was the number 1 record of the year and the best-selling single of the year. It spent more weeks on the pop charts than any other single of 1968, 19 weeks in all, and held the number 1 position for nine straight weeks. Their recording was also the longest single, at seven minutes and 11 seconds, played on American radio at the time, and the longest fade-out of any pop record, at about three minutes. Within another year, The Beatles had broken up for good, though the official announcement wasn't made until early 1970.

RAINDROPS KEEP FALLIN' ON MY HEAD
1969

Words by Hal David, Music by Burt Bacharach. The breezy, angular tunes of Bacharach and David have left an indelible mark on American pop music. They found a style of song that seemed classic and rooted to the standards era, but with the freshness of the rock era in them. "Raindrops Keep Fallin' on My Head" was introduced in the 1969 film *Butch Cassidy and the Sundance Kid*, winning an Academy Award. It was sung by B.J. Thomas in the film and on a recording that hit number 1.

YOUR SONG
1970

Words and Music by Elton John and Bernie Taupin. Elton John (born Reginald Kenneth Dwight) caught the attention of critics in 1970 in a performance that featured his original music, including "Your Song." But the music was only part of what made the news. Midway through the performance, John leapt to his feet, kicked the piano bench over and performed handstands on the piano. An act was born. "Your Song," which was on the artist's debut album, simply titled "Elton John," went to number 8 on the U.S. pop charts. It's somewhat of an unusual song in John's output; he's recorded relatively few love songs.

IT'S TOO LATE
1971

Words by Toni Stern, Music by Carole King. "It's Too Late" appeared on Carole King's enormously successful *Tapestry* album. Prior to the release of *Tapestry*, King was known primarily as a songwriter. With the album she made a name for herself as a performer as well. "It's Too Late" hit number 1 on the charts, winning a Grammy for Record of the Year.

ROCKY MOUNTAIN HIGH
1972

Words and Music by John Denver and Michael Taylor. "Rocky Mountain High," now the unofficial theme song of Colorado, was the title song of one of John Denver's four platinum albums. Twelve other Denver albums went gold. Following his death in a plane crash in 1997, Denver was hailed by Sony as one of the five top artists of all time. He was named Colorado's Poet Laureate in 1974, in great part on the basis of this song.

KILLING ME SOFTLY WITH HIS SONG
1973

Words by Norman Gimbel, Music by Charles Fox. Although this song was introduced by Lori Lieberman, it is Roberta Flack's number 1 recording that became a hit. Her rendition won a Grammy for Song of the Year and Record of the Year. In the 1990s, The Fugees scored a hit with a remake of the famous song.

DON'T LET THE SUN GO DOWN ON ME
1974

Words and Music by Elton John and Bernie Taupin. Long before international rock fans knew anything of Elton John and Bernie Taupin, the pair was churning out songs for other musicians. Taupin would write lyrics all day, sometimes at the rate of a song per hour. He would deliver packages of them to John who would immediately set them to music. When John began performing the tunes himself, it was with a flamboyant delivery that was compared to that of Jerry Lee Lewis. As all the world knows, John easily exceeded any previous artist's over-the-top style in his live concerts. He became the first act since The Beatles to have four albums in the American Top Ten at the same time. "Don't Let the Sun Go Down on Me" went gold for John, peaking at number 2 on the U.S. charts. A 1992 version recorded by Elton John and George Michael went to number 1.

CAN'T SMILE WITHOUT YOU
1975

Words and Music by Chris Arnold, David Martin and Geoff Morrow. Trained at Juilliard, Barry Manilow, who started out writing jingles, made a name for himself as a composer, arranger, performer, and producer. Early in his career he was Bette Midler's accompanist, and produced her first two albums. Manilow's pop songs of the '70s brought him international fame. After his first album went platinum, twelve more followed suit, including two that went multi-platinum. In 1977 Manilow had five albums on the charts at once, something accomplished only twice before, by Frank Sinatra and Johnny Mathis.

TONIGHT'S THE NIGHT
1976

Words and Music by Rod Stewart. When "Tonight's the Night," from Rod Stewart's A Night on the Town album, first hit U.S. airwaves it got late night play if at all. Across the country, radio program directors opted not to air the song, finding its lyric too sexually explicit. But public demand won out. Once the song was on the air it soared to number 1 on the charts.

HOW DEEP IS YOUR LOVE
1977

Words and Music by Barry Gibb, Maurice Gibb and Robin Gibb. The Gibb brothers, once poster boys for disco, have become one of the wealthiest groups in the pop industry. Sons of a British bandleader, the brothers have had an uncanny ability to sniff out trends and incorporate them into their ever-changing act. "How Deep Is Your Love," a disco ballad, was introduced on the soundtrack of Saturday Night Fever, with the single going gold almost immediately after the movie's release.

DUST IN THE WIND
1978

Words and Music by Kerry Livgren. Although dismissed by early critics as rehashed British progressive rock, the complex classic rock sound of Kansas was a hit with audiences. Formed in Topeka, Kansas, the band began by playing local clubs, with very limited success. The group's first two albums sold a few hundred thousand copies. But in 1977 their album Leftoverture, containing the hit "Carry On Wayward Son," sold more than three million copies. Point of Know Return, containing "Dust in the Wind," went triple platinum. "Dust in the Wind" hit number 6 on the charts. The mellow, acoustic sound of the recording is unlike most of the band's harder edged material.

Y.M.C.A.
1979

Words and Music by Henri Belolo, Jacques Morali and Victor Willis. The Village People, complete with overplayed stereotypes and double-entendre lyrics, were a joke that most of America didn't get. The obviously gay themes of their tunes went right past many of those who were dancing in the flashing lights of disco clubs. "Y.M.C.A." was a platinum record for the group. Although they faded from view in the U.S. by the early '80s, the group maintained a large international following for several years. "Y.M.C.A." is still one of the most popular party songs, and can be heard at nearly every major sporting event.

SAILING
1980

Words and Music by Christopher Cross. The singer-songwriter appeared on the national pop scene in 1980 with the album Christopher Cross. The album went quadruple platinum with four of its songs hitting the Top 20, including "Sailing." The song went to number 1. Cross won five Grammy Awards that year, including Album of the Year, Song of the Year, and Record of the Year. He had one more huge hit with "Arthur's Theme (The Best That You Can Do)" from the film Arthur, and a couple of other respectable singles before fading from view.

PHYSICAL
1981

Words and Music by Stephen Kipner and Terry Shaddick. "Physical," from Olivia Newton-John's album of the same name, was part of a deliberate image change for the once squeaky-clean singer. In 1974 Newton-John won Female Vocalist of the Year from the Country Music Association, which caused some members to quit in protest. In 1978 she appeared opposite John Travolta in *Grease*, the most profitable movie musical made to date. The image change she underwent in *Grease* carried over into her musical act. From that point on the world saw a sexier, rock-oriented Olivia. "Physical" hit number 1 on the charts, with the album going platinum. It was a notable video of its era, with Newton-John among a bunch of near naked gym hunks.

CHARIOTS OF FIRE
1982

Music by Vangelis. "Chariots of Fire," that inspirational anthem, was on the U.S. charts for 15 weeks. The instrumental composition was recorded by keyboardist/composer Vangelis (a pseudonym for Evangelos Odyssey Papathanassiou). Vangelis won an Academy Award for the score to *Chariots of Fire*, a film about two athletes striving for glory in the 1924 Olympic Games.

TIME AFTER TIME
1983

Words and Music by Cyndi Lauper and Rob Hyman. Cyndi Lauper hit the rock scene with a splash in 1983. Her debut album, *She's So Unusual*, had four Top Five singles, including "Time After Time." This was a first for a woman in the music industry. Lauper, sporting a childlike voice and a tattered, urban image, used the new medium of MTV to propel herself to stardom. Sometimes lost in the hubbub was her excellent songwriting, of which this song is a prime example. The jazz duo Tuck & Patti recorded a memorable rendition of "Time After Time," and more than most songs of the rock era, it has become a standard among performers in various styles. Inoj had a top-ten hit with a new rendition in 1998.

I JUST CALLED TO SAY I LOVE YOU
1984

Words and Music by Stevie Wonder. Before finding a second life in advertising for long distance telephone service, Stevie Wonder's "I Just Called to Say I Love You" was a number 1 hit. It's a cheerful love song, typical of Wonder's songwriting. The song was introduced in the 1984 film *The Woman in Red*. Wonder took home an Academy Award for the song, as well as a Grammy for Song of the Year.

WE BUILT THIS CITY
1985

Words by Bernie Taupin, Dennis Lambert, Martin Page and Peter Wolf, Music by Lambert, Page and Wolf. Introduced by Starship, on the platinum album *Knee Deep in the Hoopla*, "We Built This City" was a number 1 hit. Starship was the last incarnation of the long-lived rock franchise known first as Jefferson Airplane and later as Jefferson Starship. The only common denominator in these editions of the band was singer Grace Slick.

GLORY OF LOVE
1986

Words and Music by Peter Cetera, David Foster and Diane Nini. Former lead singer for the band Chicago, Peter Cetera set out on his own in 1985. The following year he scored a number 1 hit with "Glory of Love," and hit the charts with several other tunes. But his solo albums never hit the Top Twenty. This song, heard on the soundtrack of the film *Karate Kid II*, was nominated for an Academy Award and a Golden Globe. Cetera's distinctive, high voice seemed perfect for the romantic ballads he so often recorded.

I STILL HAVEN'T FOUND WHAT I'M LOOKING FOR
1987

Words and Music by U2. Known as one of the most adventurous and innovative acts in pop music, U2 had a number 1 hit with "I Still Haven't Found What I'm Looking For" from the album *The Joshua Tree*. Formed in Dublin, Ireland, the band was the most widely followed rock act of the '80s, making the cover of *Time* magazine in 1987. The group remained popular into the '90s, releasing the album *Pop* in 1997 and *Best of 1980-1990* in 1998.

KOKOMO
1988

Words and Music by Mike Love, Scott McKenzie, Terry Melcher and John Phillips. In the early '60s The Beach Boys epitomized California pop/rock. Now America's most famous nostalgia act, they have sold nearly 70 million records worldwide. The happy-go-lucky "Kokomo" was introduced in the Tom Cruise film *Cocktail* (1988), becoming a hit single. The Beach Boys were inducted into the Rock and Roll Hall of Fame in 1988.

UNDER THE SEA
1989

Words by Howard Ashman, Music by Alan Menken. The happy calypso song was written for the first animated blockbuster in the Disney renaissance. *The Little Mermaid* was the studio's first feature-length animated fairytale since 1959. "Under the Sea" won an Academy Award and a Golden Globe. Ashman and Menken made musical magic again, working together on Disney's *Beauty and the Beast* (1991). The pair wrote three songs for *Aladdin* (1992) before Ashman's untimely death ended their partnership.

HOW AM I SUPPOSED TO LIVE WITHOUT YOU
1990

Words and Music by Michael Bolton and Doug James. "How Am I Supposed to Live Without You" first charted in 1983, in a recording by Laura Branigan. She took the song to number 12 on the pop charts and number 1 on the adult contemporary charts. It wasn't until co-composer Michael Bolton recorded the song himself that it soared to number 1 on the pop charts.

SOMEDAY
1991

Words and Music by Mariah Carey and Ben Margulies. "Someday" appeared on Mariah Carey's 1990 debut album, *Mariah Carey*. The album brought rave reviews for the young singer and her incredible vocal range. Nearly all of Carey's subsequent singles have gone to the number 1 spot on the charts. In 1998 she even released an album entitled *#1's*, featuring "Someday" and other chart-topping hits.

END OF THE ROAD
1992

Words and Music by Babyface (Kenneth B. Edmonds), Antonio M. Reid and Daryl L. Simmons. Babyface emerged as the most important pop songwriter of the 1990s. His songs have become hits for such stars as Michael Jackson, Gladys Knight, Sheena Easton, Aretha Franklin, Paula Abdul, and Whitney Houston. "End of the Road," which was written for Boyz II Men, became one of the best-selling hits of all time. It surpassed Elvis Presley's "Heartbreak Hotel" in the length of its stay in the number 1 spot on the *Billboard* Hot 100 chart.

FIELDS OF GOLD
1993

Words and Music by Sting (a.k.a. Gordon Sumner). When Sting's band, The Police, was at the height of its success, Sting himself disbanded the group. Always antsy for a new challenge, Sting found success in recordings with jazz musician Branford Marsalis, appeared in numerous films and starred on a Broadway revival of *The Threepenny Opera*. His solo recording career has been a steady stream of hits. "Fields of Gold," from Sting's 1993 album *Ten Summoner's Tales*, was released again in 1994 as the title track of an anthology album.

CAN YOU FEEL THE LOVE TONIGHT
1994

Words by Tim Rice, Music by Elton John. Famous for his flamboyant costumes and keyboard-heavy rock music, Elton John found a new audience with Disney's animated feature *The Lion King*. Disney executives asked lyricist Tim Rice who his first choice would be as a songwriter. Rice responded, "Elton John would be fantastic." Disney's producers thought John would turn them down, but he jumped at the chance. His songs were an instant hit with the children at whom the movie was directed. "Can You Feel the Love Tonight" also appealed to adult listeners, making it to number 4 on the pop charts. This song won an Academy Award for Best Song.

EXHALE (SHOOP SHOOP)
1995

Words and Music by Babyface (Kenneth B. Edmonds). Singer Whitney Houston became a movie star in *The Bodyguard*, and her film career continued with *Waiting to Exhale*, the story of four African-American women and their search for love. The soundtrack album won an Image Award in 1996. "Exhale (Shoop Shoop)" was nominated for the MTV Movie Award for Best Movie Song, but the award went to "Sittin' Up in My Room," also from this film.

I FINALLY FOUND SOMEONE
1996

Words and Music by Barbra Streisand, Marvin Hamlisch, R.J. Lange and Bryan Adams. Streisand herself sang the song on the soundtrack to the film *The Mirror Has Two Faces*, a romantic comedy about two intellectuals who marry on the theory of friendship is best, but wind up falling in love. The song was nominated for an Academy Award and a Golden Globe. It won the A.S.C.A.P. Award for Most Performed Songs from Motion Pictures.

BUTTERFLY KISSES
1997

Words and Music by Robert Mason Carlisle and Randy Keith Thomas. "Butterfly Kisses" was a surprising crossover hit for country/gospel singer Bob Carlisle. Written as a love song to his daughter, it was released just before Father's Day on an album entitled *Shades of Grace*. When the song took off, the album was released again under the title *Butterfly Kisses*. The song won Carlisle a number of awards including a Grammy for Best Country Song, a Gospel Music Association Dove Award for Southern Gospel Recorded Song of the Year, and an American Music Award for New Country Artist.

YOU'RE STILL THE ONE
1998

Words and Music by Robert John Lange and Shania Twain. Born Eileen Regina Edwards, Shania Twain created her name using her stepfather's surname, Twian, and the Ojibway word meaning "I'm on my way." It took a few years for Nashville to warm up to Twain, with her glamour and pop influences. After her huge success on the pop charts, as well as the country charts, no one could question her place in Nashville anymore. The Canadian singer won numerous awards with this song, including Grammy Awards for Best Country Song and Best Country Vocal Performance, a Billboard Music Award for Best-Selling Country Single, a Blockbuster Entertainment Award for Favorite Single, and a BMI Pop Song of the Year Award.

YOU'LL BE IN MY HEART
1999

Words and Music by Phil Collins. Following in the successful footsteps of Elton John, rock musician Phil Collins took a turn at writing songs for Disney's animated feature *Tarzan*™, contributing five songs to the film. The former lead singer and drummer of the band Genesis, Collins scored an instant hit with "You'll Be in My Heart," and was presented with a star on the Hollywood Walk of Fame. He recorded the song in French, German, Italian and two dialects of Spanish, marking the first time that a Disney animated feature was released with international versions of songs by the same recording artist. Unlike previous Disney musicals where the characters sing the songs, Collins himself sings all the songs on the soundtrack.

1900
A Bird in a Gilded Cage

Registration 10
Rhythm: Waltz

Words by Arthur J. Lamb
Music by Harry Von Tilzer

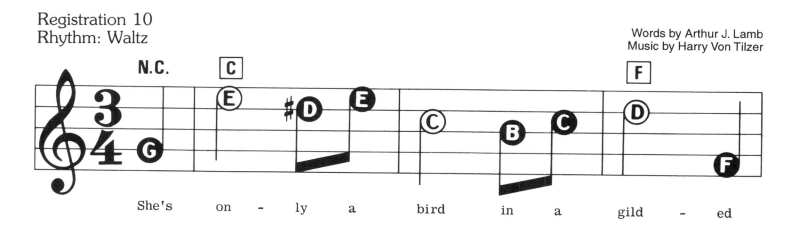

She's on - ly a bird in a gild - ed

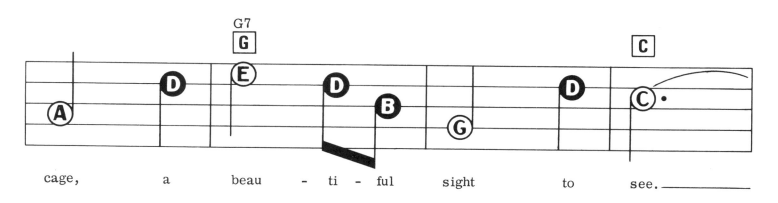

cage, a beau - ti - ful sight to see.

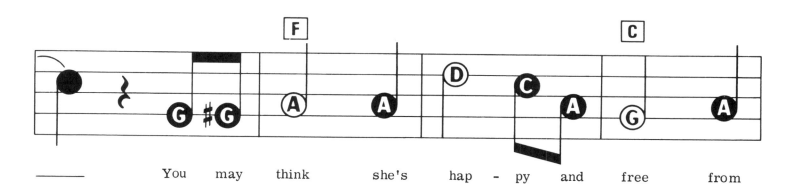

You may think she's hap - py and free from

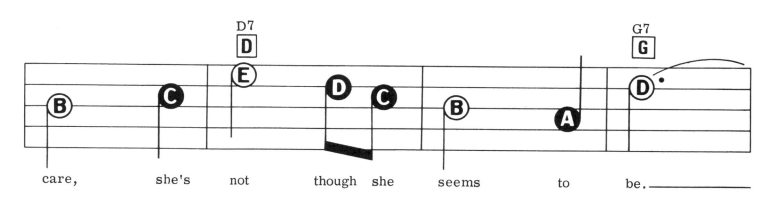

care, she's not though she seems to be.

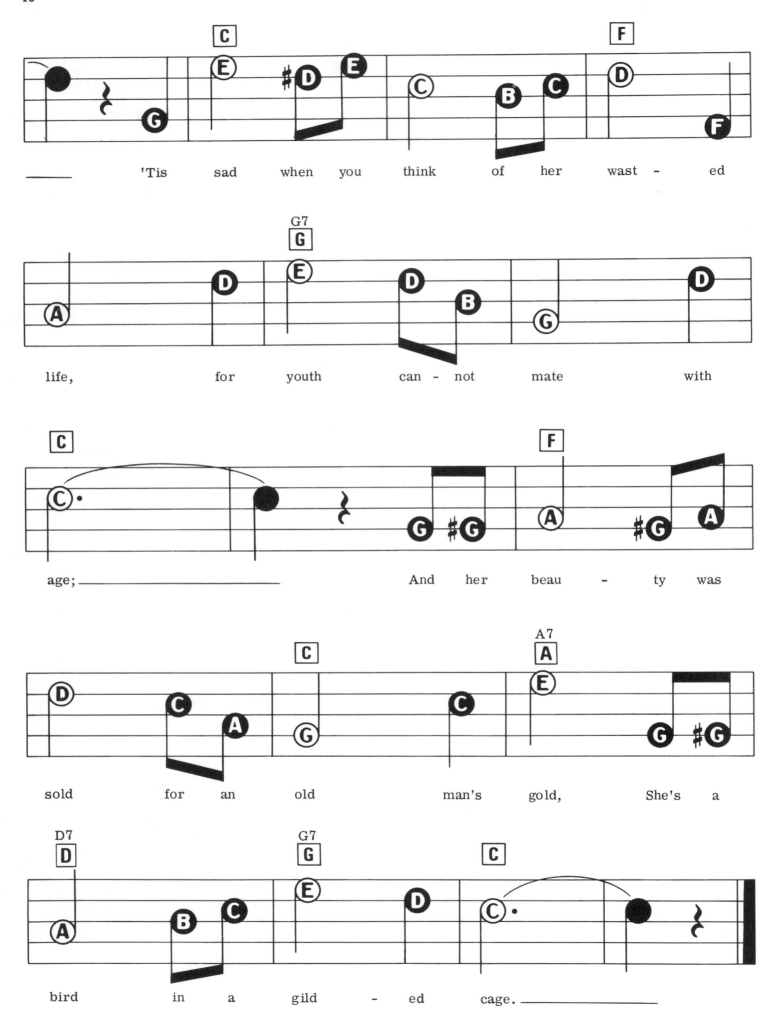

1901
The American Patrol

Registration 4
Rhythm: March

Music by F.W. Meacham

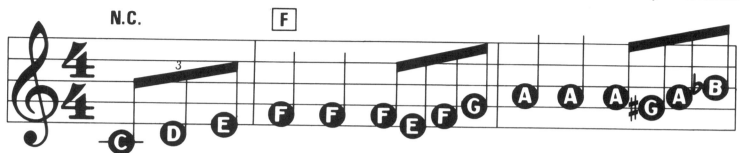

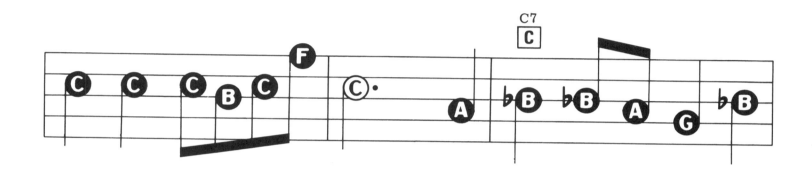

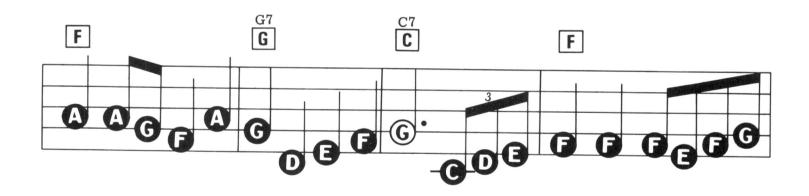

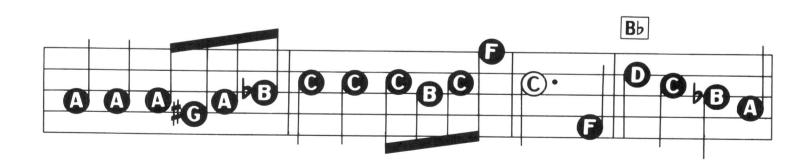

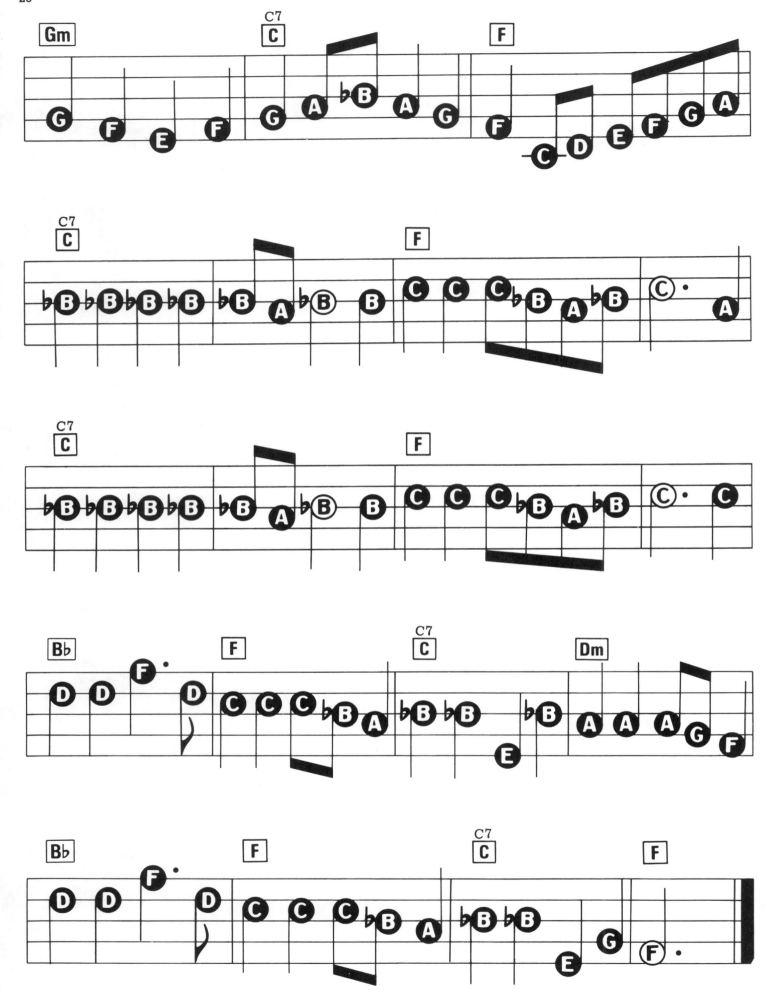

1902
On a Sunday Afternoon

Registration 2
Rhythm: Waltz

Words by Andrew B. Sterling
Music by Harry Von Tilzer

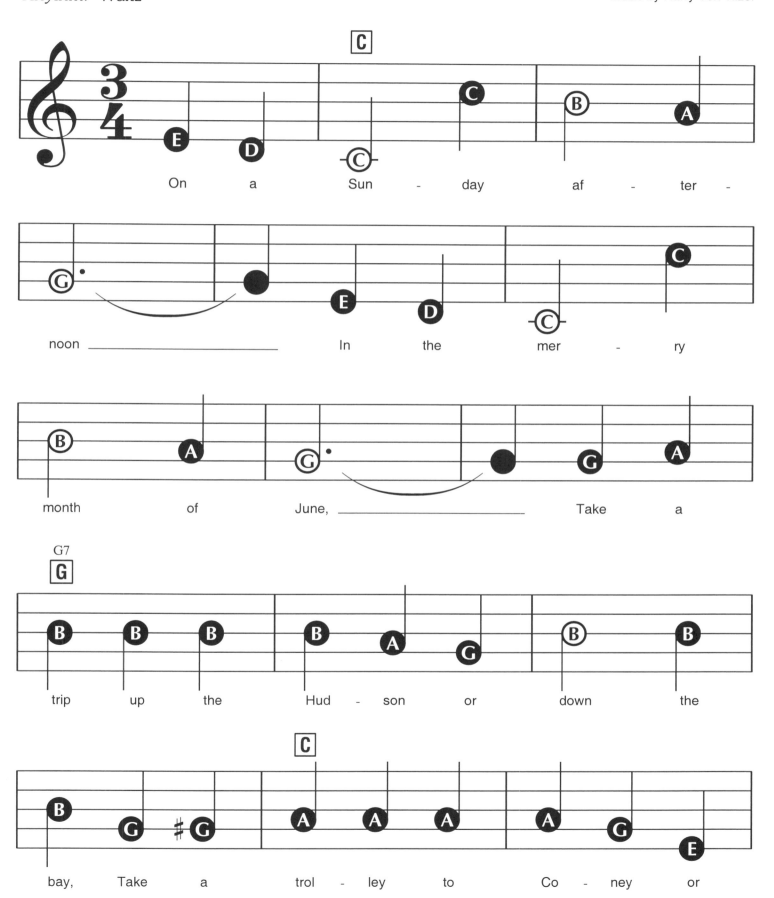

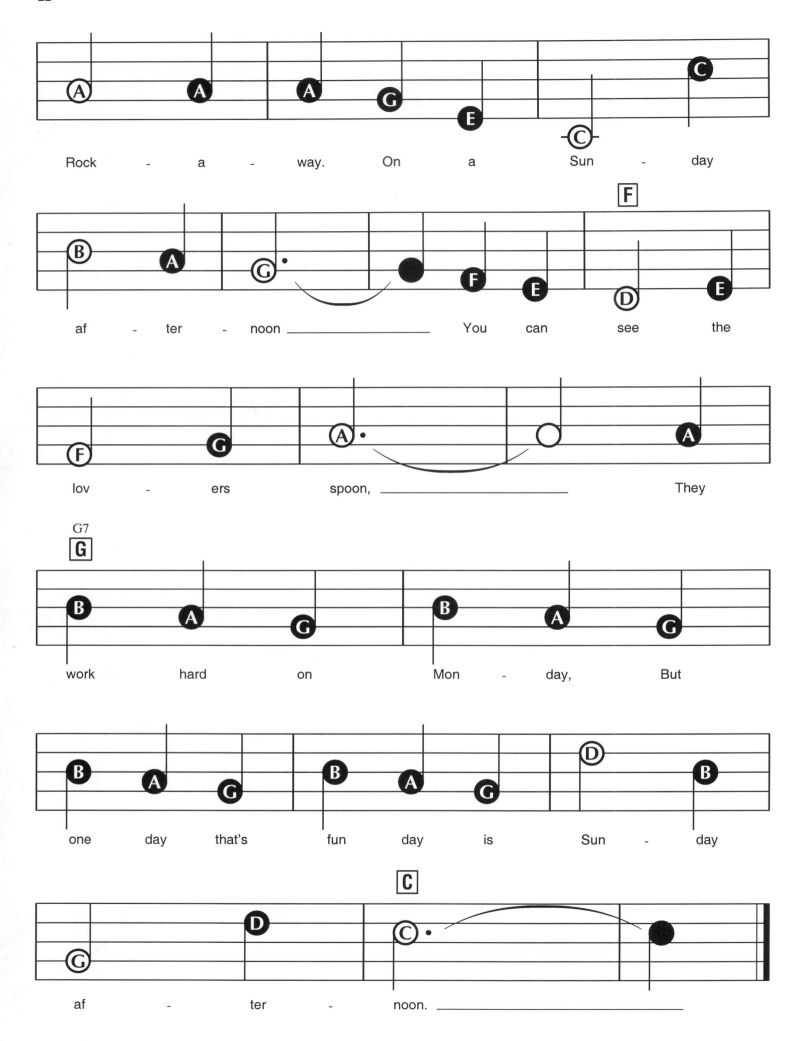

22

1903
In the Good Old Summertime
from IN THE GOOD OLD SUMMERTIME

Registration 5
Rhythm: Waltz

Words by Ren Shields
Music by George Evans

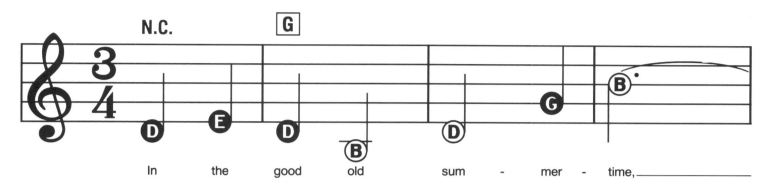

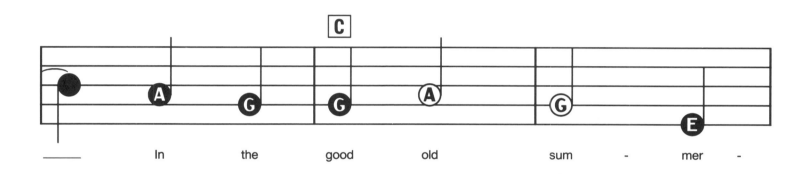

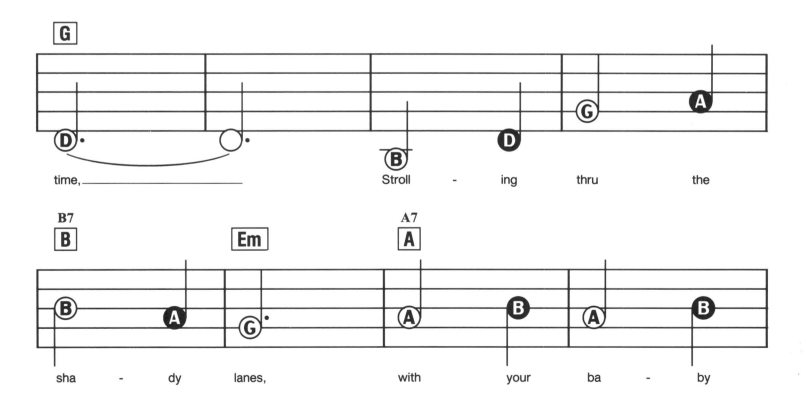

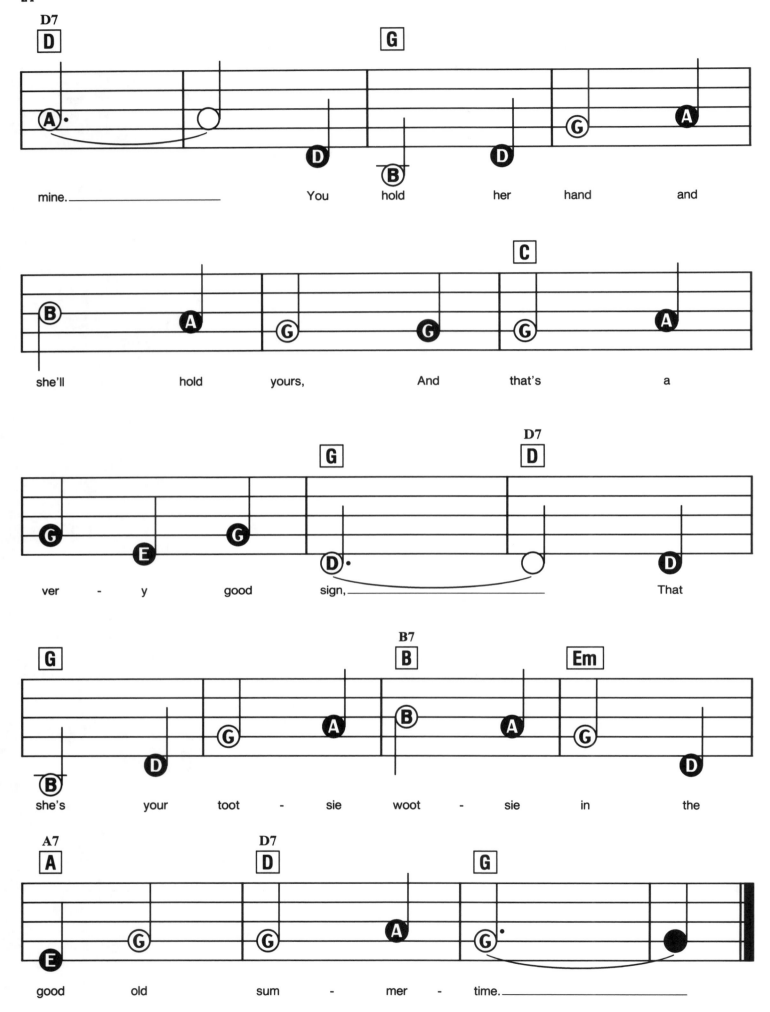

1904
Give My Regards to Broadway

Registration 2
Rhythm: Swing or Shuffle

Words and Music by
George M. Cohan

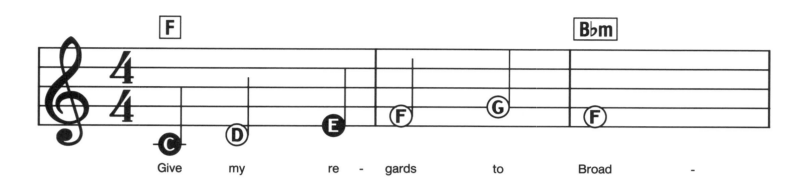

Give my re - gards to Broad -

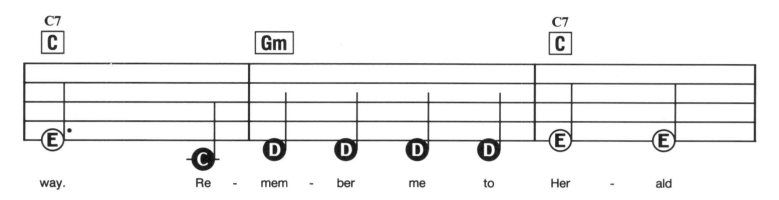

way. Re - mem - ber me to Her - ald

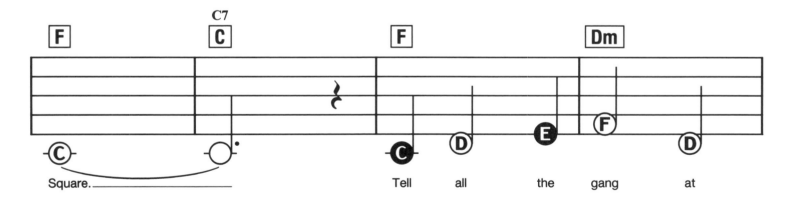

Square. Tell all the gang at

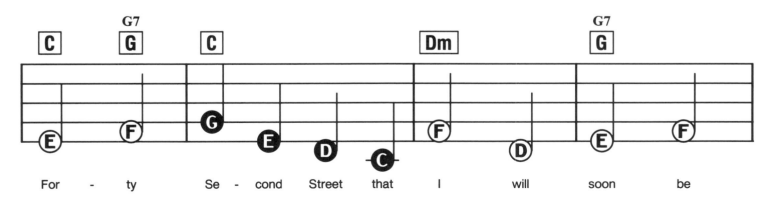

For - ty Se - cond Street that I will soon be

26

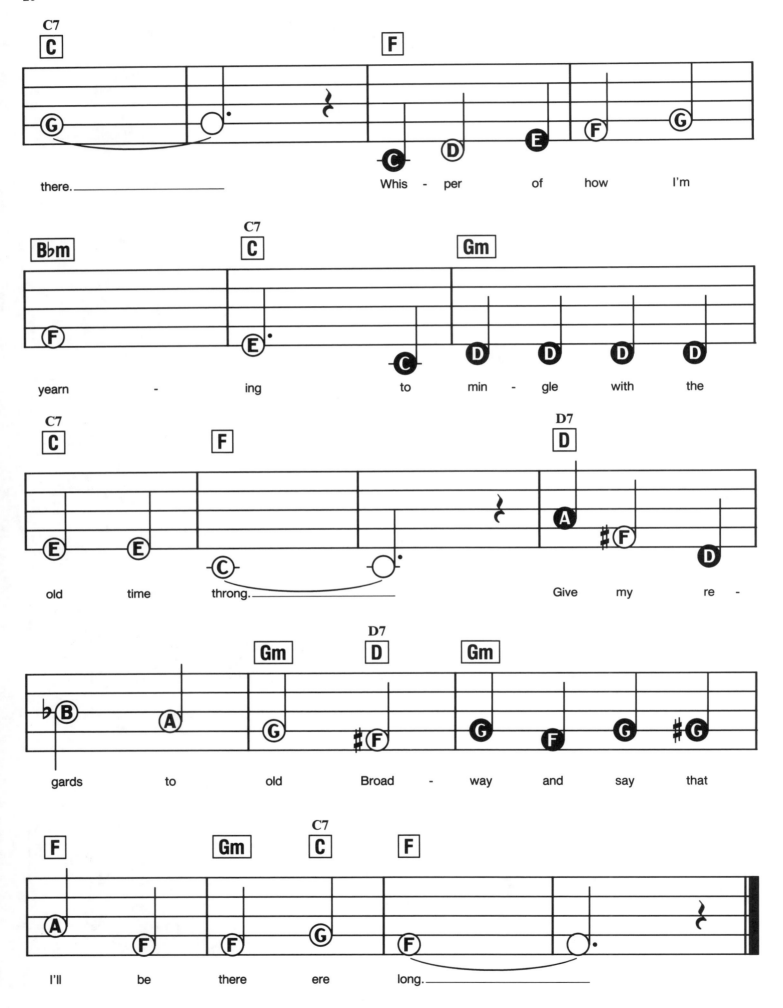

1905
In My Merry Oldsmobile

Registration 4
Rhythm: Waltz

Words by Vincent Bryan
Music by Gus Edwards

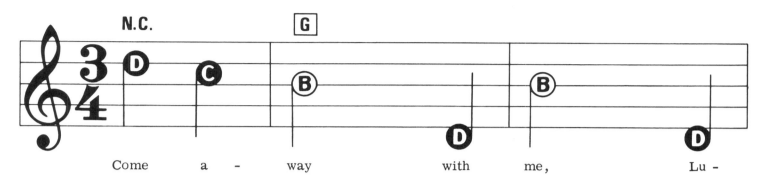

Come a - way with me, Lu -

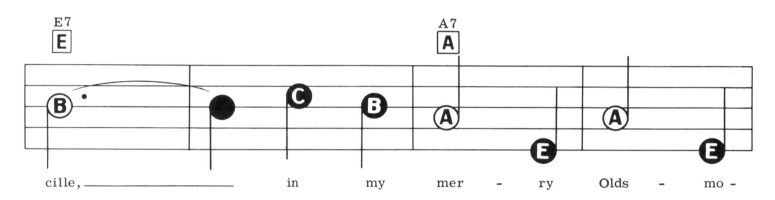

cille, _____ in my mer - ry Olds - mo -

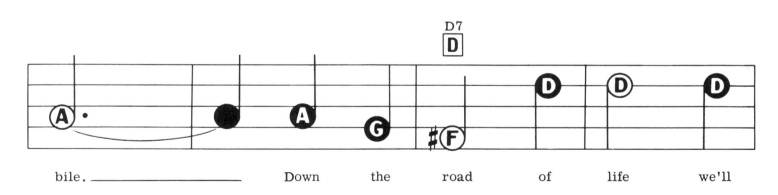

bile. _____ Down the road of life we'll

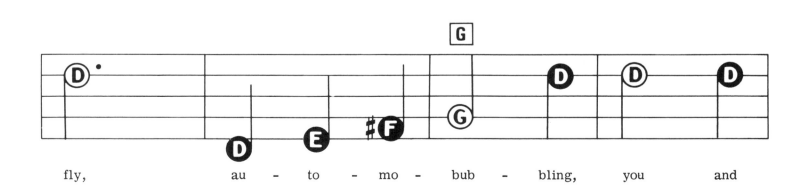

fly, au - to - mo - bub - bling, you and

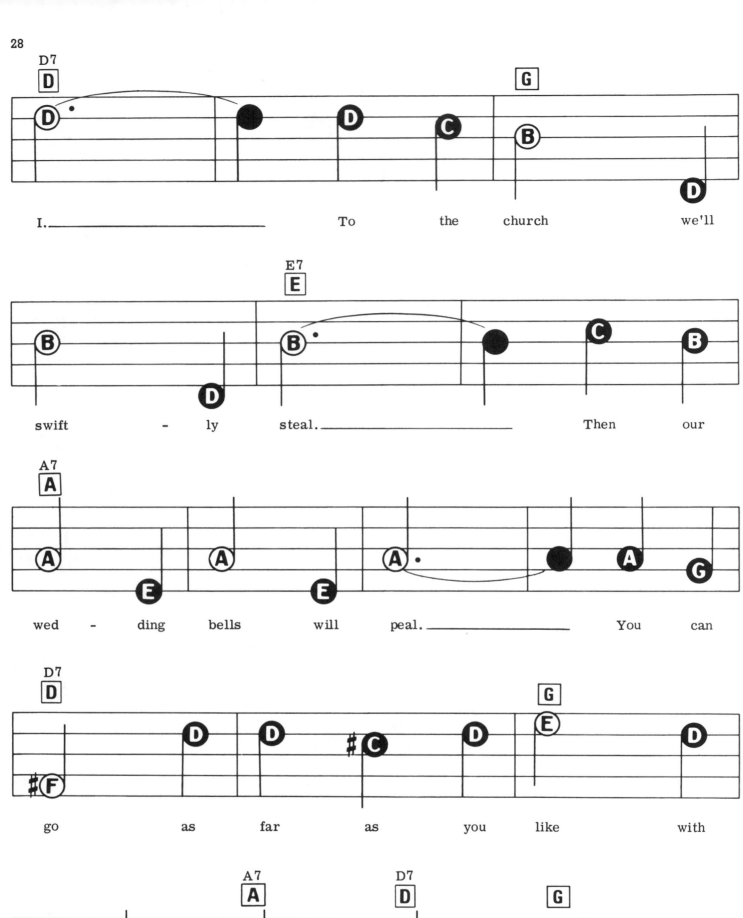

I._____ To the church we'll swift - ly steal._____ Then our wed - ding bells will peal._____ You can go as far as you like with

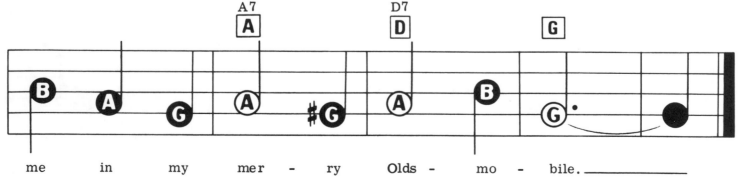

me in my mer - ry Olds - mo - bile._____

1906
I Love You Truly

Registration 10
Rhythm: Waltz

Words and Music by
Carrie Jacobs-Bond

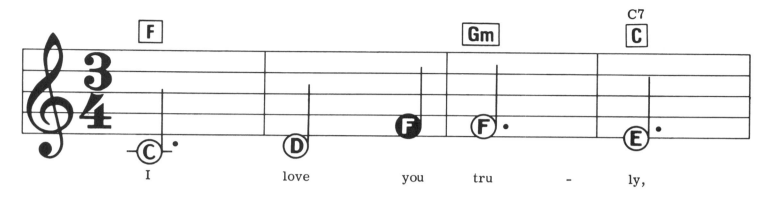

I love you tru - ly,

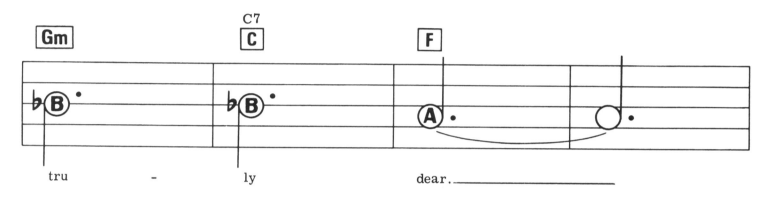

tru - ly dear._____

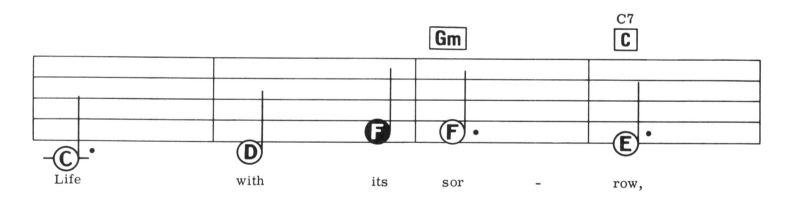

Life with its sor - row,

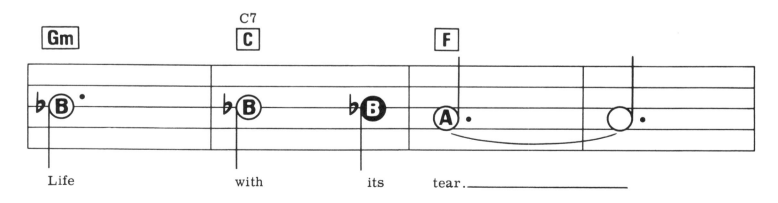

Life with its tear._____

30

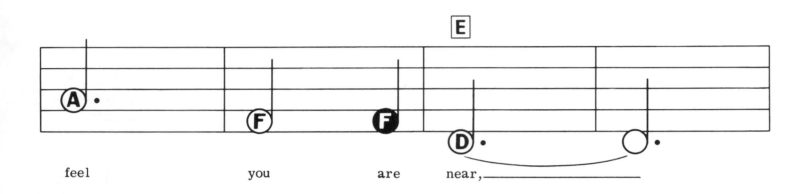

Fades in - to dreams,_____ when I

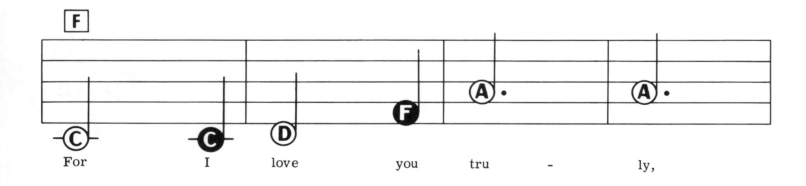

feel you are near,_____

For I love you tru - ly,

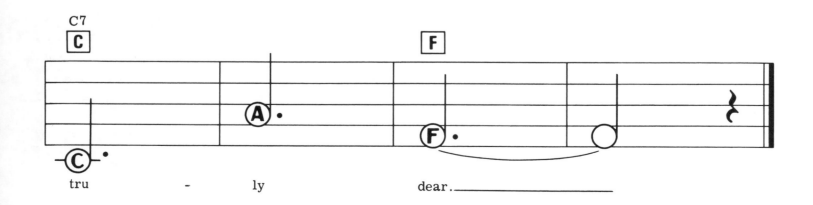

tru - ly dear._____

1907
My Gal Sal

Registration 7
Rhythm: Swing

Words and Music by
Paul Dresser

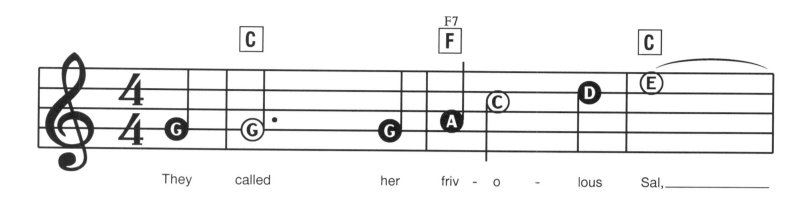

They called her friv - o - lous Sal, _____

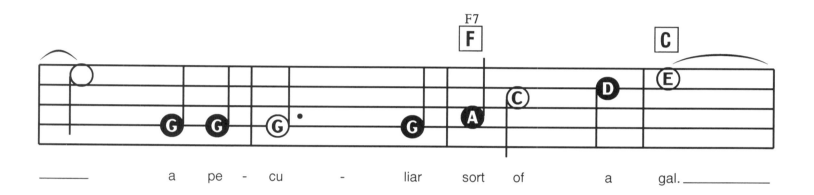

_____ a pe - cu - liar sort of a gal. _____

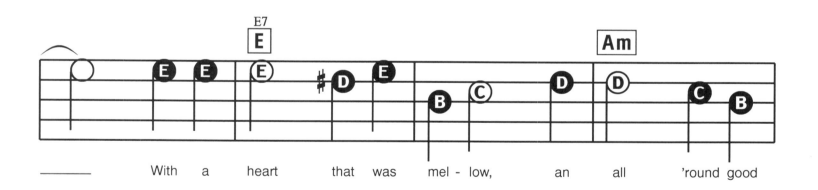

_____ With a heart that was mel - low, an all 'round good

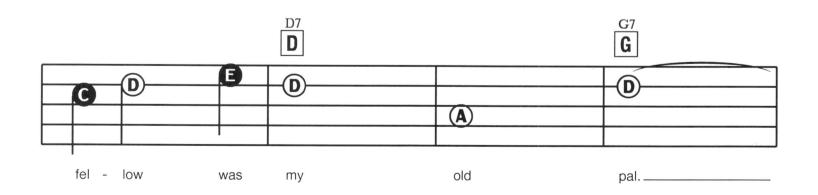

fel - low was my old pal. _____

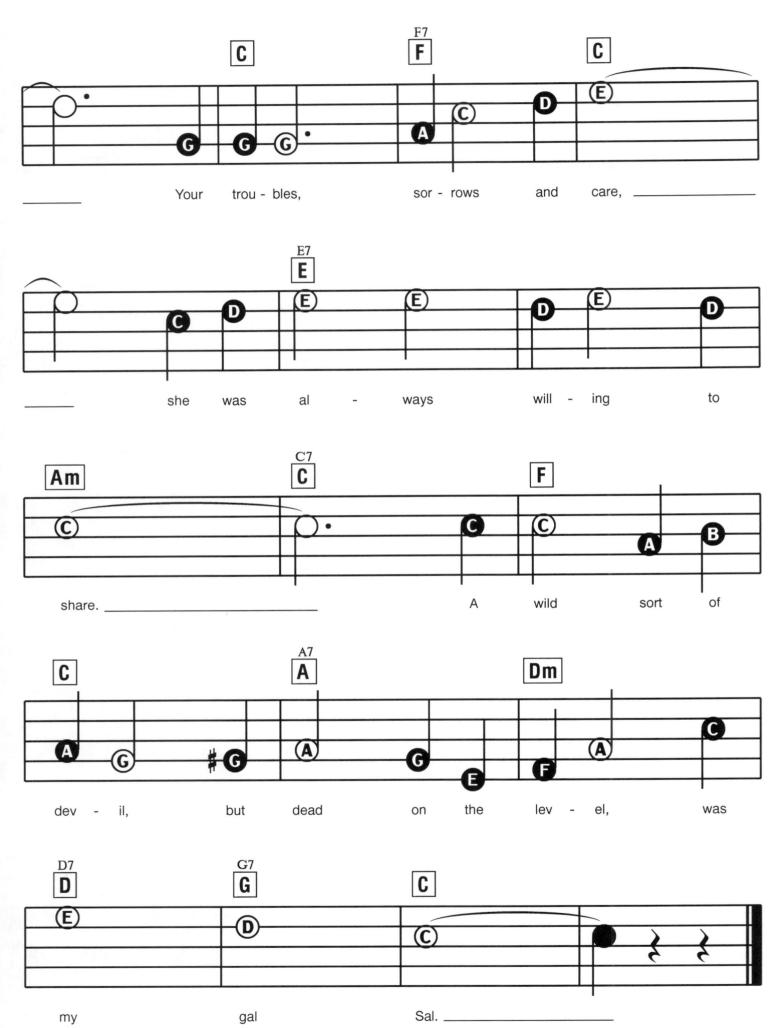

1908
Cuddle Up a Little Closer, Lovey Mine
from THE THREE TWINS

Registration 3
Rhythm: Swing

Words by Otto Harbach
Music by Karl Hoschna

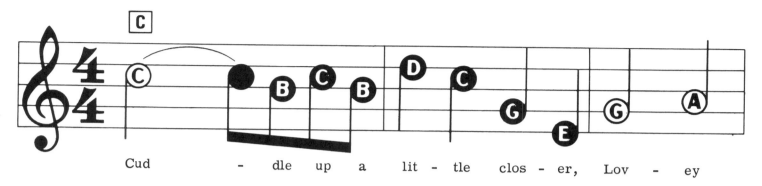

Cud - dle up a lit - tle clos - er, Lov - ey

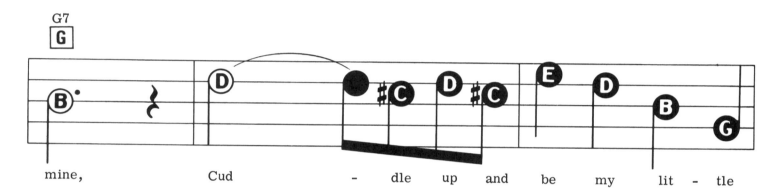

mine, Cud - dle up and be my lit - tle

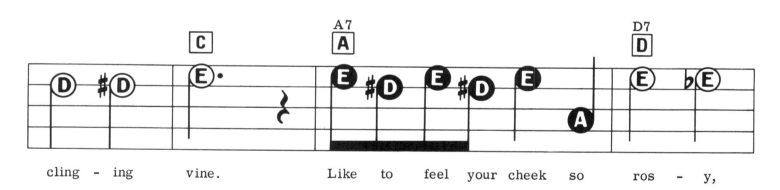

cling - ing vine. Like to feel your cheek so ros - y,

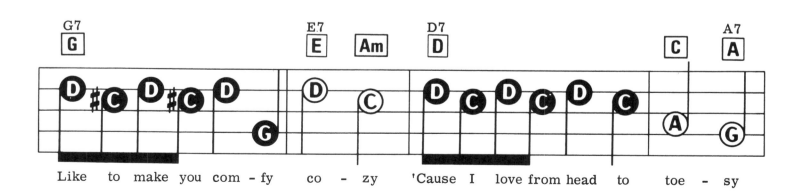

Like to make you com - fy co - zy 'Cause I love from head to toe - sy

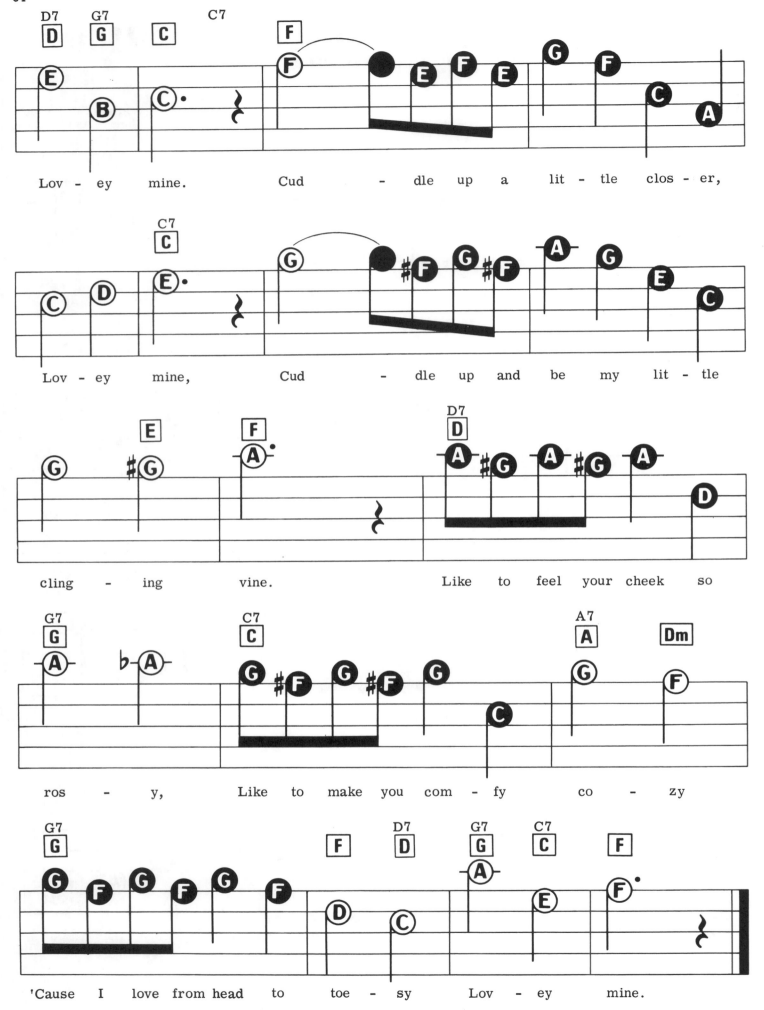

1909
By the Light of the Silvery Moon

Registration 2
Rhythm: Swing

Lyrics by Ed Madden
Music by Gus Edwards

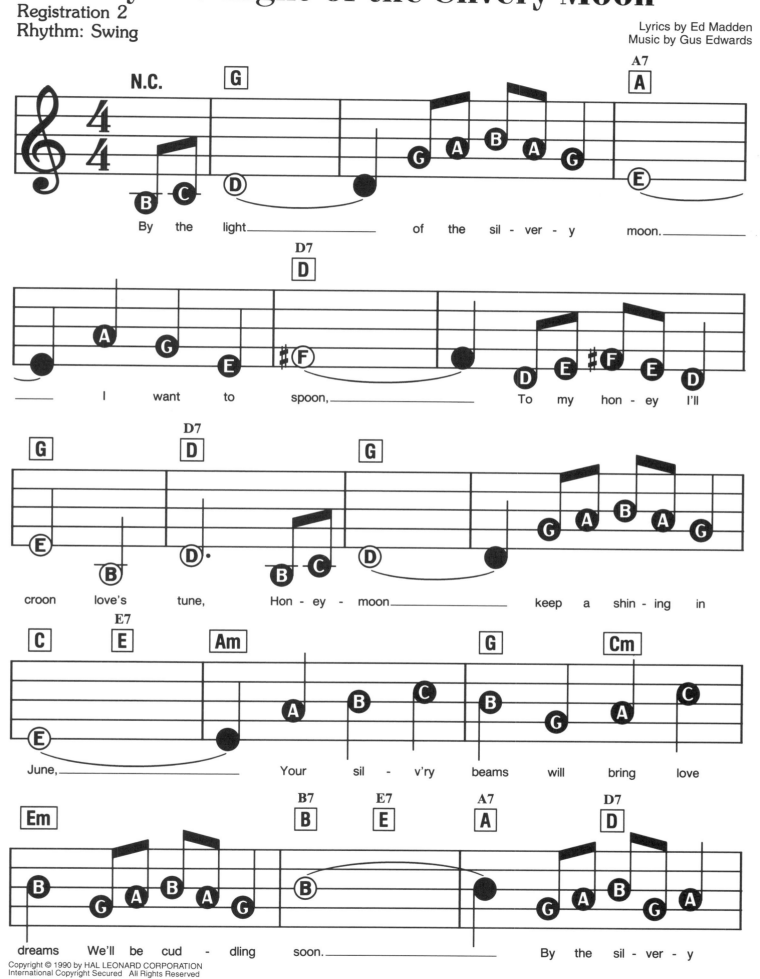

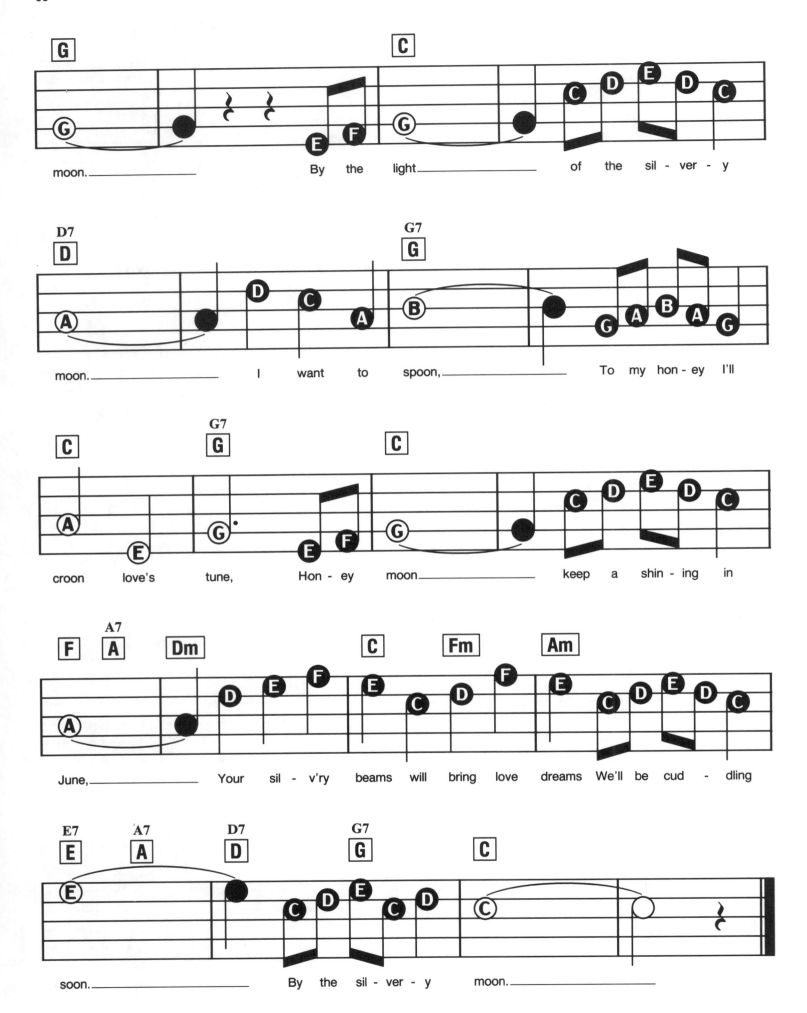

1910
Meet Me Tonight in Dreamland

Registration 5
Rhythm: Waltz

Words by Beth Slater Whitson
Music by Leo Friedman

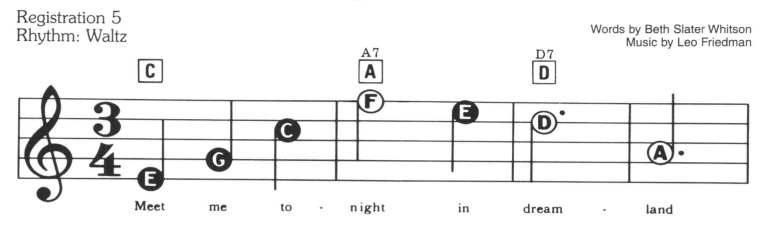

Meet me to - night in dream - land

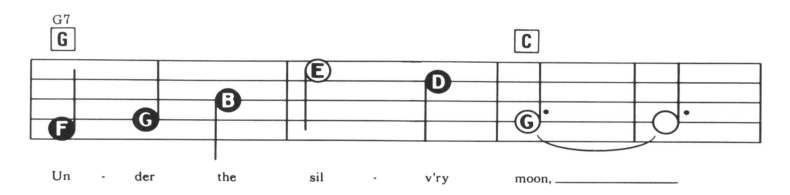

Un - der the sil - v'ry moon, _____

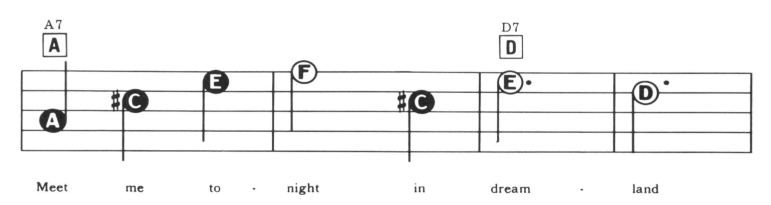

Meet me to - night in dream - land

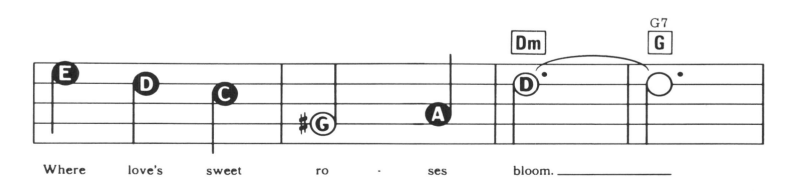

Where love's sweet ro - ses bloom. _____

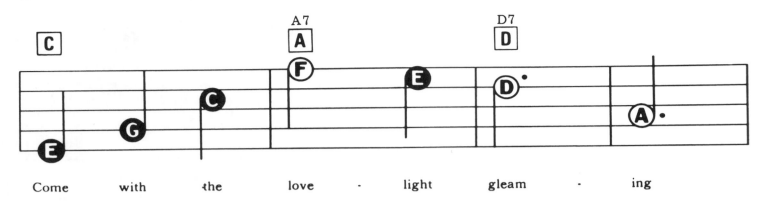

Come with the love - light gleam - ing

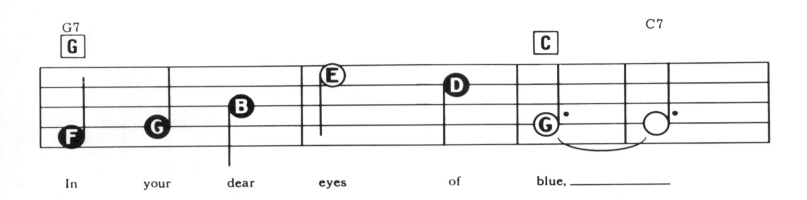

In your dear eyes of blue, _____

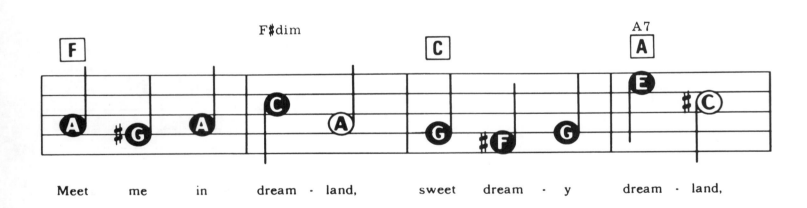

Meet me in dream - land, sweet dream - y dream - land,

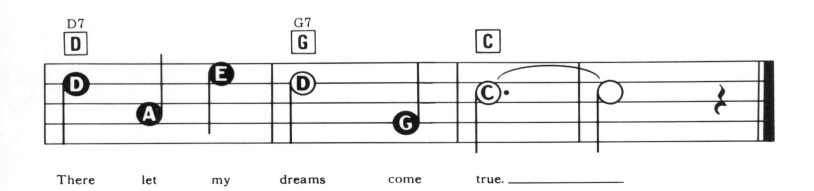

There let my dreams come true. _____

1911
Put Your Arms Around Me, Honey

Registration 9
Rhythm: Fox Trot

Words by Junie McCree
Music by Albert Von Tilzer

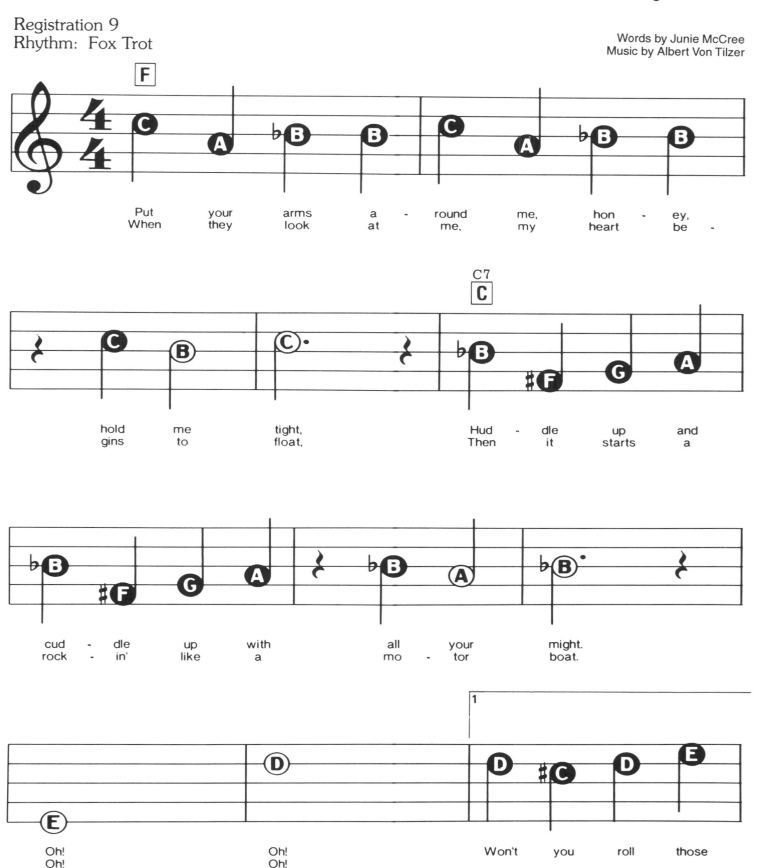

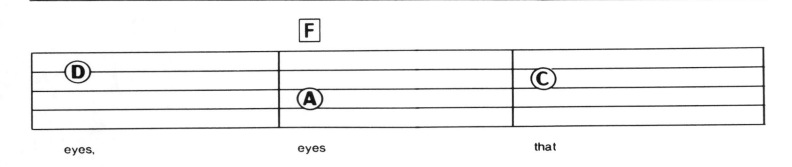

eyes,   eyes   that

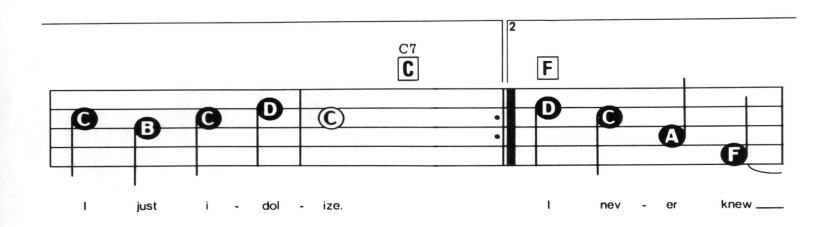

I   just   i - dol - ize.   I   nev - er   knew _____

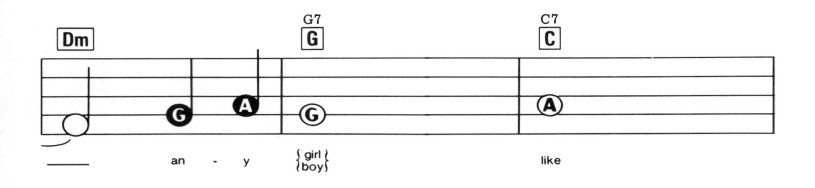

_____   an - y   {girl}{boy}   like

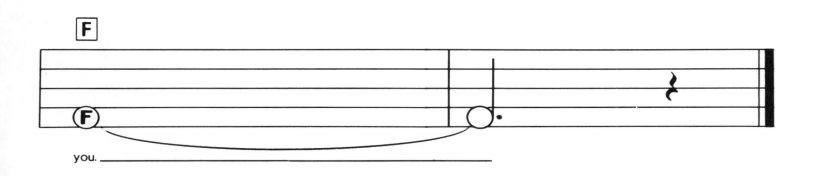

you. _____

1912
My Melancholy Baby

Registration 3
Rhythm: Swing

Words by George Norton
Music by Ernie Burnett

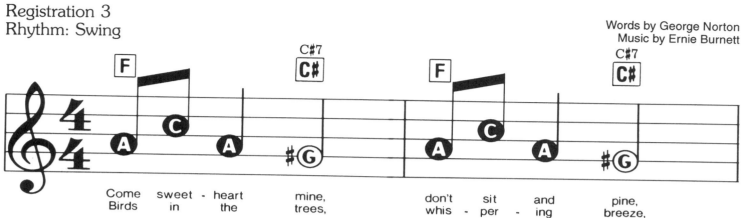

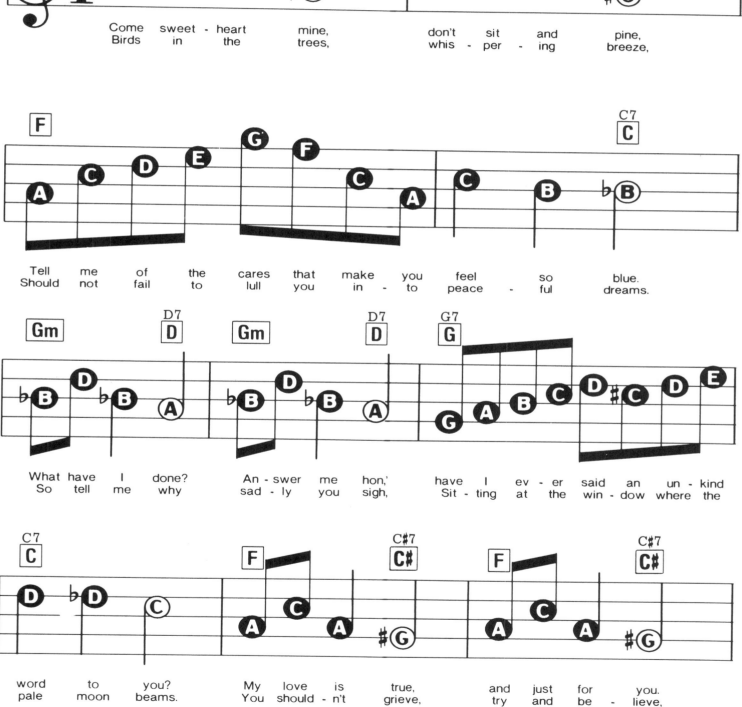

42

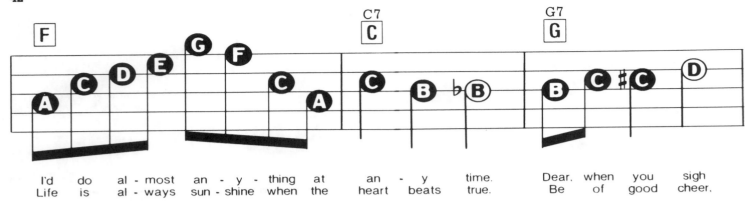

I'd do al-most an-y-thing at an-y time. Dear, when you sigh
Life is al-ways sun-shine when the heart beats true. Be of good cheer,

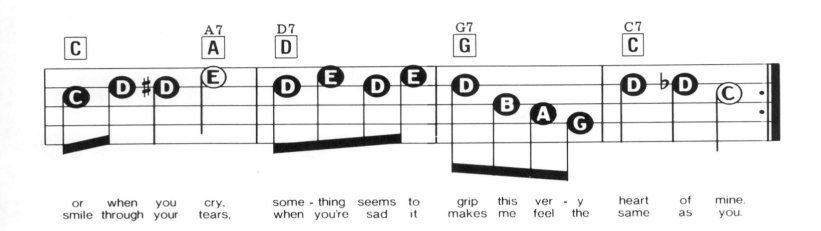

or when you cry, some-thing seems to grip this ver-y heart of mine.
smile through your tears, when you're sad it makes me feel the same as you.

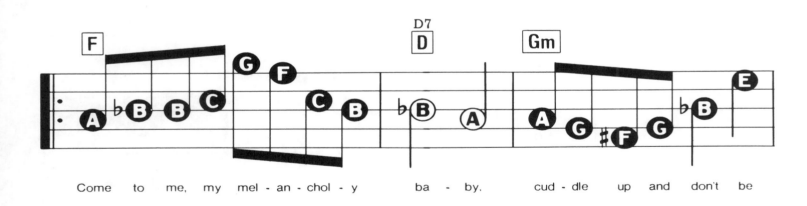

Come to me, my mel-an-chol-y ba-by. cud-dle up and don't be

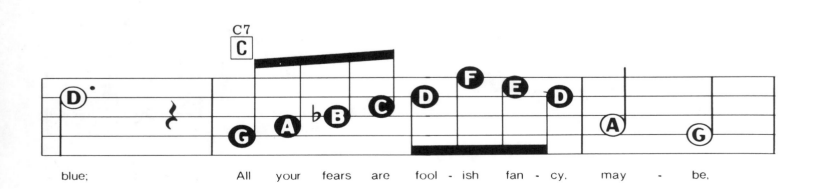

blue; All your fears are fool-ish fan-cy, may-be,

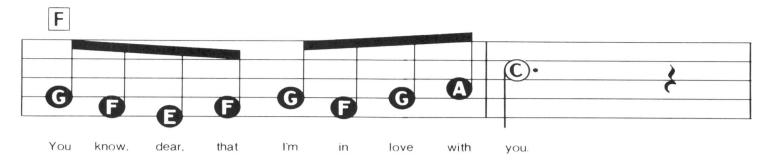

You know, dear, that I'm in love with you.

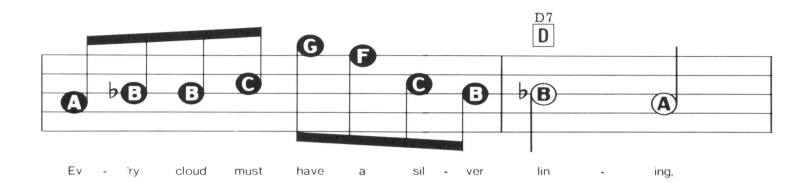

Ev - 'ry cloud must have a sil - ver lin - ing,

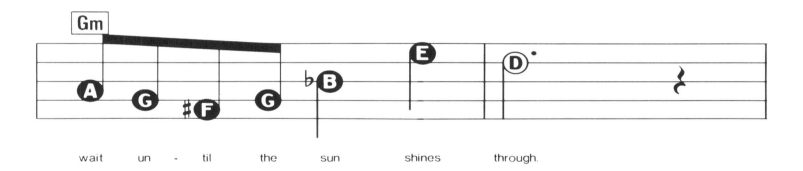

wait un - til the sun shines through.

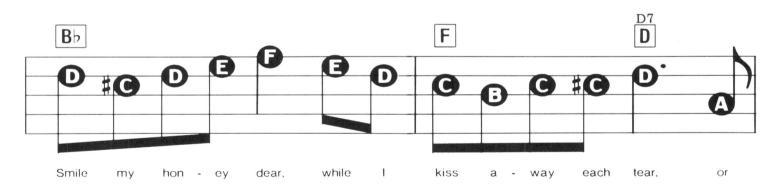

Smile my hon - ey dear, while I kiss a - way each tear, or

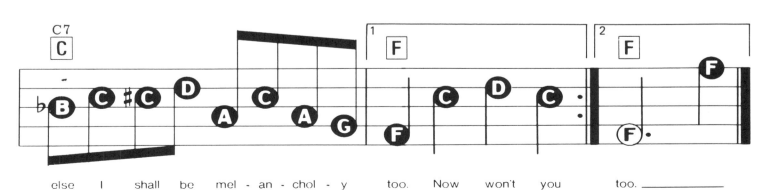

else I shall be mel - an - chol - y too. Now won't you too. _____

1913
Peg O' My Heart

Registration 2
Rhythm: Fox Trot or Swing

Words by Alfred Bryan
Music by Fred Fisher

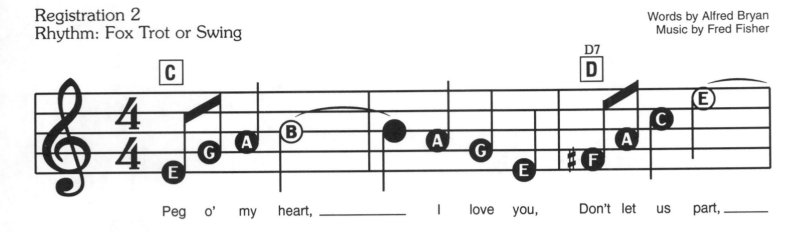

Peg o' my heart, _____ I love you, Don't let us part, _____

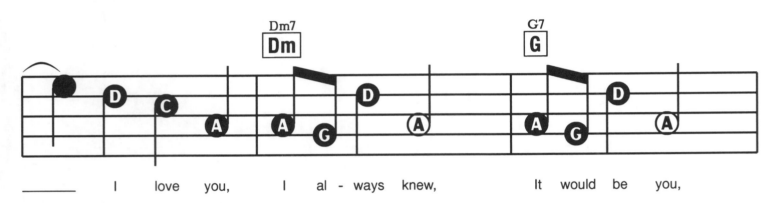

_____ I love you, I al - ways knew, It would be you,

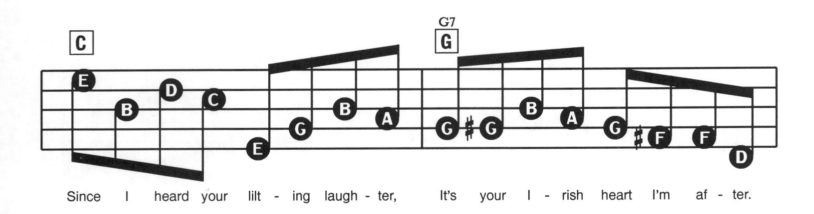

Since I heard your lilt - ing laugh - ter, It's your I - rish heart I'm af - ter.

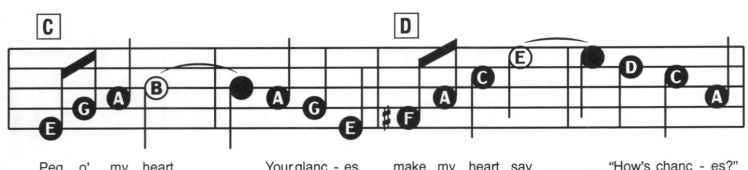

Peg o' my heart, _____ Your glanc - es make my heart say _____ "How's chanc - es?"

1914
Ballin' the Jack

Registration 9
Rhythm: Swing or Fox Trot

Words by Jim Burris
Music by Chris Smith

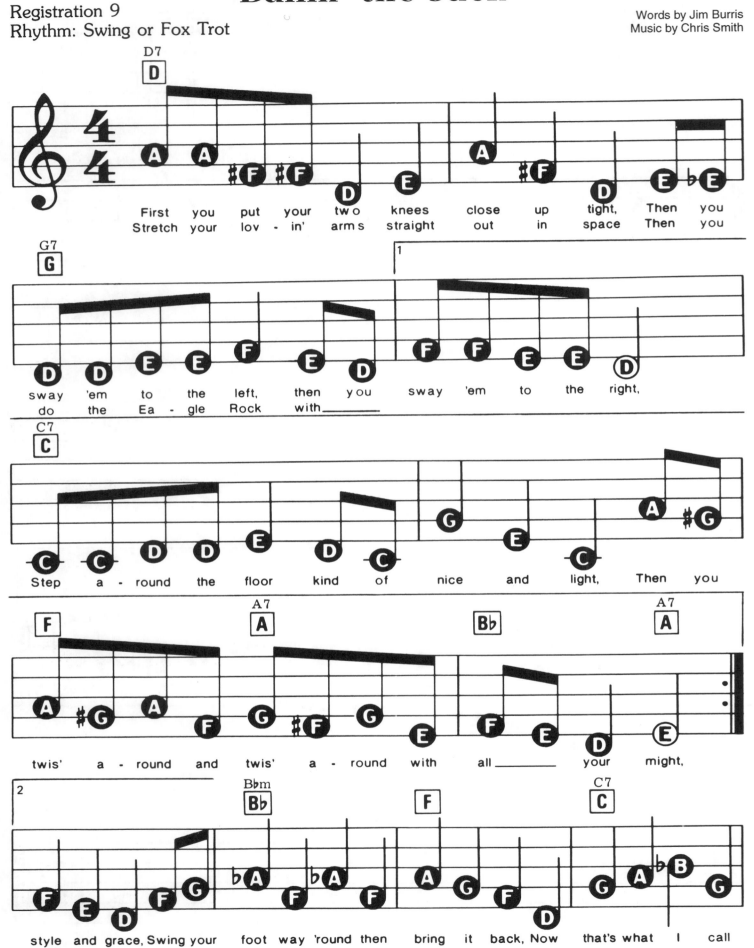

1915

They Didn't Believe Me

from THE GIRL FROM UTAH

Registration 2
Rhythm: Ballad or Swing

Words by Herbert Reynolds
Music by Jerome Kern

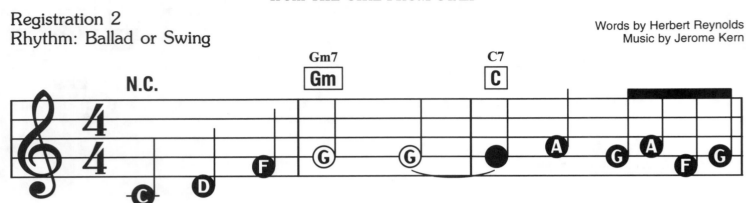

And when I told them_____ How beau - ti - ful you

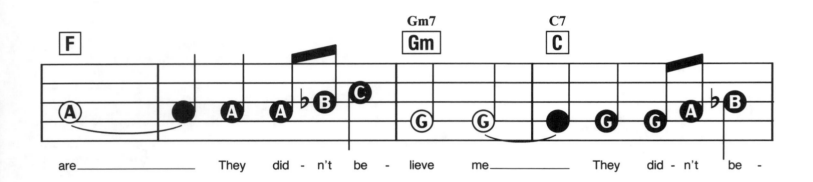

are_____ They did - n't be - lieve me_____ They did - n't be -

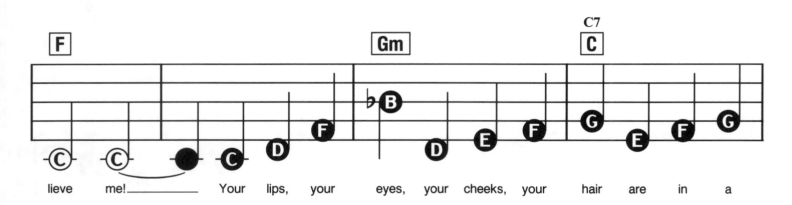

lieve me!_____ Your lips, your eyes, your cheeks, your hair are in a

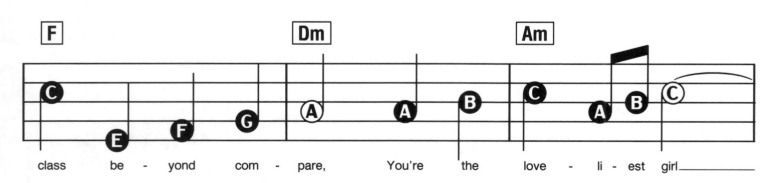

class be - yond com - pare, You're the love - li - est girl_____

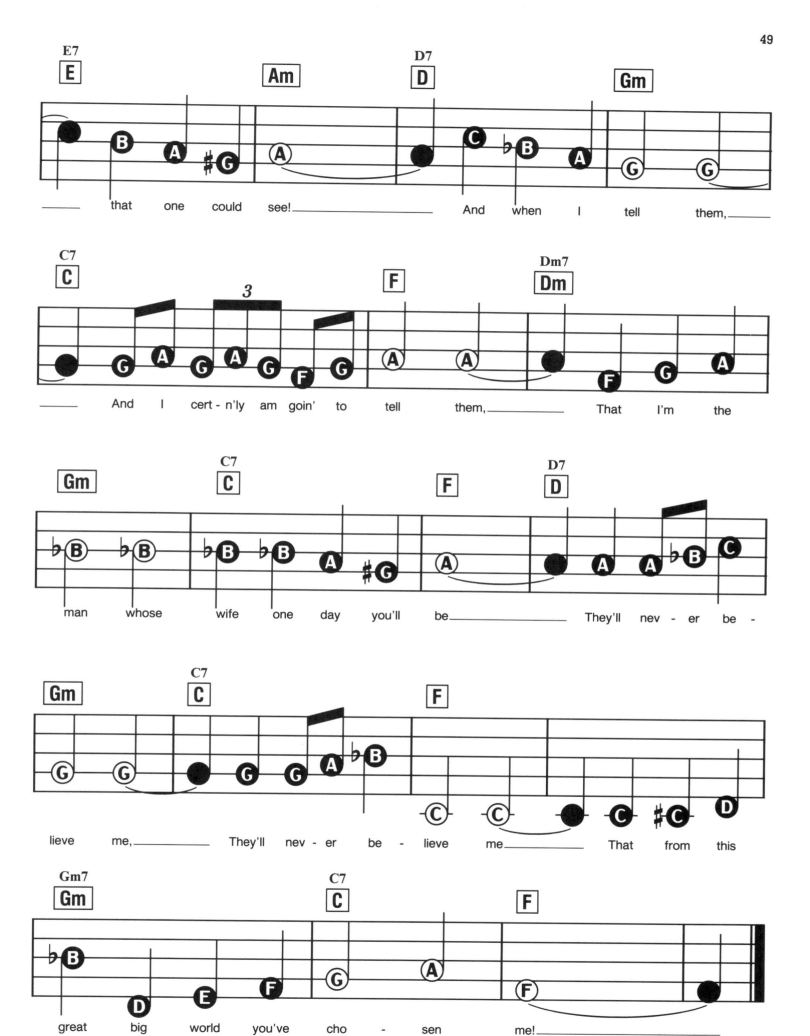

1916

I Love a Piano
from the Stage Production STOP! LOOK! LISTEN!

Registration 8
Rhythm: Swing

Words and Music by
Irving Berlin

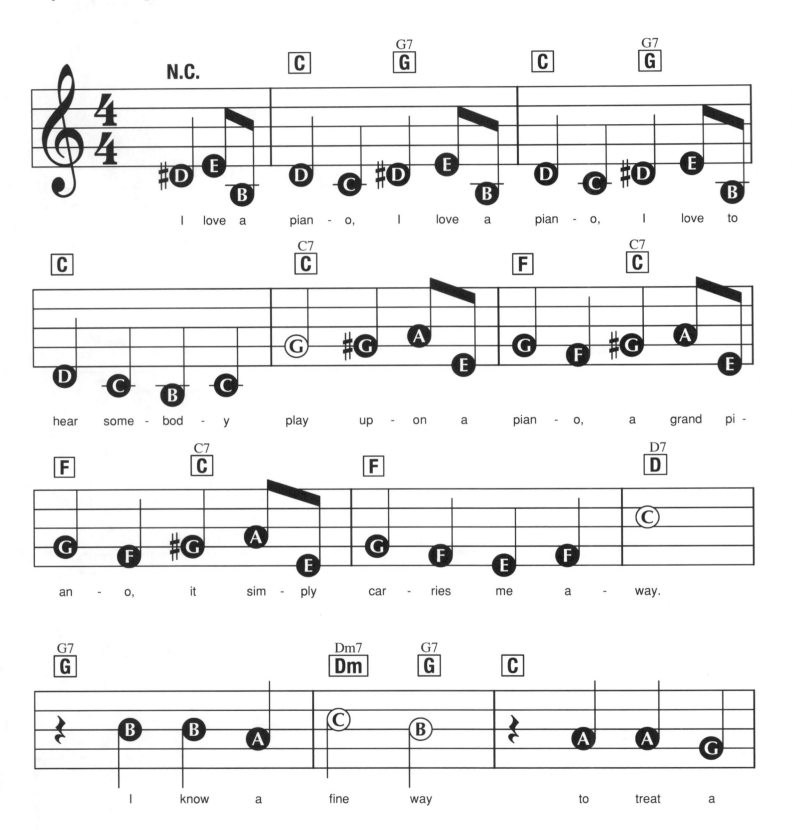

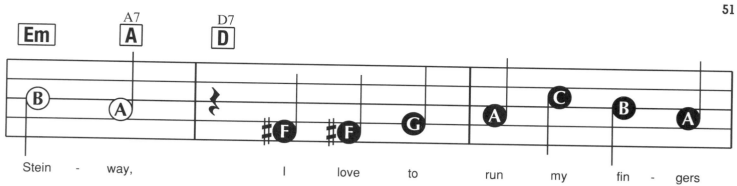

Stein - way, I love to run my fin - gers

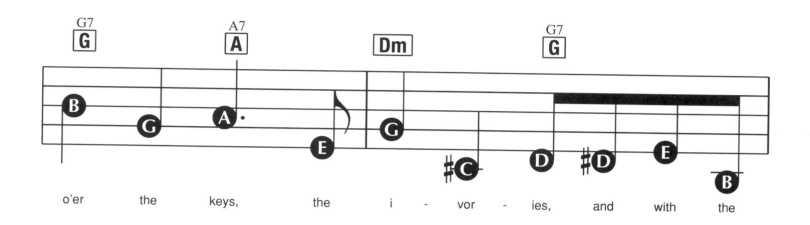

o'er the keys, the i - vor - ies, and with the

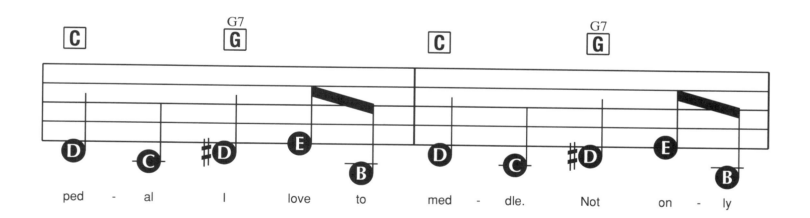

ped - al I love to med - dle. Not on - ly

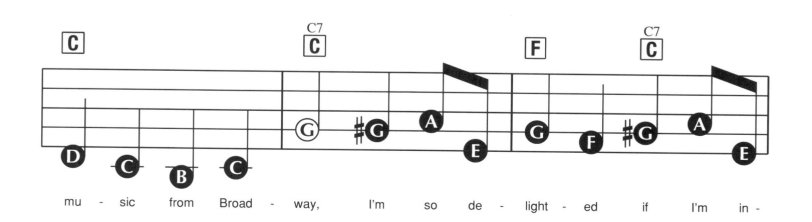

mu - sic from Broad - way, I'm so de - light - ed if I'm in -

52

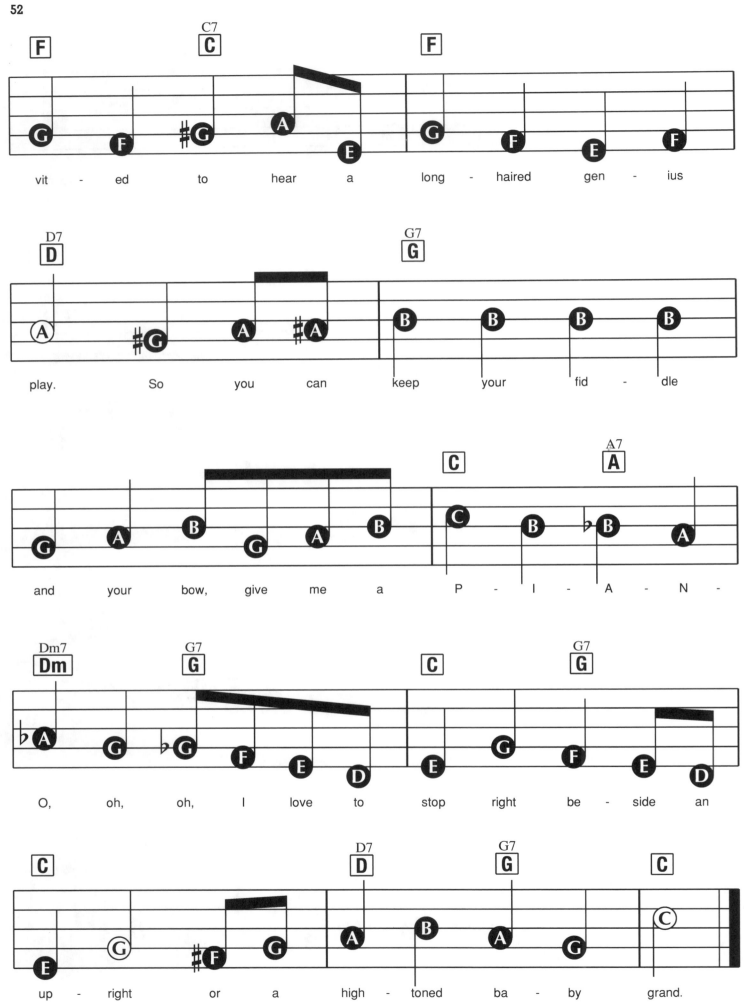

For Me and My Gal

1917

Registration 3
Rhythm: Swing

Words by Edgar Leslie and E. Ray Goetz
Music by George W. Meyer

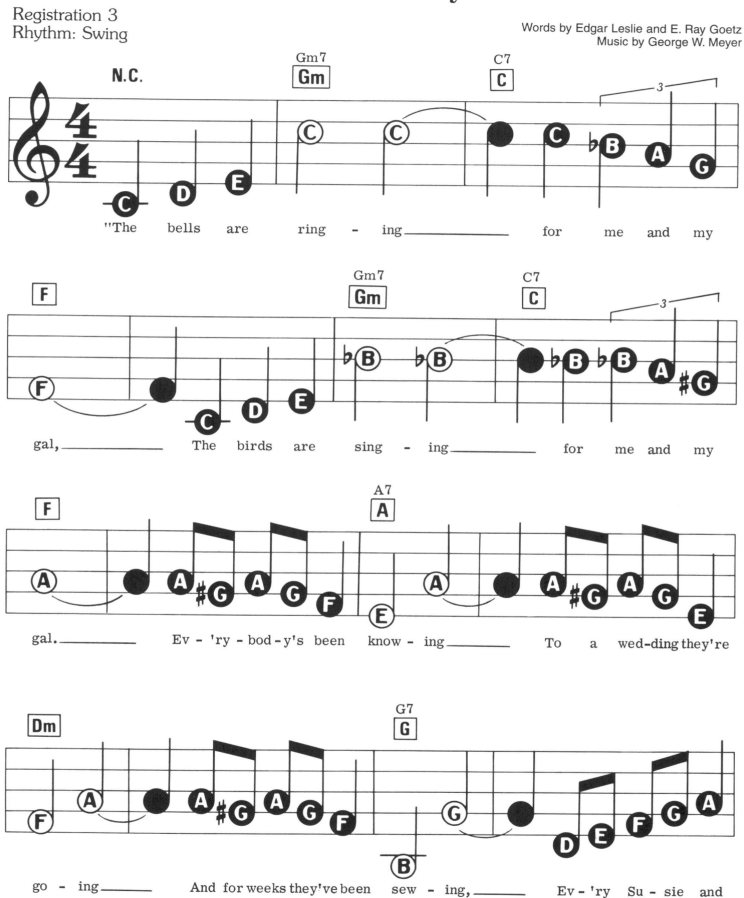

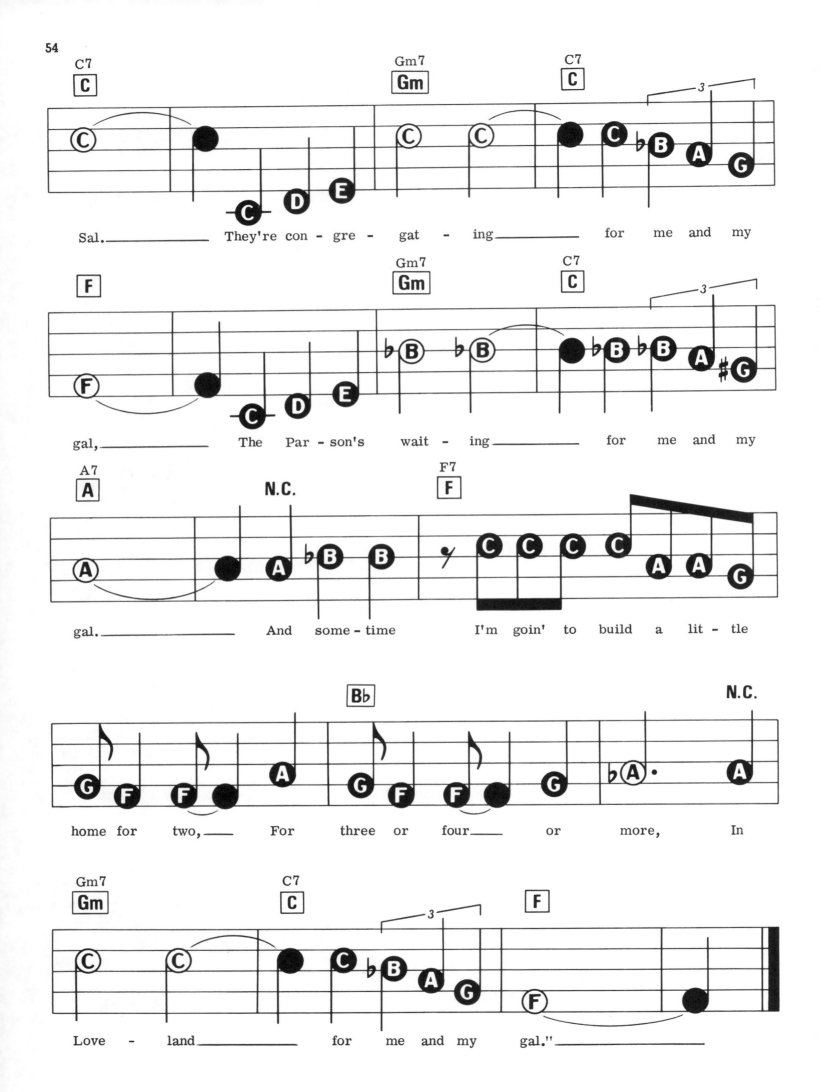

1918
The Caissons Go Rolling Along

Registration 2
Rhythm: March

Words and Music by
Edmund L. Gruber

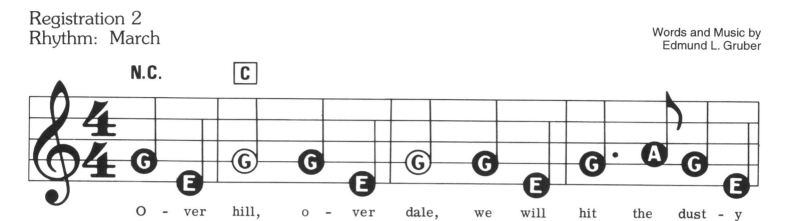

O - ver hill, o - ver dale, we will hit the dust - y

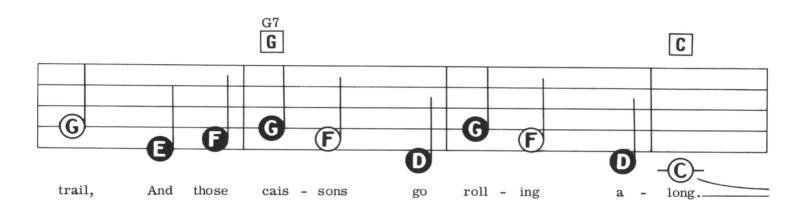

trail, And those cais - sons go roll - ing a - long.

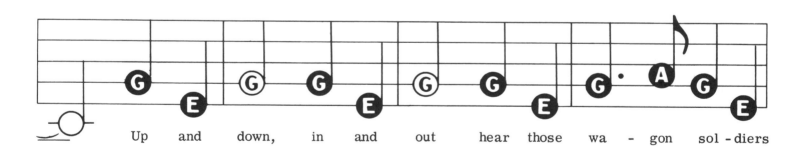

Up and down, in and out hear those wa - gon sol - diers

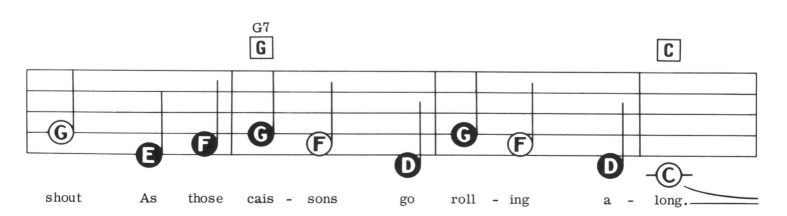

shout As those cais - sons go roll - ing a - long.

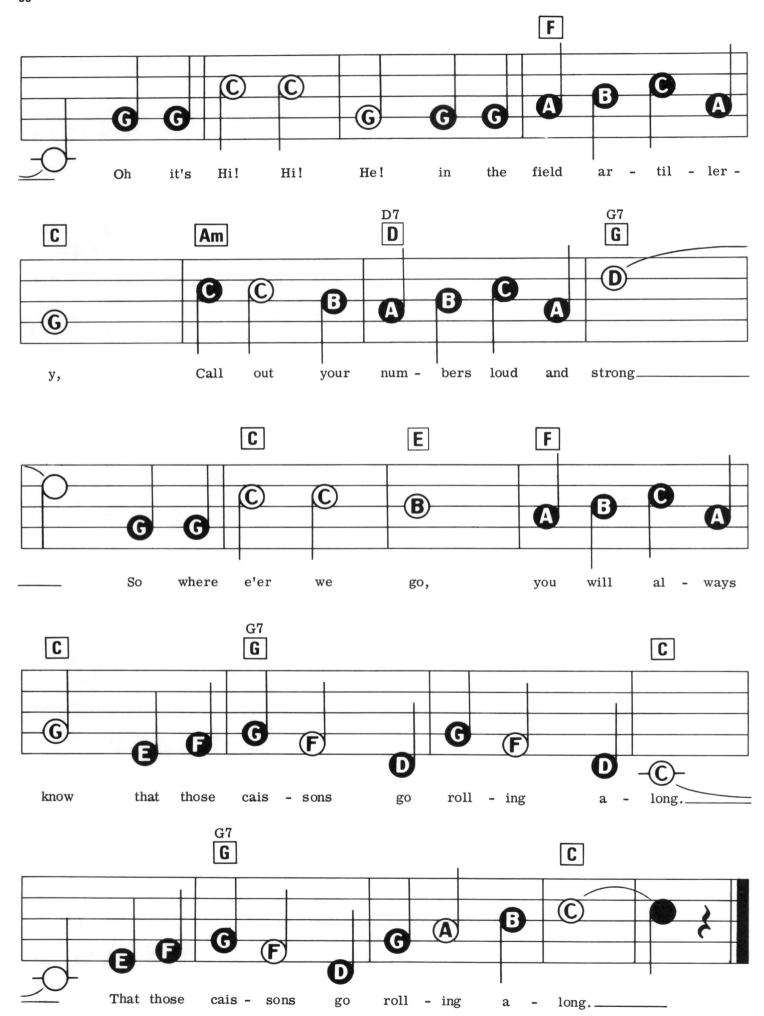

1919
After You've Gone
from ONE MO' TIME

Registration 8
Rhythm: Swing

Words by Henry Creamer
Music by Turner Layton

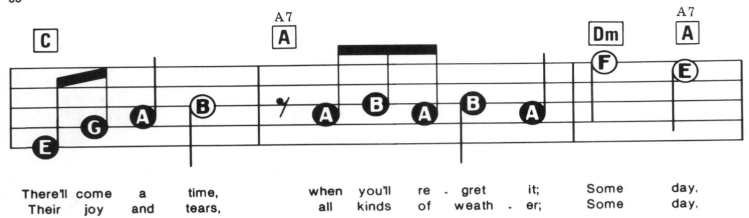

There'll come a time, when you'll re - gret it; Some day,
Their joy and tears, all kinds of weath - er; Some day,

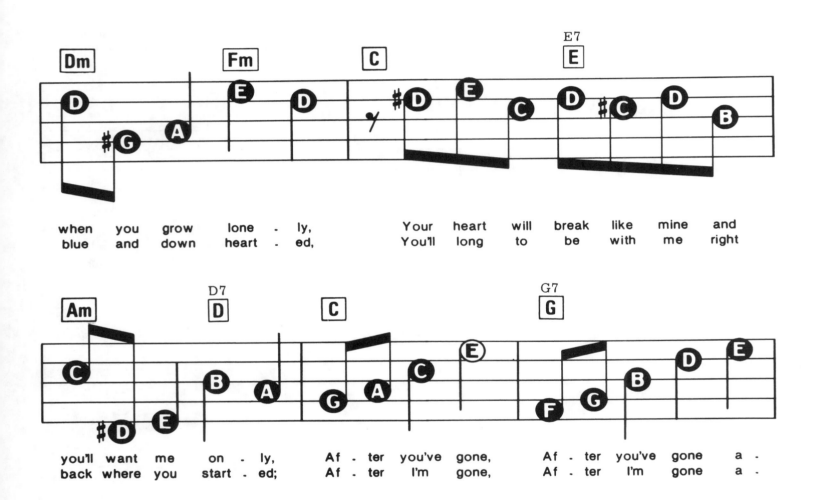

when you grow lone - ly, Your heart will break like mine and
blue and down heart - ed, You'll long to be with me right

you'll want me on - ly, Af - ter you've gone,
back where you start - ed; Af - ter I'm gone,

Af - ter you've gone a -
Af - ter I'm gone a -

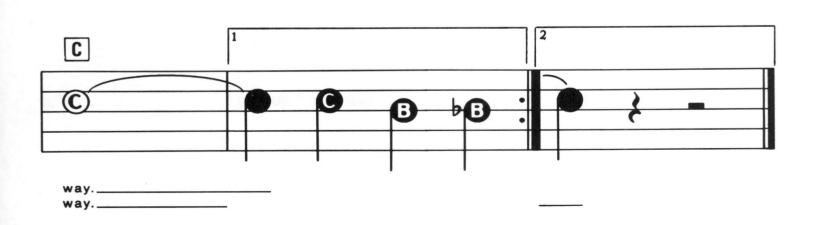

way. _____
way. _____

1920
Whispering

Registration 4
Rhythm: Fox Trot or Swing

Words and Music by Richard Coburn,
John Schonberger and Vincent Rose

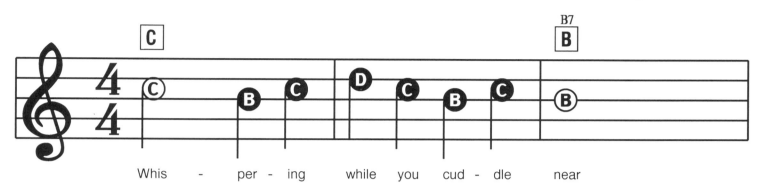

Whis - per - ing while you cud - dle near

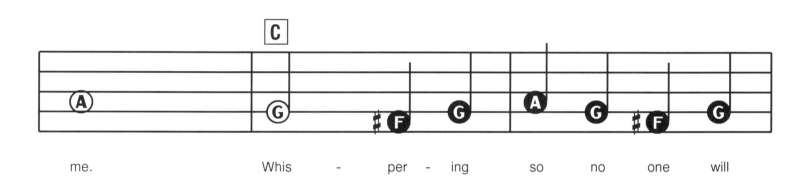

me. Whis - per - ing so no one will

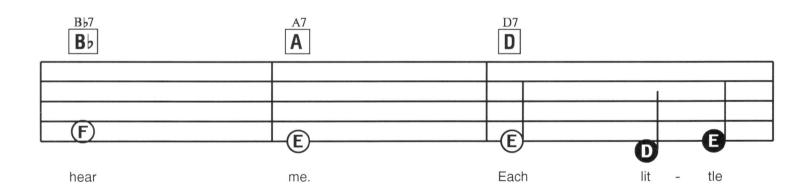

hear me. Each lit - tle

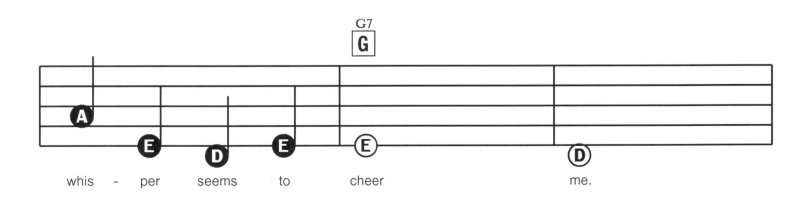

whis - per seems to cheer me.

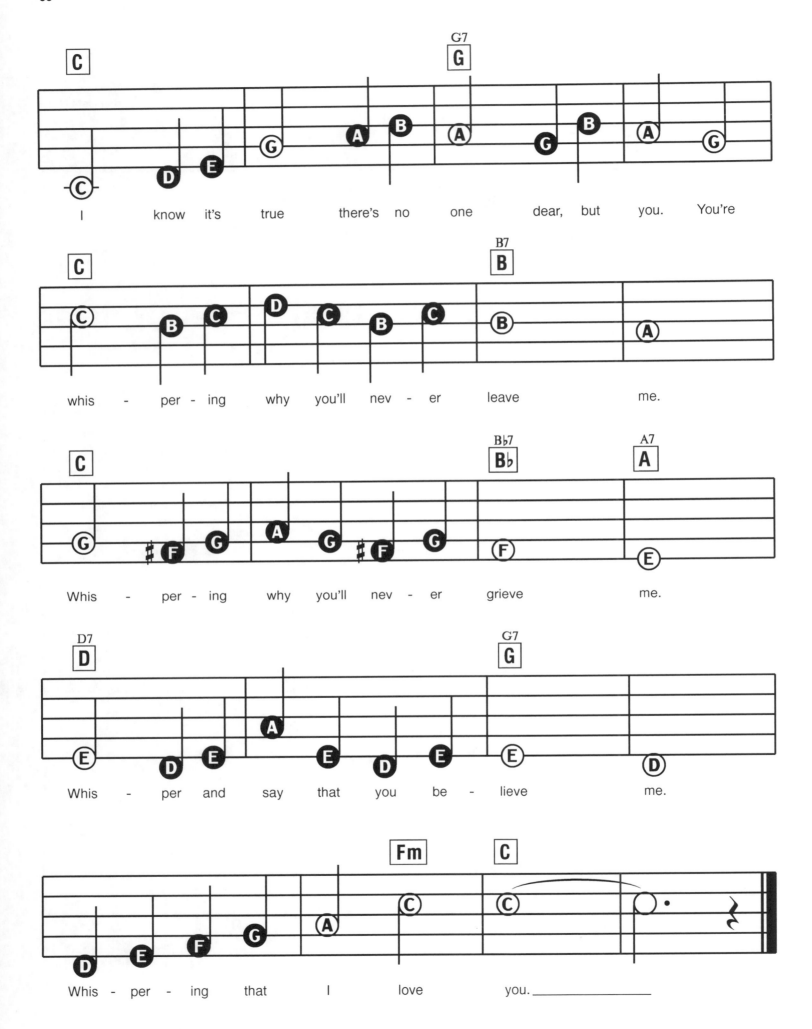

1921
Look for the Silver Lining
from SALLY

Registration 2
Rhythm: Fox Trot or Swing

Words by Buddy DeSylva
Music by Jerome Kern

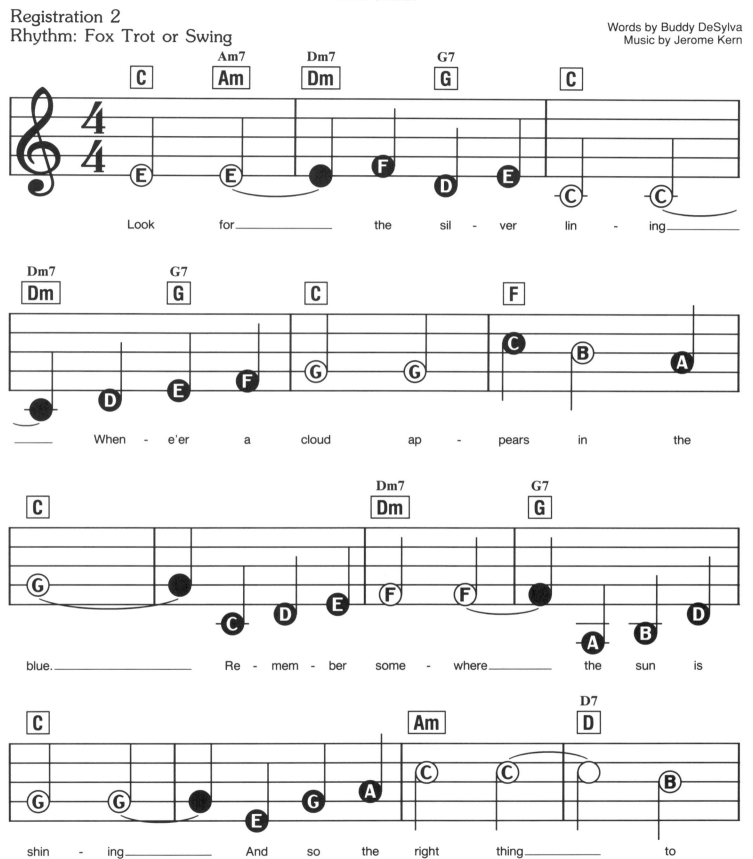

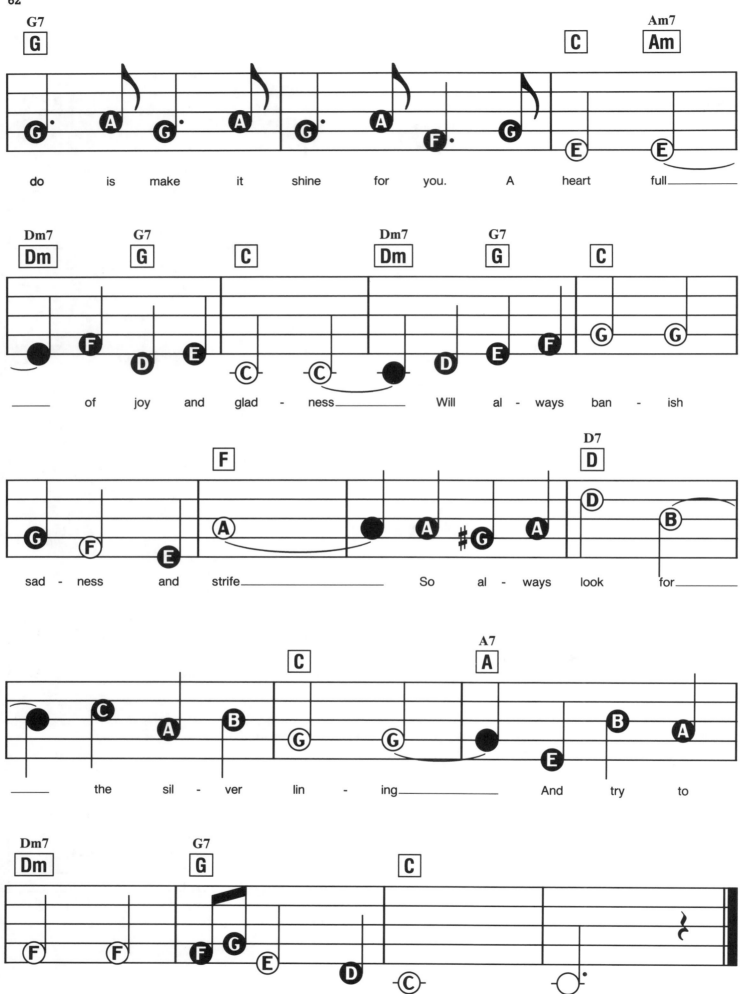

1922
April Showers
from BOMBO

Registration 9
Rhythm: Fox Trot

Words by B.G. DeSylva
Music by Louis Silvers

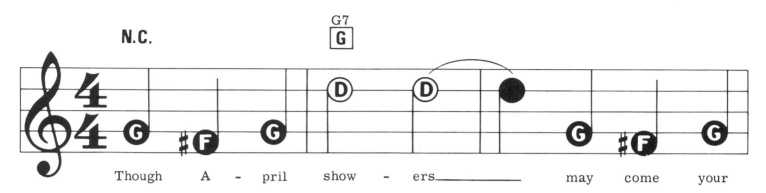

Though A - pril show - ers_____ may come your

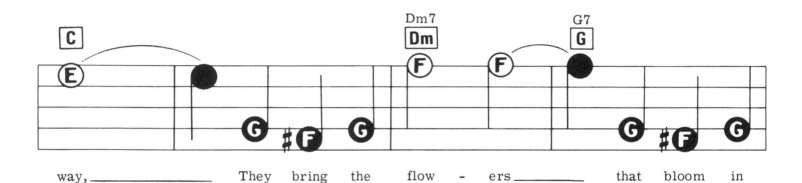

way,_____ They bring the flow - ers_____ that bloom in

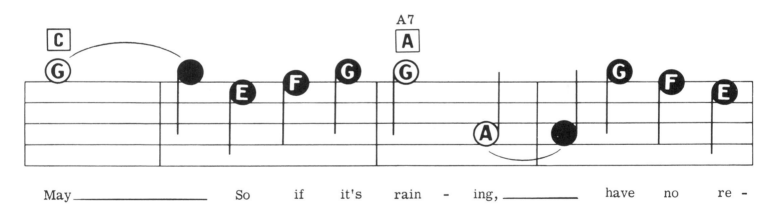

May_____ So if it's rain - ing,_____ have no re -

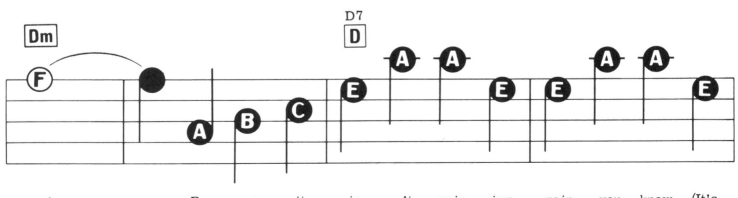

grets_____ Be - cause it is - n't rain - ing rain you know, (It's

64

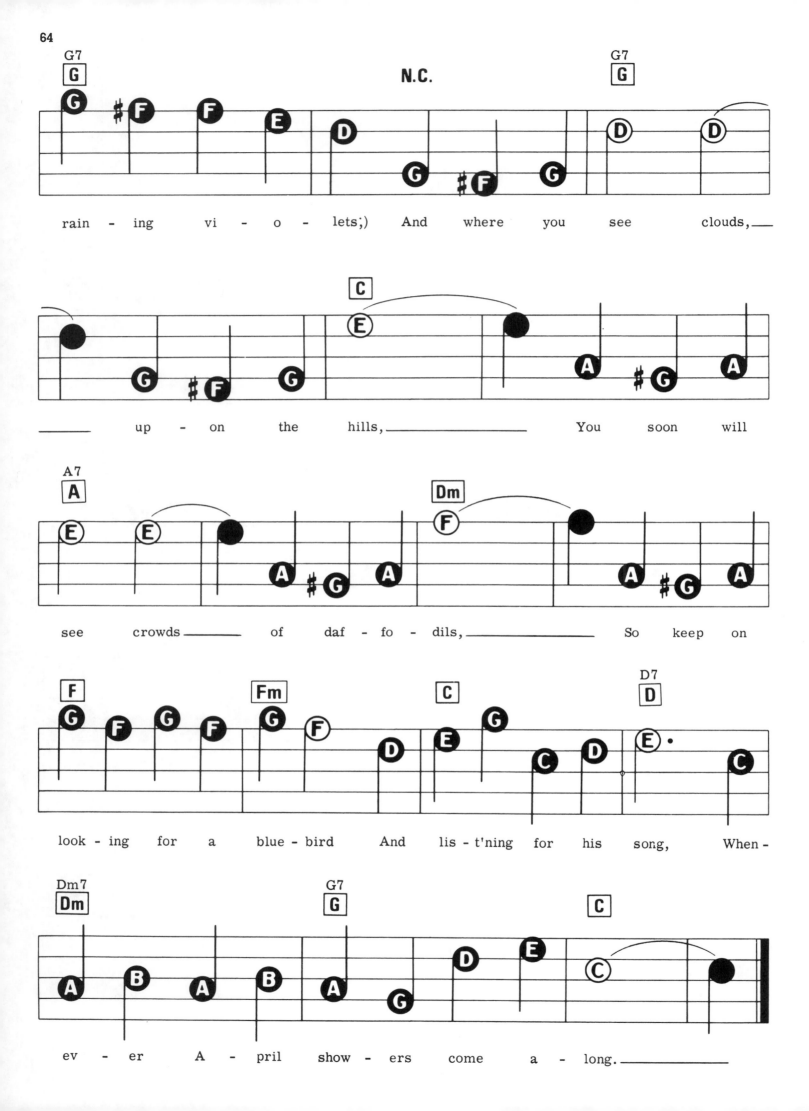

1923
Toot, Toot, Tootsie!
(Good-bye!)

Registration 4
Rhythm: Swing

Words and Music by Gus Kahn, Ernie Erdman,
Dan Russo and Ted Fiorito

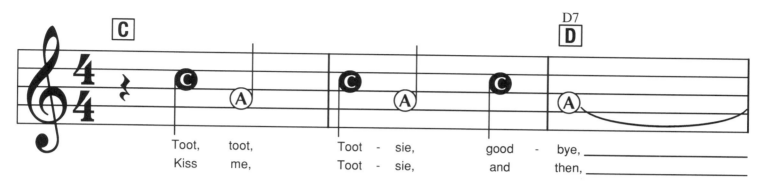

Toot,   toot,   Toot - sie,   good - bye, _____
Kiss   me,   Toot - sie,   and   then, _____

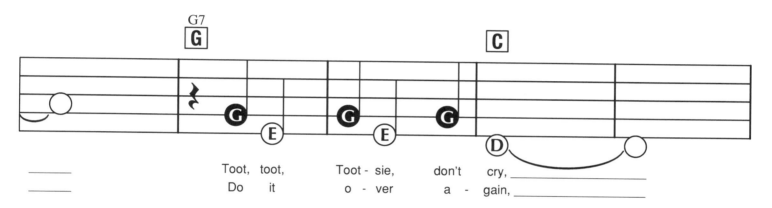

_____   Toot, toot,   Toot - sie,   don't   cry, _____
_____   Do   it   o - ver   a - gain, _____

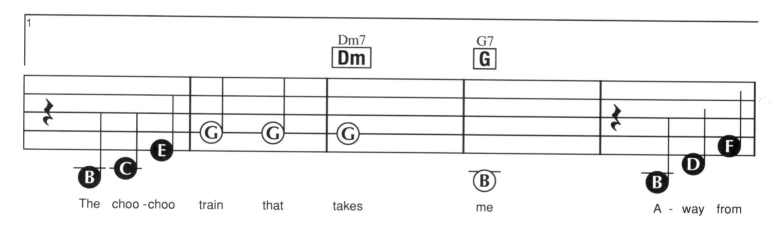

The choo -choo train   that   takes   me   A - way from

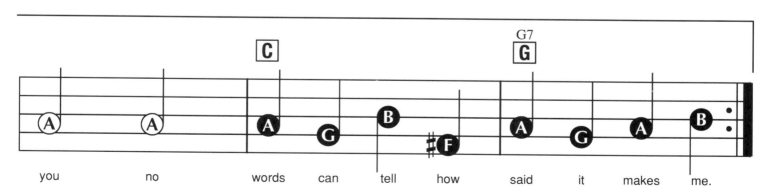

you   no   words   can   tell   how   said   it   makes   me.

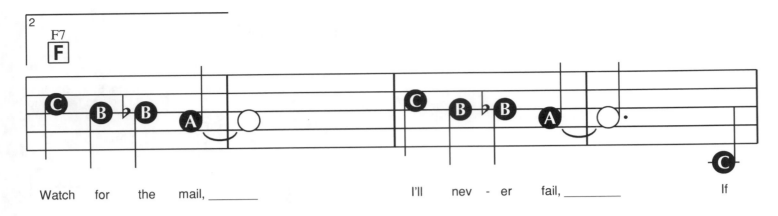

Watch for the mail, _____ I'll nev - er fail, _____ If

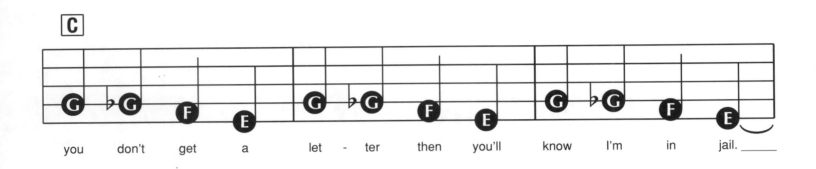

you don't get a let - ter then you'll know I'm in jail. _____

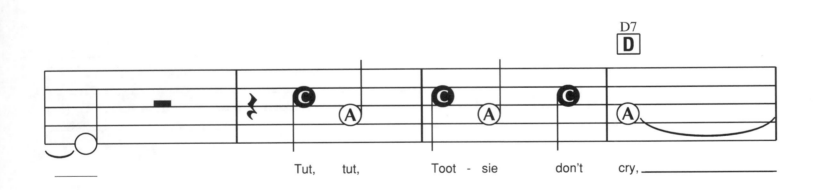

_____ Tut, tut, Toot - sie don't cry, _____

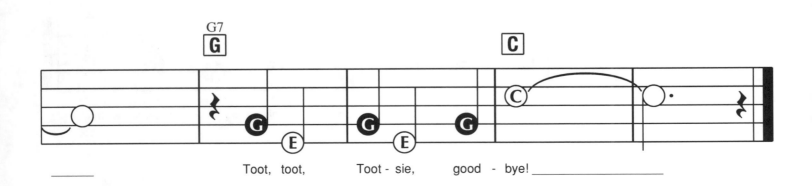

_____ Toot, toot, Toot - sie, good - bye! _____

1924
California, Here I Come

Registration 5
Rhythm: Swing or Jazz

Words and Music by Al Jolson,
B.G. DeSylva and Joseph Meyer

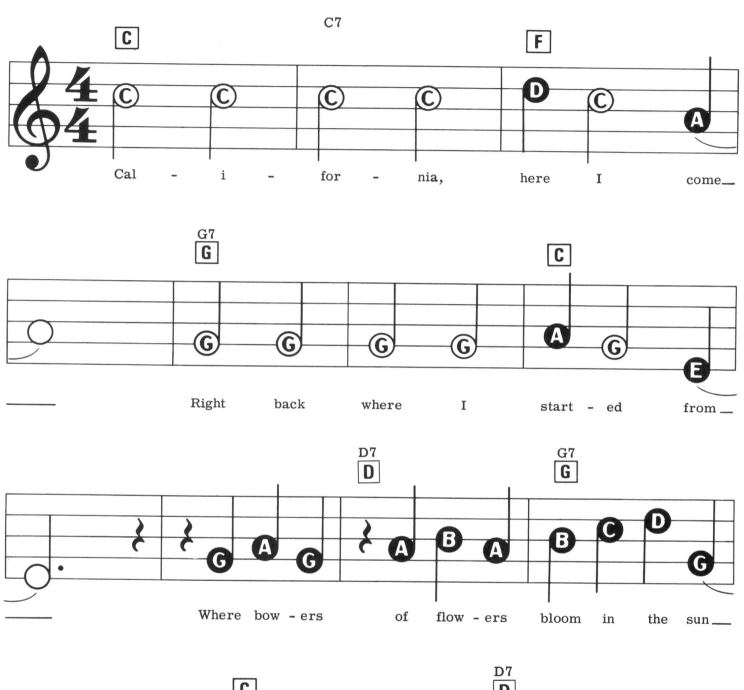

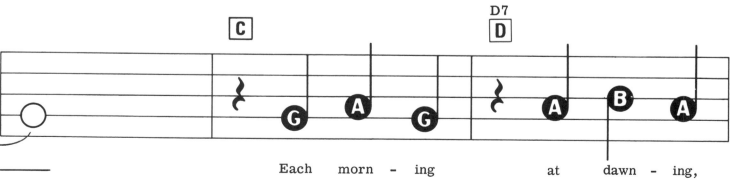

1925
Manhattan
from the Broadway Musical THE GARRICK GAIETIES

Registration 7
Rhythm: Fox Trot

Words by Lorenz Hart
Music by Richard Rodgers

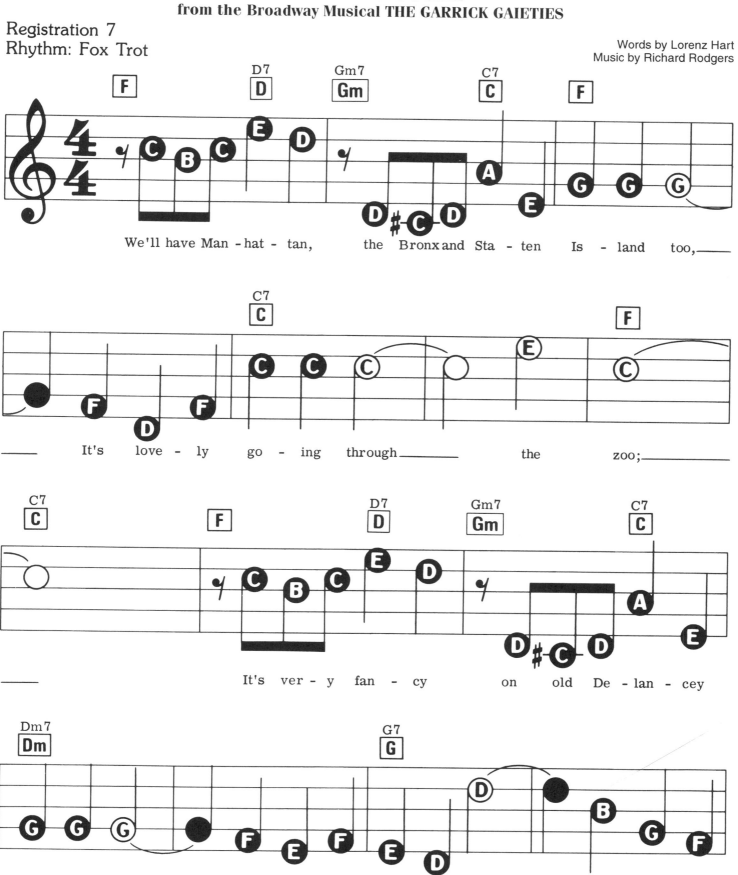

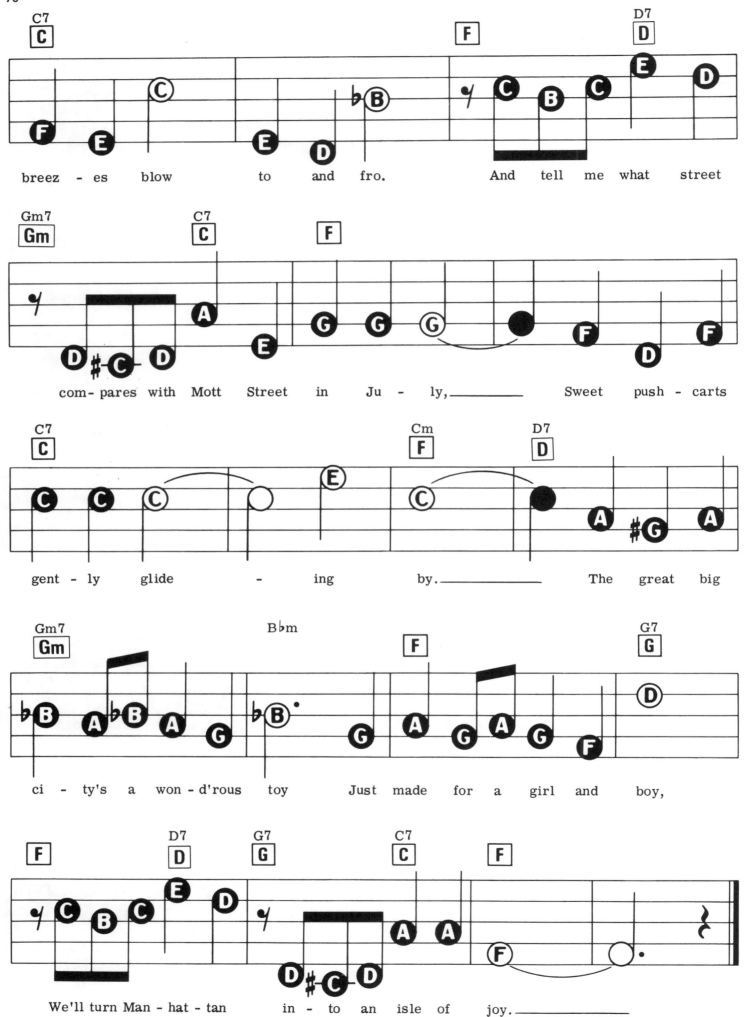

1926

Five Foot Two, Eyes of Blue
(Has Anybody Seen My Girl?)

Registration 9
Rhythm: Fox Trot

Words by Joe Young and Sam Lewis
Music by Ray Henderson

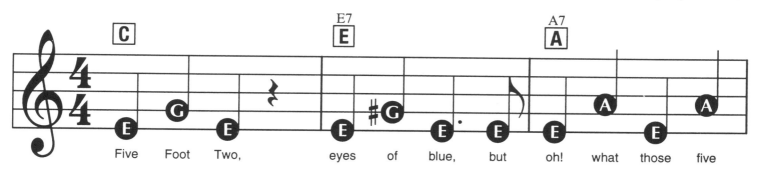

Five Foot Two, eyes of blue, but oh! what those five

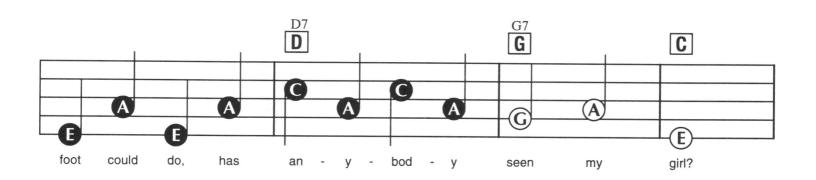

foot could do, has an - y - bod - y seen my girl?

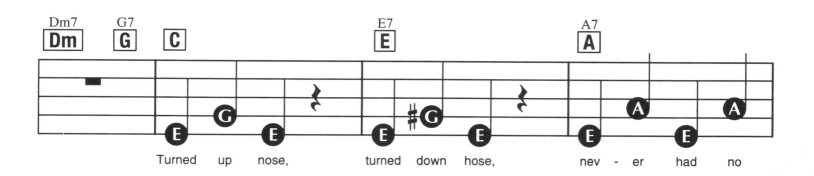

Turned up nose, turned down hose, nev - er had no

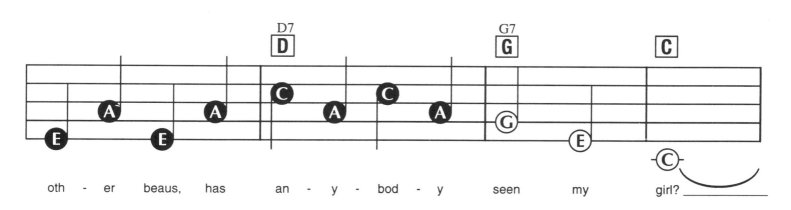

oth - er beaus, has an - y - bod - y seen my girl? _____

72

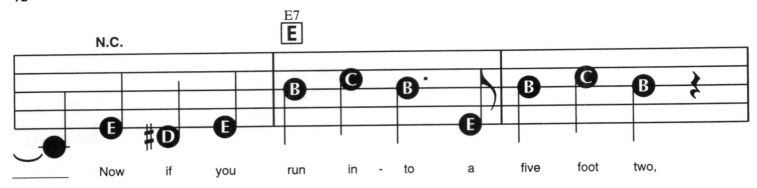

Now if you run in - to a five foot two,

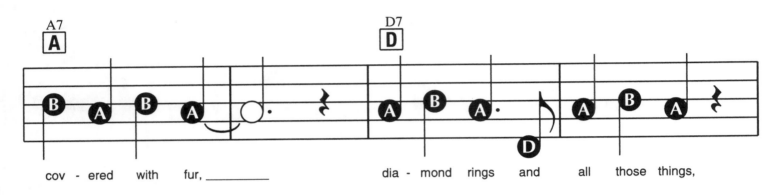

cov - ered with fur, _____ dia - mond rings and all those things,

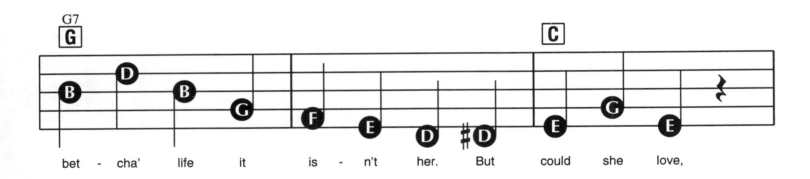

bet - cha' life it is - n't her. But could she love,

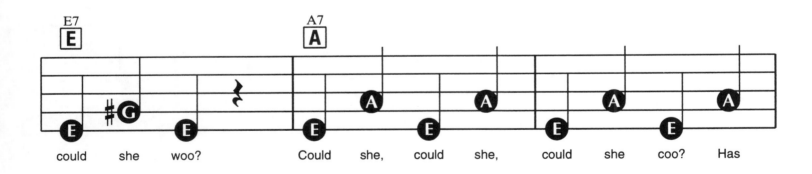

could she woo? Could she, could she, could she coo? Has

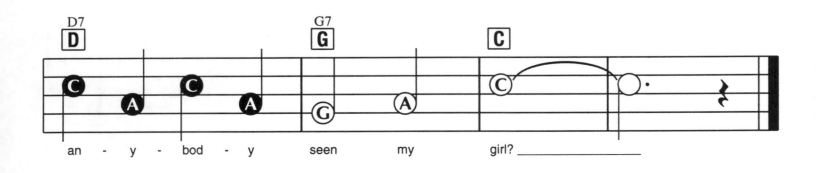

an - y - bod - y seen my girl? _____

1927
Blue Skies
from BETSY

Registration 8
Rhythm: Fox Trot or Swing

Words and Music by
Irving Berlin

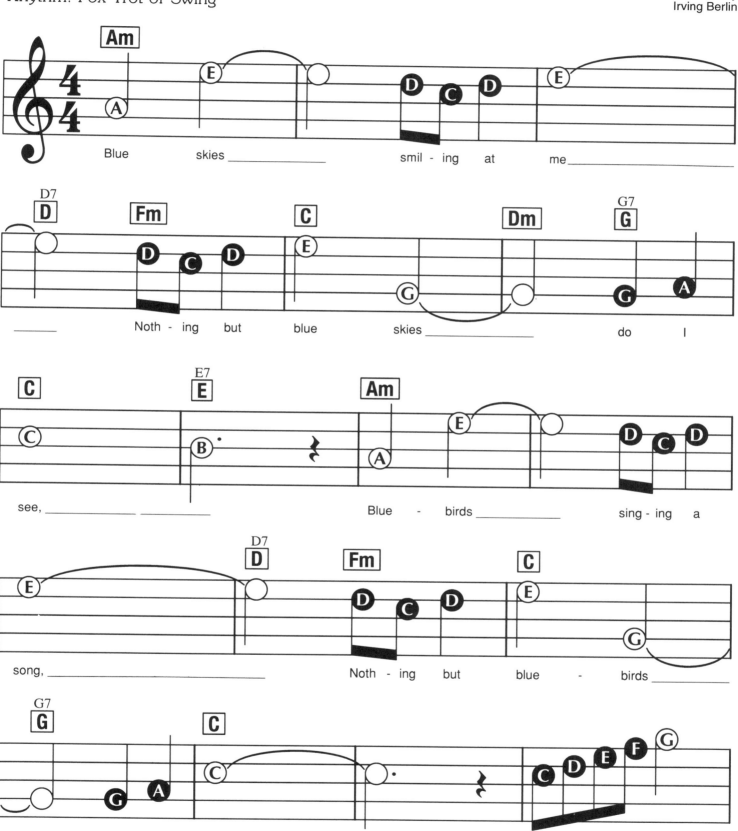

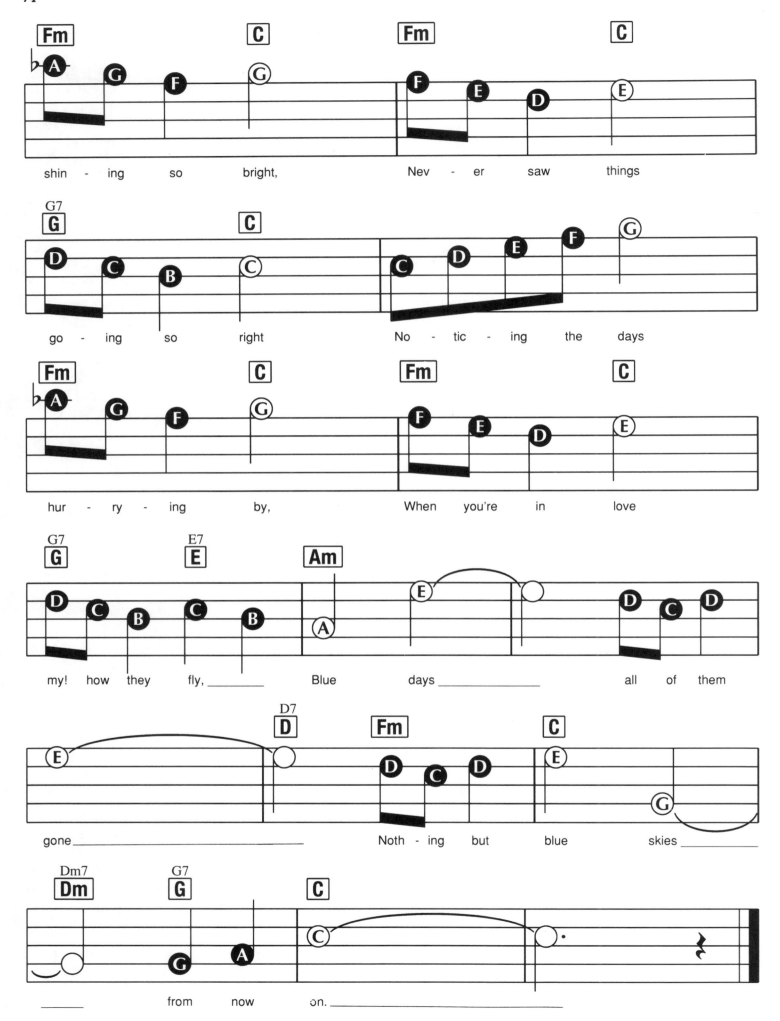

1928
I Can't Give You Anything but Love
from BLACKBIRDS OF 1928

Registration 5
Rhythm: Swing or Jazz

Words by Dorothy Fields
Music by Jimmy McHugh

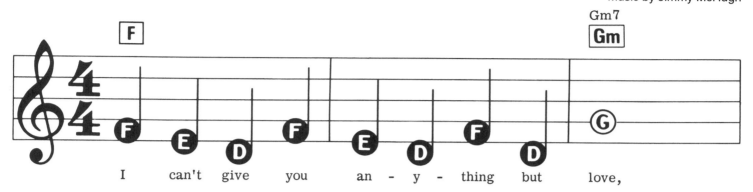

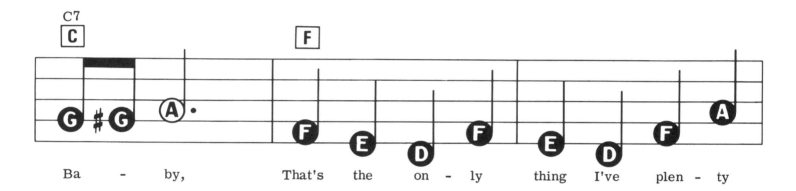

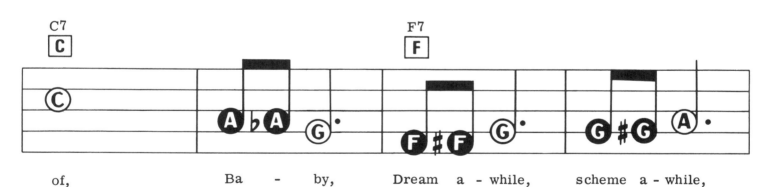

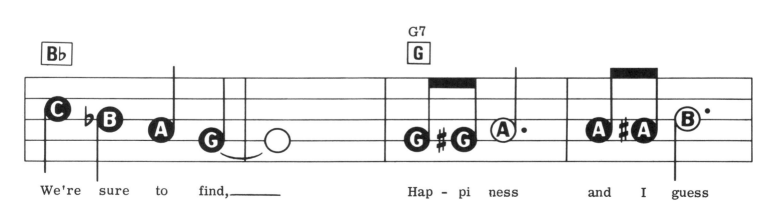

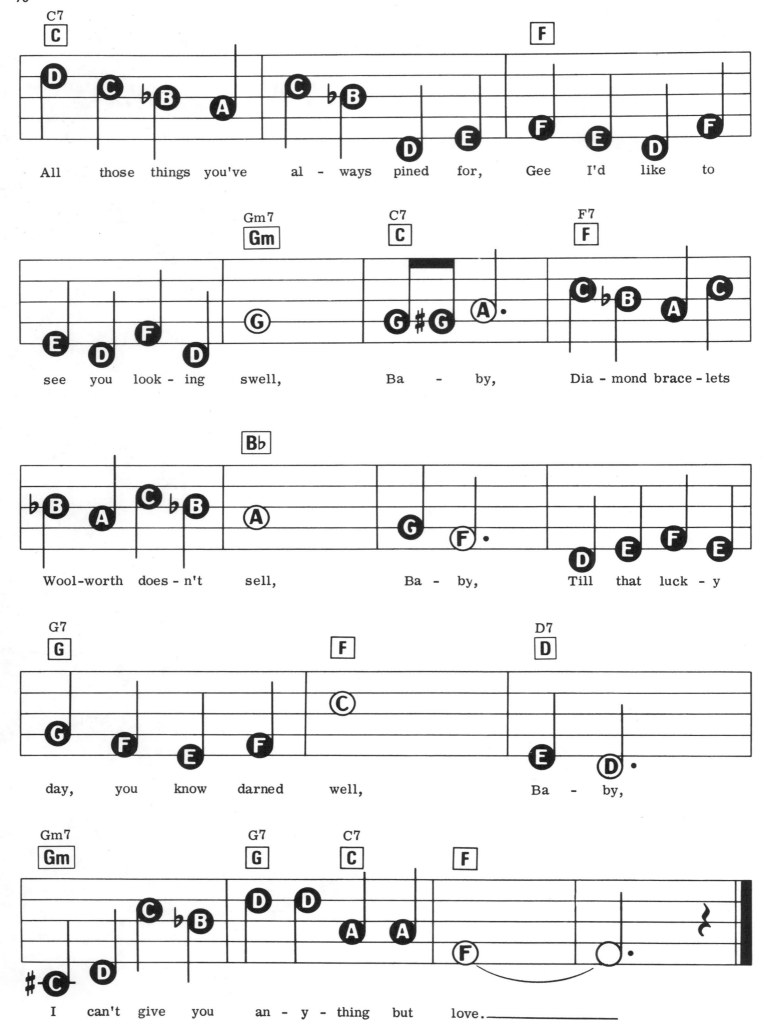

1929
More Than You Know

Registration 8
Rhythm: Fox Trot

Words by William Rose and Edward Eliscu
Music by Vincent Youmans

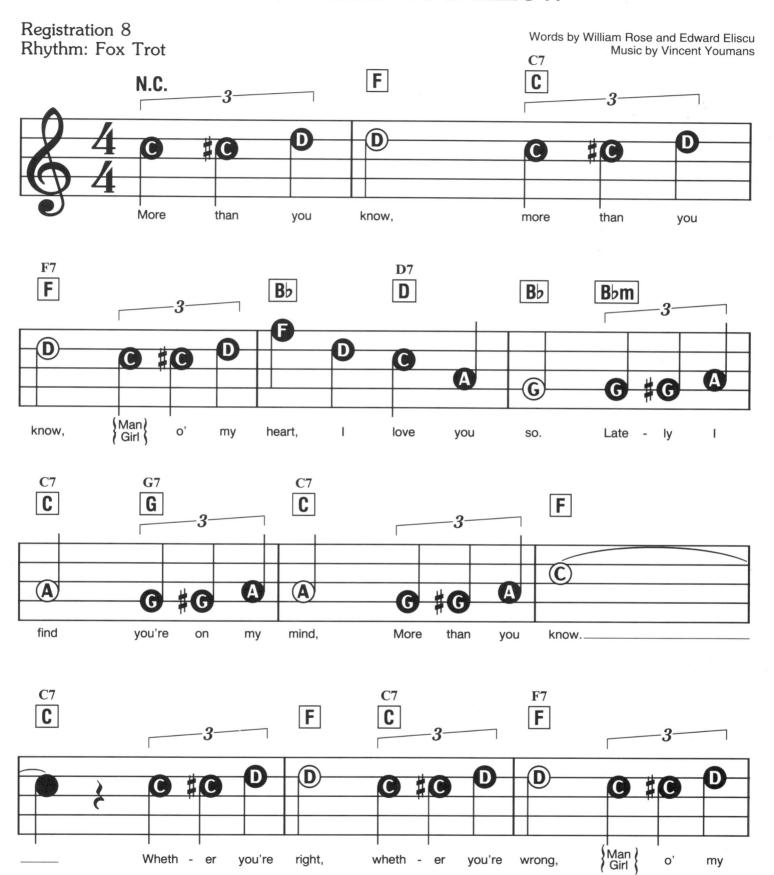

78

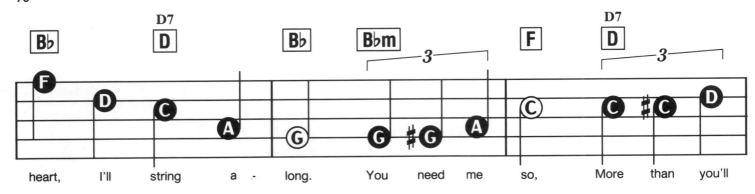

heart, I'll string a - long. You need me so, More than you'll

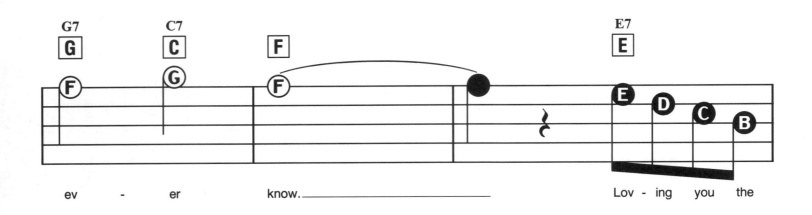

ev - er know._____ Lov - ing you the

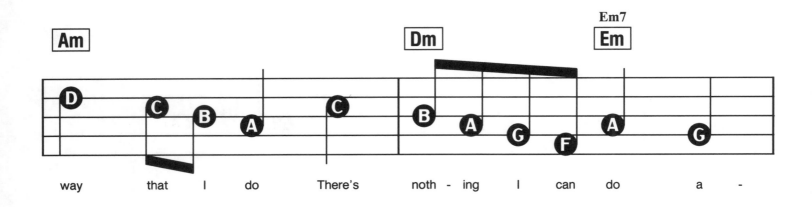

way that I do There's noth - ing I can do a -

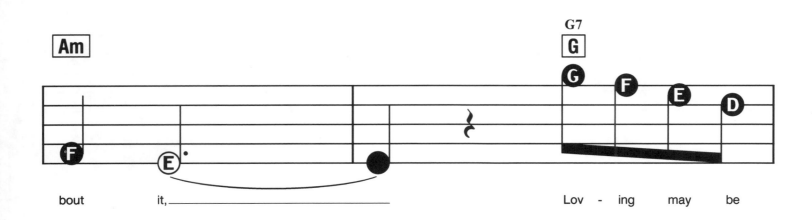

bout it,_____ Lov - ing may be

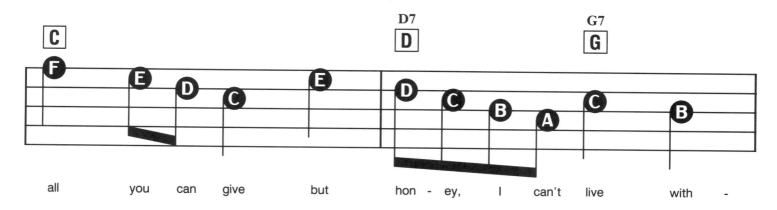

all you can give but hon - ey, I can't live with -

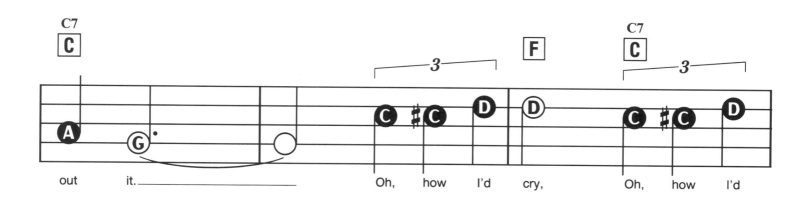

out it. Oh, how I'd cry, Oh, how I'd

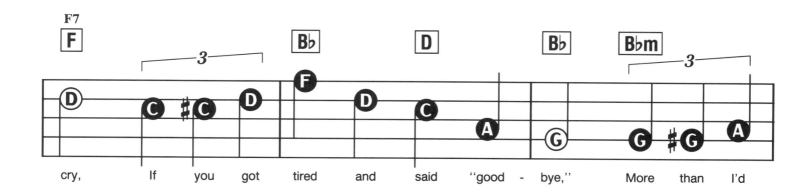

cry, If you got tired and said "good - bye," More than I'd

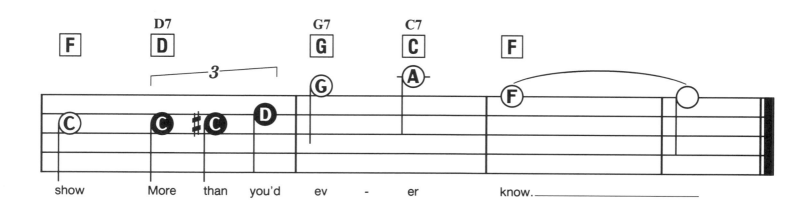

show More than you'd ev - er know.

1930
Puttin' on the Ritz
from the Motion Picture PUTTIN' ON THE RITZ

Registration 7
Rhythm: Fox Trot or Swing

Words and Music by
Irving Berlin

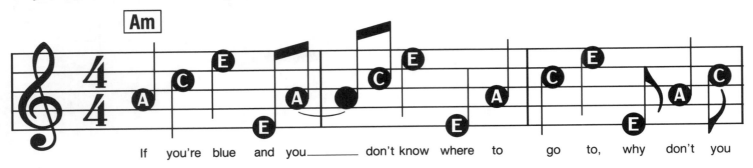

If you're blue and you_____ don't know where to go to, why don't you

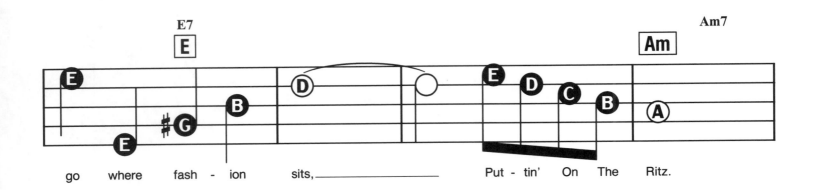

go where fash - ion sits,_____ Put - tin' On The Ritz.

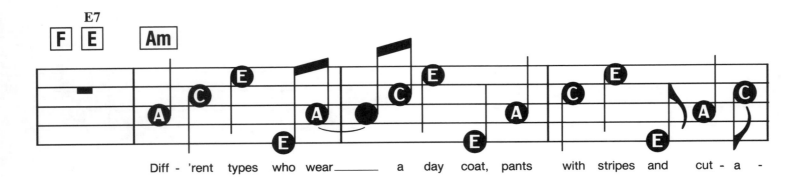

Diff - 'rent types who wear_____ a day coat, pants with stripes and cut - a -

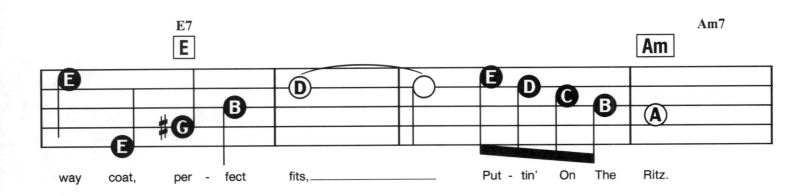

way coat, per - fect fits,_____ Put - tin' On The Ritz.

81

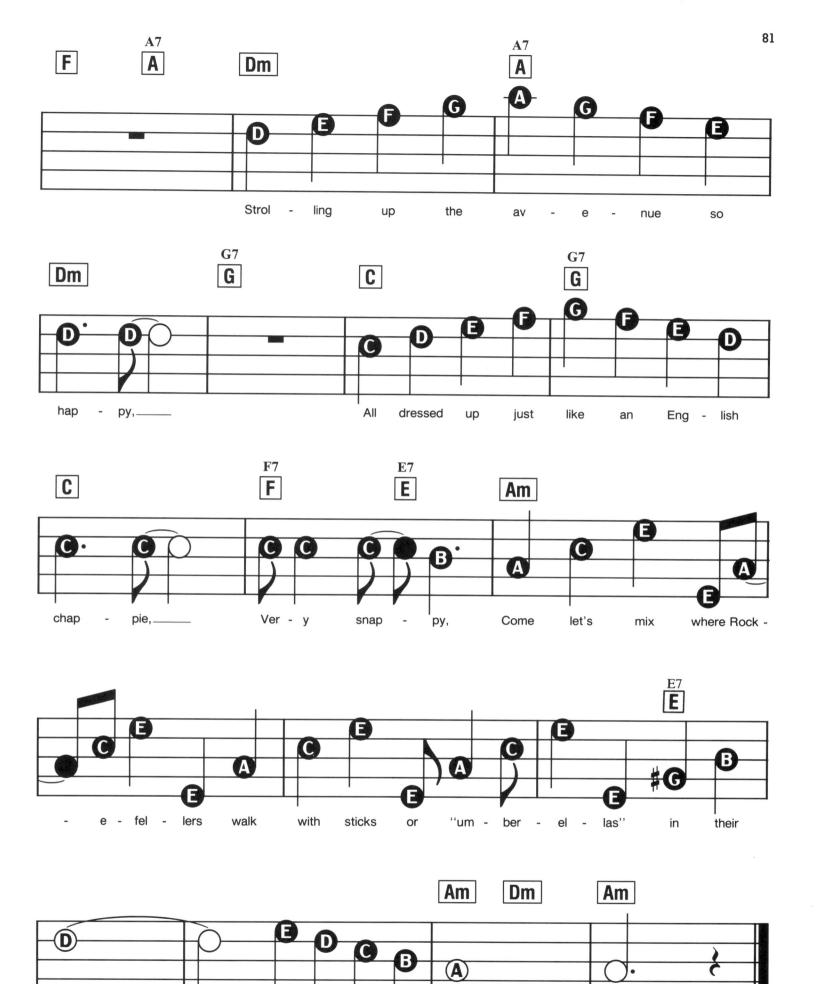

1931
Just a Gigolo

Original German Text by Julius Brammer
English Words by Irving Caesar
Music by Leonello Casucci

Registration 7
Rhythm: Swing or Jazz

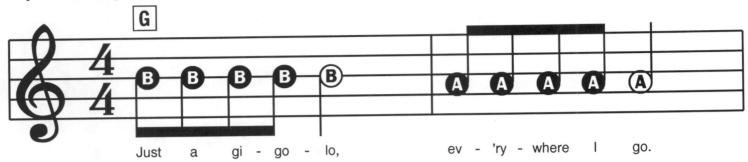

Just a gi - go - lo, ev - 'ry - where I go.

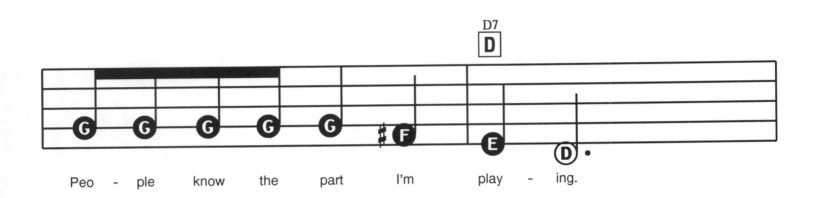

Peo - ple know the part I'm play - ing.

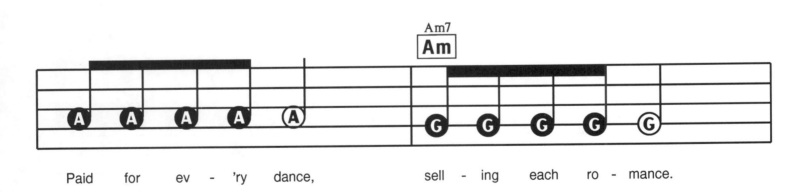

Paid for ev - 'ry dance, sell - ing each ro - mance.

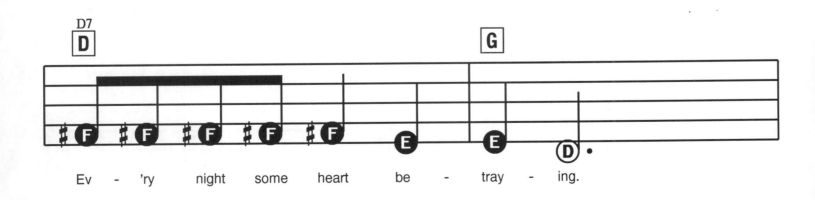

Ev - 'ry night some heart be - tray - ing.

83

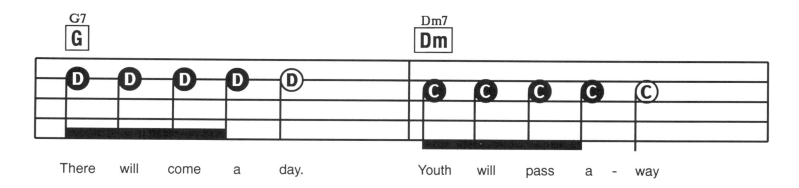

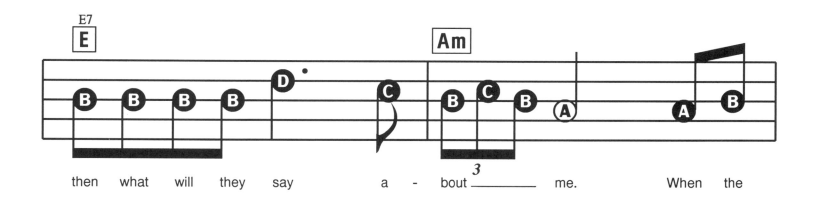

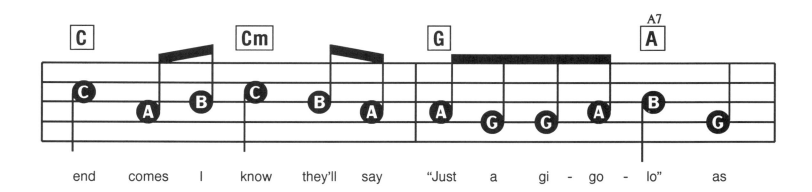

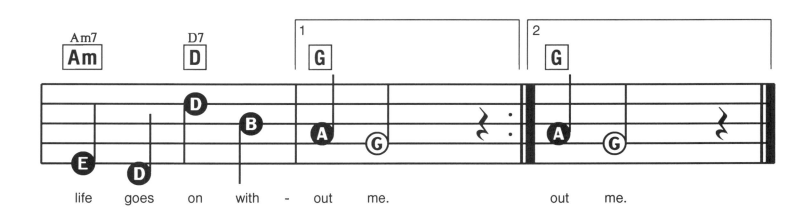

1932
How Deep Is the Ocean
(How High Is the Sky)

Registration 4
Rhythm: Fox Trot or Swing

Words and Music by
Irving Berlin

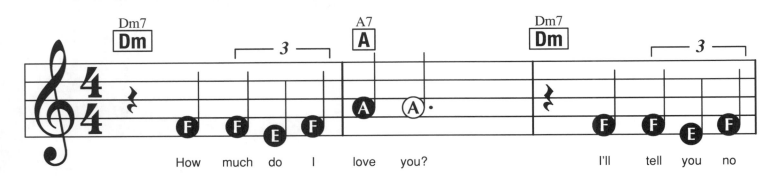

How much do I love you? I'll tell you no

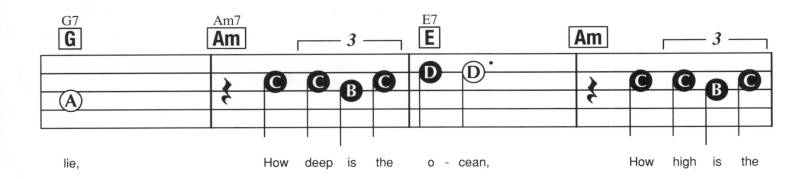

lie, How deep is the o - cean, How high is the

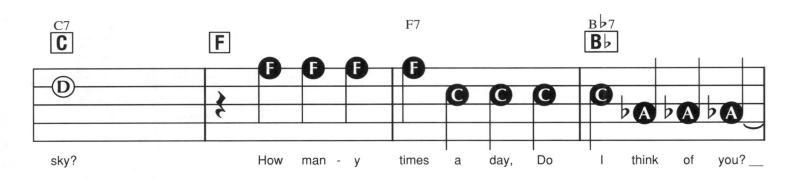

sky? How man - y times a day, Do I think of you? __

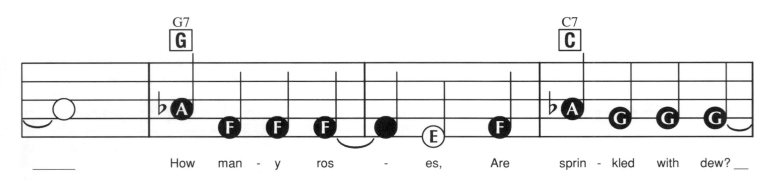

_____ How man - y ros - es, Are sprin - kled with dew? __

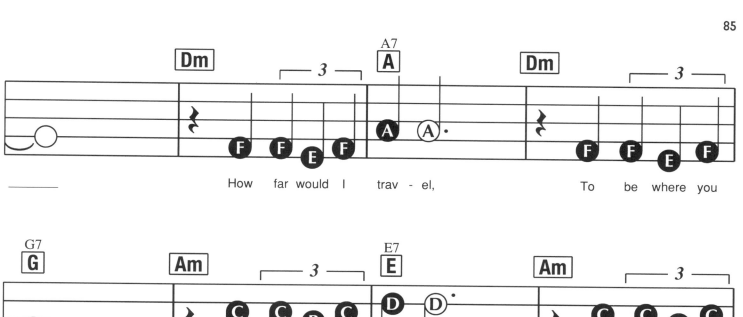

How far would I trav - el, To be where you

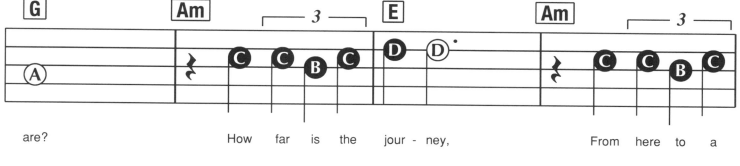

are? How far is the jour - ney, From here to a

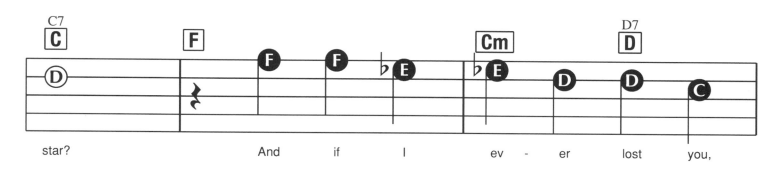

star? And if I ev - er lost you,

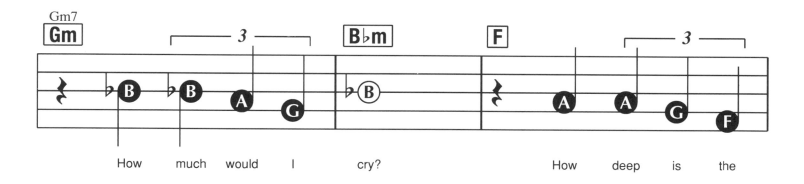

How much would I cry? How deep is the

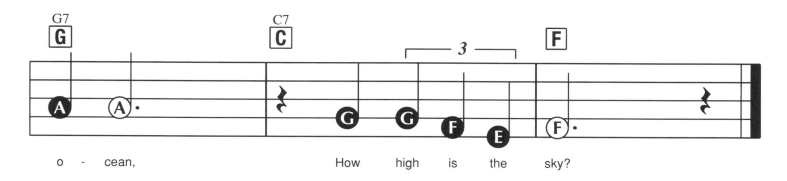

o - cean, How high is the sky?

1933
Did You Ever See a Dream Walking?
from SITTING PRETTY

Words by Mack Gordon
Music by Harry Revel

Registration 1
Rhythm: Fox Trot

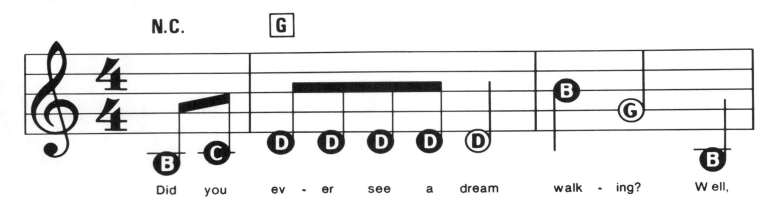

Did you ev - er see a dream walk - ing? Well,

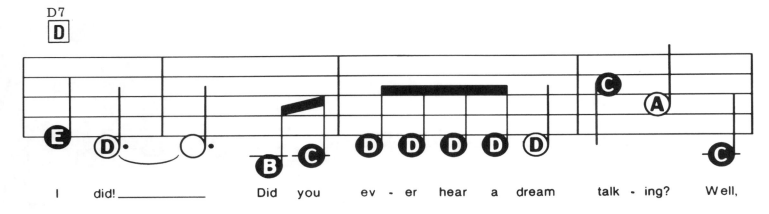

I did! _____ Did you ev - er hear a dream talk - ing? Well,

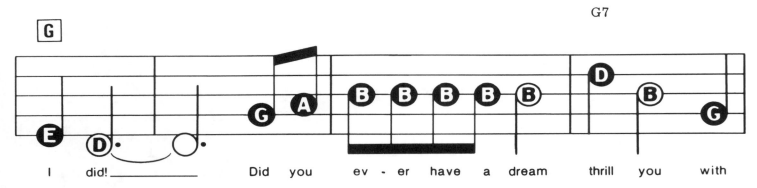

I did! _____ Did you ev - er have a dream thrill you with

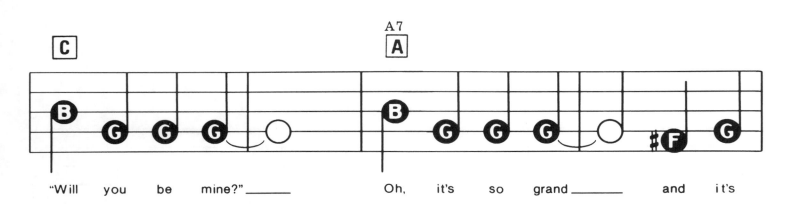

"Will you be mine?" _____ Oh, it's so grand _____ and it's

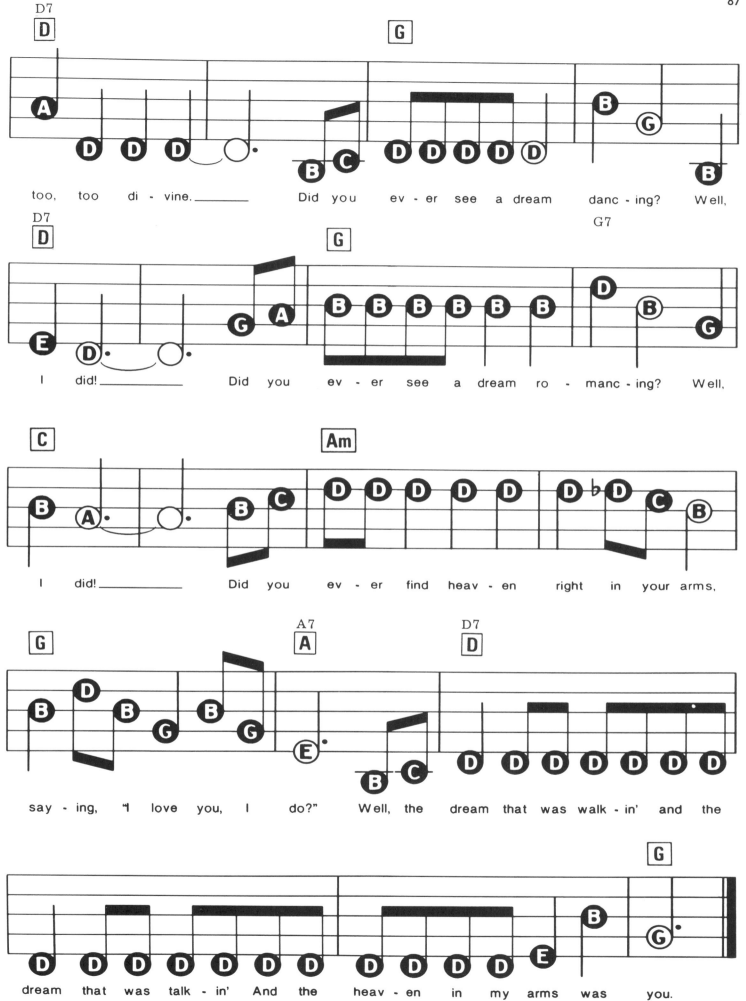

1934
Smoke Gets in Your Eyes
from ROBERTA

Registration 10
Rhythm: Fox Trot or Swing

Words by Otto Harbach
Music by Jerome Kern

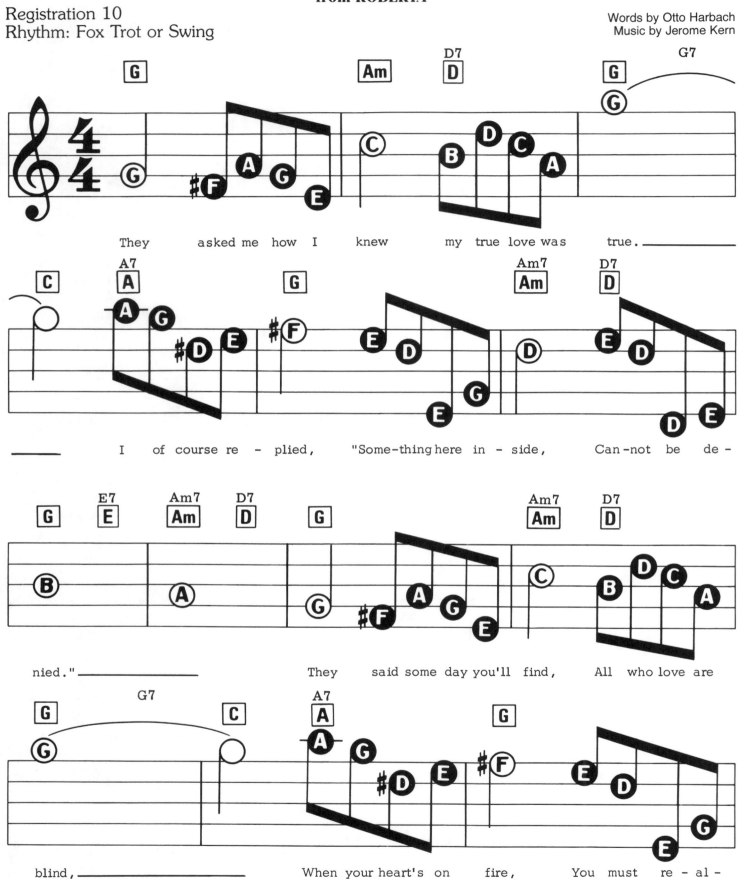

89

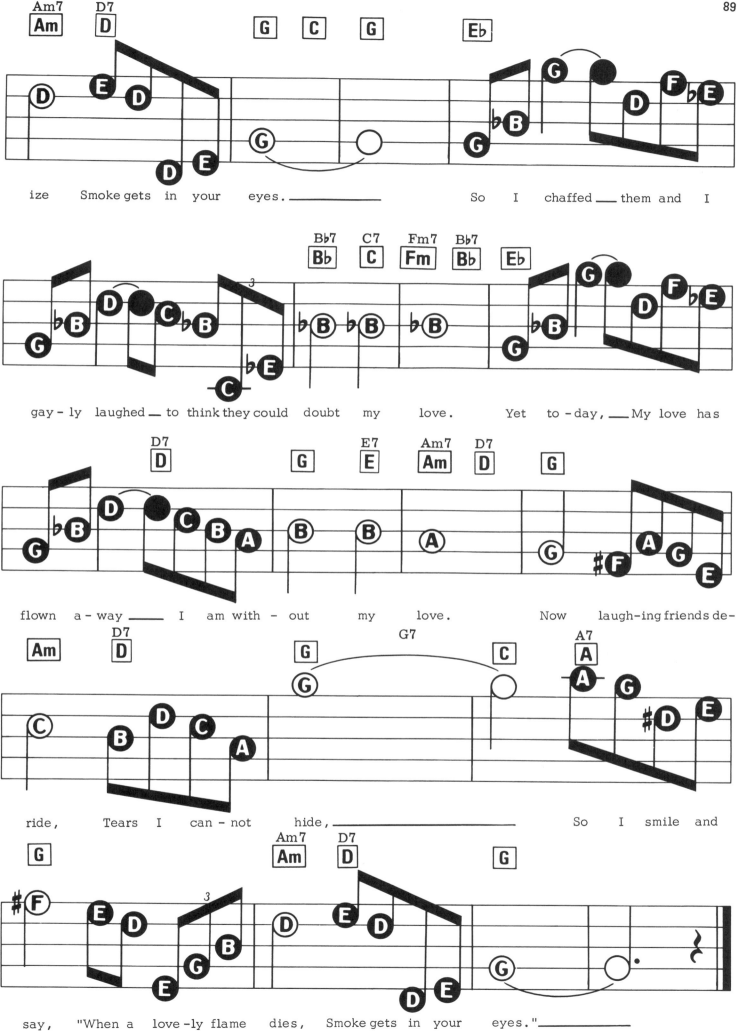

1935
My Romance
from JUMBO

Registration 5
Rhythm: Fox Trot or Ballad

Words by Lorenz Hart
Music by Richard Rodgers

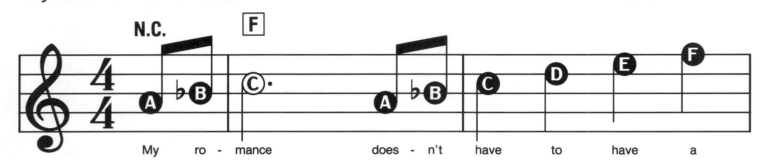

My ro - mance does - n't have to have a

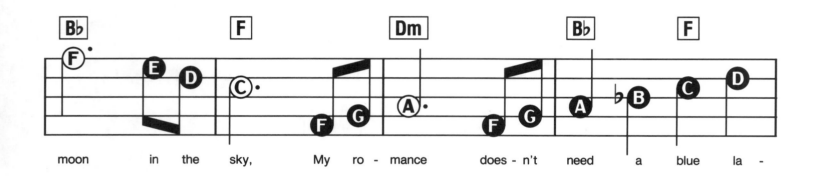

moon in the sky, My ro - mance does - n't need a blue la -

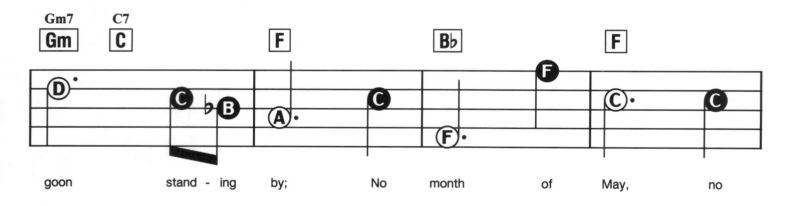

goon stand - ing by; No month of May, no

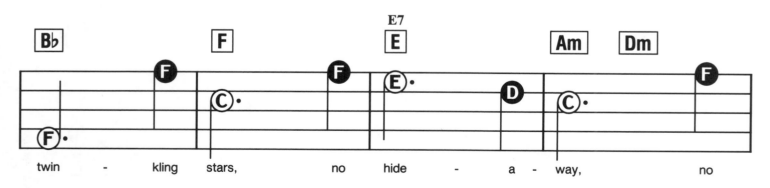

twin - kling stars, no hide - a - way, no

91

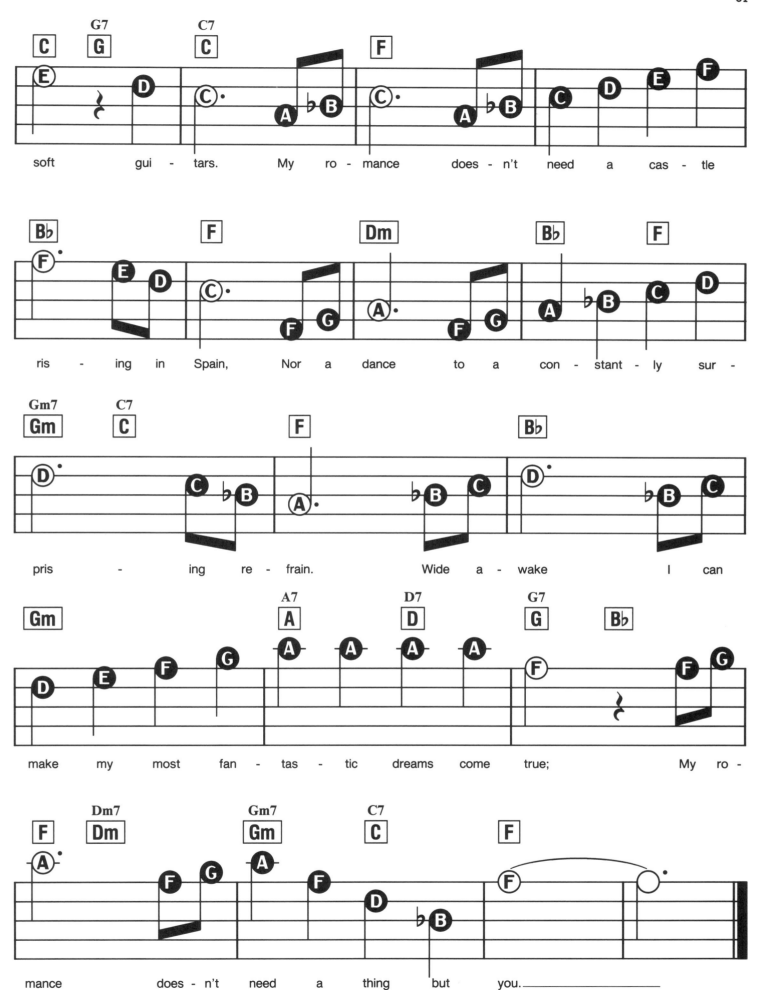

1936
The Way You Look Tonight
from SWING TIME

Registration 3
Rhythm: Fox Trot or Swing

Words by Dorothy Fields
Music by Jerome Kern

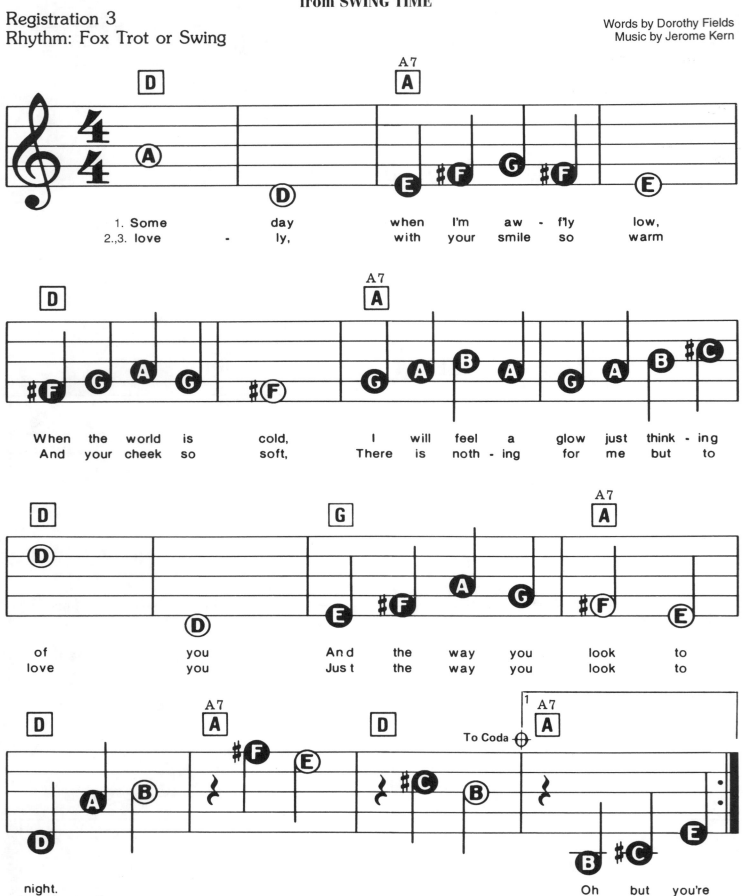

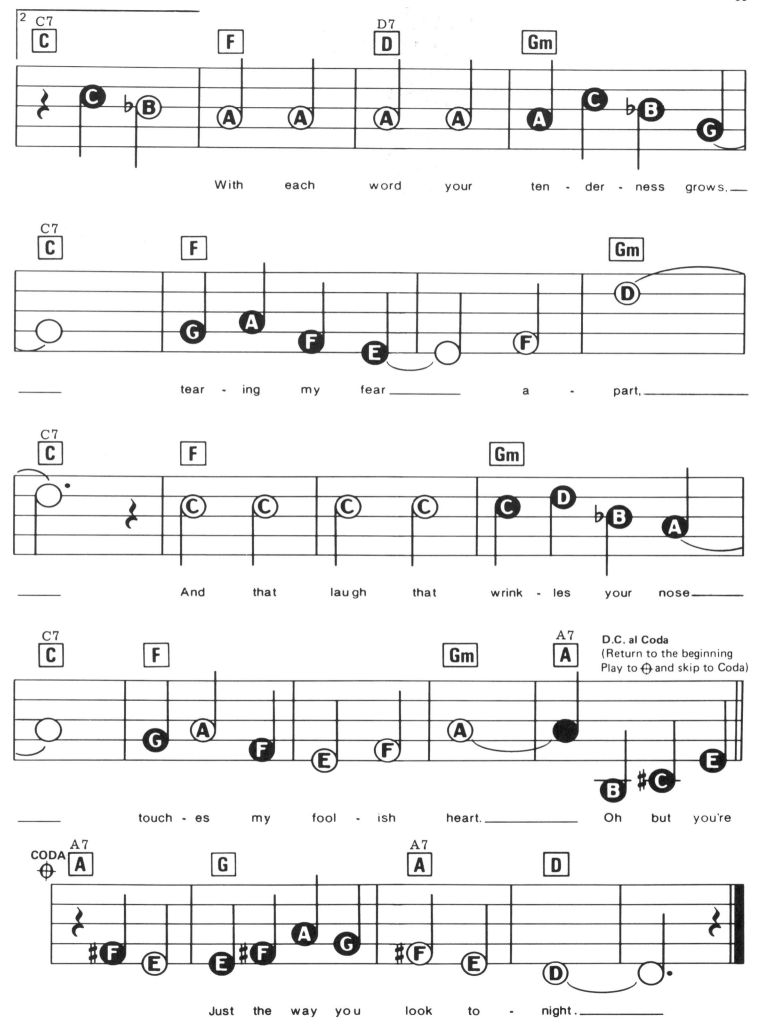

1937
Caravan
from SOPHISTICATED LADIES

Registration 7
Rhythm: Ballad or Fox Trot

Words and Music by Duke Ellington,
Irving Mills and Juan Tizol

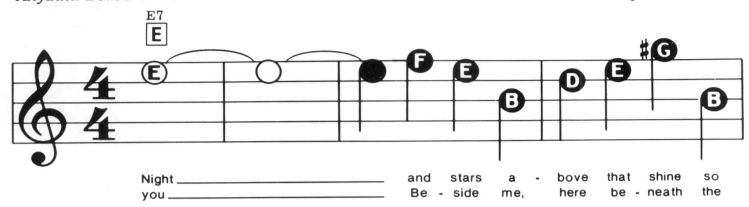

Night _____ and stars a - bove that shine so
you _____ Be - side me, here be - neath the

bright _____ The mys - t'ry of their fad - ing
blue _____ My dream of love is com - ing

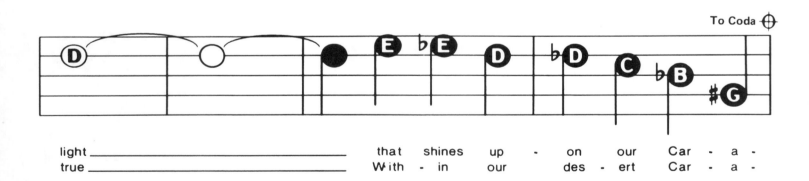

light _____ that shines up - on our Car - a -
true _____ With - in our des - ert Car - a -

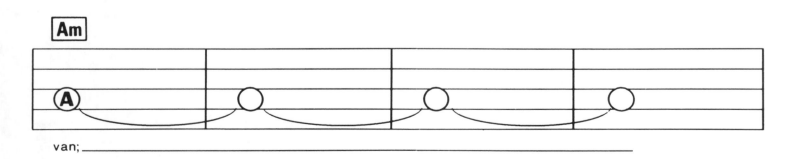

van; _____

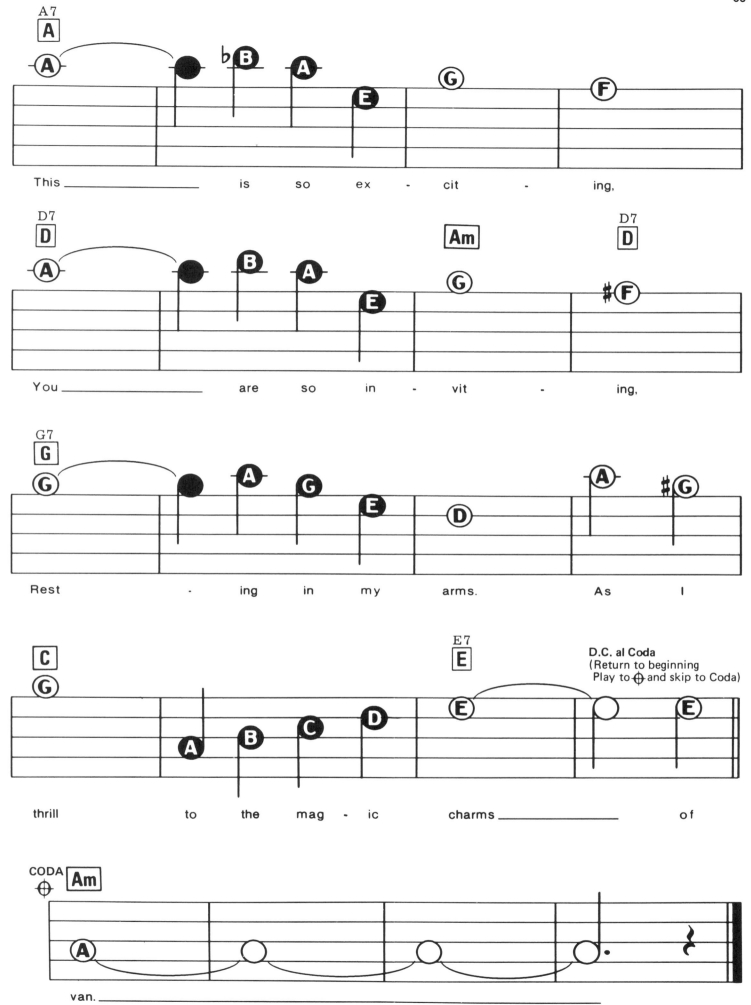

1938
Thanks for the Memory
from the Paramount Picture BIG BROADCAST OF 1938

Registration 3
Rhythm: Swing

Words and Music by Leo Robin
and Ralph Rainger

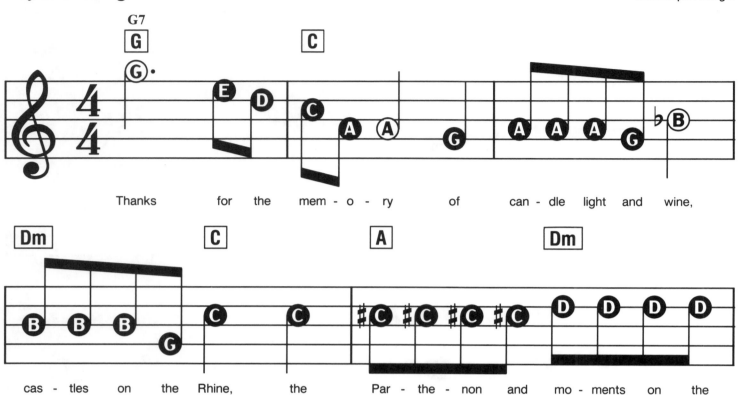

Thanks for the mem-o-ry of can-dle light and wine,

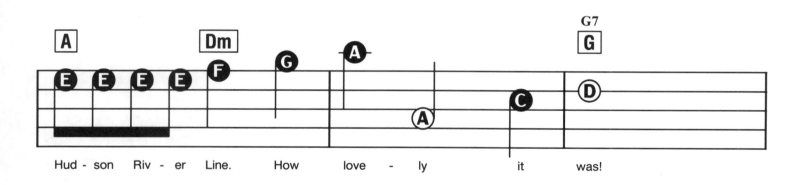

cas-tles on the Rhine, the Par-the-non and mo-ments on the

Hud-son Riv-er Line. How love-ly it was!

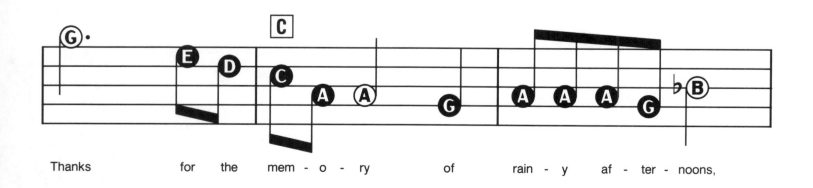

Thanks for the mem-o-ry of rain-y af-ter-noons,

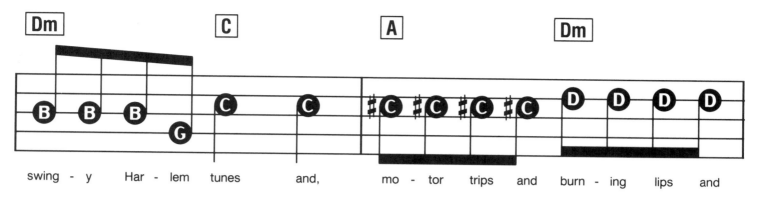

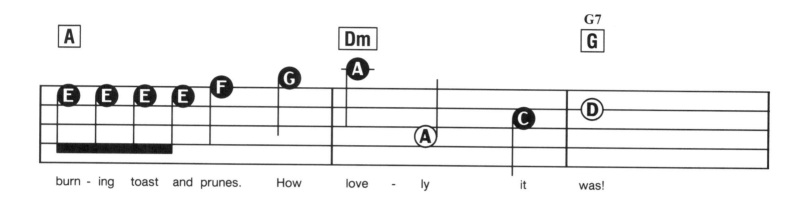

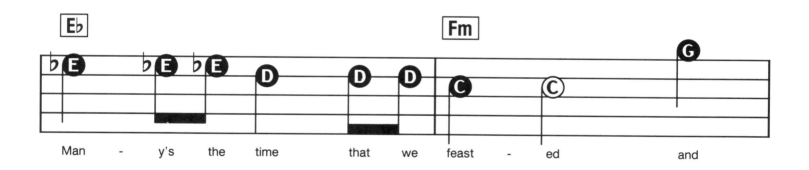

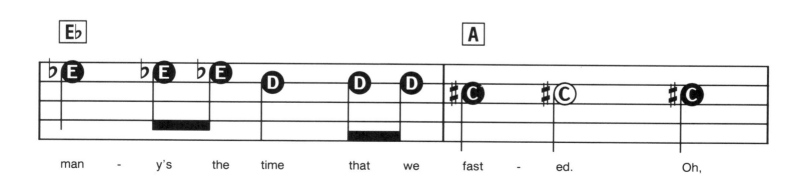

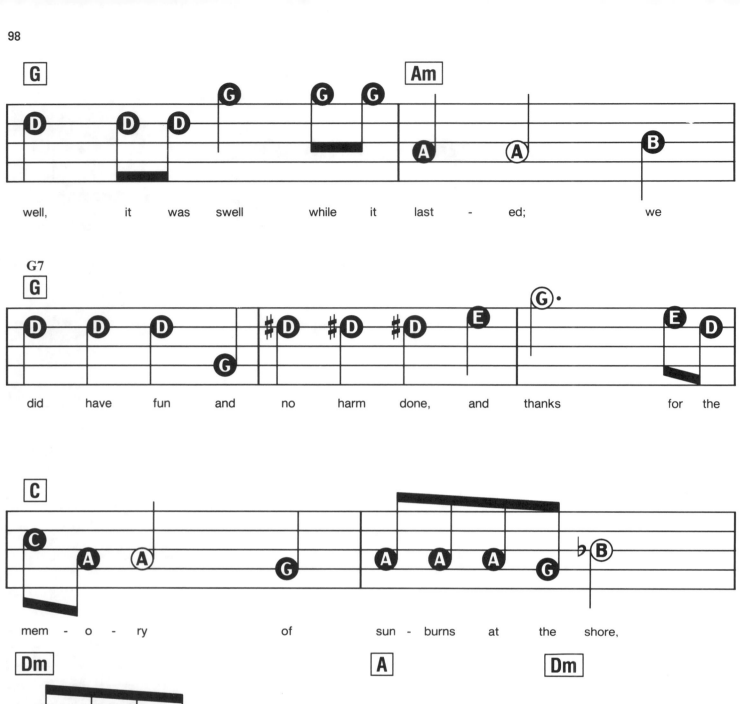

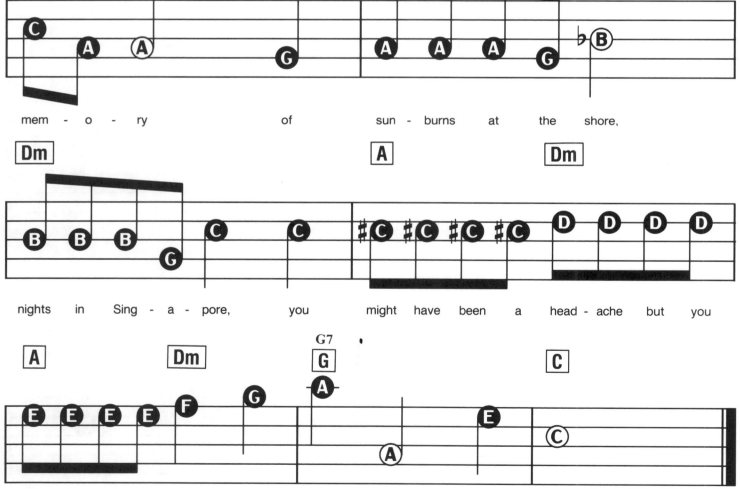

1939

Beer Barrel Polka
(Roll Out the Barrel)
Based on the European success "Skoda Lasky"*

Registration 5
Rhythm: Polka or March

By Lew Brown, Wladimir A. Timm,
Jaromir Vejvoda and Vasek Zeman

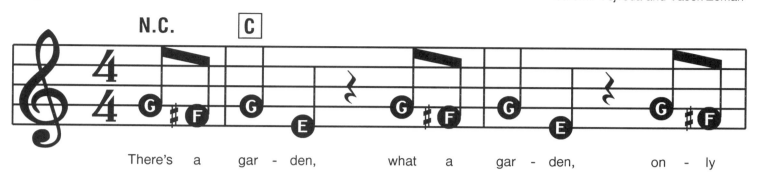

There's a   gar - den,   what a   gar - den,   on - ly

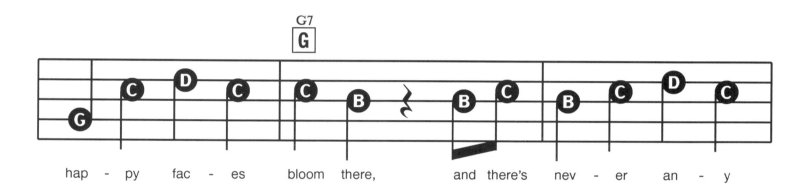

hap - py   fac - es   bloom there,   and there's   nev - er   an - y

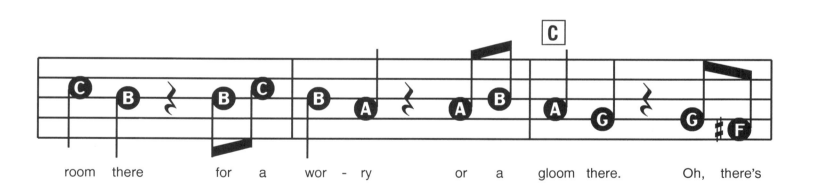

room there   for   a   wor - ry   or a   gloom there.   Oh, there's

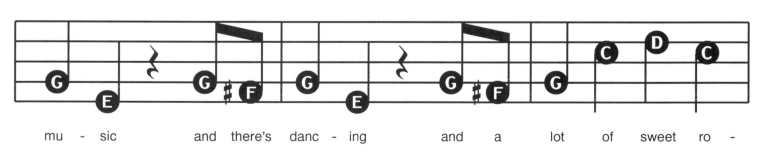

mu - sic   and there's   danc - ing   and a   lot   of   sweet   ro -

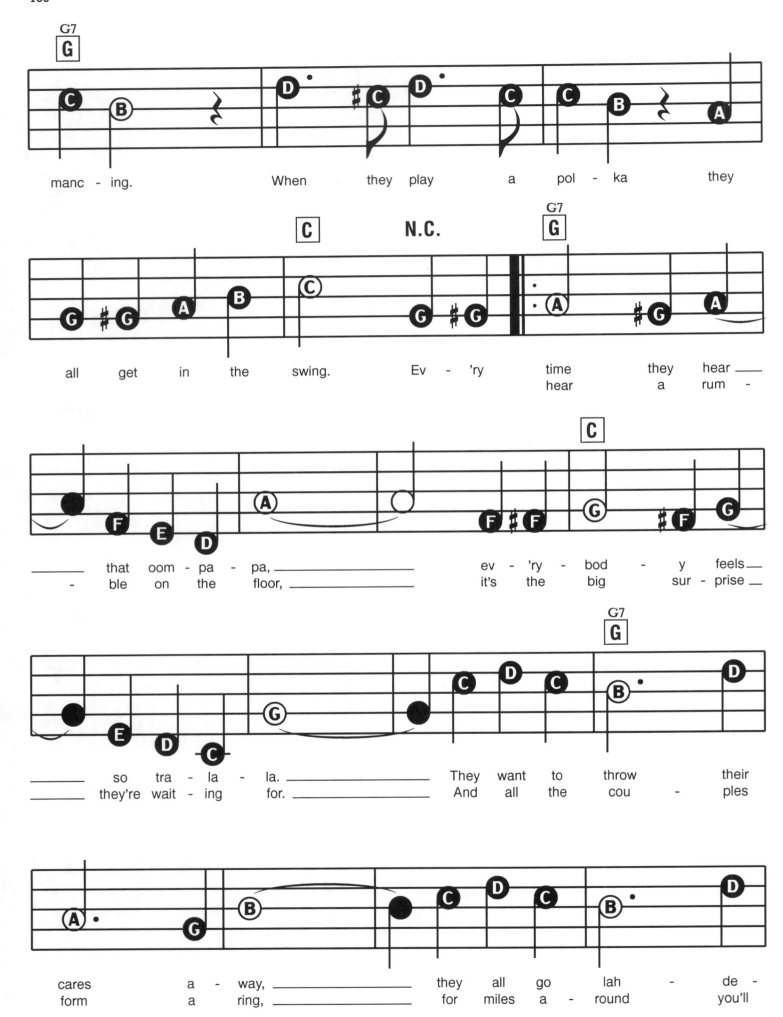

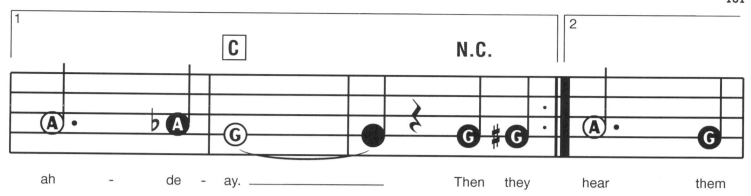

ah - de - ay. _____ Then they hear them

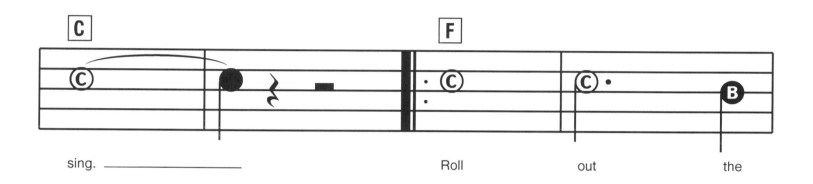

sing. _____ Roll out the

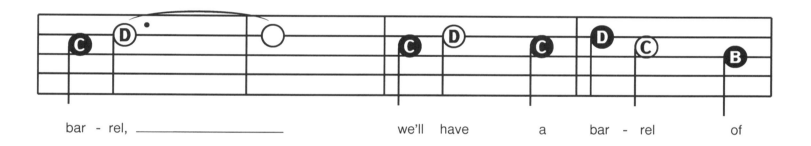

bar - rel, _____ we'll have a bar - rel of

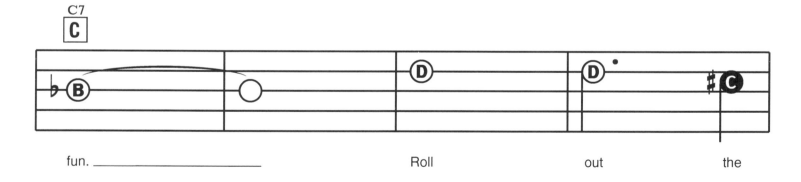

fun. _____ Roll out the

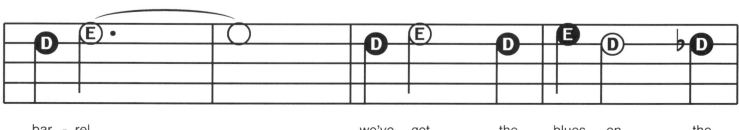

bar - rel, _____ we've got the blues on the

102

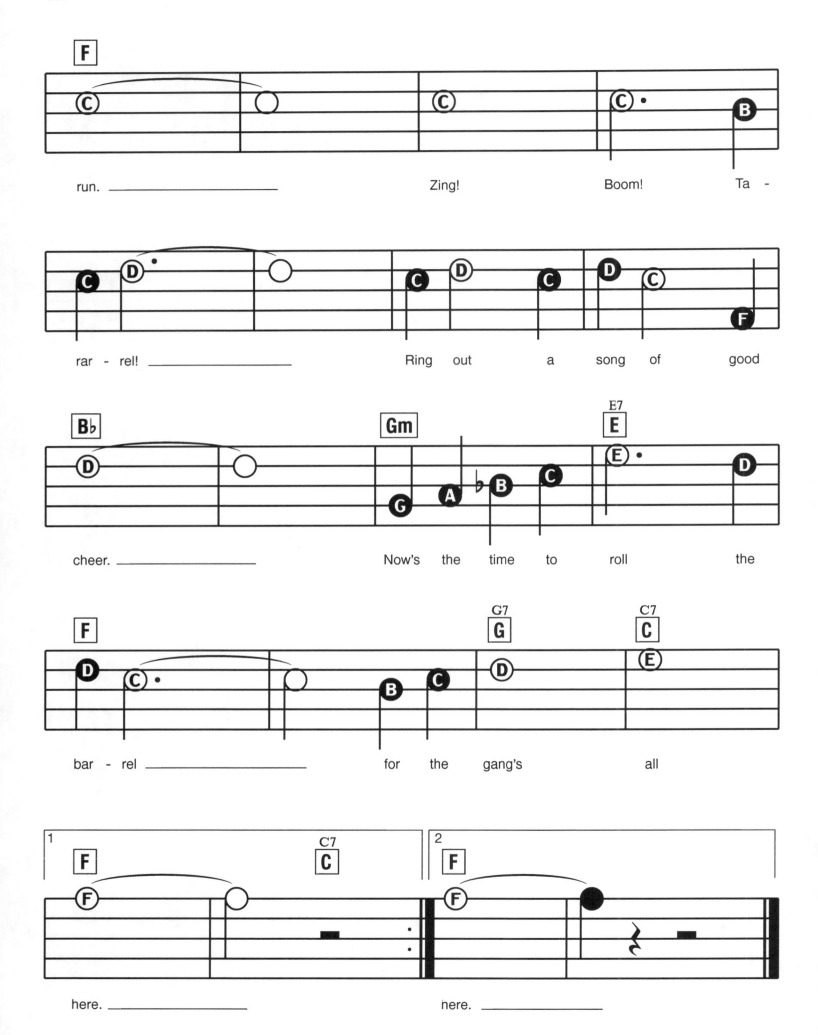

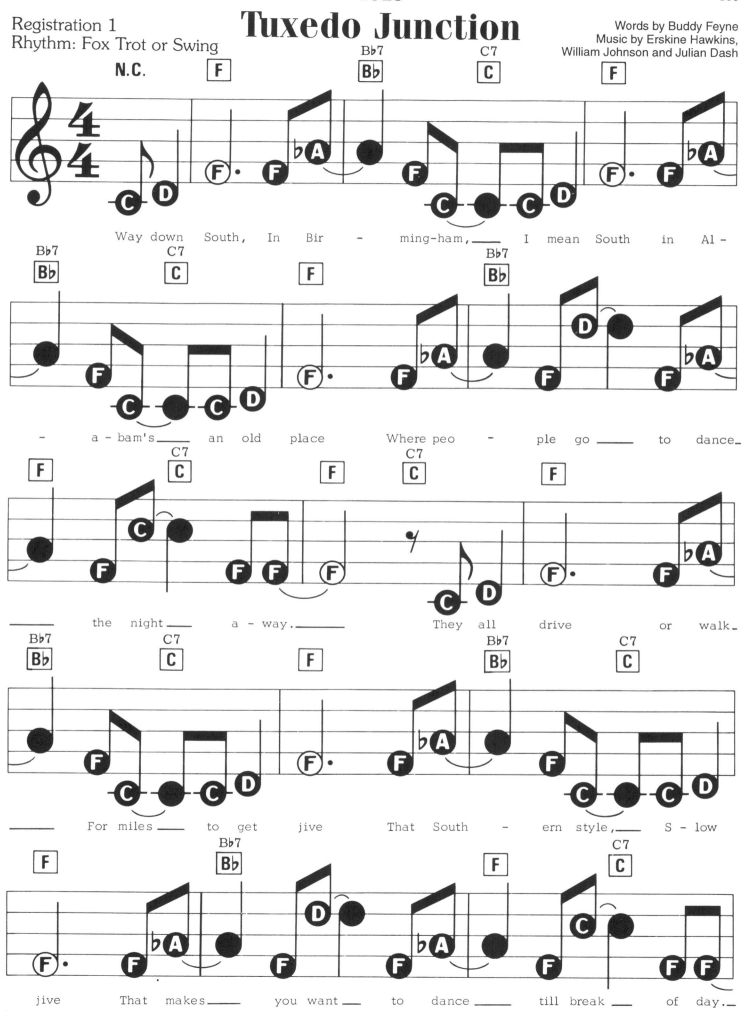

104

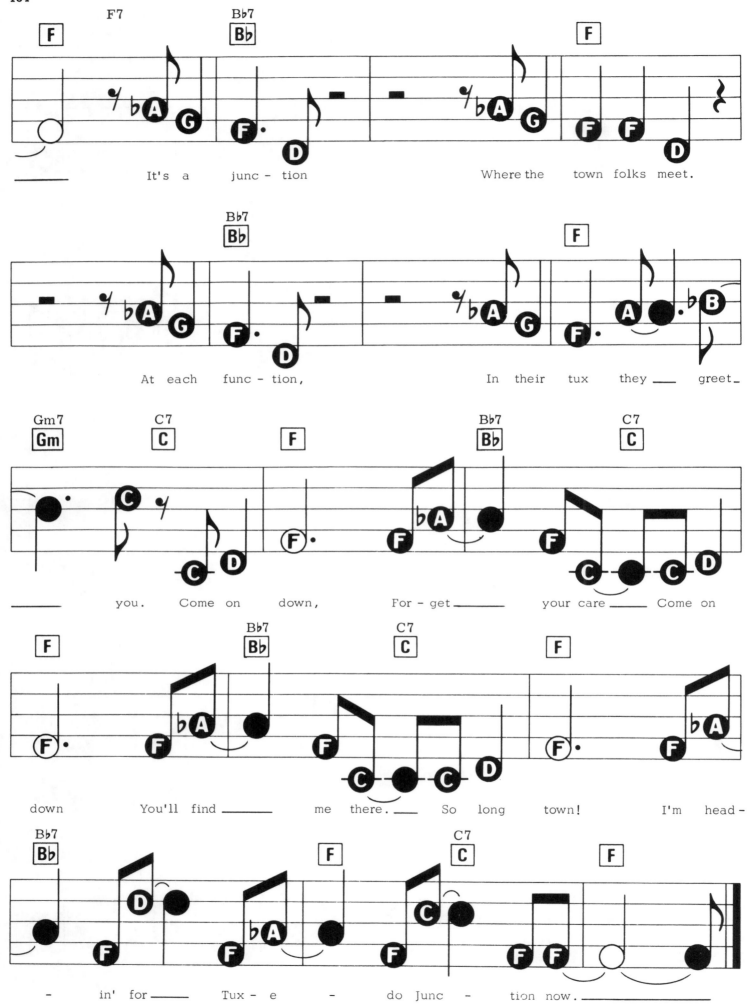

1941
Aquellos ojos verdes
(Green Eyes)

Registration 3
Rhythm: Rhumba or Latin

Music by Nilo Menendez
Spanish Words by Adolfo Utrera
English Words by E. Rivera and E. Woods

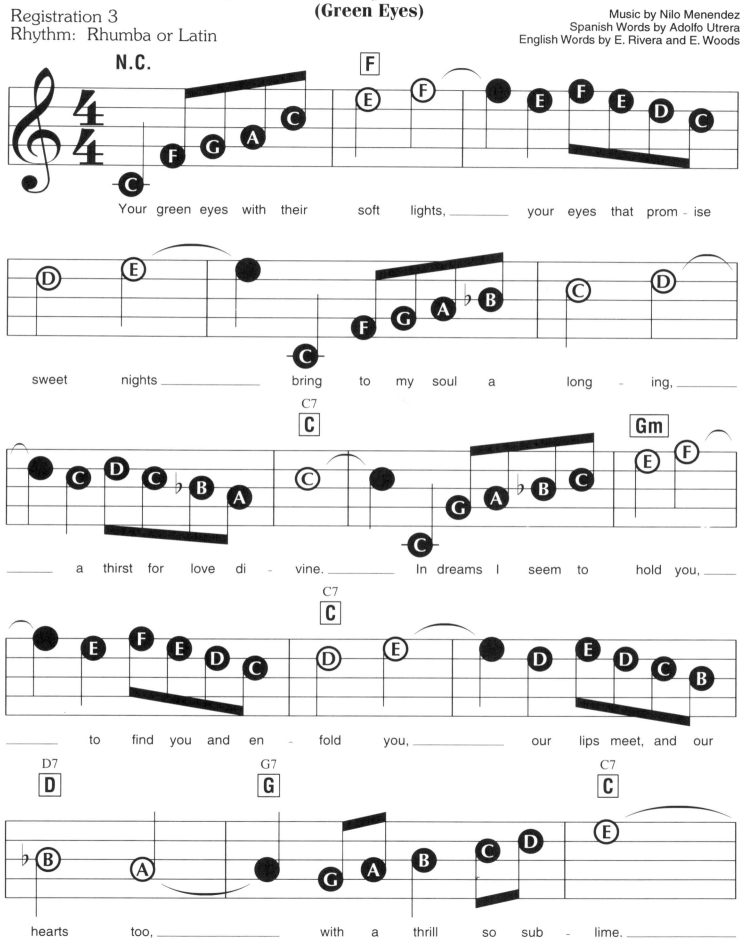

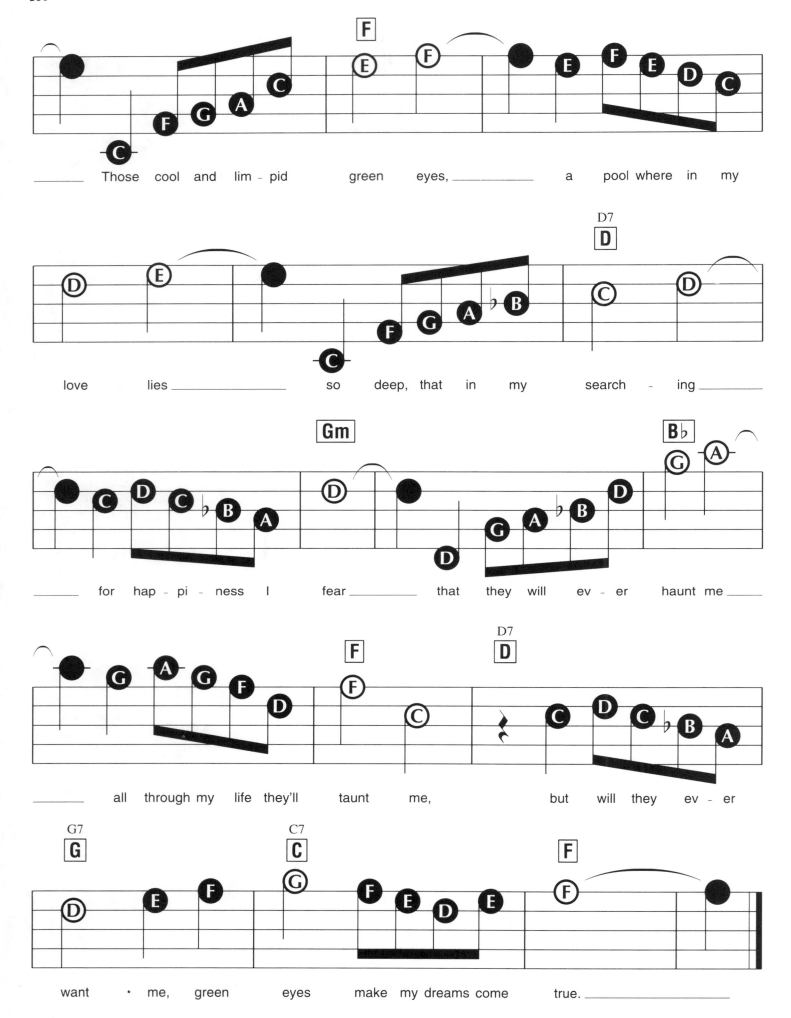

1942
Don't Sit Under the Apple Tree
(With Anyone Else but Me)

Registration 2
Rhythm: Swing

Words and Music by Lew Brown,
Sam H. Stept and Charlie Tobias

F

F F F F G A A A. B C C C D C

Don't sit un-der the ap-ple tree {
Don't go walk-ing down lov-ers' lane {

with an-y-one else but

Gm7 / Gm   C7 / C   F

A B B B C B G A A A B A

me, an-y-one else but me, an-y-one else but

C7 / C   F

F C C C F F F F G A A A. B

me. No! No! No! { Just re-mem-ber that I've been true to
{ Don't start show-ing that off your charms in

D7 / D   Gm7 / Gm   C7 / C

C C C D C A. D G G F E

no-bod-y else but you, so just be true to
some-bod-y else-'s arms, You must be true to

1. F   F
me.

2. F   F7   F
me. I'm

1943
That Old Black Magic
from the Paramount Picture STAR SPANGLED RHYTHM

Registration 1
Rhythm: Fox Trot or Swing

Words by Johnny Mercer
Music by Harold Arlen

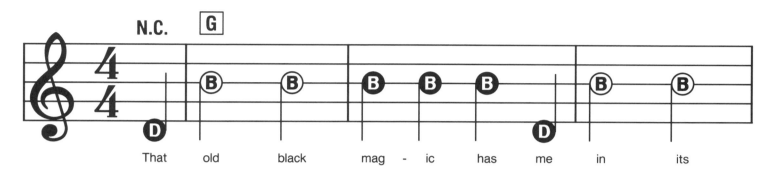

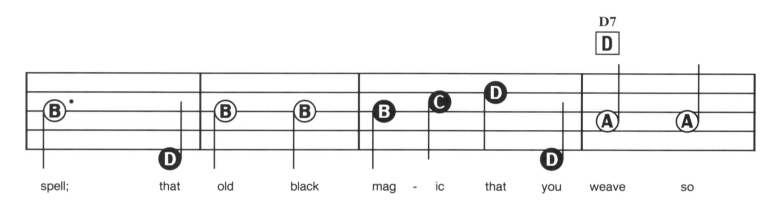

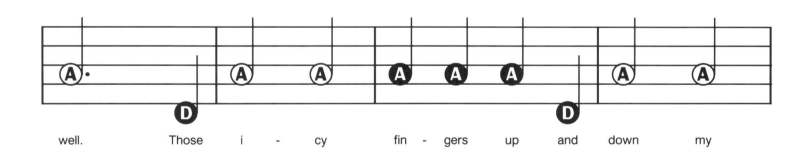

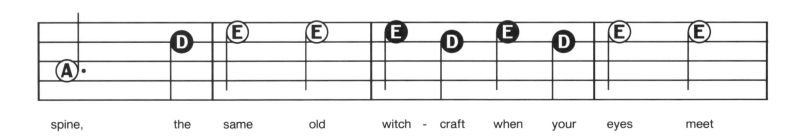

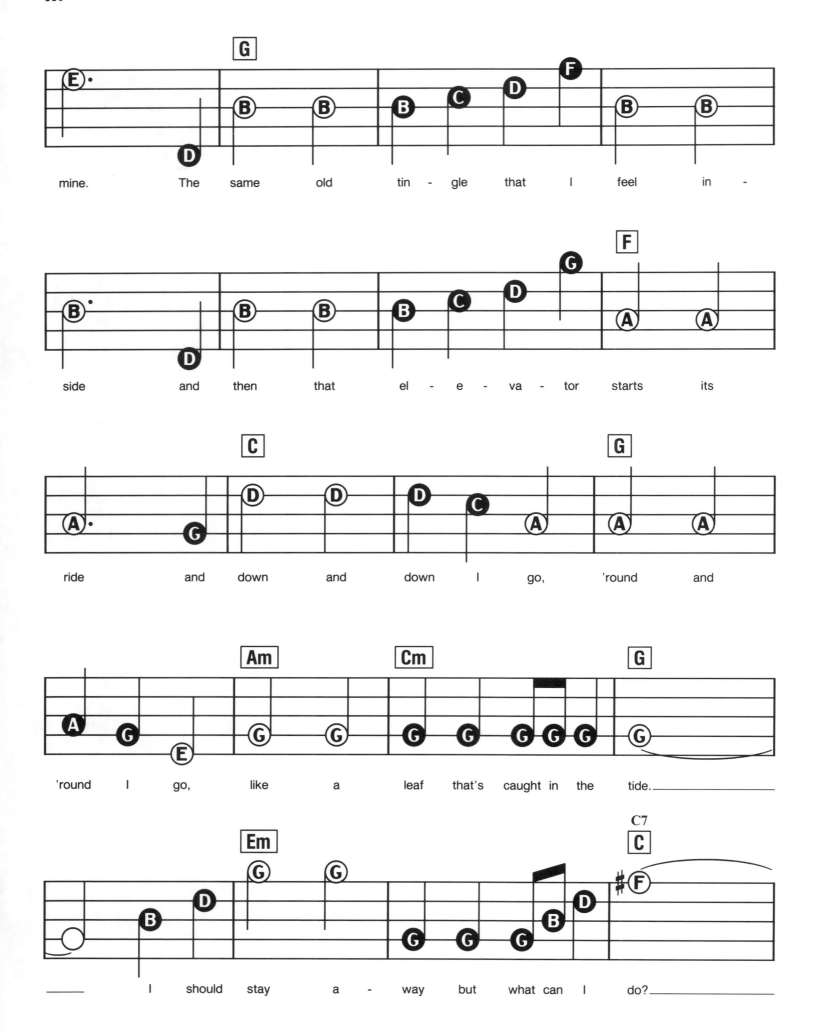

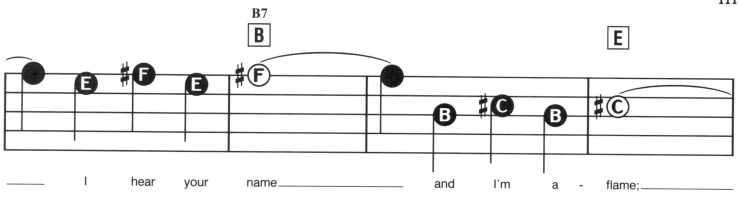

I hear your name_____ and I'm a - flame;_____

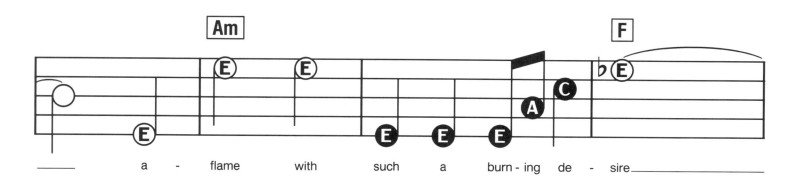

_____ a - flame with such a burn - ing de - sire_____

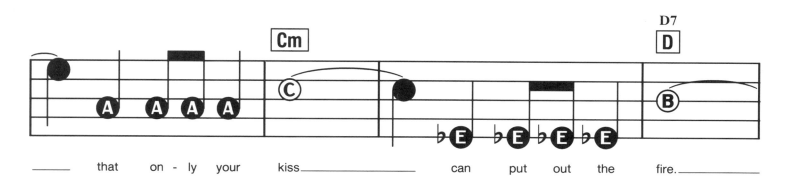

_____ that on - ly your kiss_____ can put out the fire._____

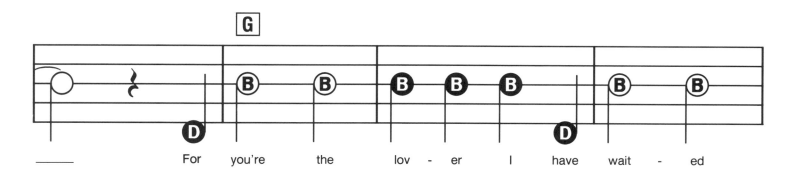

_____ For you're the lov - er I have wait - ed

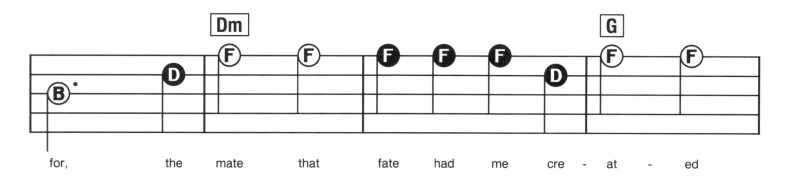

for, the mate that fate had me cre - at - ed

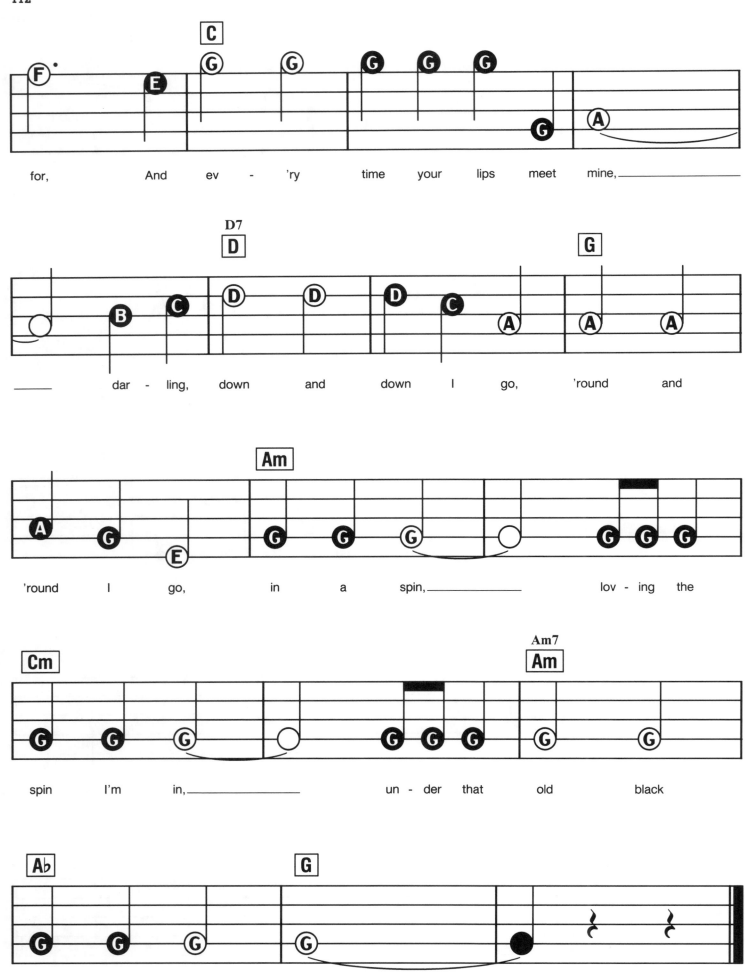

1944
Mairzy Doats

Registration 5
Rhythm: Fox Trot or Swing

Words and Music by Milton Drake,
Al Hoffman and Jerry Livingston

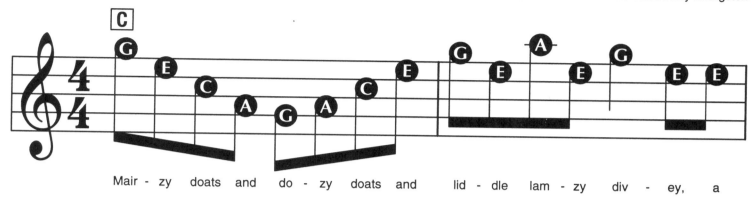

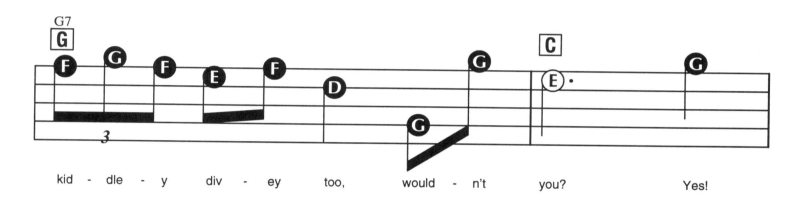

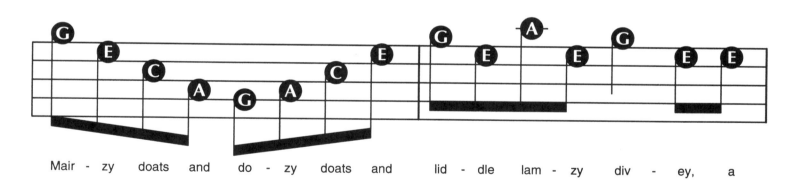

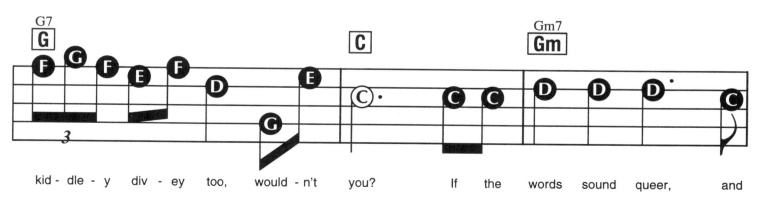

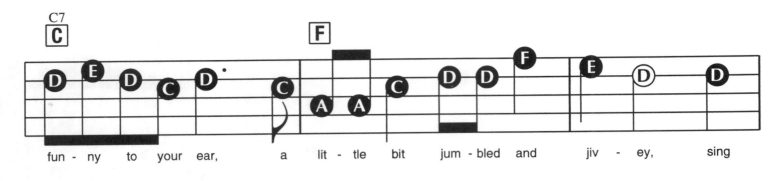

fun - ny to your ear, a lit - tle bit jum - bled and jiv - ey, sing

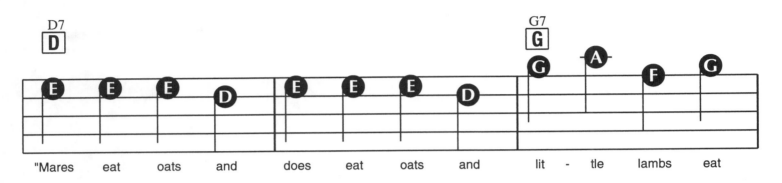

"Mares eat oats and does eat oats and lit - tle lambs eat

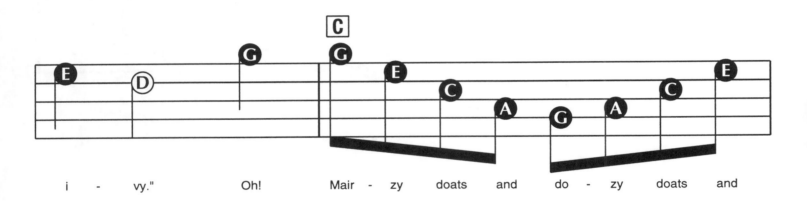

i - vy." Oh! Mair - zy doats and do - zy doats and

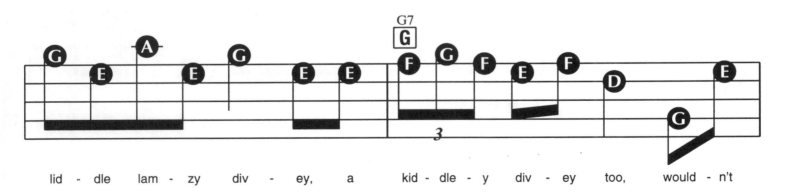

lid - dle lam - zy div - ey, a kid - dle - y div - ey too, would - n't

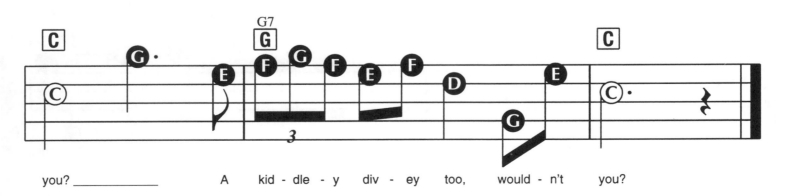

you? _____ A kid - dle - y div - ey too, would - n't you?

1945
Candy

Registration 4
Rhythm: Fox Trot or Swing

By Alex Kramer,
Joan Whitney and Mack David

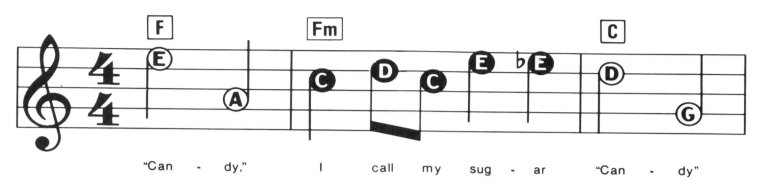

"Can - dy," I call my sug - ar "Can - dy"

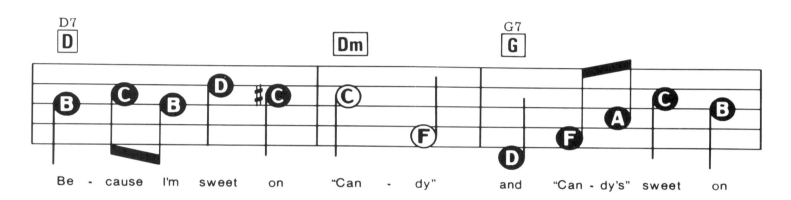

Be - cause I'm sweet on "Can - dy" and "Can - dy's" sweet on

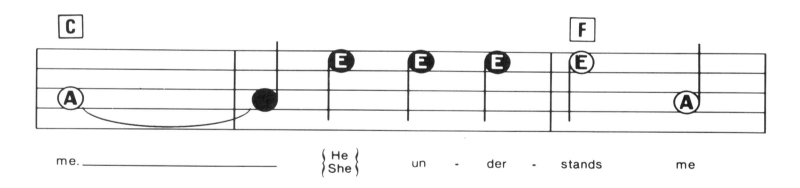

me. _____ {He / She} un - der - stands me

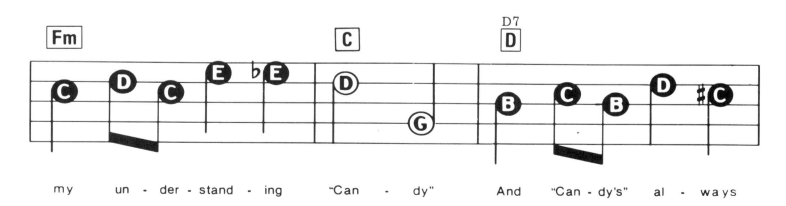

my un - der - stand - ing "Can - dy" And "Can - dy's" al - ways

116

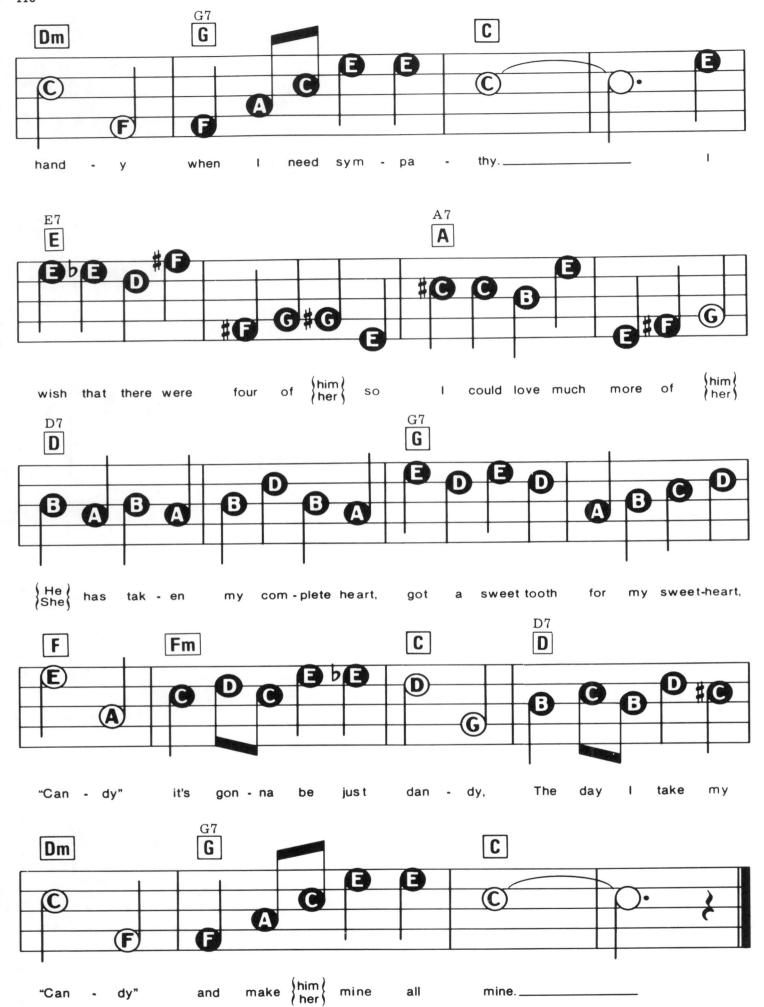

1946
Route 66

Registration 7
Rhythm: Swing

By Bobby Troup

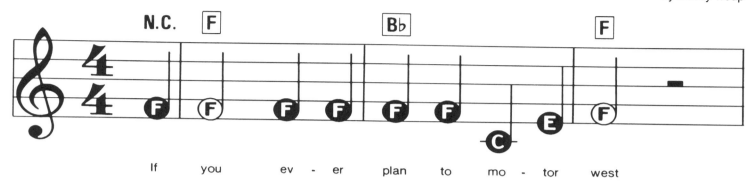

If you ev - er plan to mo - tor west

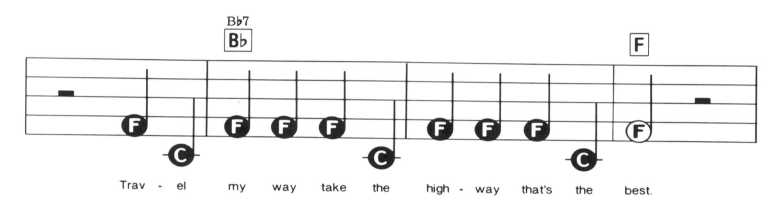

Trav - el my way take the high - way that's the best.

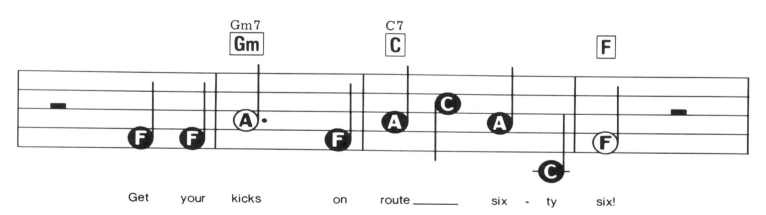

Get your kicks on route ____ six - ty six!

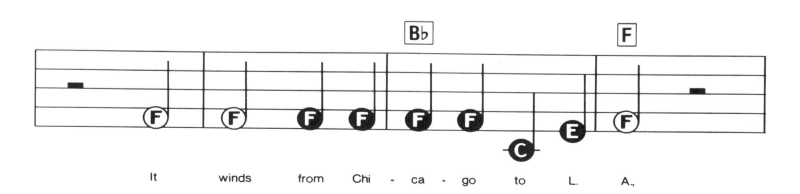

It winds from Chi - ca - go to L. A.,

118

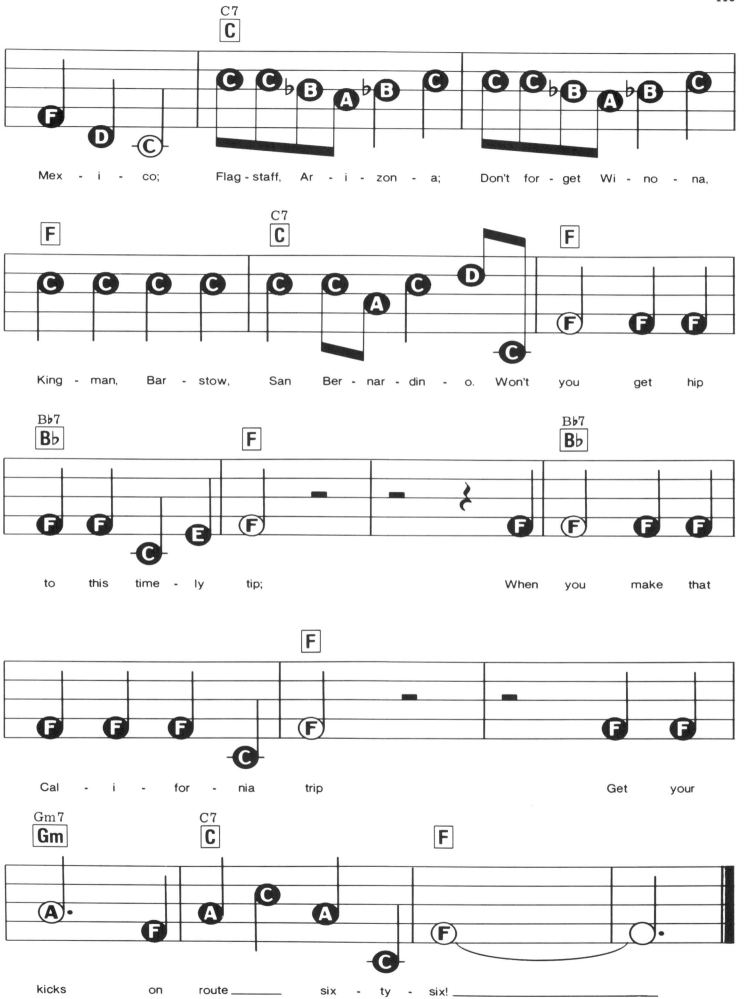

1947

Beyond the Sea

Registration 7
Rhythm: Slow Rock or Ballad

English Lyrics by Jack Lawrence
Music and French Lyrics by Charles Trenet

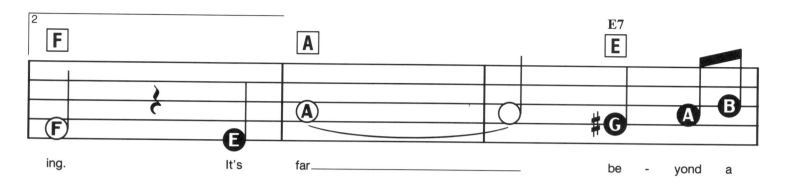

ing. It's far_____ be - yond a

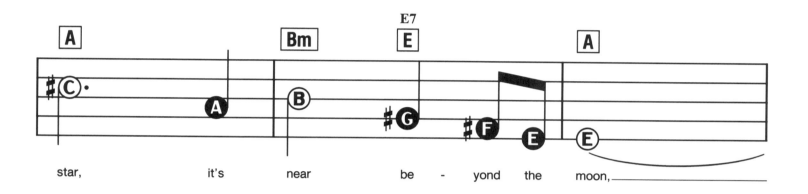

star, it's near be - yond the moon,_____

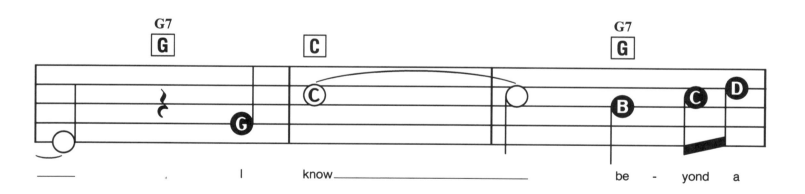

_____ I know_____ be - yond a

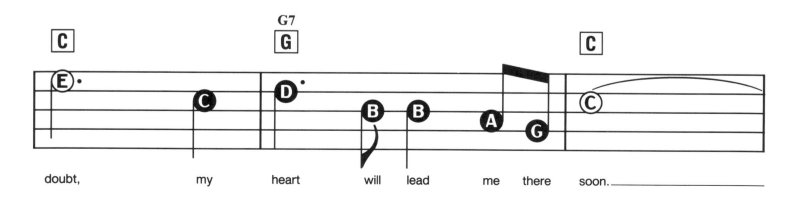

doubt, my heart will lead me there soon._____

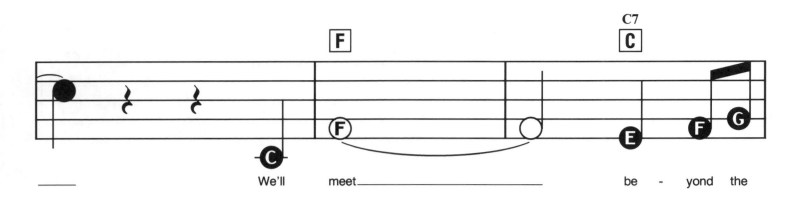

We'll meet_____ be - yond the

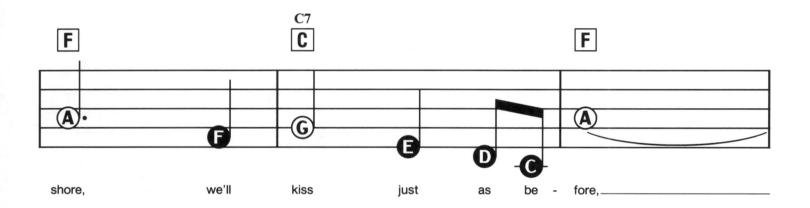

shore, we'll kiss just as be - fore,_____

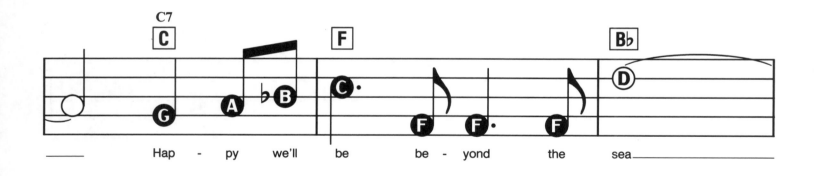

_____ Hap - py we'll be be - yond the sea_____

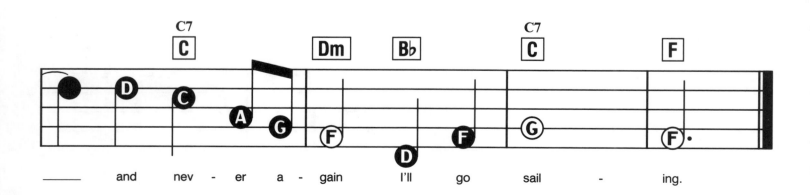

_____ and nev - er a - gain I'll go sail - ing.

1948
Buttons and Bows
from the Paramount Picture PALEFACE

Registration 4
Rhythm: Swing

Words and Music by Jay Livingston
and Ray Evans

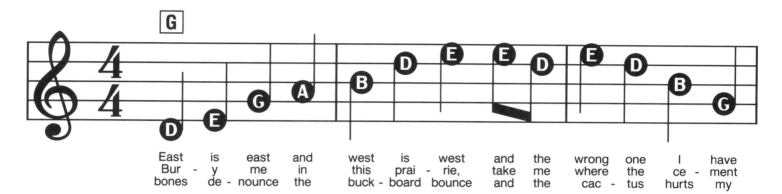

East is east and the west is west and the wrong one I have
Bur - y me in this prai - rie, take me where the ce - ment
bones de - nounce the buck - board bounce and the cac - tus hurts my

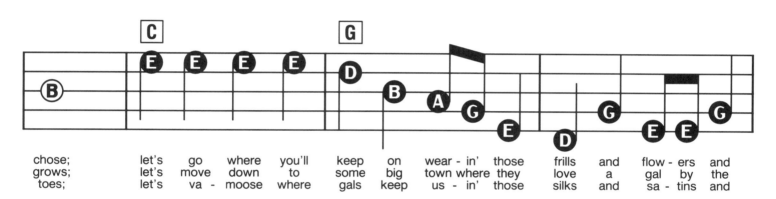

chose; let's go where you'll keep on wear - in' those frills and flow - ers and
grows; let's move down to town where they love a gal by the
toes; let's va - moose where gals keep us - in' those silks and sa - tins and

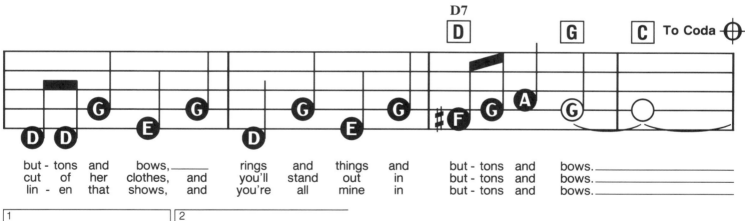

but - tons and bows, rings and things and but - tons and bows.
cut of her clothes, and you'll stand out in but - tons and bows.
lin - en that shows, and you're all mine in but - tons and bows.

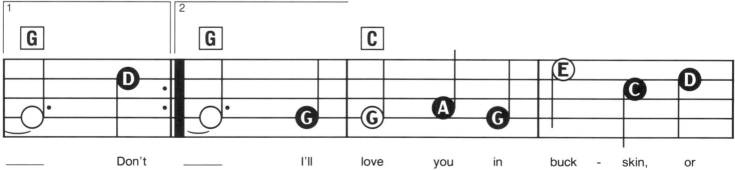

Don't I'll love you in buck - skin, or

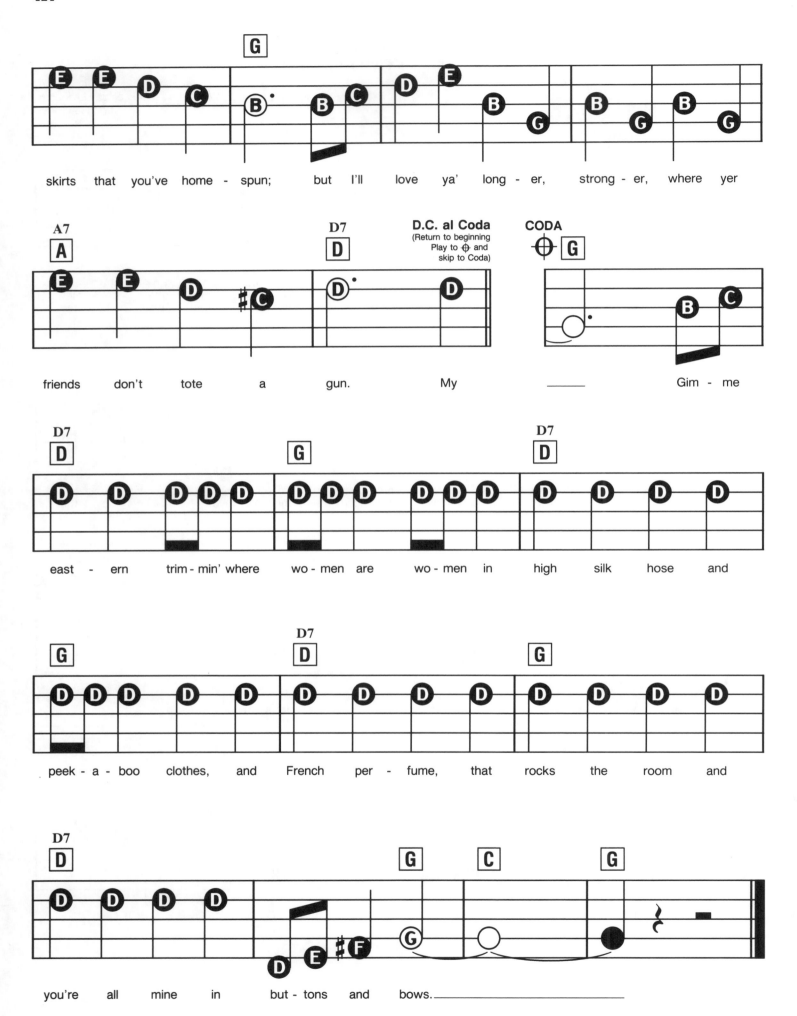

124

1949
(Ghost)
Riders in the Sky
(A Cowboy Legend)
from RIDERS IN THE SKY

Registration 10
Rhythm: March or Polka

By Stan Jones

126

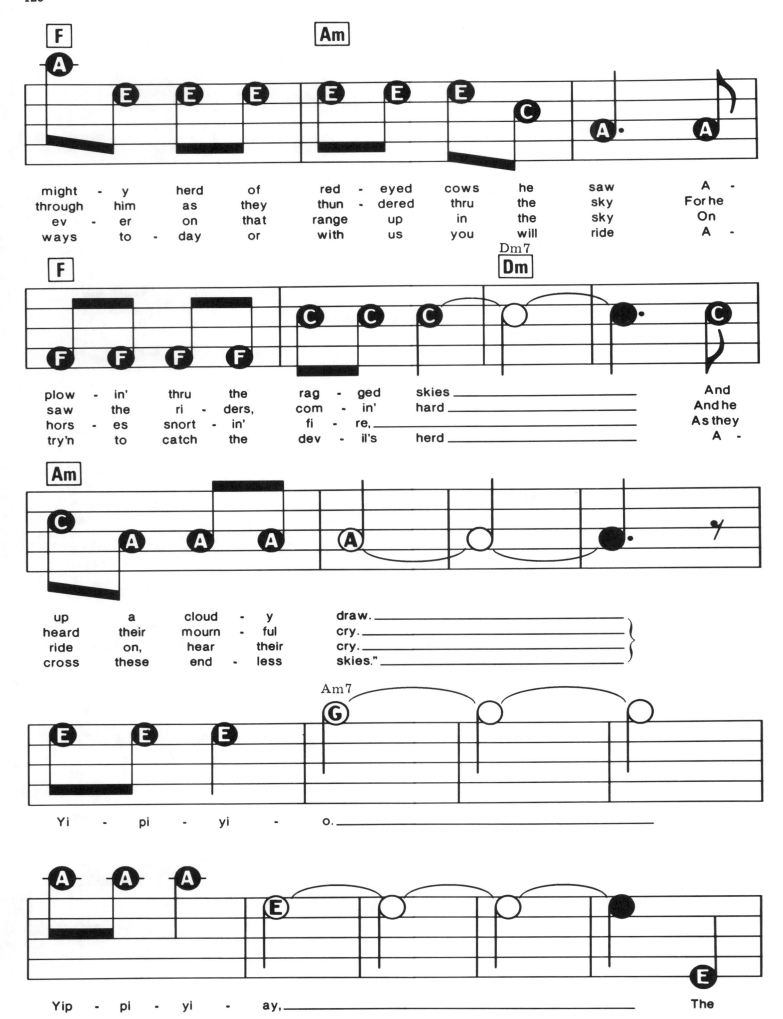

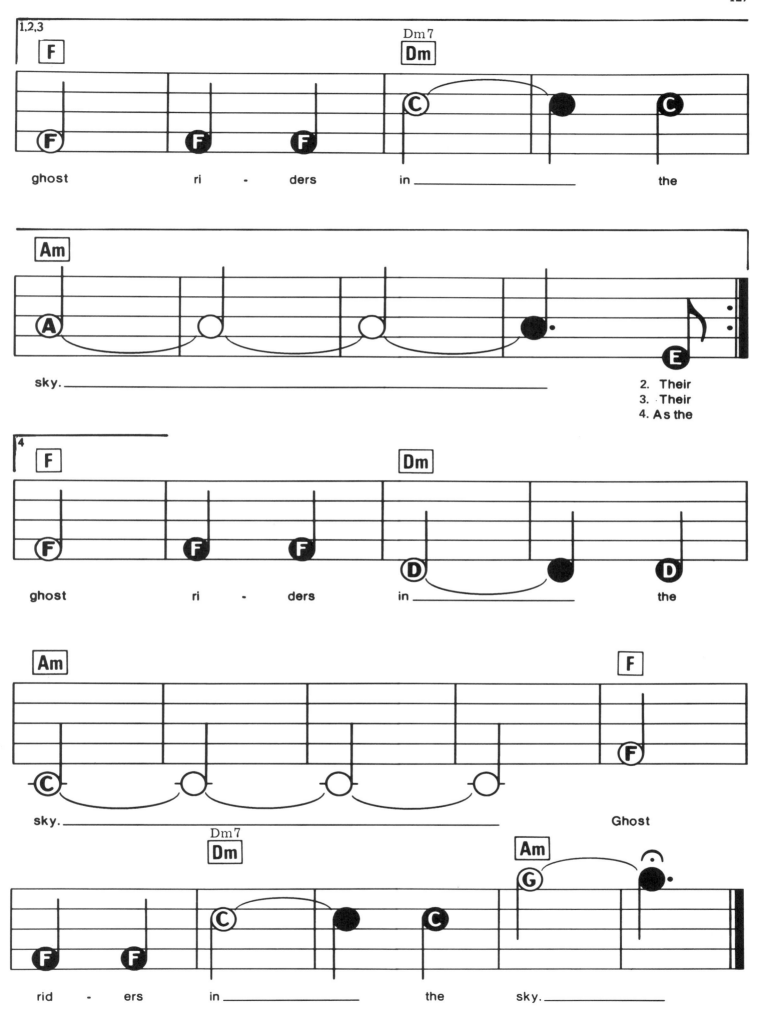

1950
Mona Lisa
from the Paramount Picture CAPTAIN CAREY, U.S.A.

Registration 9
Rhythm: Swing or 8 Beat

Words and Music by Jay Livingston
and Ray Evans

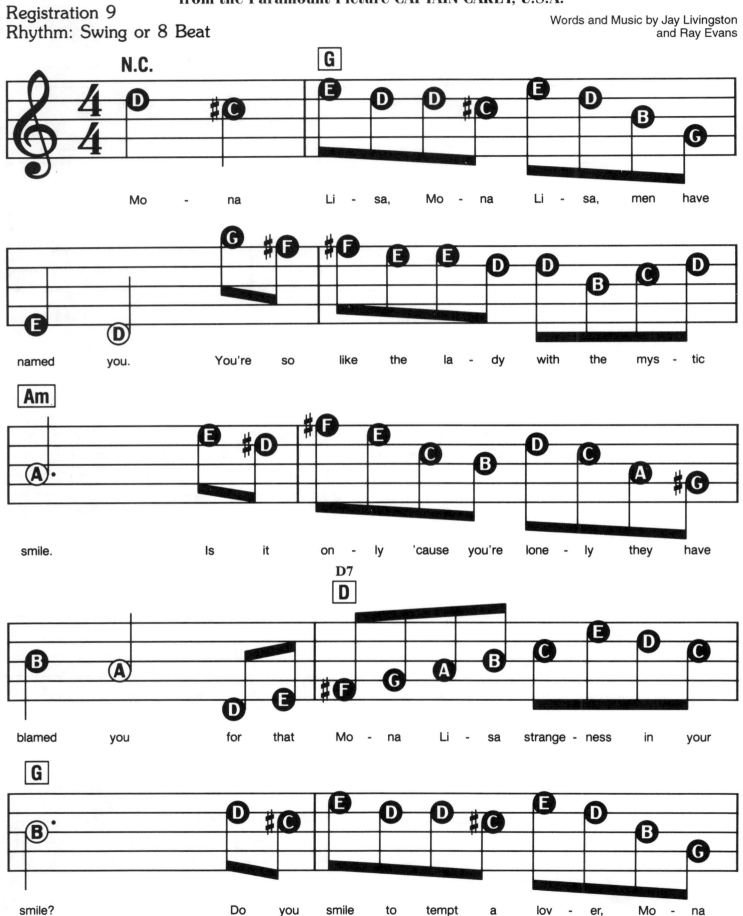

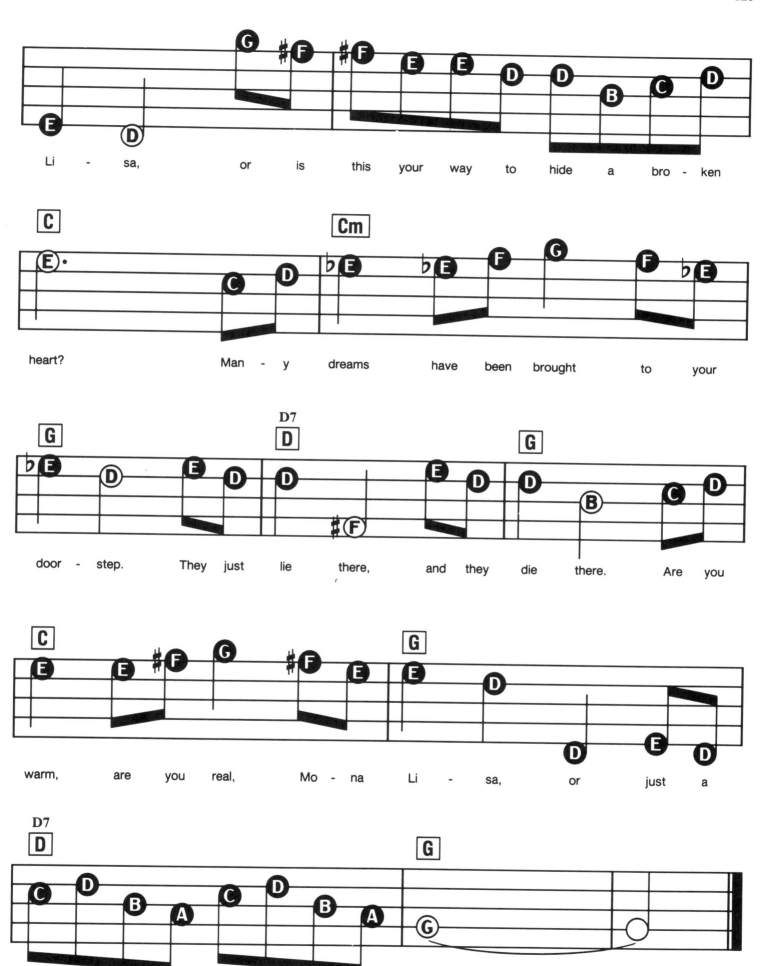

1951
Cry

Registration 1
Rhythm: Swing

Words and Music by
Churchill Kohlman

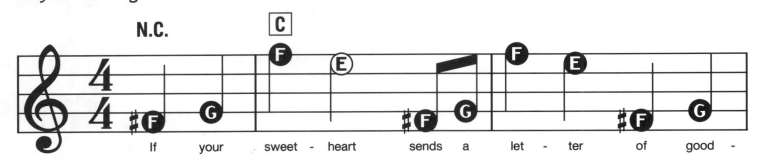

If your sweet - heart sends a let - ter of good -

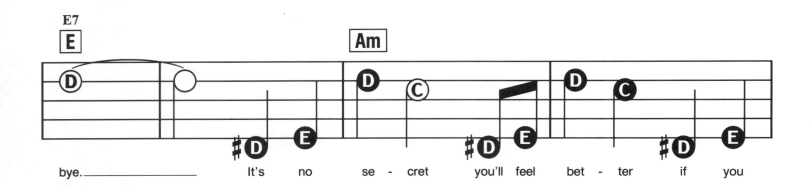

bye. It's no se - cret you'll feel bet - ter if you

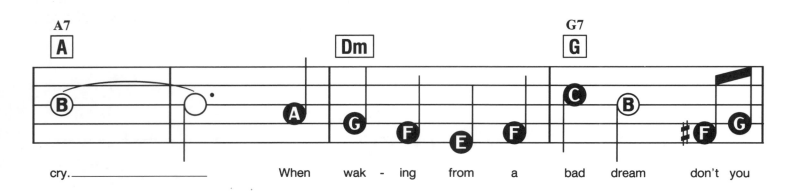

cry. When wak - ing from a bad dream don't you

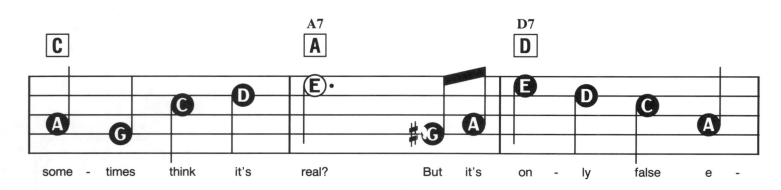

some - times think it's real? But it's on - ly false e -

131

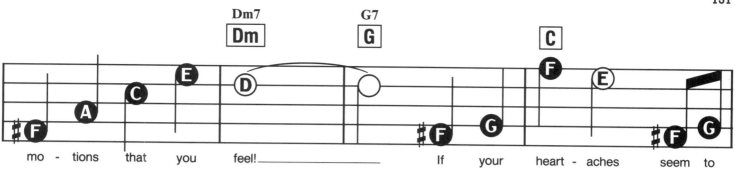

mo - tions that you feel!_____ If your heart - aches seem to

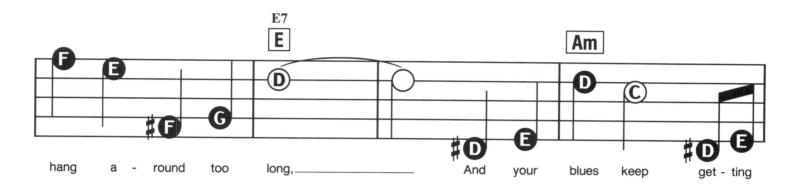

hang a - round too long,_____ And your blues keep get - ting

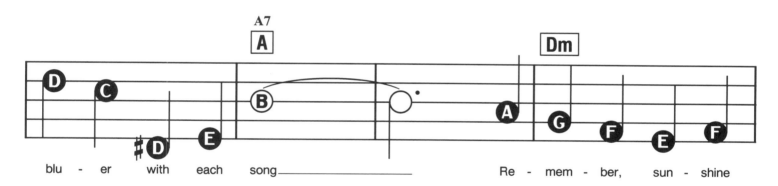

blu - er with each song_____ Re - mem - ber, sun - shine

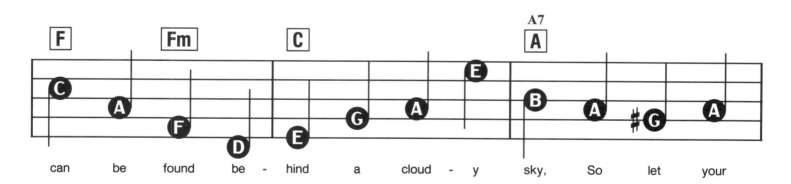

can be found be - hind a cloud - y sky, So let your

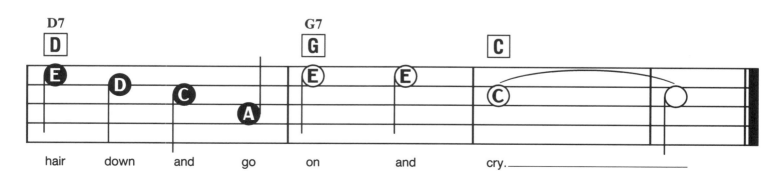

hair down and go on and cry._____

1952
Your Cheatin' Heart

Registration 5
Rhythm: Fox Trot or Swing

Words and Music by
Hank Williams

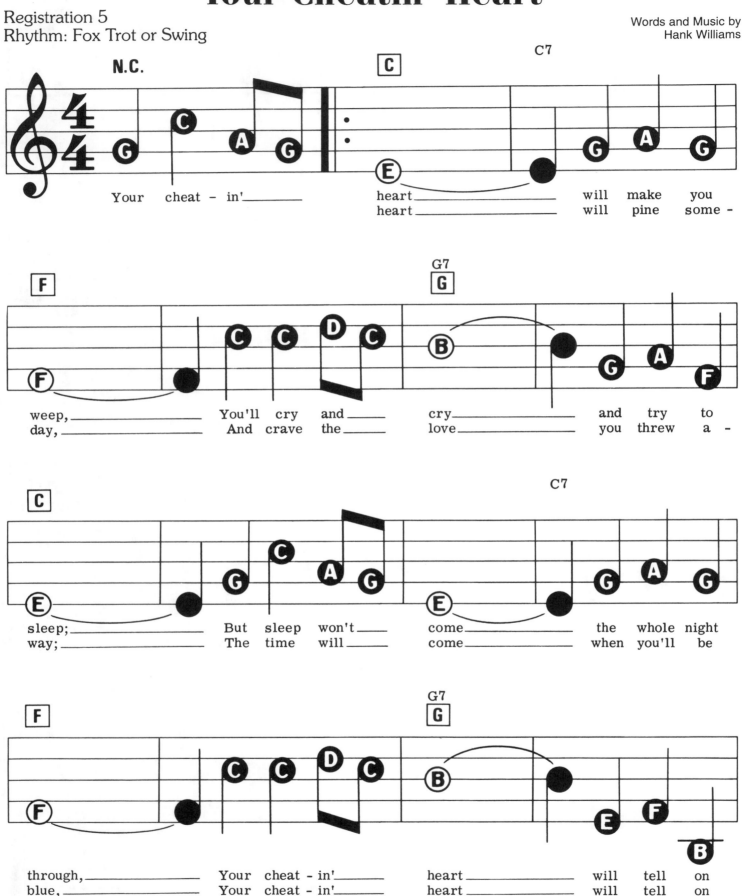

133

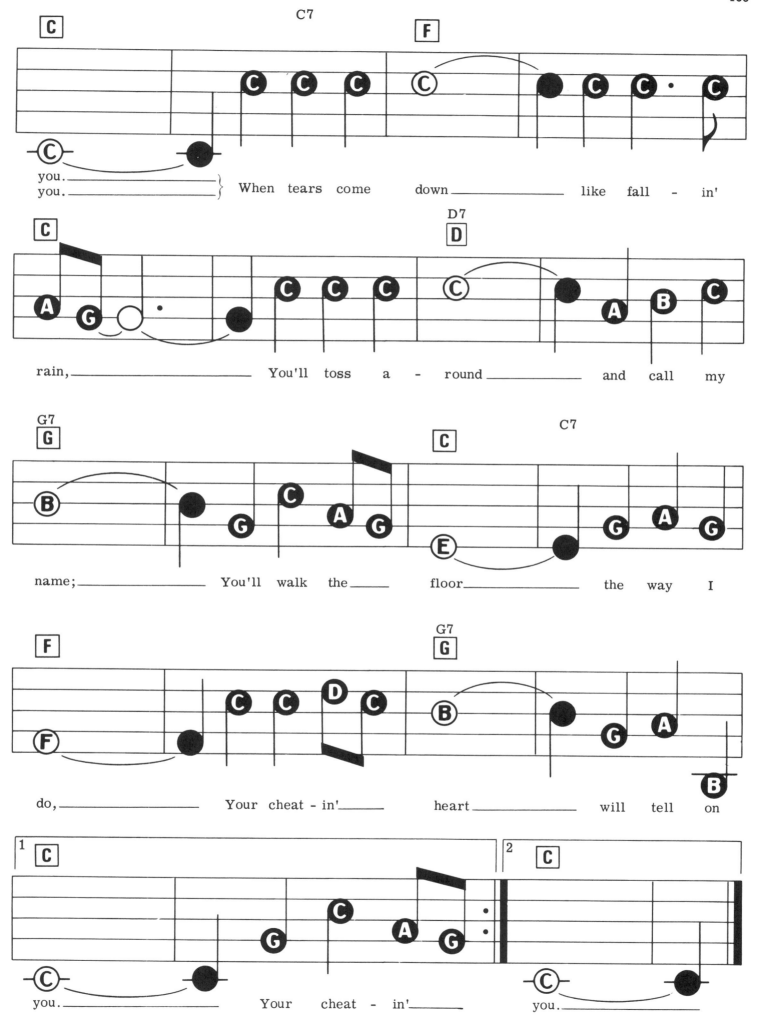

1953
I Love Paris
from CAN-CAN

Registration 9
Rhythm: Fox Trot

Words and Music by
Cole Porter

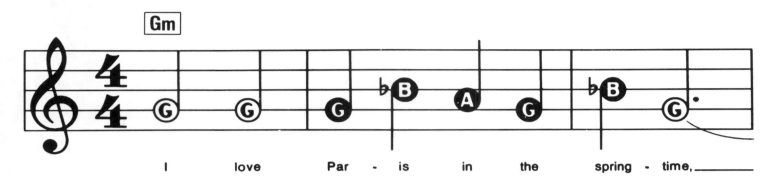

I love Par - is in the spring - time, _____

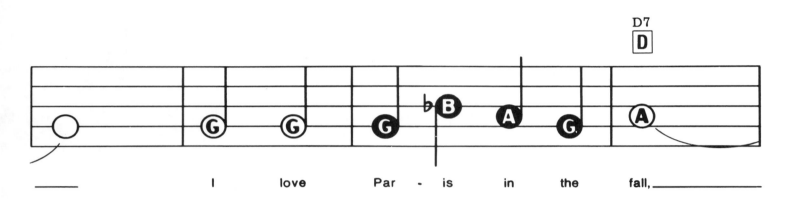

_____ I love Par - is in the fall, _____

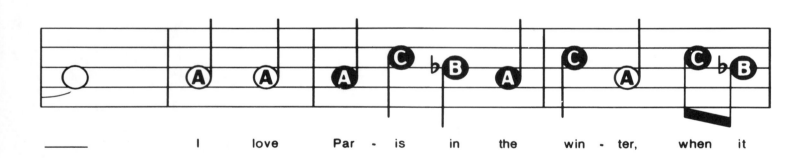

_____ I love Par - is in the win - ter, when it

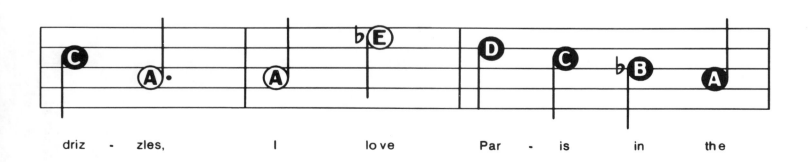

driz - zles, I love Par - is in the

135

sum - mer, when it siz - zles, I love

Pa - ris ev - 'ry mo - ment,_____

ev - 'ry mo - ment of the year,_____

I love Par - is, why, oh why do I love Par - is?

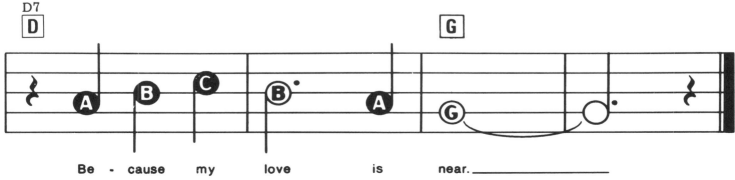

Be - cause my love is near._____

1954

Shake, Rattle and Roll

Registration 8
Rhythm: Rock or Jazz Rock

Words and Music by
Charles Calhoun

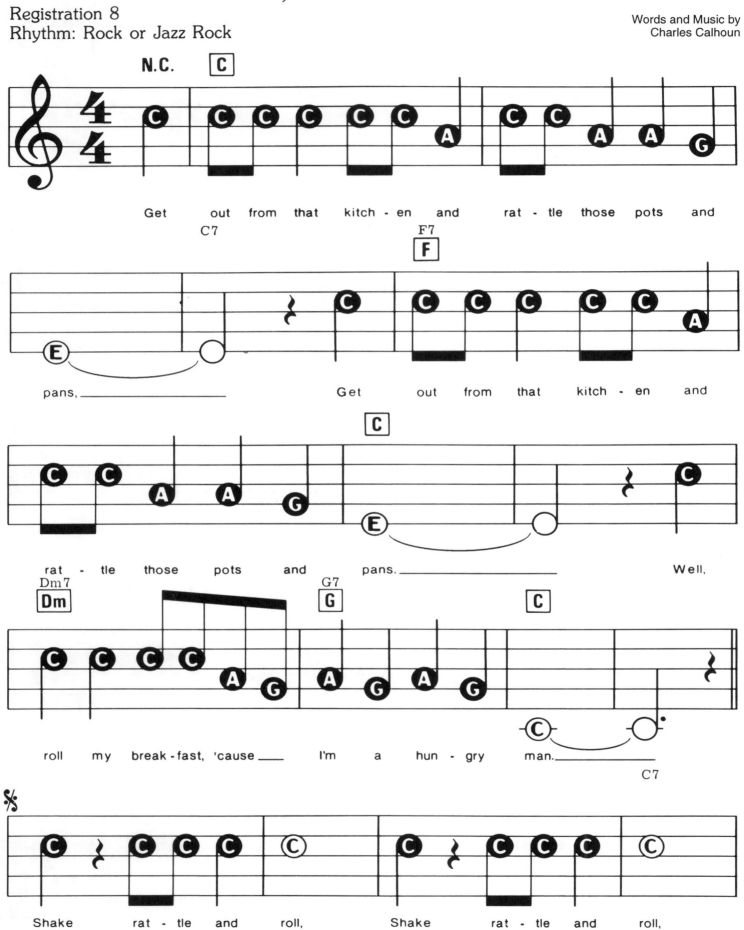

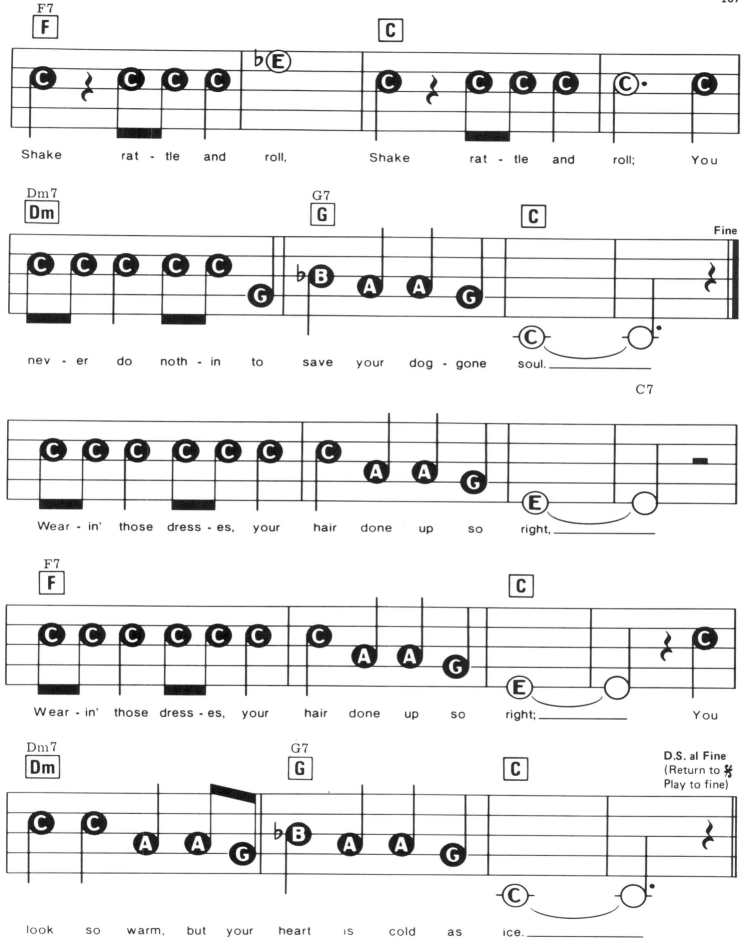

1955
Autumn Leaves
(Les Feuilles Mortes)

Registration 2
Rhythm: Fox Trot or Swing

English lyric by Johnny Mercer
French lyric by Jacques Prevert
Music by Joseph Kosma

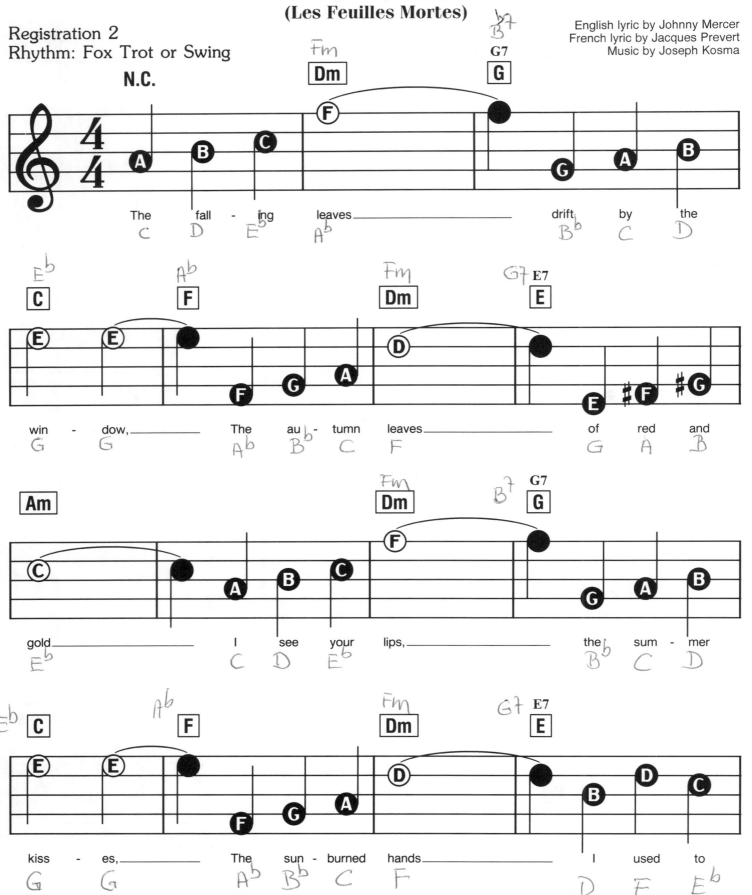

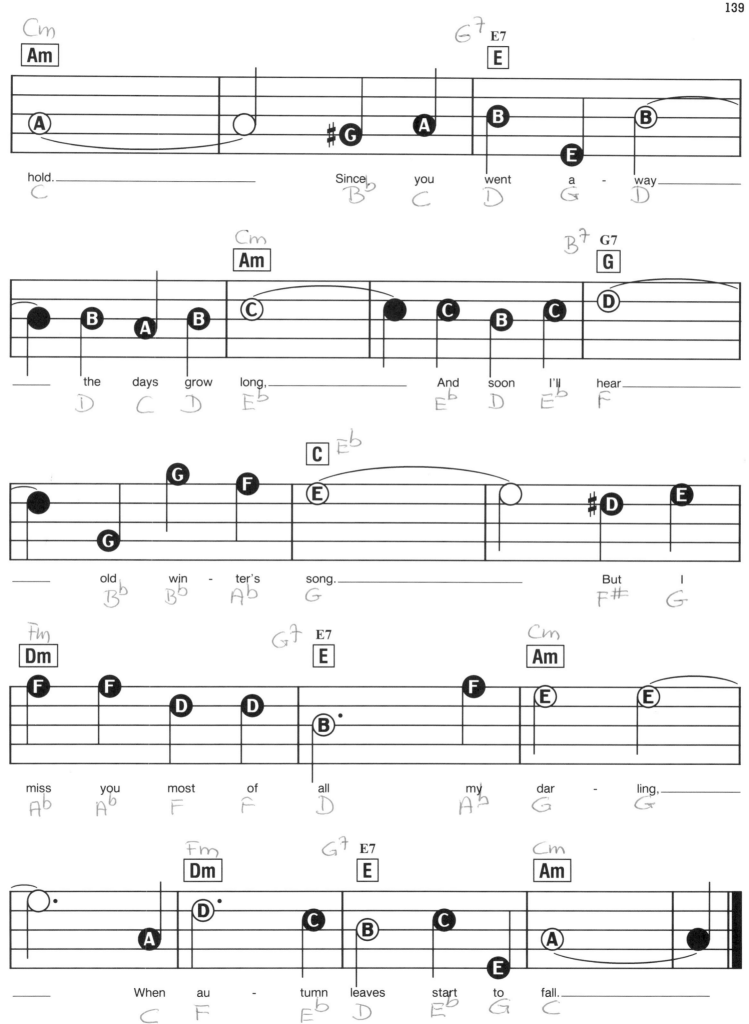

1956
The Great Pretender

Registration 4
Rhythm: Fox Trot or Swing

Words and Music by
Buck Ram

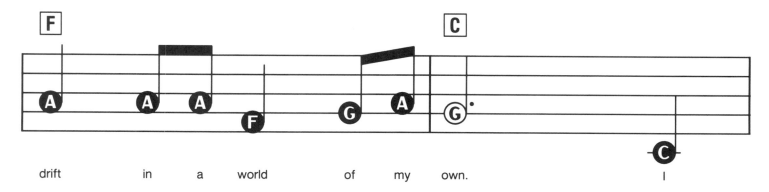

drift in a world of my own. I

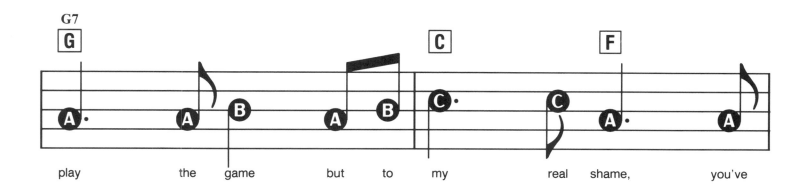

play the game but to my real shame, you've

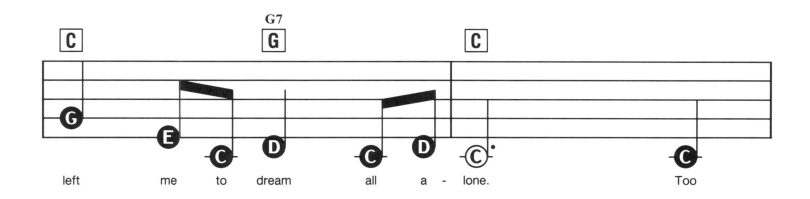

left me to dream all a - lone. Too

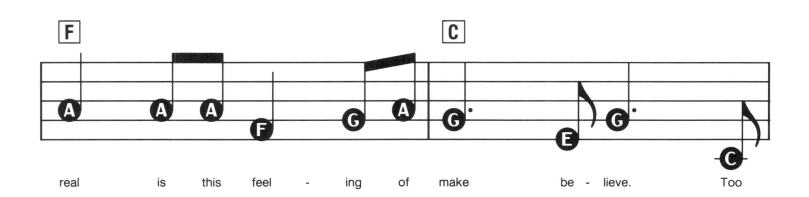

real is this feel - ing of make be - lieve. Too

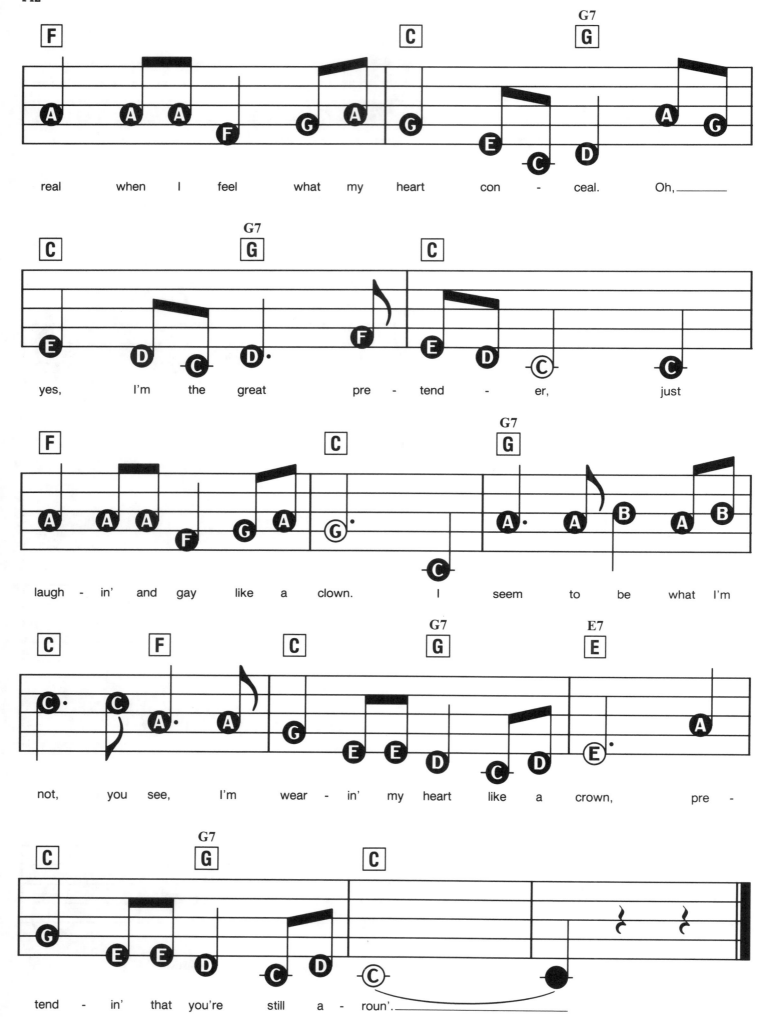

1957
All Shook Up

Registration 5
Rhythm: Rock

Words and Music by Otis Blackwell
and Elvis Presley

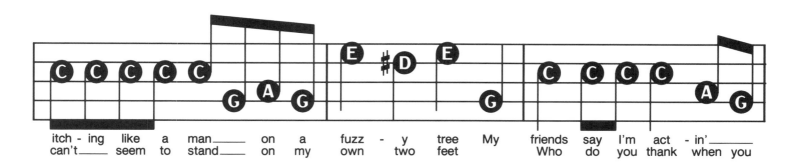

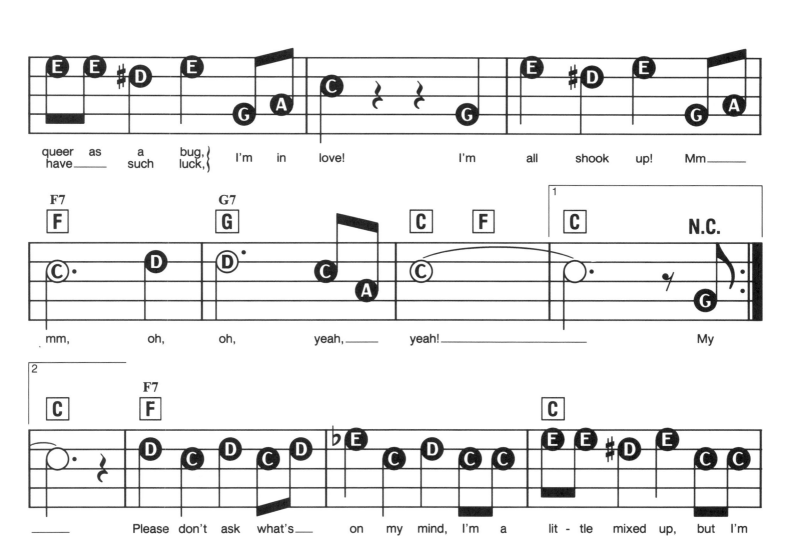

144

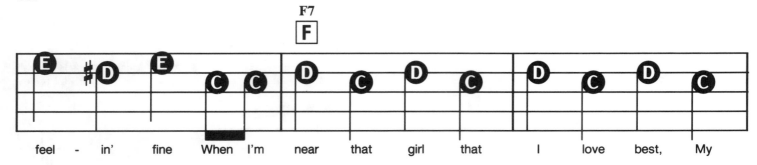

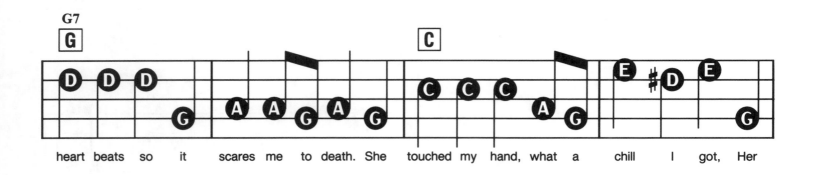

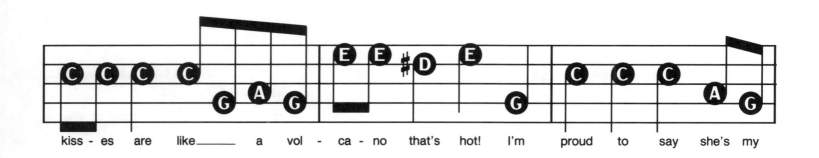

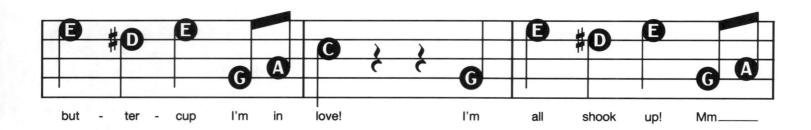

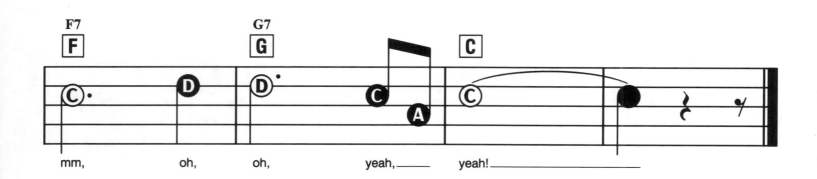

1958
I Can't Stop Loving You

Registration 8
Rhythm: Swing or Fox Trot

Words and Music by
Don Gibson

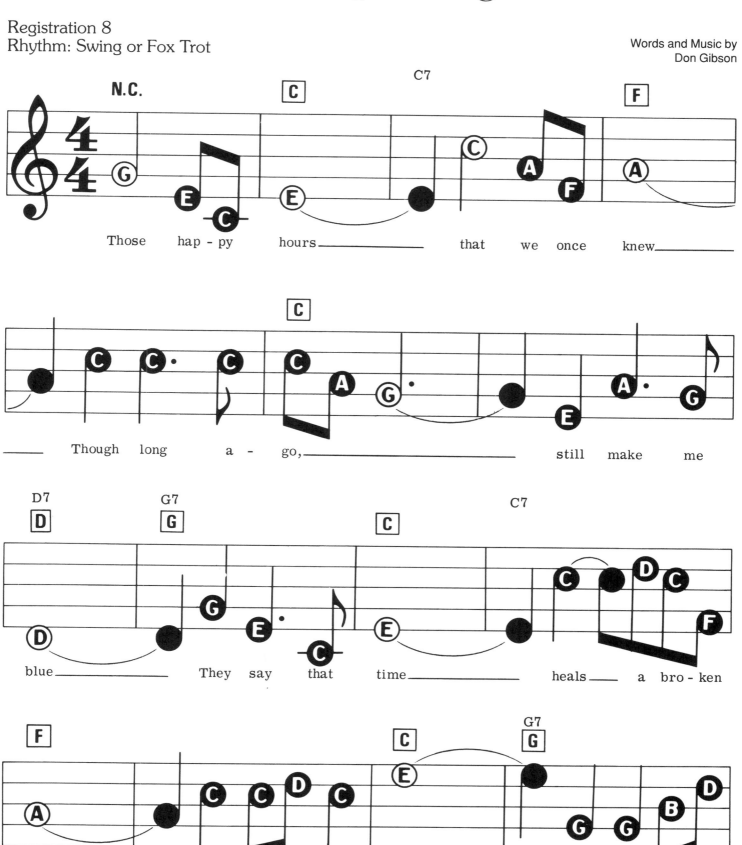

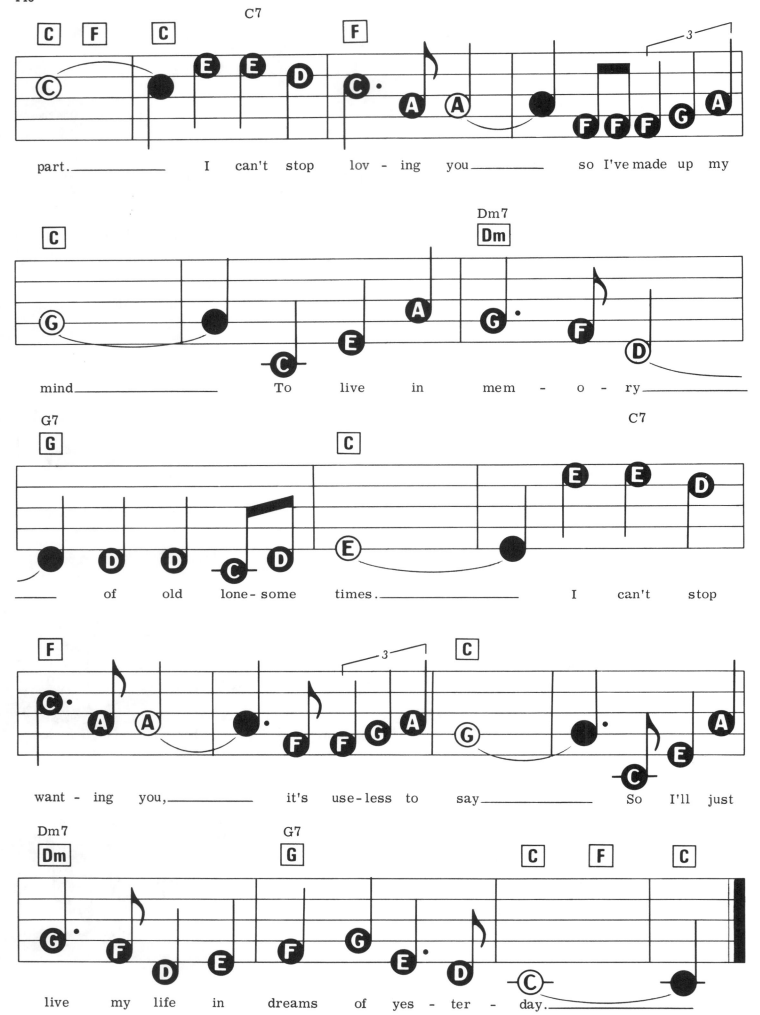

1959
Kansas City

Registration 4
Rhythm: Shuffle or Swing

Words and Music by Jerry Leiber
and Mike Stoller

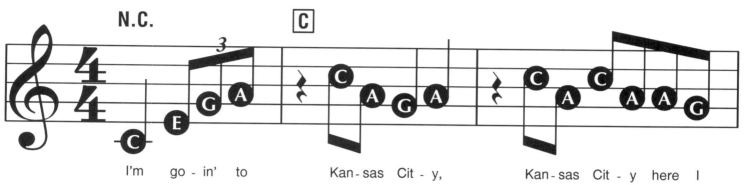

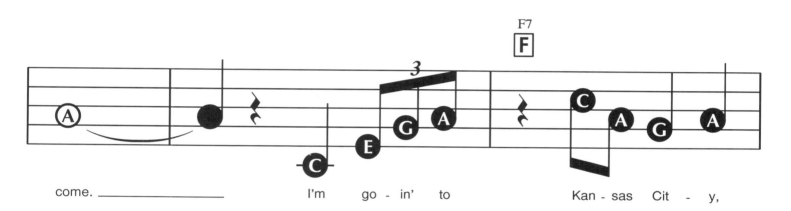

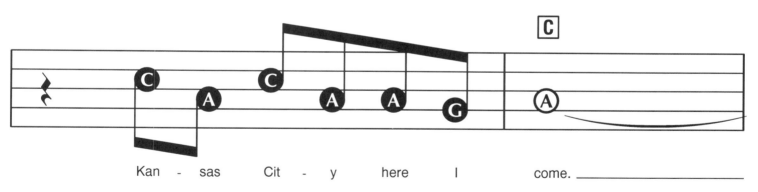

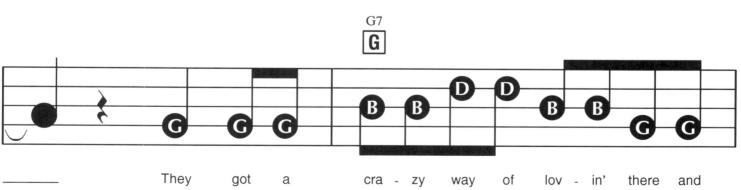

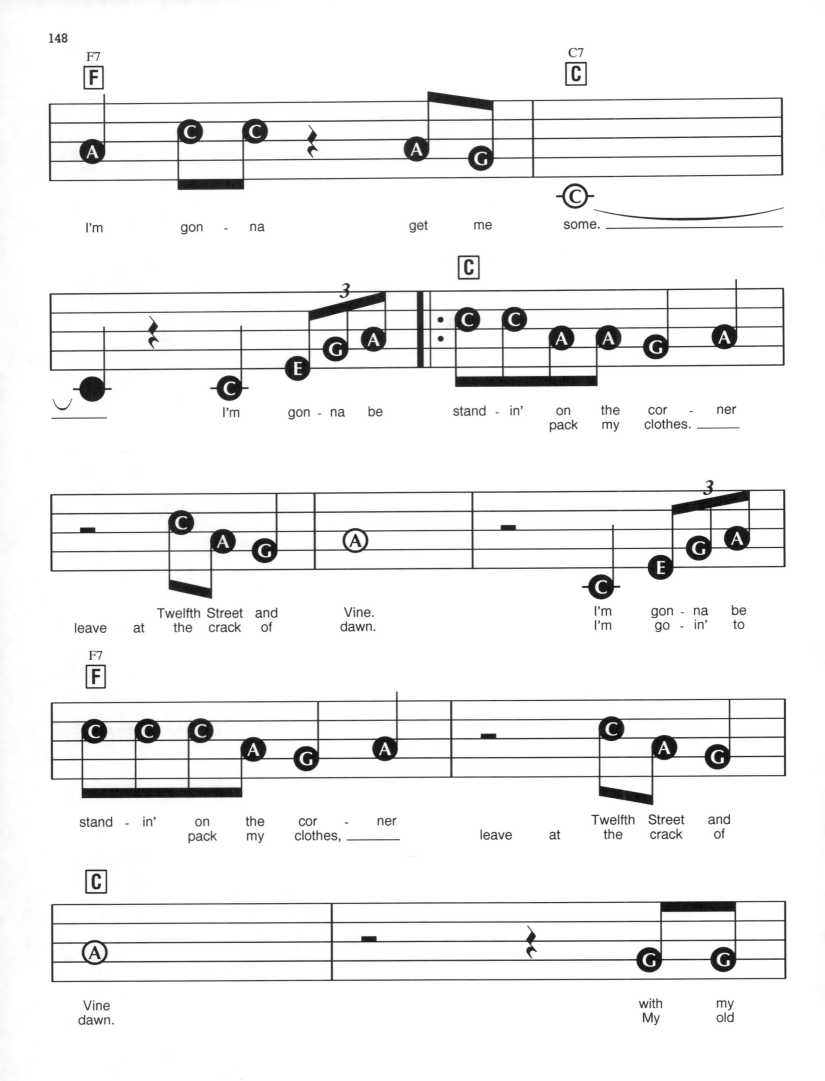

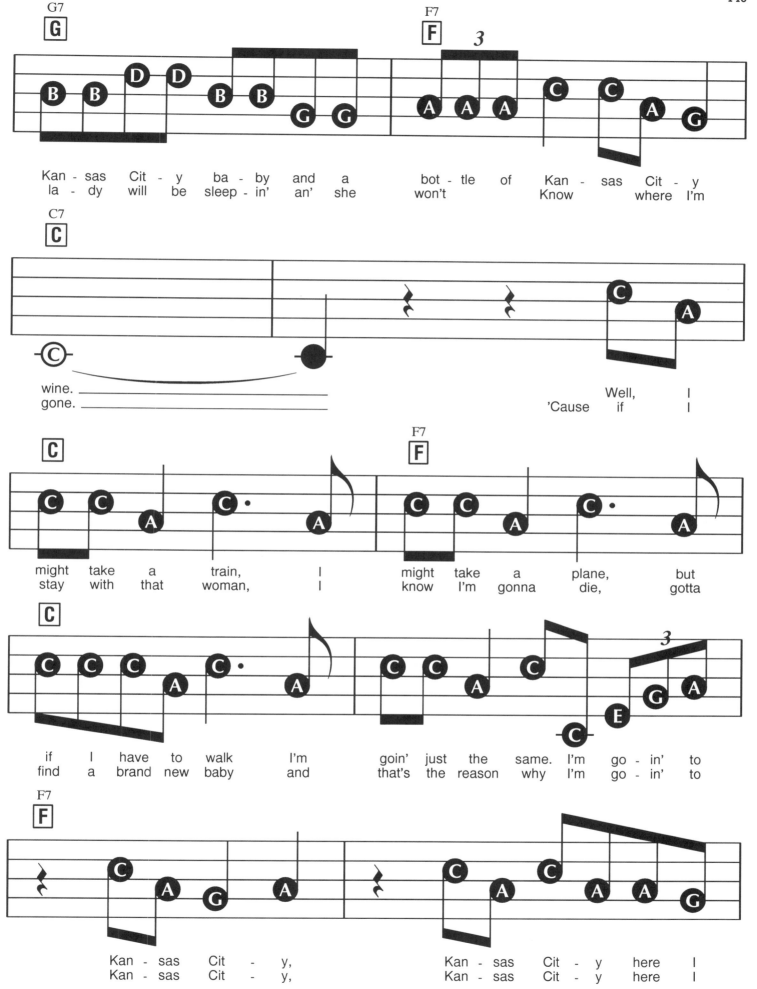

150

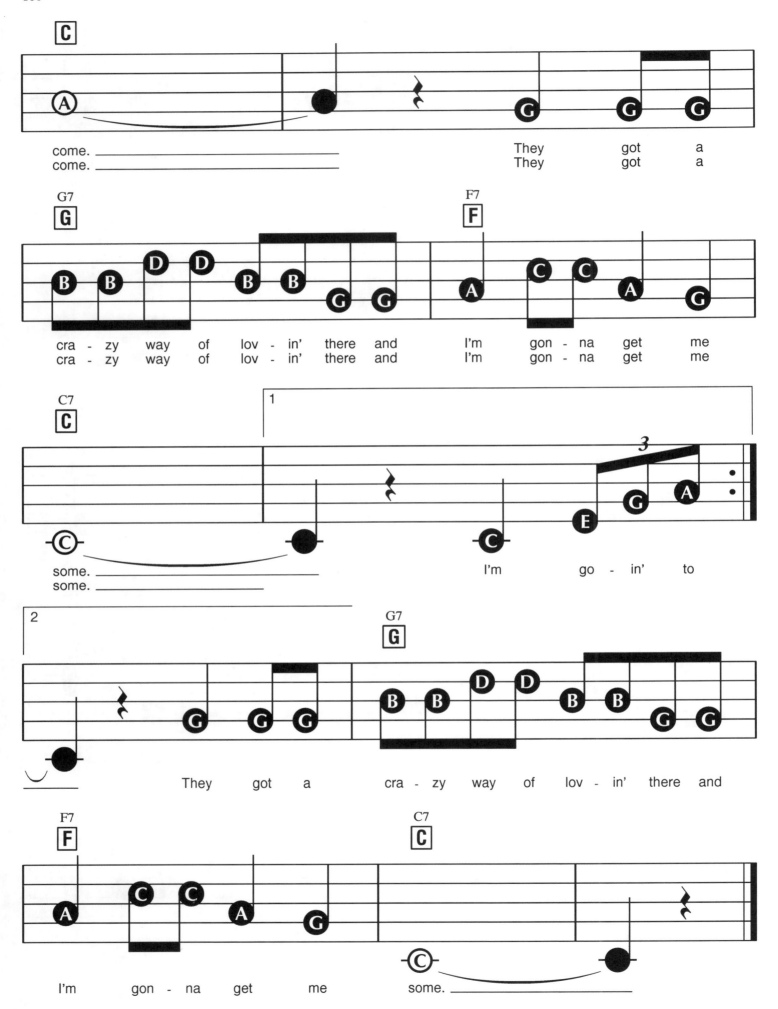

1960
If Ever I Would Leave You
from CAMELOT

Words by Alan Jay Lerner
Music by Frederick Loewe

Registration 5

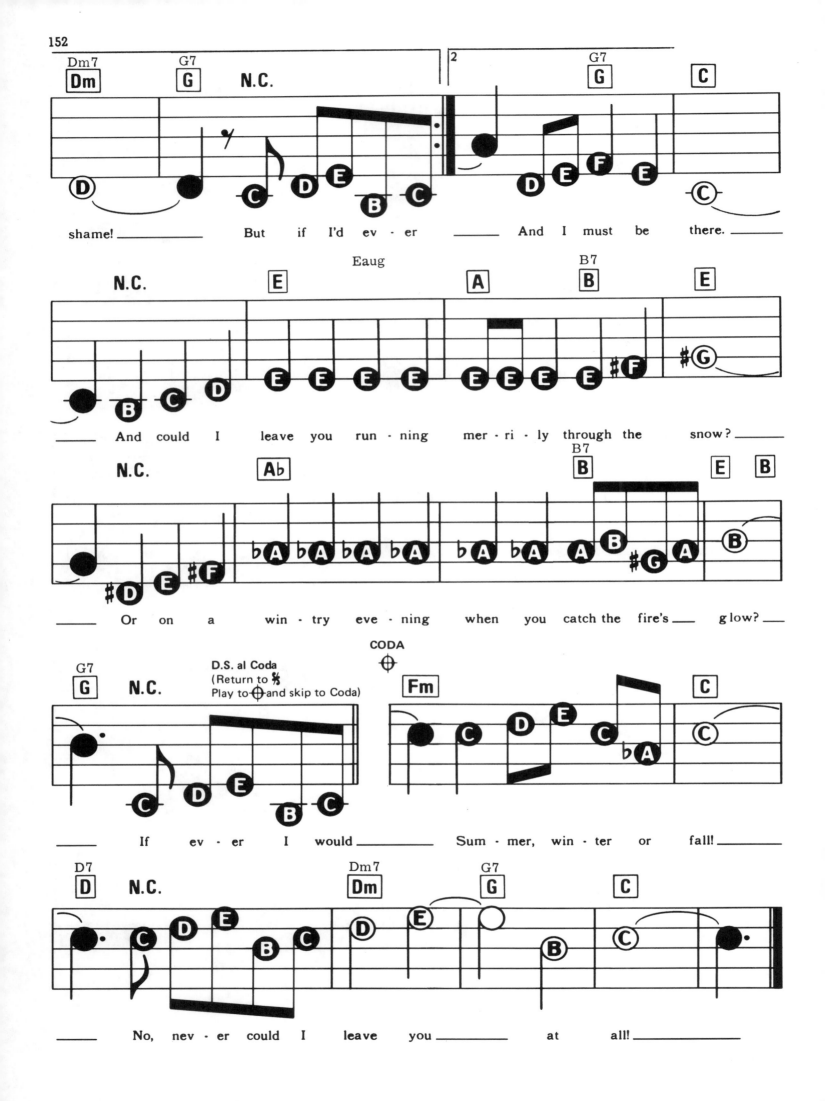

1961
Runaway

Registration 4
Rhythm: Rock

Words and Music by Del Shannon
and Max Crook

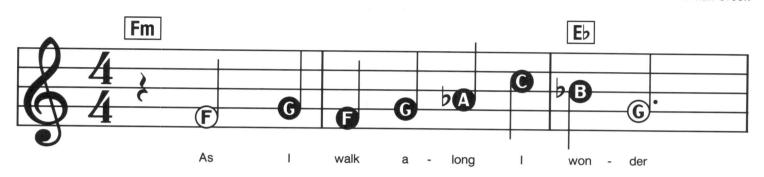

As I walk a - long I won - der

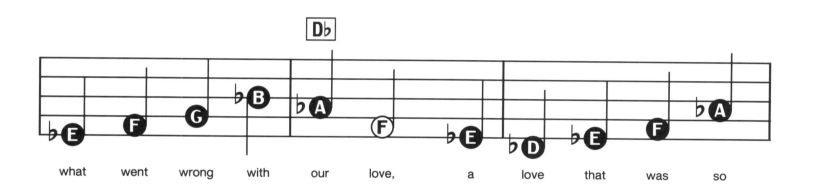

what went wrong with our love, a love that was so

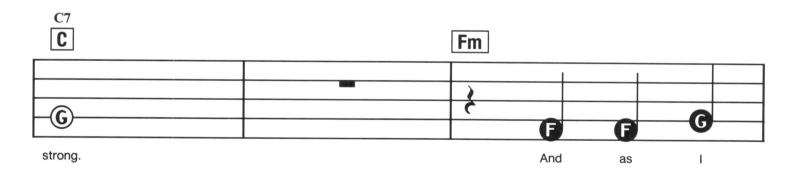

strong. And as I

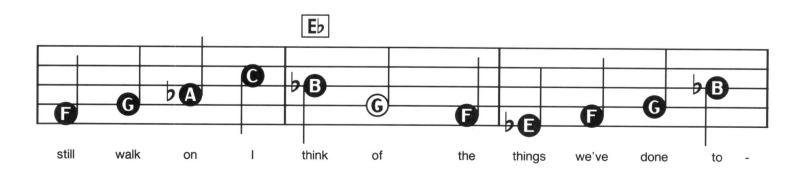

still walk on I think of the things we've done to -

154

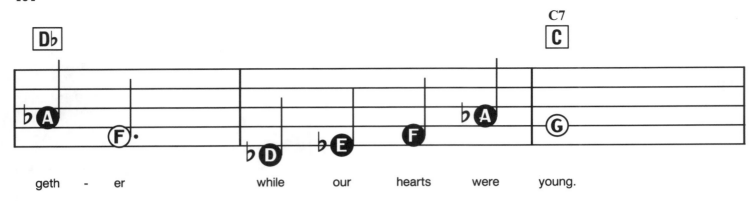

geth - er   while   our   hearts   were   young.

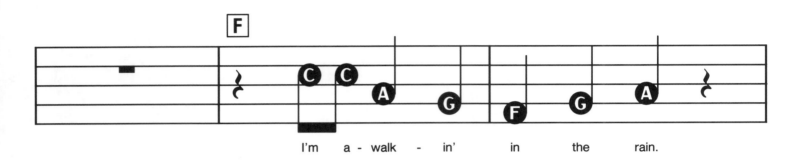

I'm   a - walk - in'   in   the   rain.

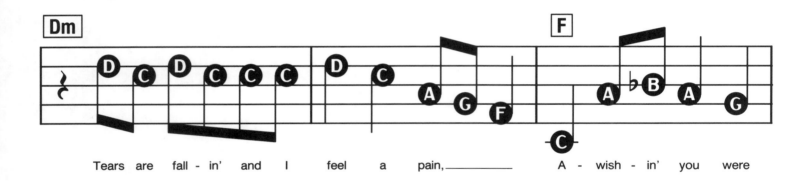

Tears   are   fall - in'   and   I   feel   a   pain,_____   A - wish - in'   you   were

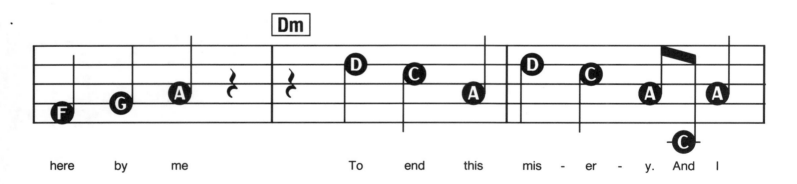

here   by   me   To   end   this   mis - er - y.   And   I

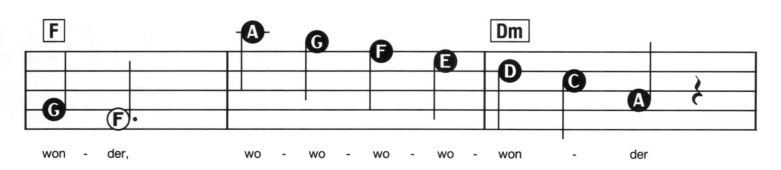

won - der,   wo - wo - wo - wo - won - der

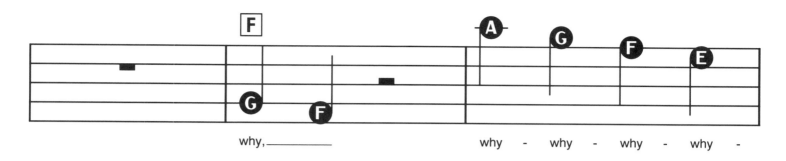

why,_____ why - why - why - why -

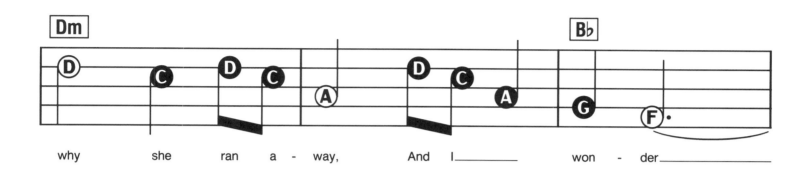

why she ran a - way, And I_____ won - der_____

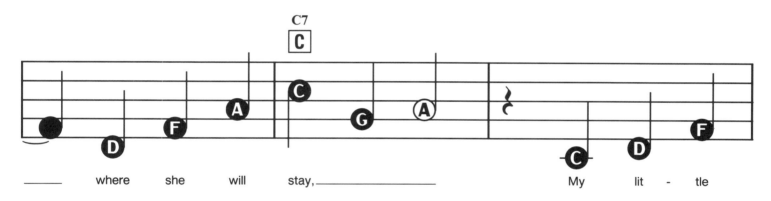

_____ where she will stay,_____ My lit - tle

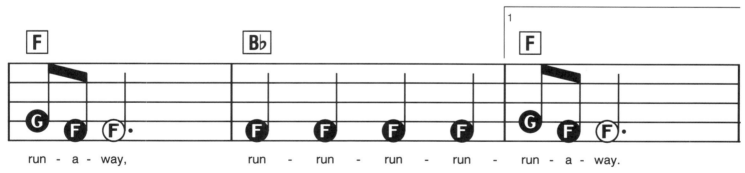

run - a - way, run - run - run - run - run - a - way.

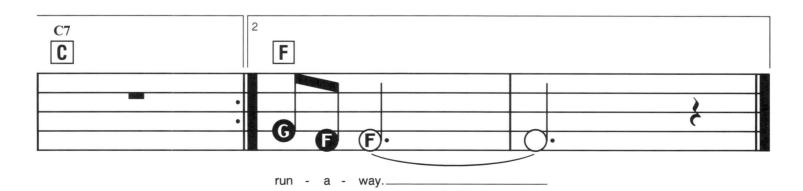

run - a - way._____

1962
I Left My Heart in San Francisco

Registration 9
Rhythm: Fox Trot

Words by Douglas Cross
Music by George Cory

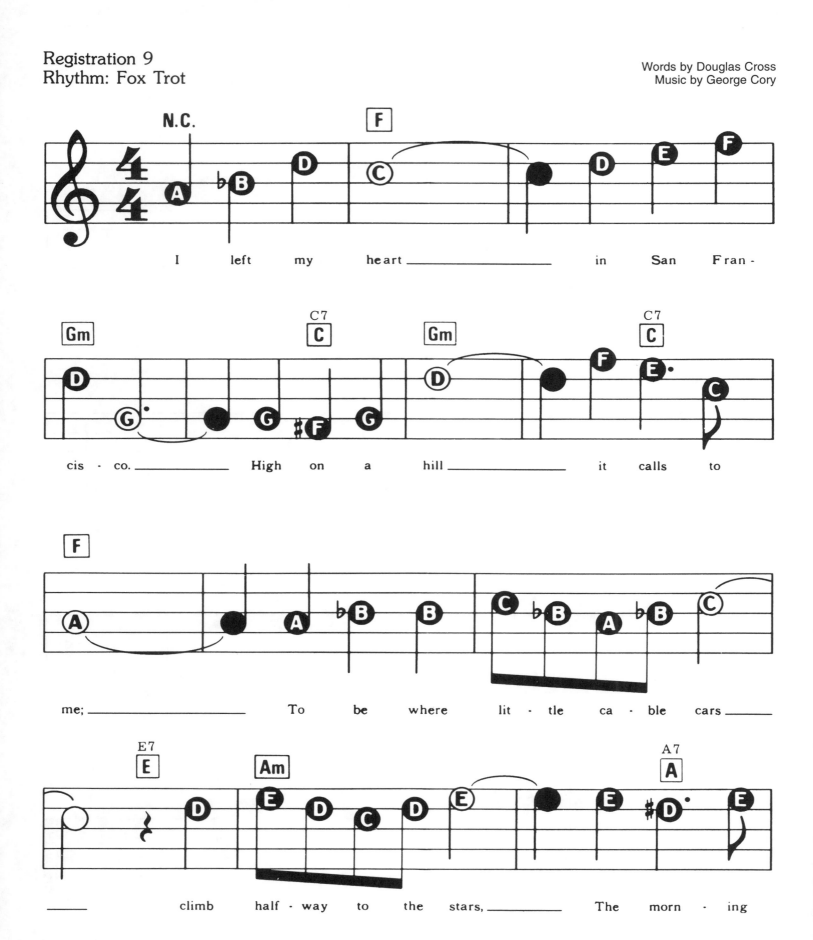

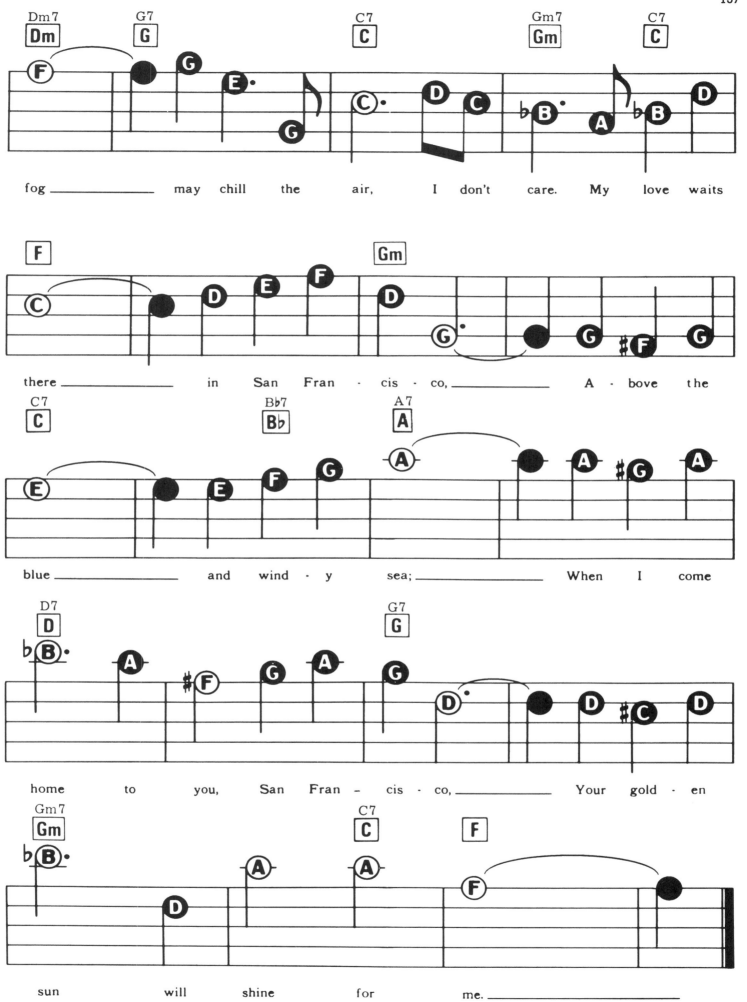

1963
Our Day Will Come

Registration 7
Rhythm: Beguine or Latin

Words by Bob Hilliard
Music by Mort Garson

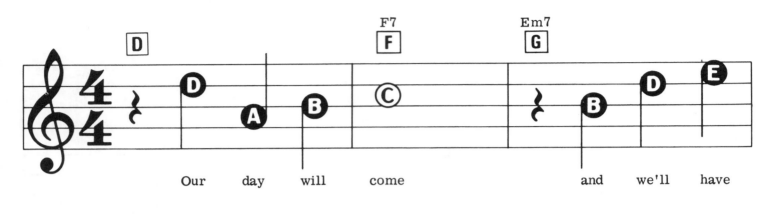

Our day will come and we'll have

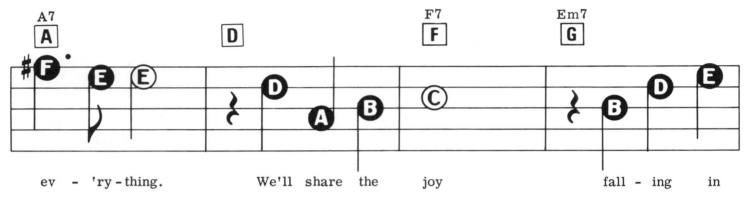

ev - 'ry-thing. We'll share the joy fall - ing in

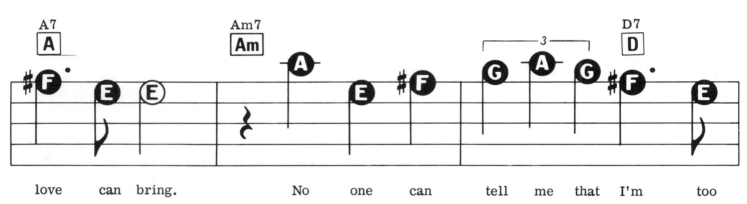

love can bring. No one can tell me that I'm too

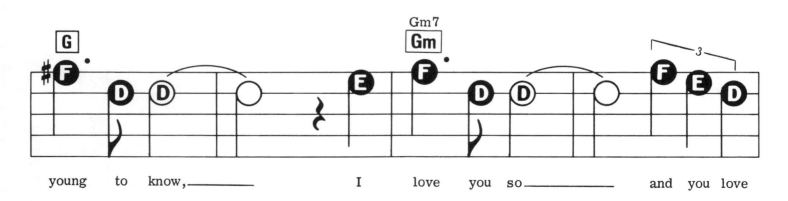

young to know, _____ I love you so _____ and you love

159

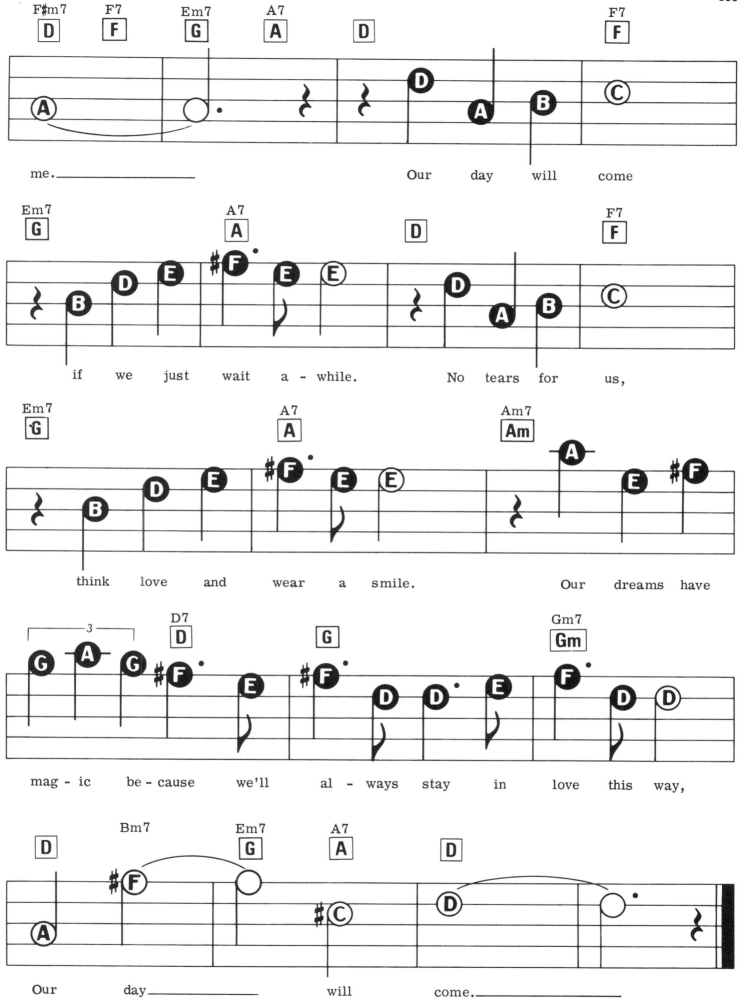

1964

The Girl from Ipanema

(Garôta De Ipanema)

Registration 4
Rhythm: Latin or Bossa Nova

Music by Antonio Carlos Jobim
English Words by Norman Gimbel
Original Words by Vinicius de Moraes

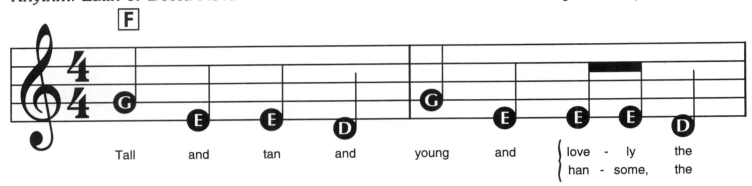

Tall   and   tan   and   young   and   { love - ly   the
                                                          han - some,   the

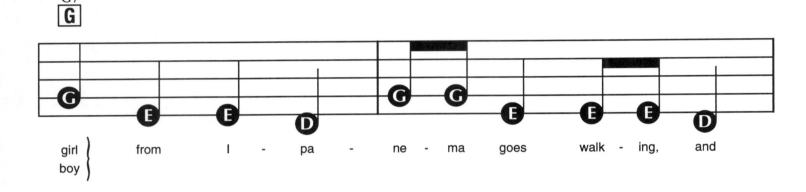

girl { from   I - pa - ne - ma   goes   walk - ing,   and
boy

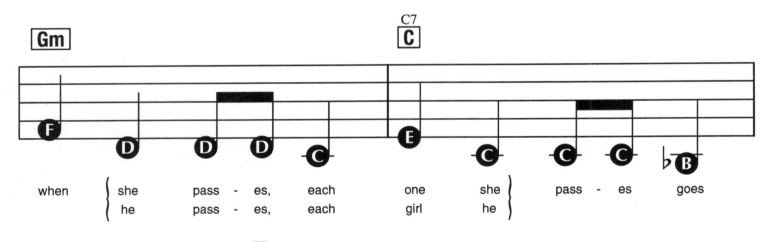

when { she   pass - es,   each   one   she { pass - es   goes
      he   pass - es,   each   girl   he

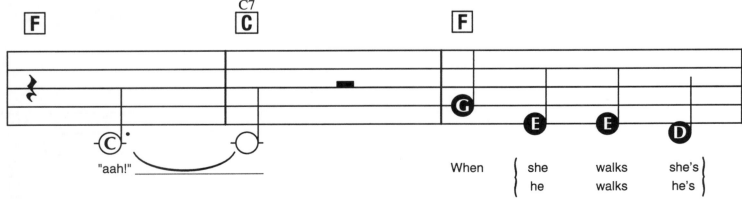

"aah!" _____

When { she   walks   she's }
      he   walks   he's

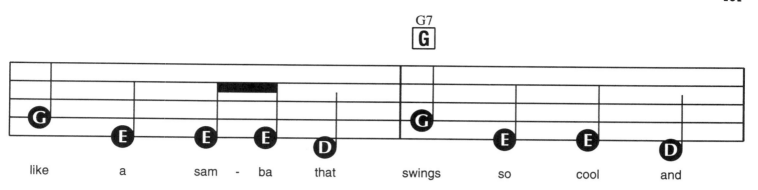

like a sam - ba that swings so cool and

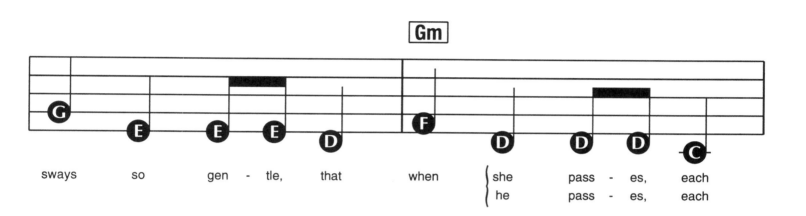

sways so gen - tle, that when { she pass - es, each
he pass - es, each

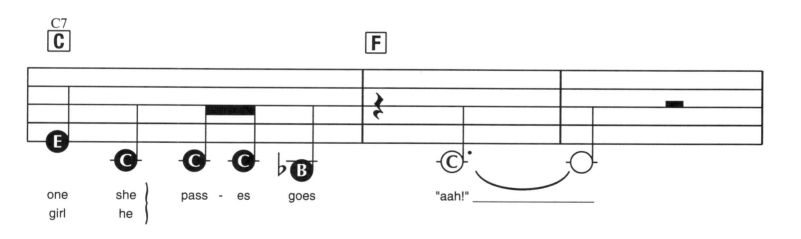

{ one she } pass - es goes "aah!" _____
girl he

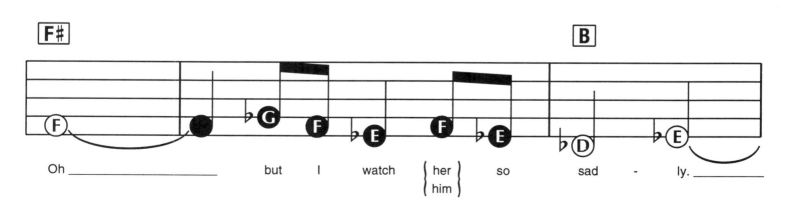

Oh _____ but I watch { her } so sad - ly. _____
him

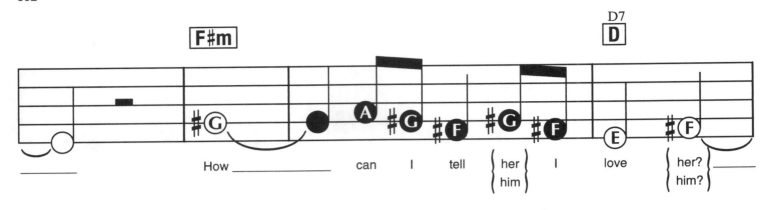

How _____ can I tell ⟨her / him⟩ I love ⟨her? / him?⟩ _____

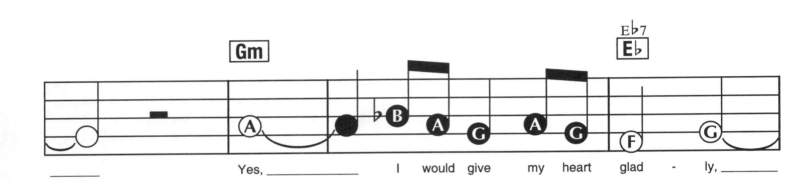

_____ Yes, _____ I would give my heart glad - ly, _____

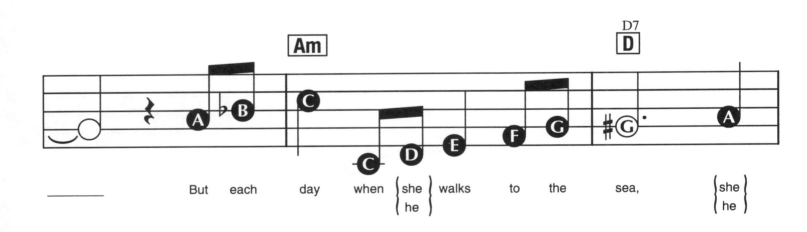

_____ But each day when ⟨she / he⟩ walks to the sea, ⟨she / he⟩

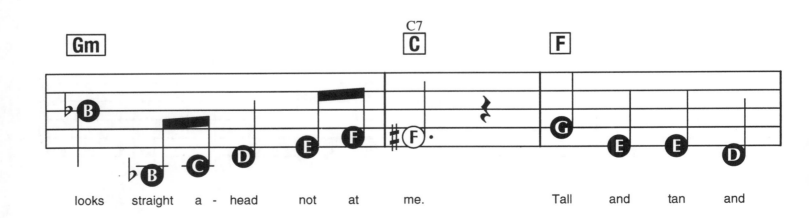

looks straight a - head not at me. Tall and tan and

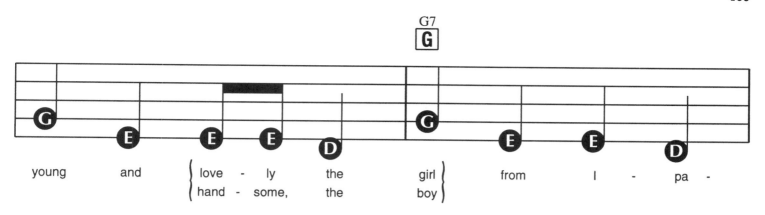

young and {love - ly the girl} / {hand - some, the boy} from I - pa -

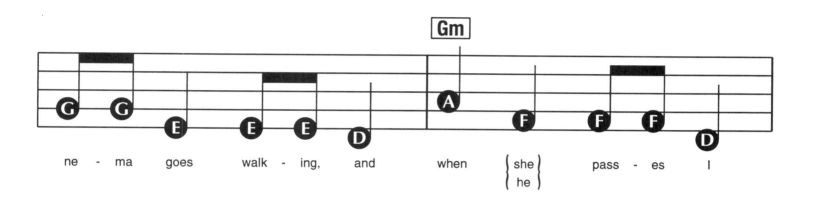

ne - ma goes walk - ing, and when {she} / {he} pass - es I

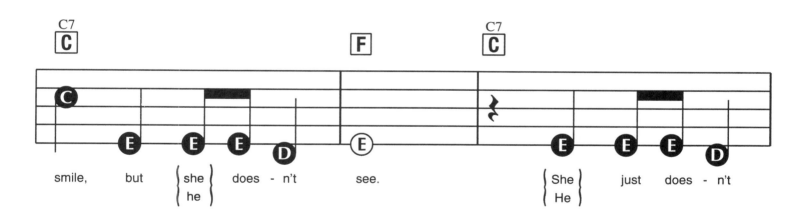

smile, but {she} / {he} does - n't see. {She} / {He} just does - n't

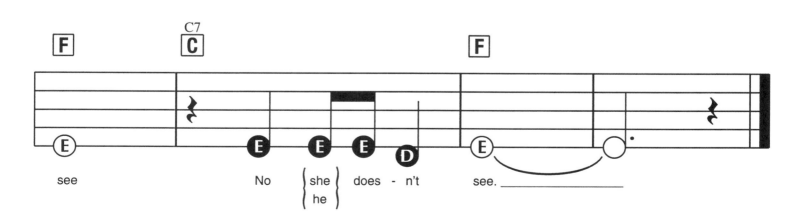

see No {she} / {he} does - n't see. _____

1965
Yesterday

Registration 2
Rhythm: Rock or Ballad

Words and Music by John Lennon
and Paul McCartney

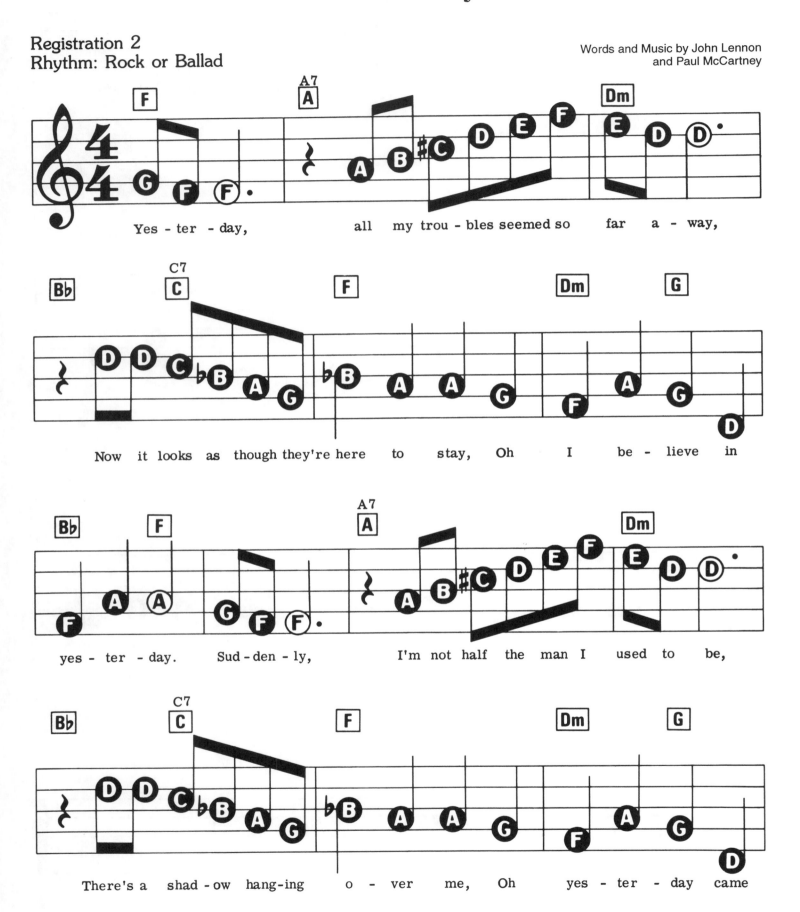

165

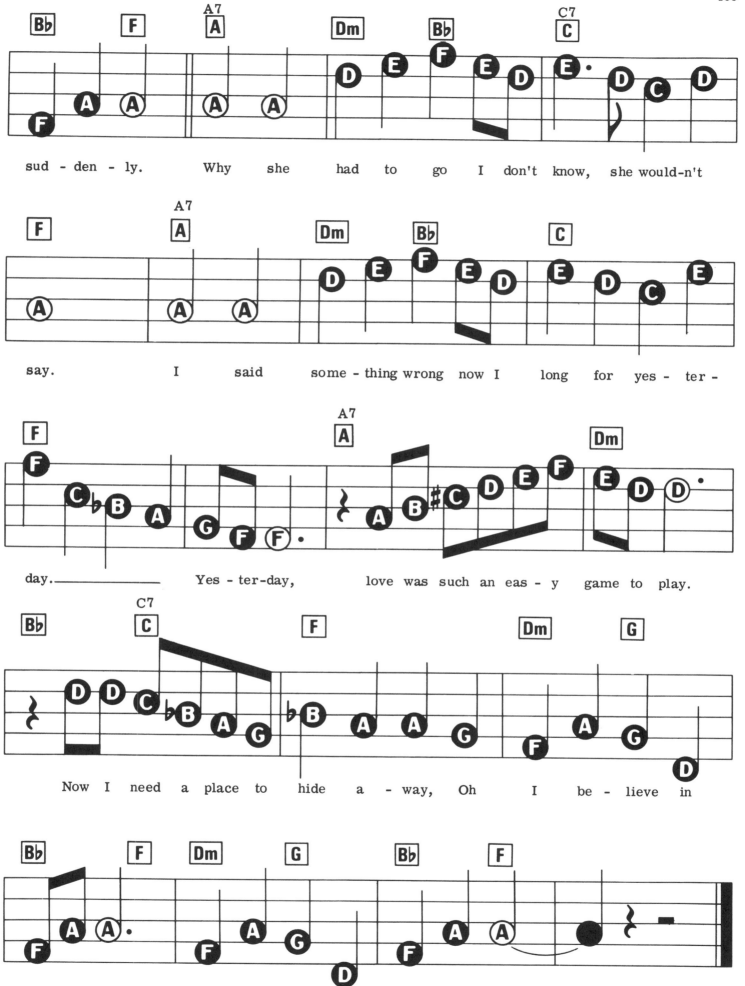

sud - den - ly. Why she had to go I don't know, she would-n't

say. I said some - thing wrong now I long for yes - ter -

day._____ Yes - ter-day, love was such an eas - y game to play.

Now I need a place to hide a - way, Oh I be - lieve in

yes - ter -day. Mm - mm - mm - mm - mm - mm - mm._____

1966
Monday, Monday

Registration 4
Rhythm: Rock

Words and Music by
John Phillips

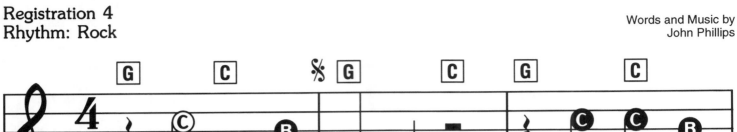

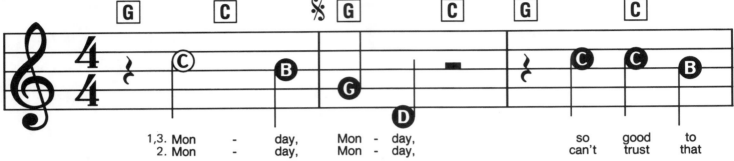

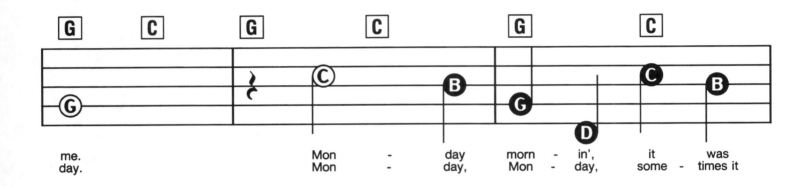

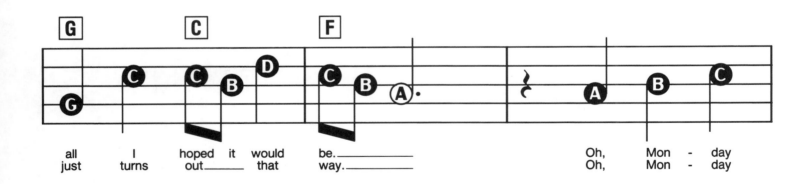

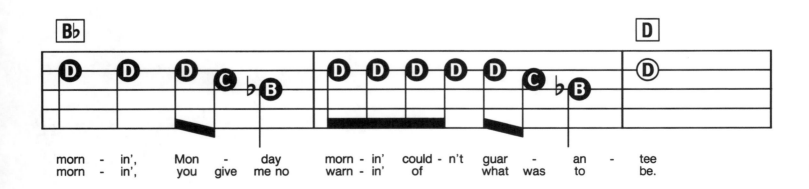

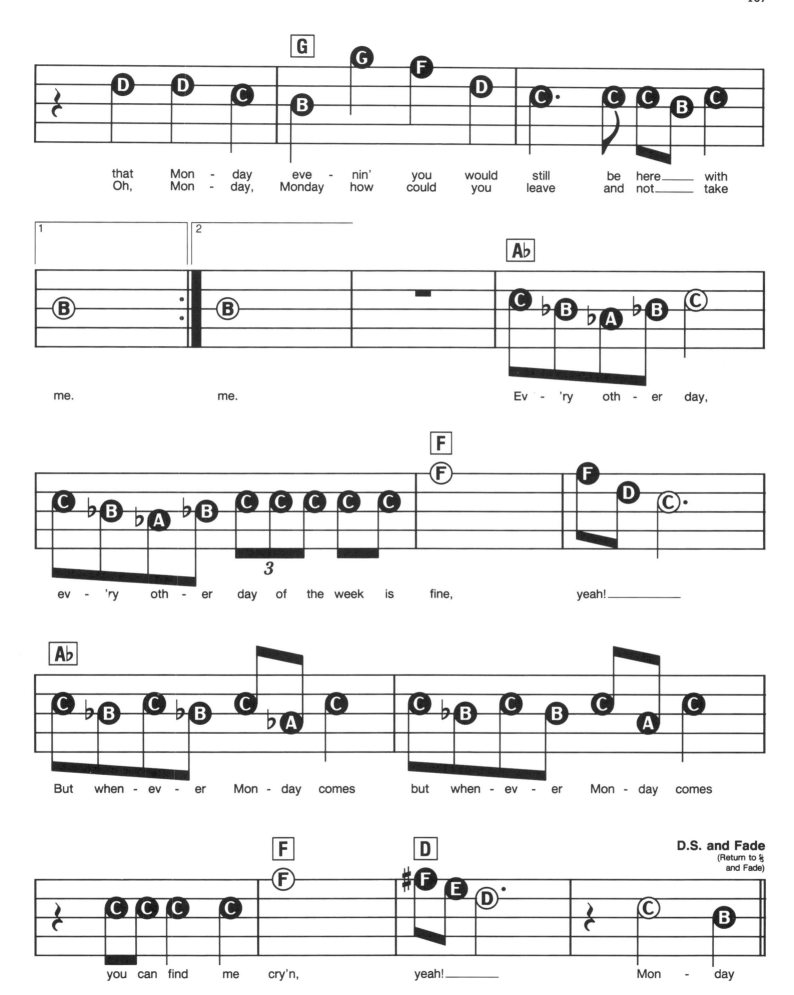

1967
Happy Together

Registration 7
Rhythm: Rock or Swing

Words and Music by Garry Bonner
and Alan Gordon

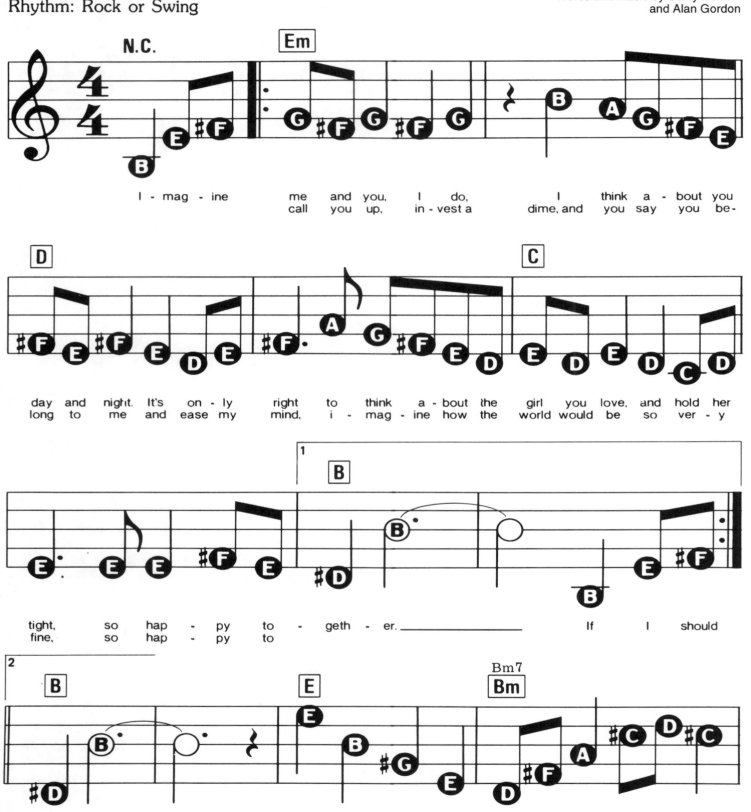

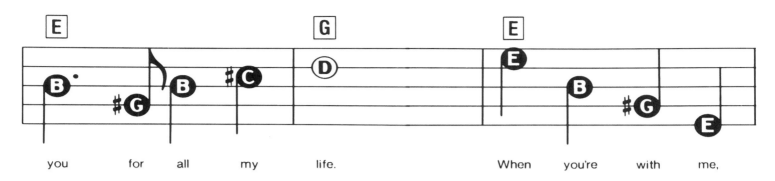

you for all my life. When you're with me,

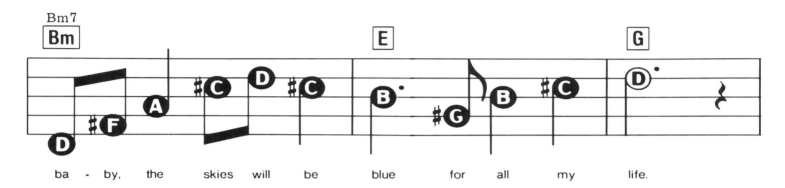

ba - by, the skies will be blue for all my life.

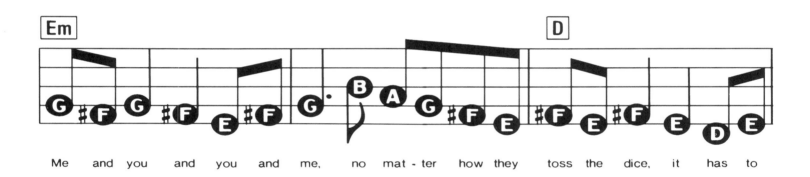

Me and you and you and me, no mat - ter how they toss the dice, it has to

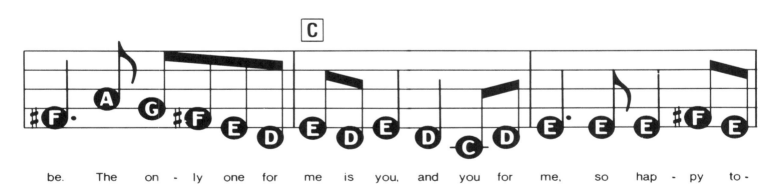

be. The on - ly one for me is you, and you for me, so hap - py to -

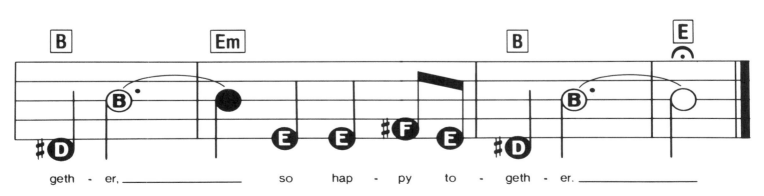

geth - er, _____ so hap - py to - geth - er. _____

1968
Hey Jude

Registration 2
Rhythm: Pops or 8 Beat

Words and Music by John Lennon
and Paul McCartney

Hey Jude, don't make it bad, Take a sad song and make it

better, _____ {Re - mem - ber to let her in - to your heart, Then you can
Re - mem - ber to let her un - der your skin, Then you'll be -

start _____ to make it _____ bet - ter. Hey Jude, don't be a-

fraid, You were made to go out and get her. _____ The

min - ute you let her un - der your skin, Then you be - gin _____ to make it _____

171

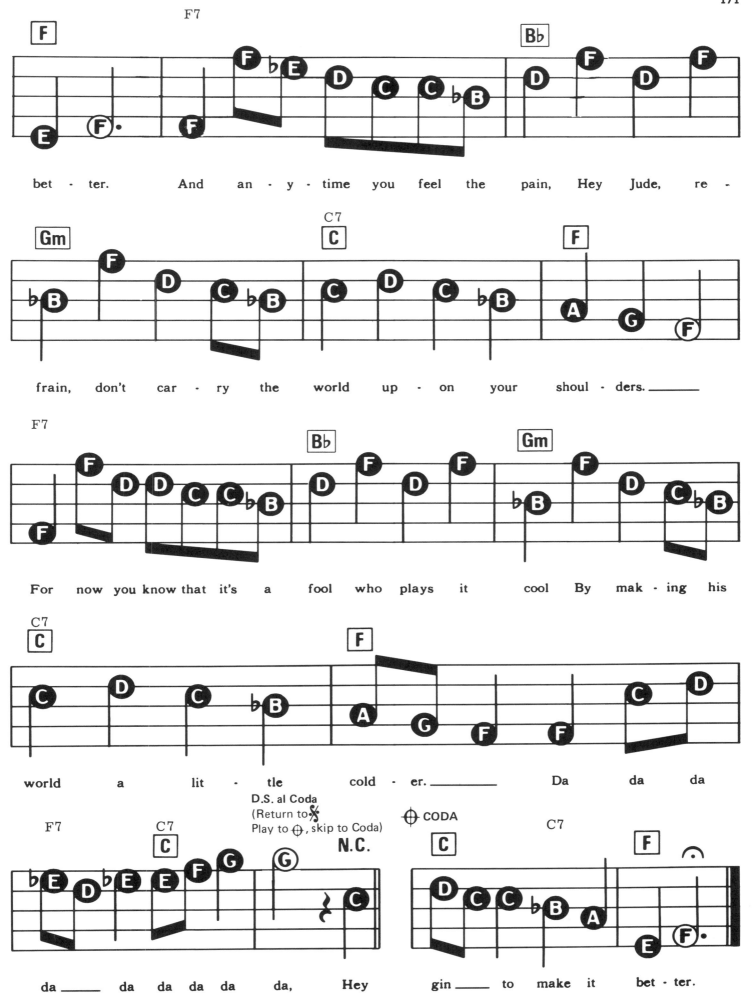

1969
Raindrops Keep Fallin' on My Head

Registration 5
Rhythm: Swing or Shuffle

Lyric by Hal David
Music by Burt Bacharach

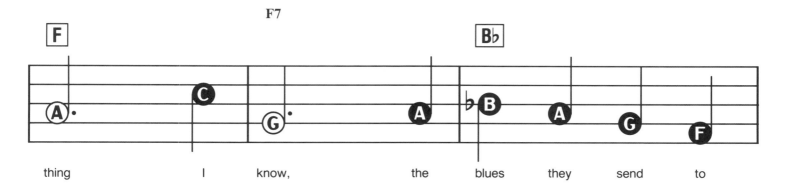

thing   I   know,   the   blues   they   send   to

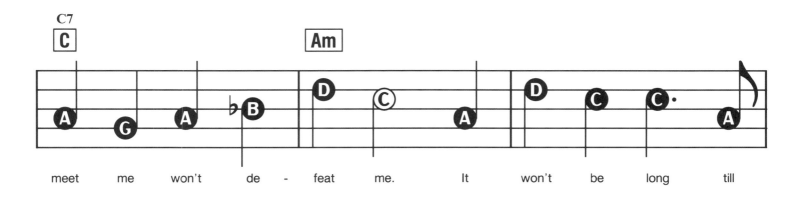

meet   me   won't   de -   feat   me.   It   won't   be   long   till

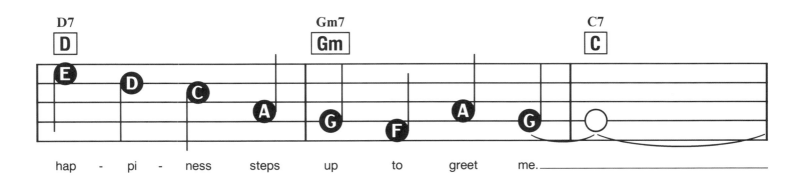

hap -   pi -   ness   steps   up   to   greet   me._____

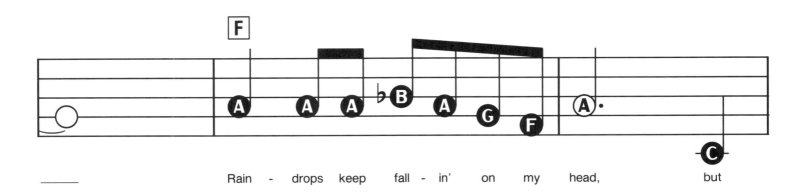

_____ Rain -   drops   keep   fall -   in'   on   my   head,   but

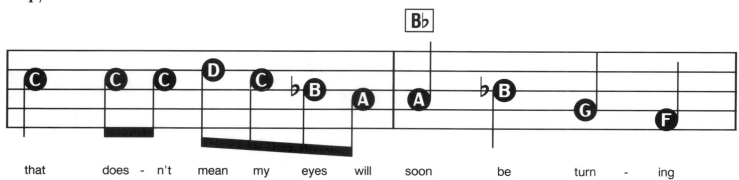

that does - n't mean my eyes will soon be turn - ing

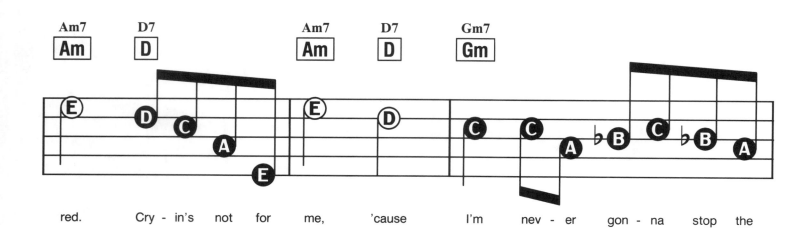

red. Cry - in's not for me, 'cause I'm nev - er gon - na stop the

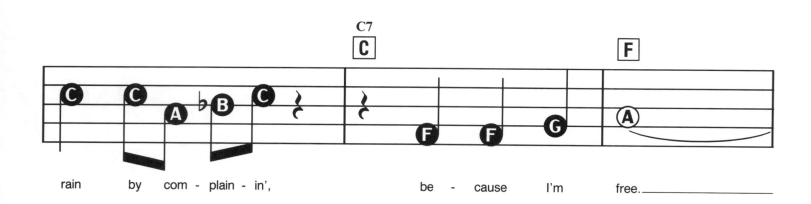

rain by com - plain - in', be - cause I'm free.____

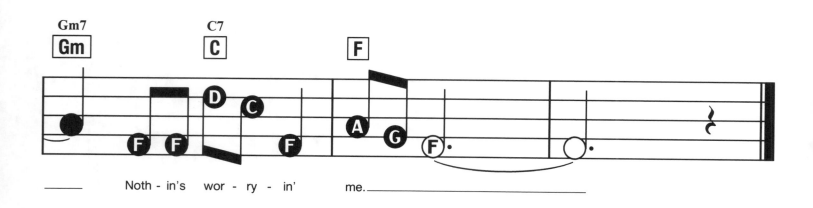

____ Noth - in's wor - ry - in' me.____

1970
Your Song

Registration 3
Rhythm: Rock or Jazz Rock

Words and Music by Elton John
and Bernie Taupin

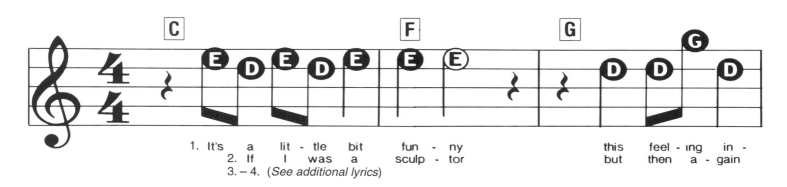

1. It's a lit - tle bit fun - ny this feel - ing in -
2. If I was a sculp - tor but then a - gain
3. – 4. (See additional lyrics)

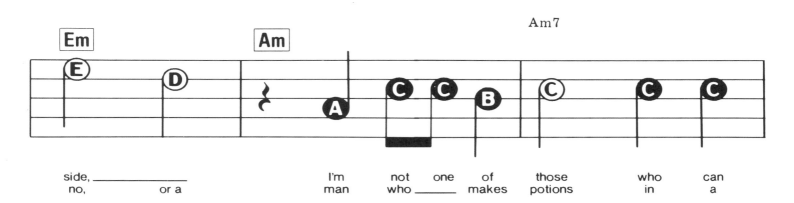

side, _____ or a I'm not one of those who can
no, or a man who _____ makes those potions who in a

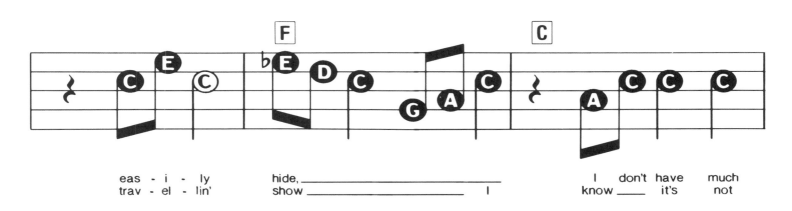

eas - i - ly hide, _____ I don't have much
trav - el - lin' show _____ I know _____ it's much not

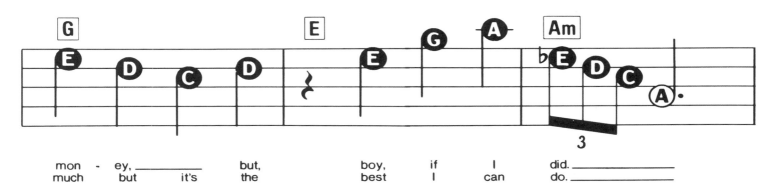

mon - ey, _____ but, boy, if I did. _____
much but it's the best I can do. _____

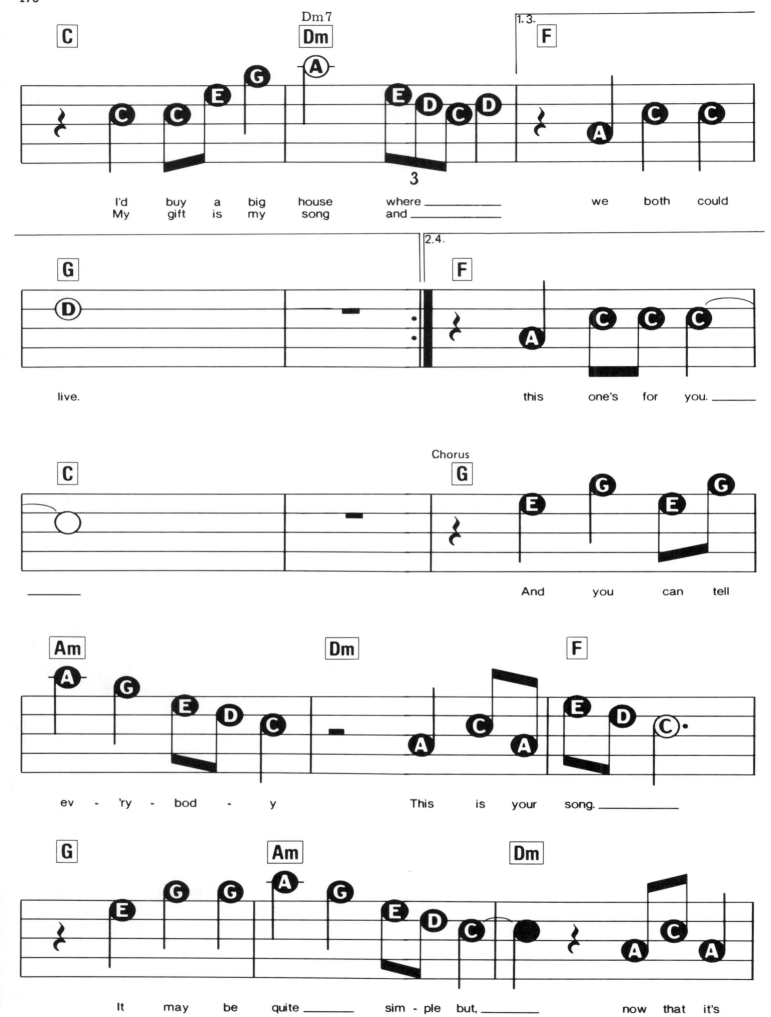

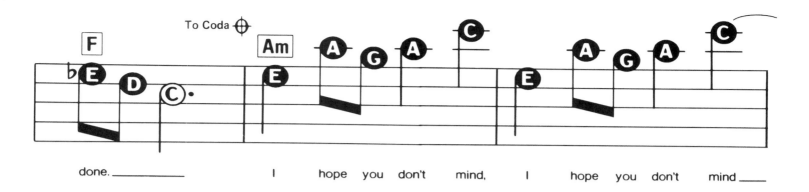

done._____ I hope you don't mind, I hope you don't mind ____

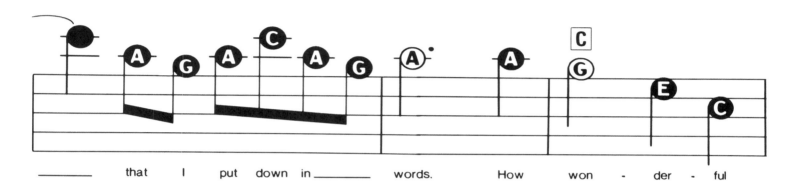

_____ that I put down in _____ words. How won - der - ful

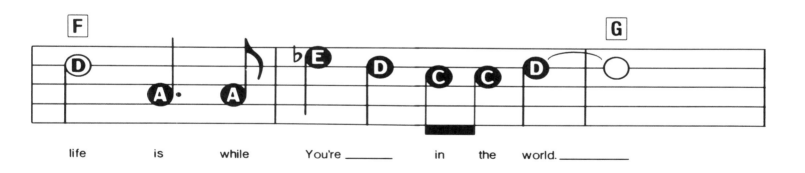

life is while You're _____ in the world._____

D.C. al Coda
(Return to beginning, take 3rd & 4th endings, Play till ⊕ and skip to Coda)

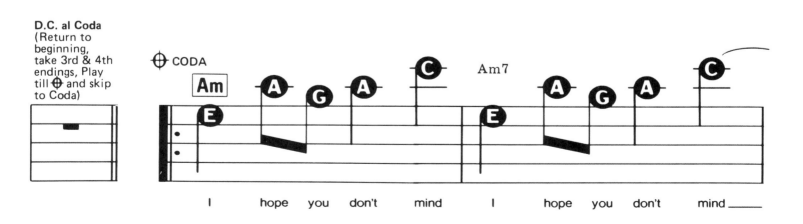

I hope you don't mind I hope you don't mind ____

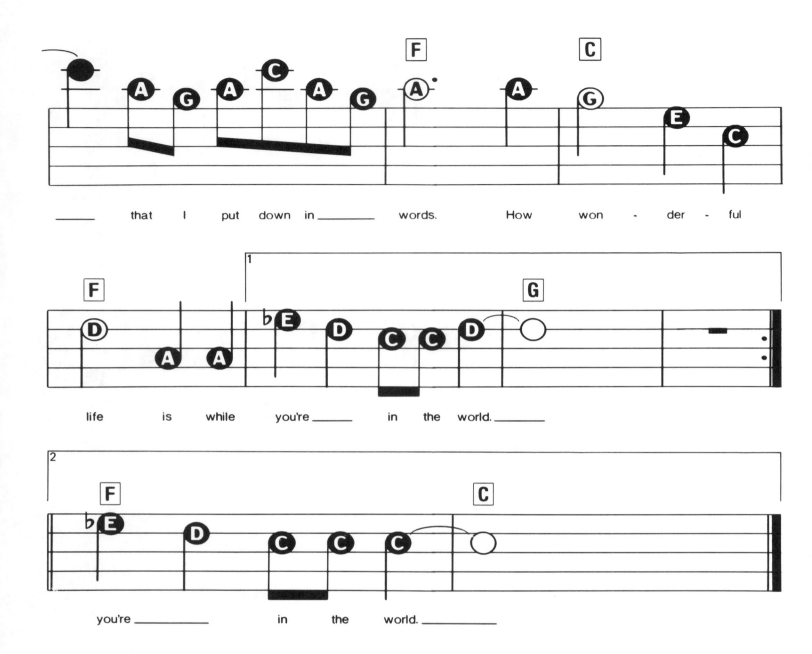

that I put down in _____ words. How won - der - ful

life is while you're _____ in the world. _____

you're _____ in the world. _____

Additional Lyrics

3. I sat on the roof and kicked off the moss.
   well a few of the verses, well they've got me quite cross,
   But the sun's been quite kind while I wrote this song,
   It's for people like you that keep it turned on.

4. So excuse me forgetting but these things I do
   You see I've forgotten if they're green or they're blue,
   Anyway the thing is what I really mean
   Yours are the sweetest eyes I've ever seen.

1971
It's Too Late

Registration 4
Rhythm: Rock

Words by Toni Stern
Music by Carole King

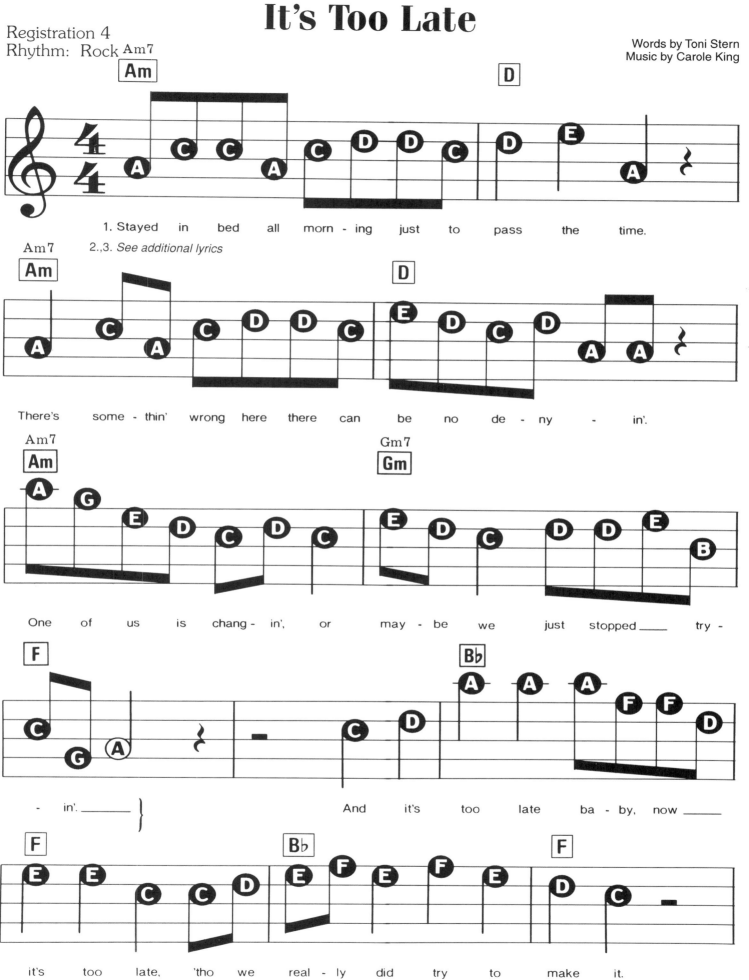

1. Stayed in bed all morn - ing just to pass the time.

2.,3. *See additional lyrics*

There's some - thin' wrong here there can be no de - ny - in'.

One of us is chang - in', or may - be we just stopped ___ try -

- in'. _____ And it's too late ba - by, now _____

it's too late, 'tho we real - ly did try to make it.

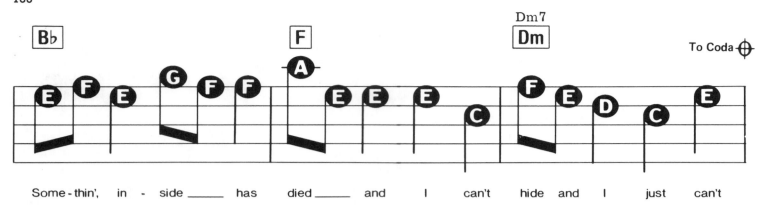

Some-thin', in - side _____ has died _____ and I can't hide and I just can't

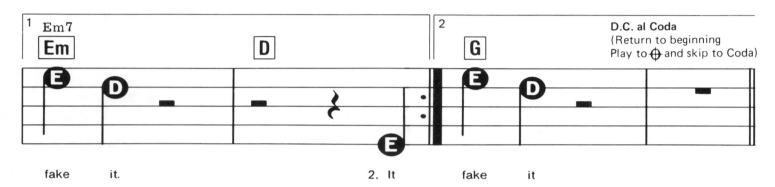

fake it.

2. It fake it

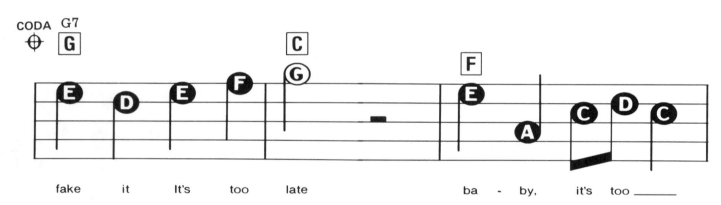

fake it It's too late ba - by, it's too _____

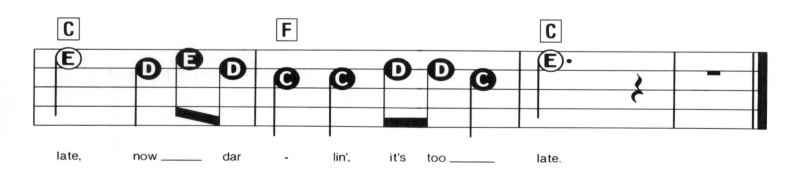

late, now _____ dar - lin', it's too _____ late.

Additional Lyrics

2. It used to be so easy living here with you;
You were light and breezy and
I knew just what to do.
Now you look so unhappy and I feel like a fool.

3. There'll be good times again for me and you;
But we just can't stay together,
Don't you feel it too?
Still I'm glad for what we had and how I once loved you.

1972
Rocky Mountain High

Registration 4
Rhythm: Country

Words by John Denver
Music by John Denver and Mike Taylor

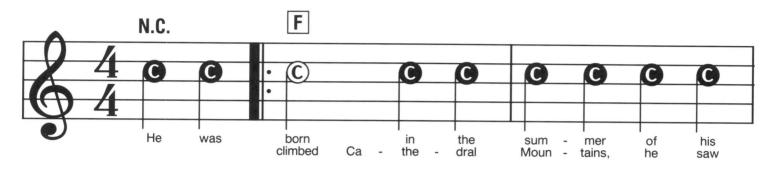

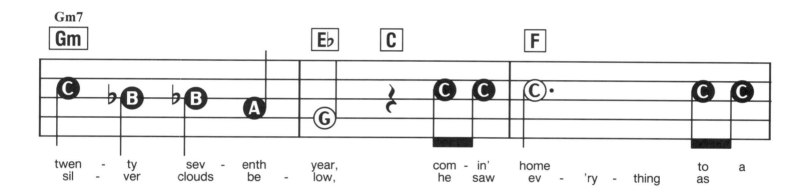

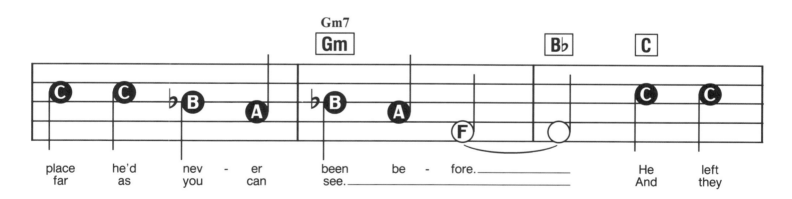

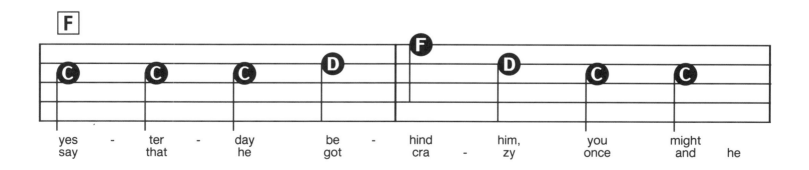

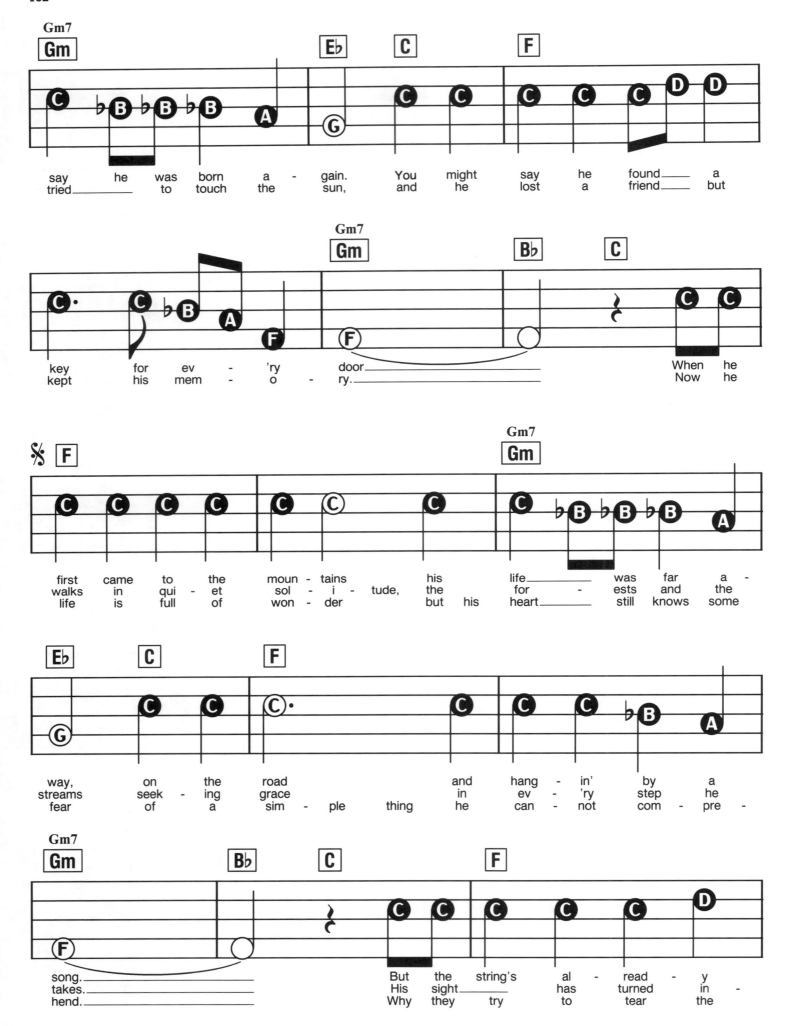

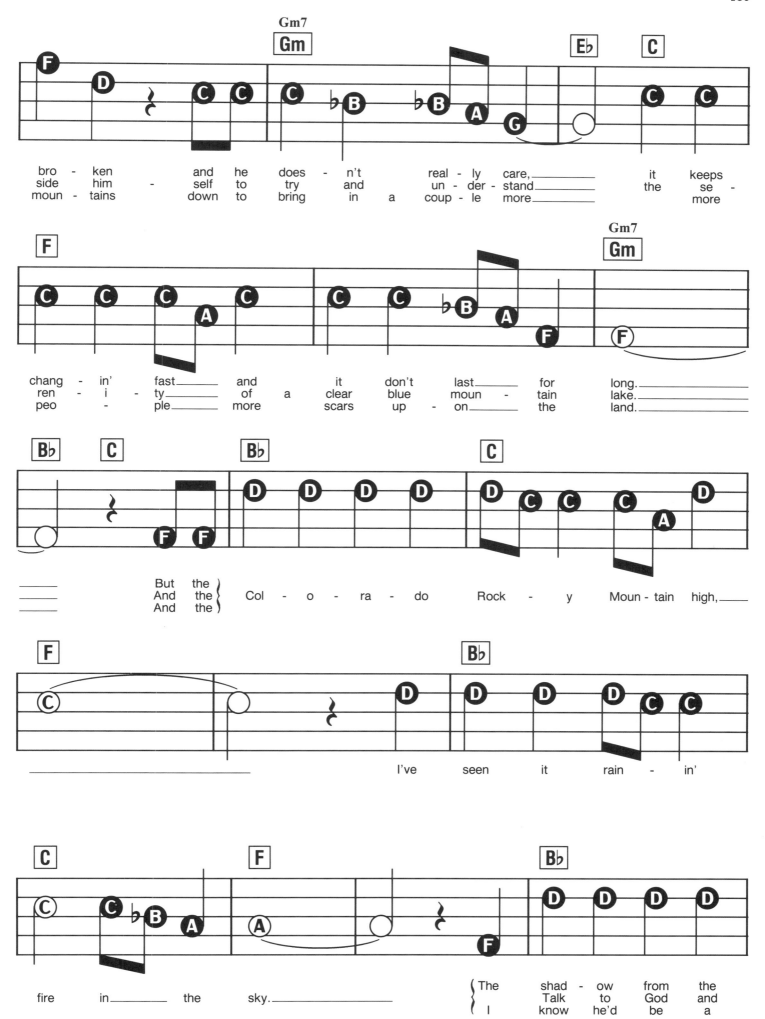

184

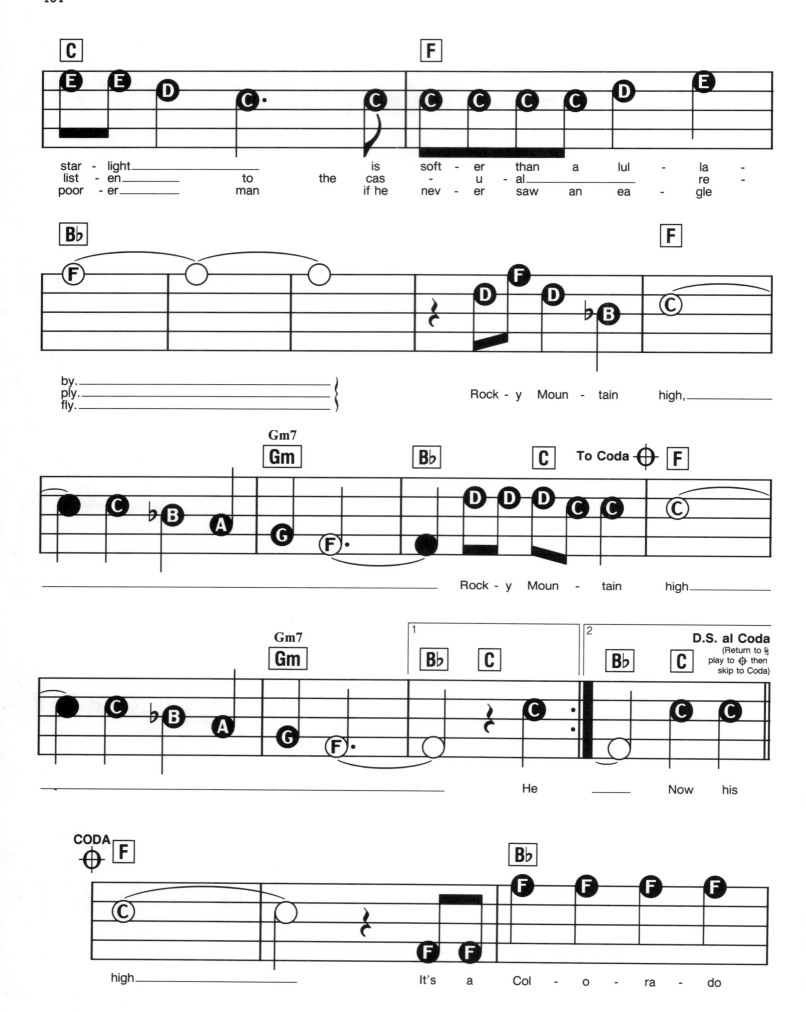

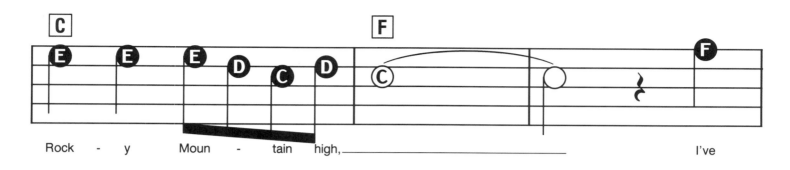

Rock - y Moun - tain high,_____ I've

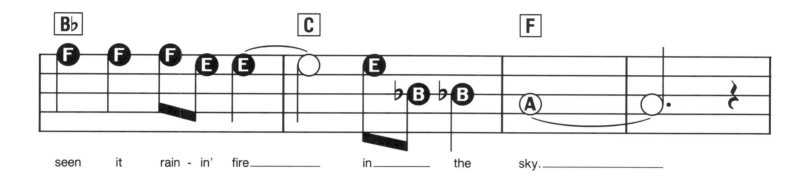

seen it rain - in' fire_____ in____ the sky._____

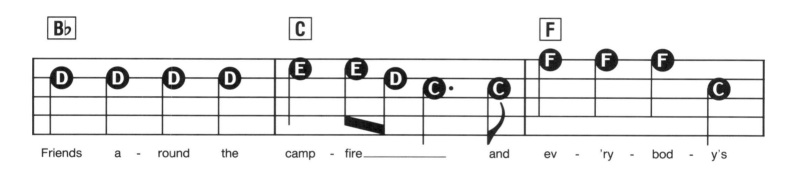

Friends a - round the camp - fire_____ and ev - 'ry - bod - y's

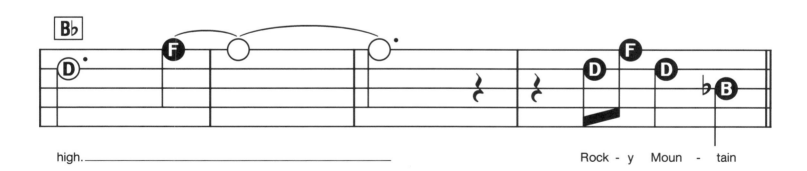

high._____ Rock - y Moun - tain

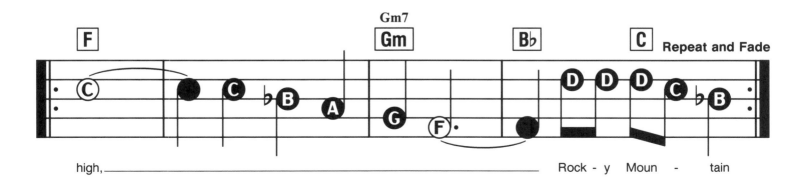

high,_____ Rock - y Moun - tain

1973
Killing Me Softly with His Song

Registration 2
Rhythm: Rock

Words by Norman Gimbel
Music by Charles Fox

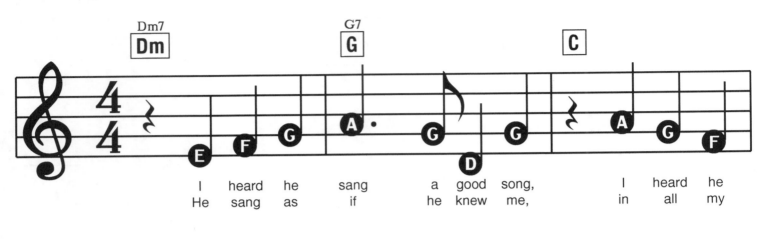

I heard he sang a good song, I heard he
He sang as if he knew me, in all my

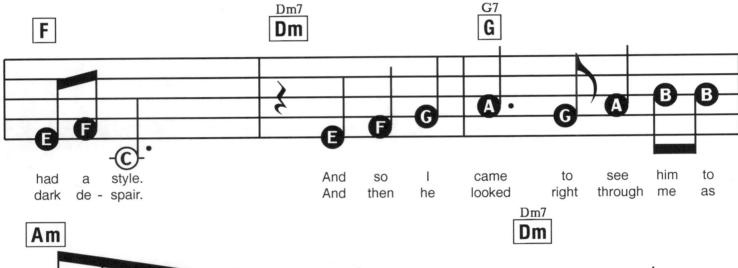

had a style. And so I came to see him to
dark de-spair. And then he looked right through me as

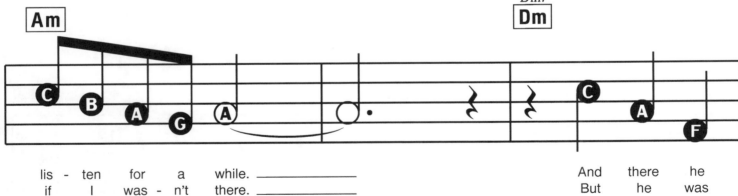

lis-ten for a while. _____ And there he
if I was-n't there. _____ But he was

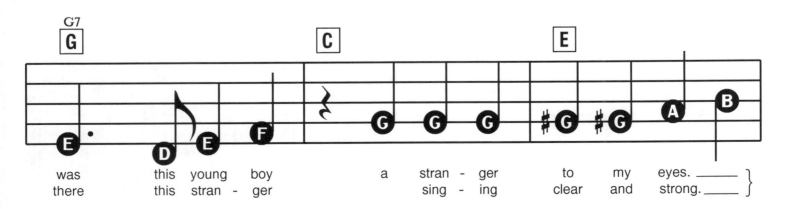

was this young boy a stran-ger to my eyes. _____
there this stran-ger sing-ing clear and strong. _____

1974
Don't Let the Sun Go Down on Me

Registration 4
Rhythm: Rock

Words and Music by Elton John
and Bernie Taupin

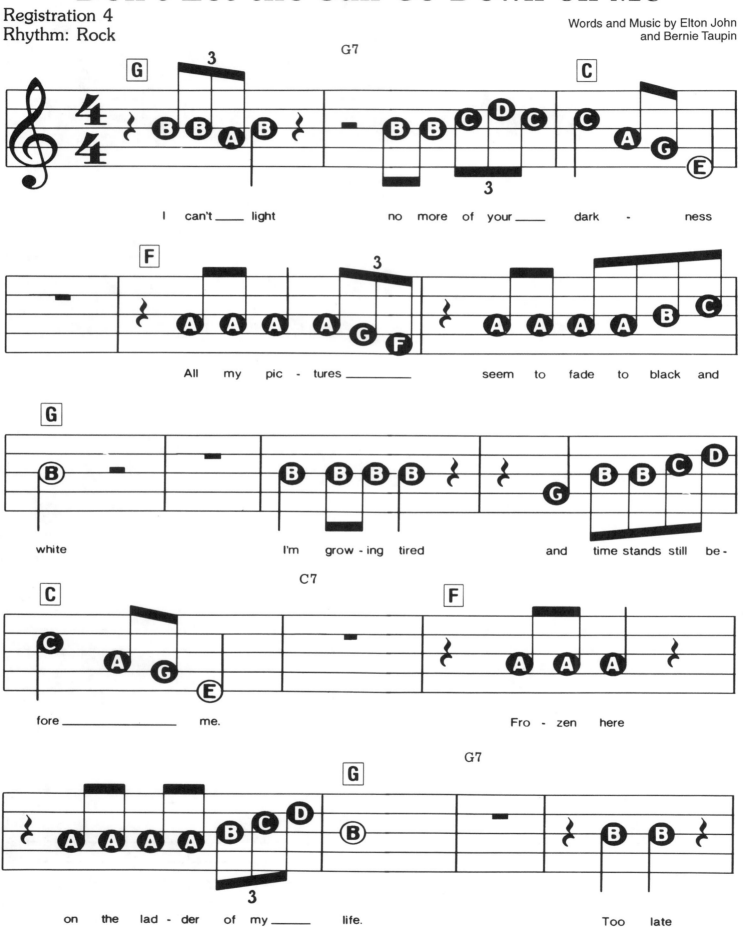

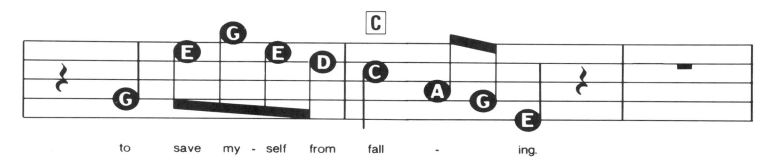

to save my - self from fall - ing.

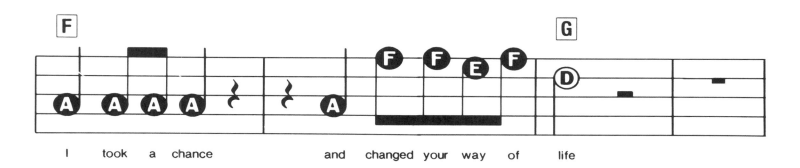

I took a chance and changed your way of life

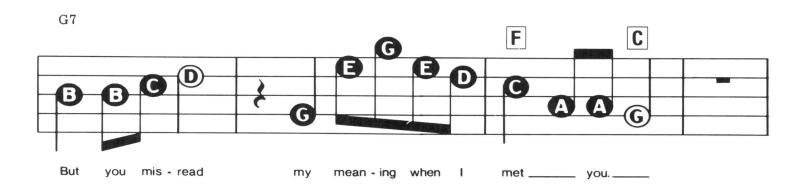

But you mis - read my mean - ing when I met you.

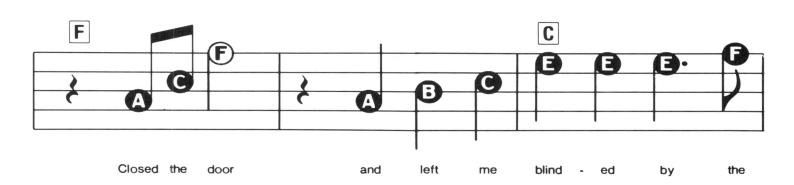

Closed the door and left me blind - ed by the

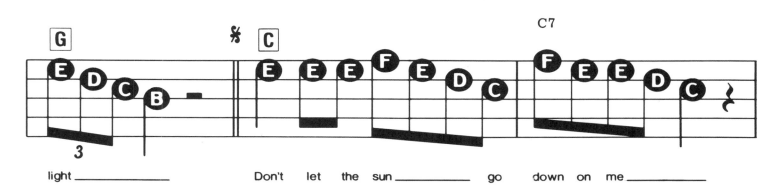

light Don't let the sun go down on me

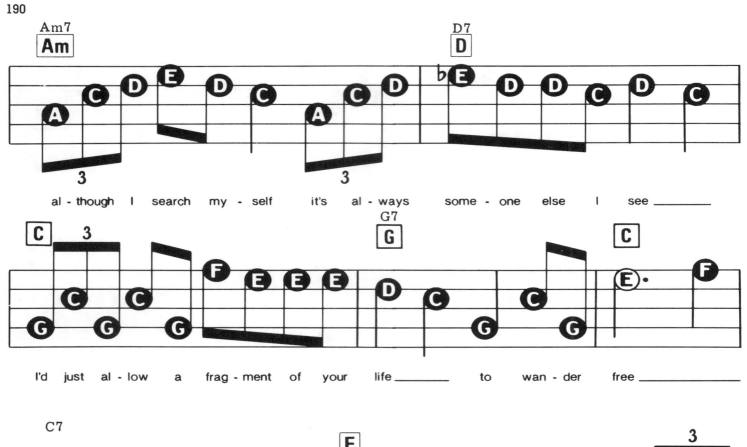

al - though I search my - self it's al - ways some - one else I see _____

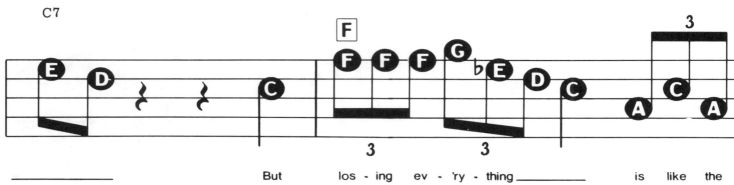

I'd just al - low a frag - ment of your life _____ to wan - der free _____

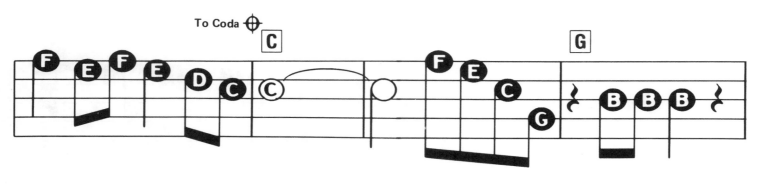

_____ But los - ing ev - 'ry - thing _____ is like the

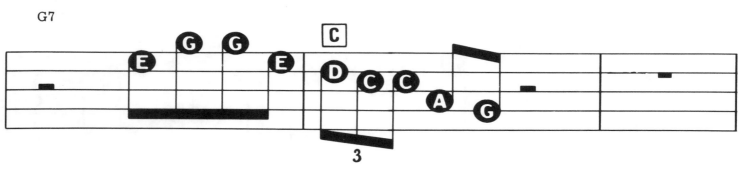

sun go - ing down on _____ me _____ I can't find

oh the right ro - man - tic line. _____

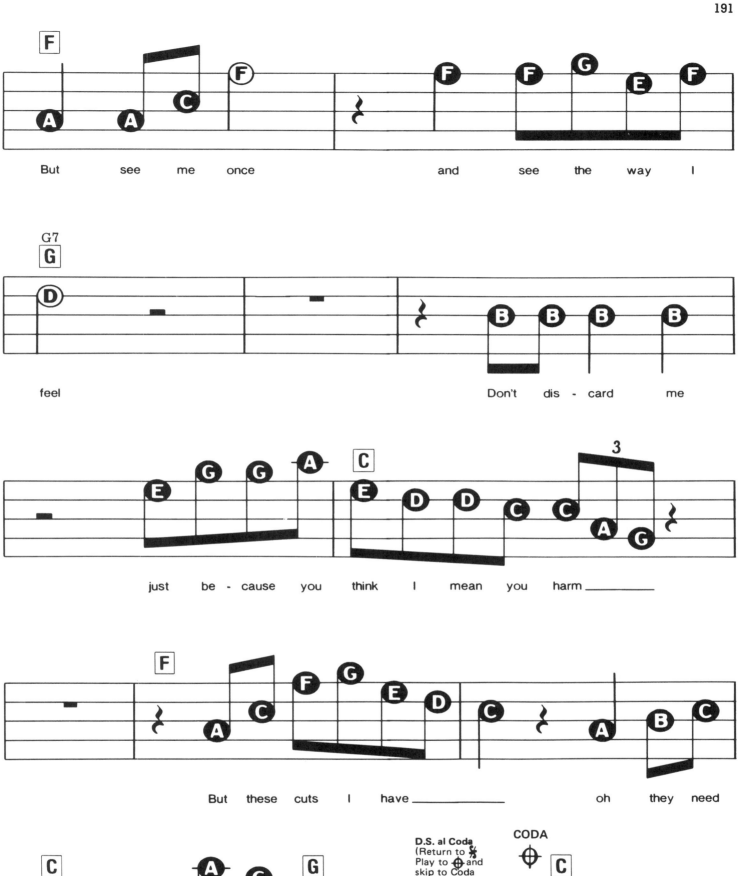

But   see   me   once   and   see   the   way   I

feel   Don't   dis - card   me

just   be - cause   you   think   I   mean   you   harm _____

But   these   cuts   I   have _____   oh   they   need

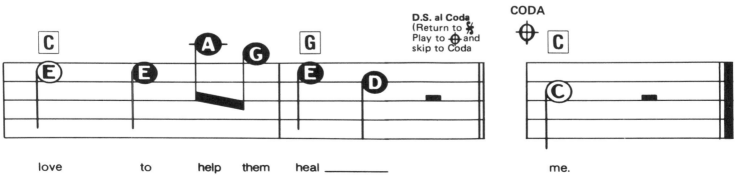

love   to   help   them   heal _____   me.

D.S. al Coda
(Return to 𝄋
Play to ⊕ and
skip to Coda

CODA

1975
Can't Smile Without You

Registration 3
Rhythm: Fox Trot or Swing

Words and Music by Chris Arnold,
David Martin and Geoff Morrow

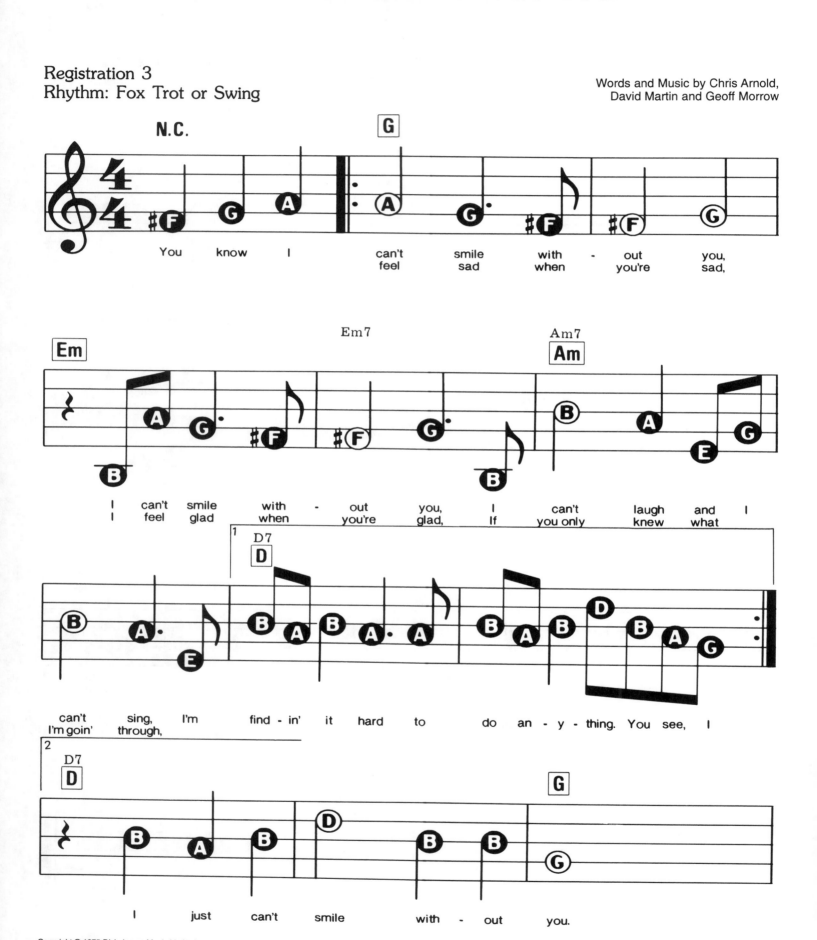

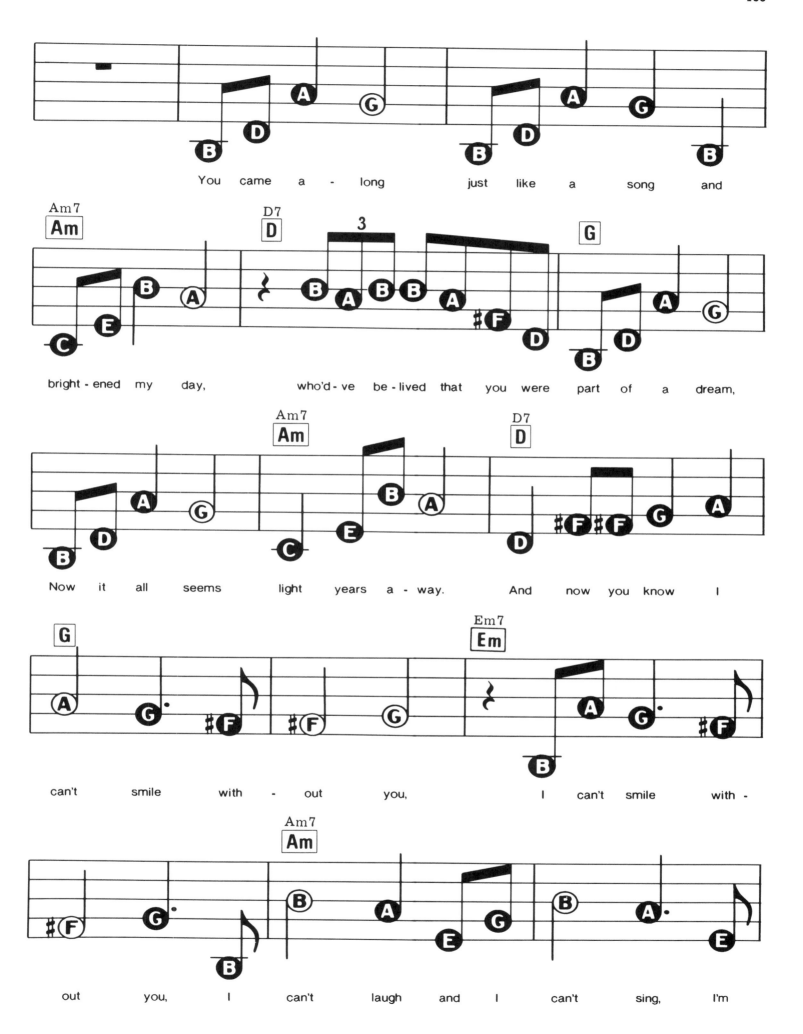

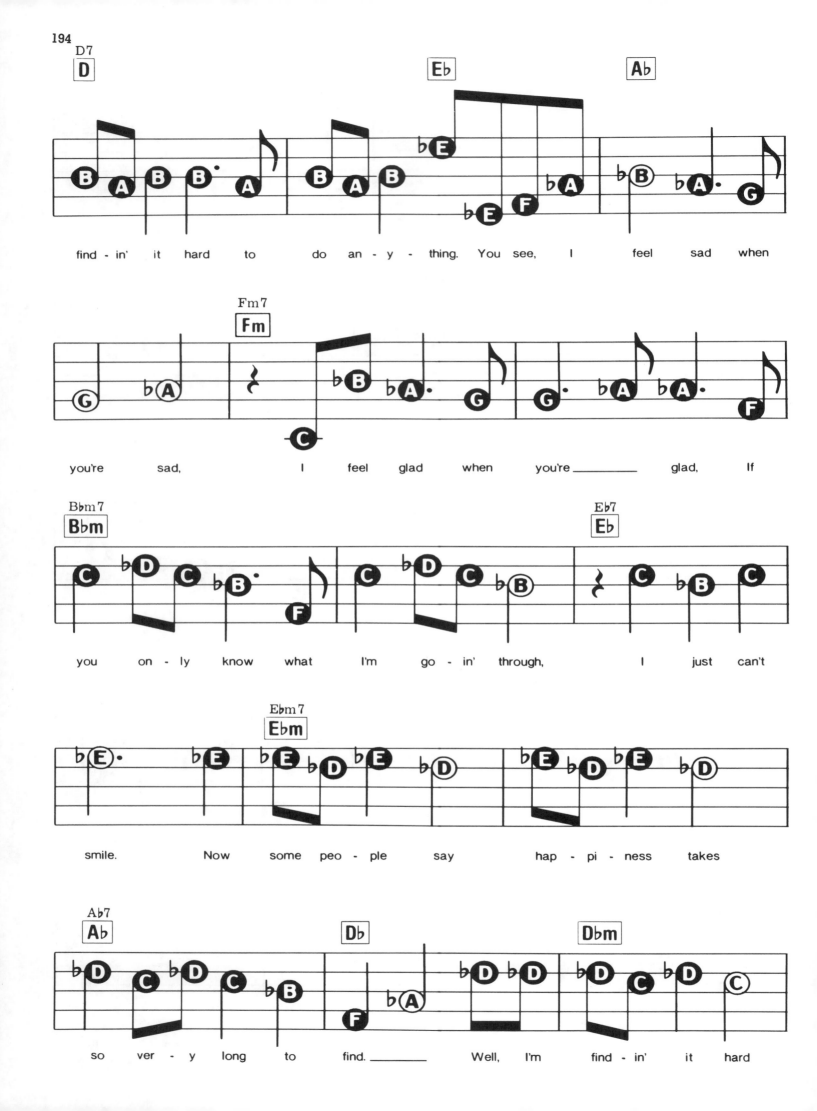

195

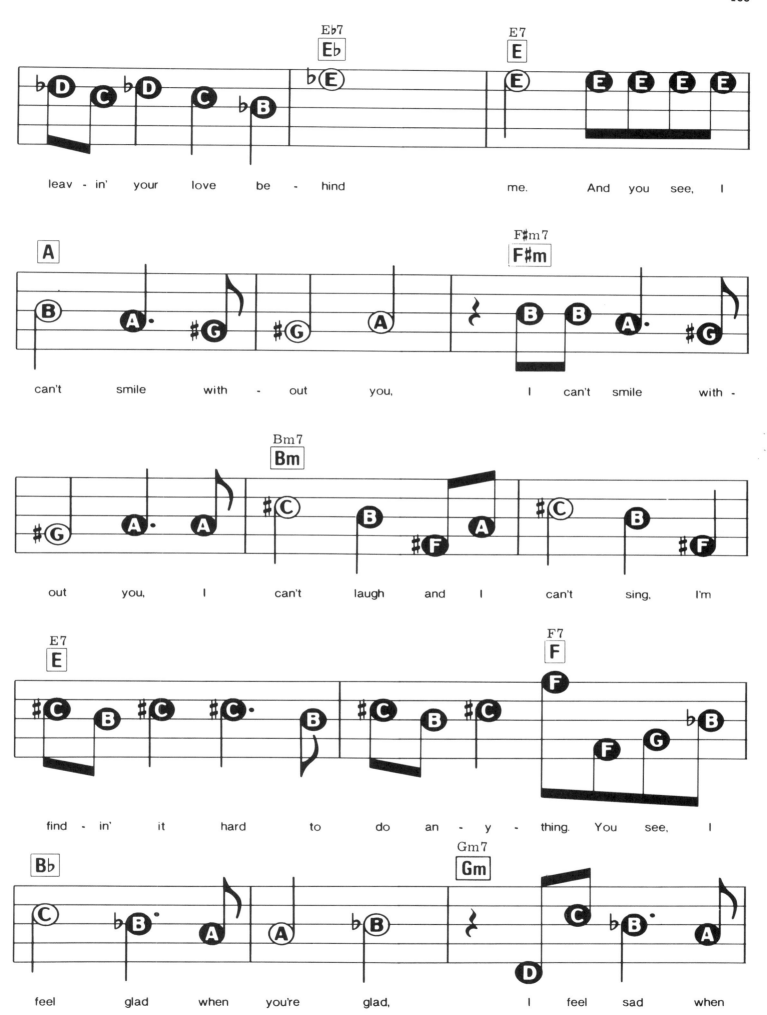

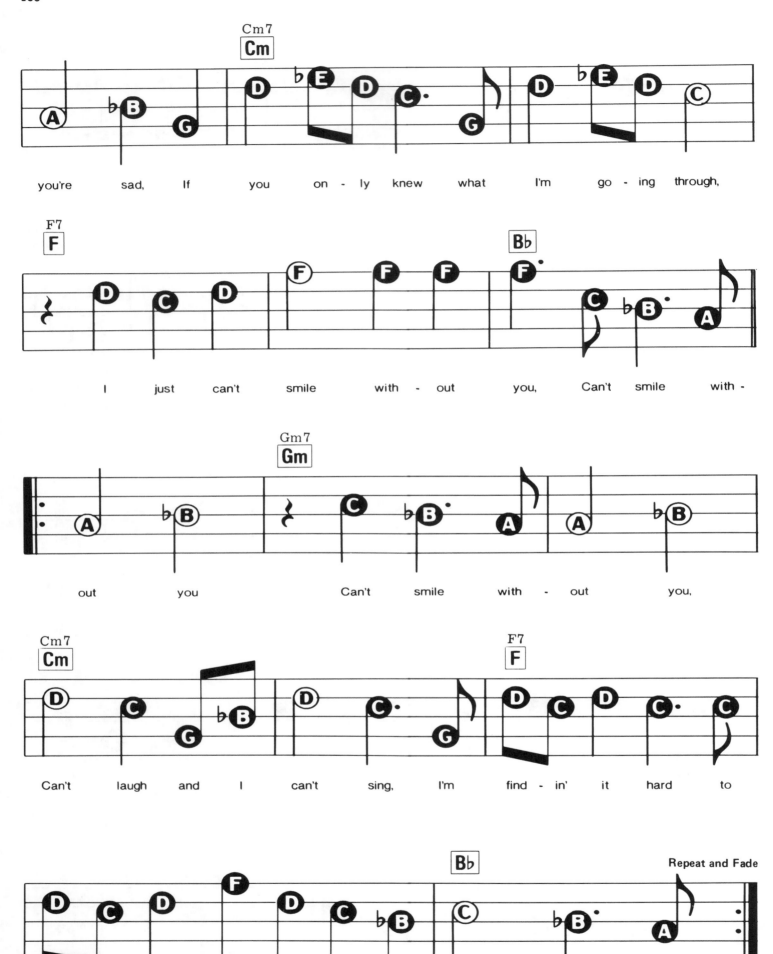

youre sad, If you on - ly knew what I'm go - ing through,

I just can't smile with - out you, Can't smile with -

out you Can't smile with - out you,

Can't laugh and I can't sing, I'm find - in' it hard to

do - an - y - thing. You see, I can't smile with -

1976
Tonight's the Night
(Gonna Be Alright)

Registration 9
Rhythm: Slow Rock or Shuffle

Words and Music by
Rod Stewart

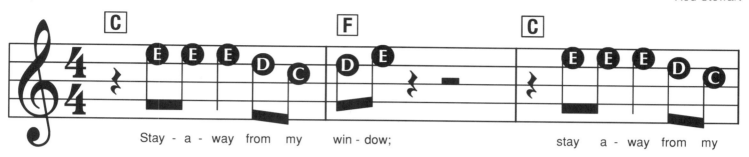

Stay - a - way from my win - dow; stay a - way from my

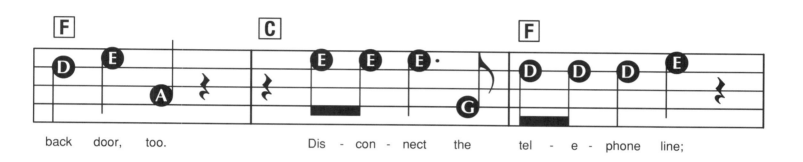

back door, too. Dis - con - nect the tel - e - phone line;

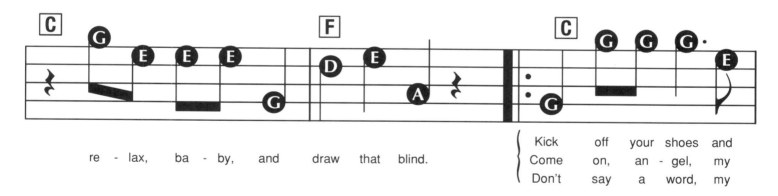

re - lax, ba - by, and draw that blind.

Kick off your shoes and
Come on, an - gel, my
Don't say a word, my

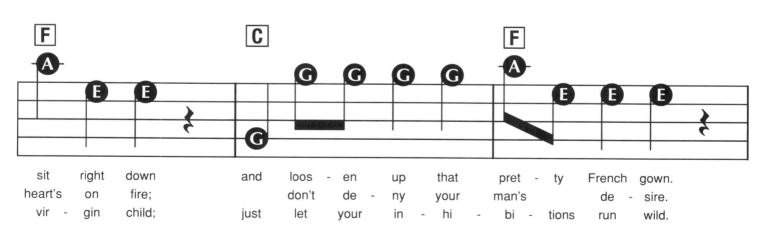

sit right down and loos - en up that pret - ty French gown.
heart's on fire; don't de - ny your man's de - sire.
vir - gin child; just let your in - hi - bi - tions run wild.

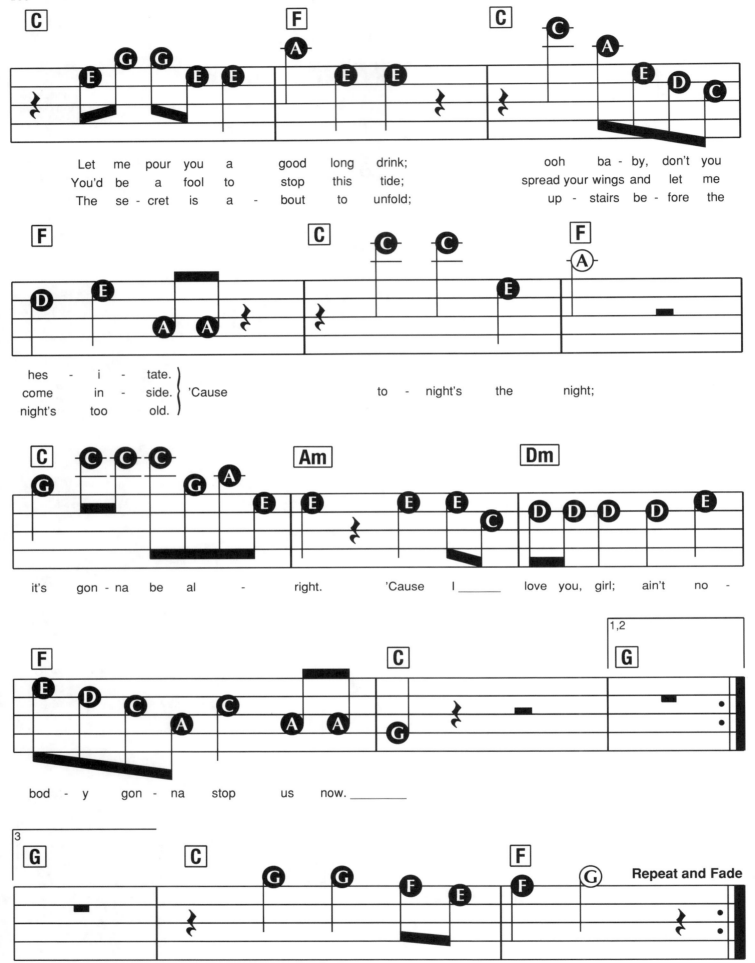

(Instrumental)

1977
How Deep Is Your Love
from the Motion Picture SATURDAY NIGHT FEVER

Registration 4
Rhythm: Rock or Disco

Words and Music by Barry Gibb,
Maurice Gibb and Robin Gibb

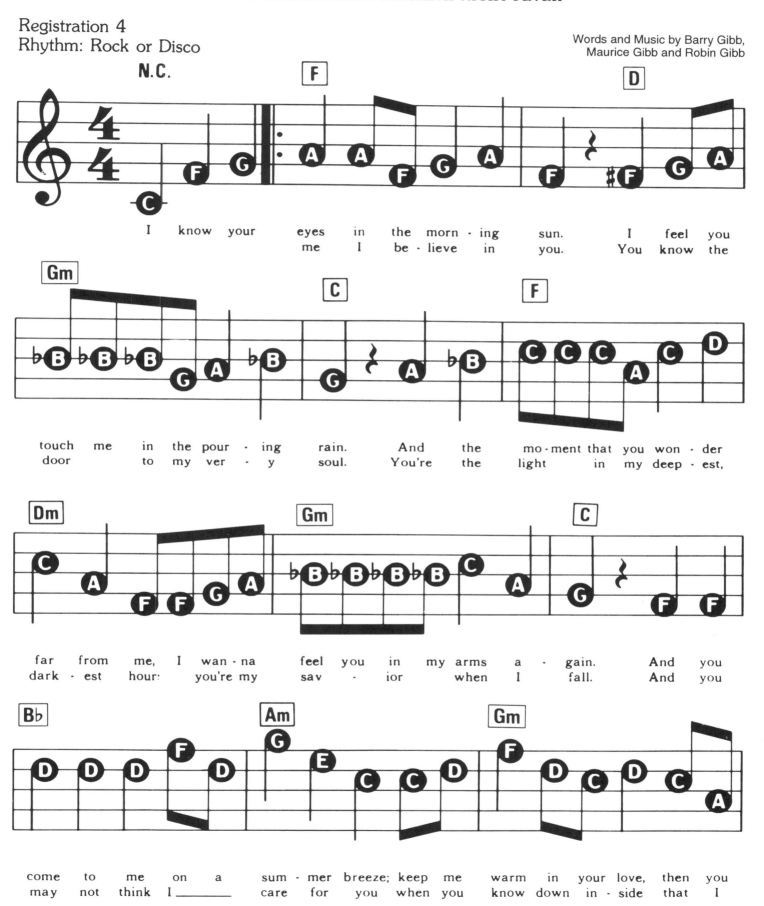

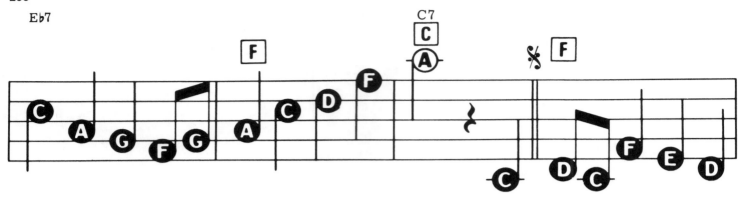

soft · ly leave.
real · ly do.
And it's me you need to show: How deep is your love? How

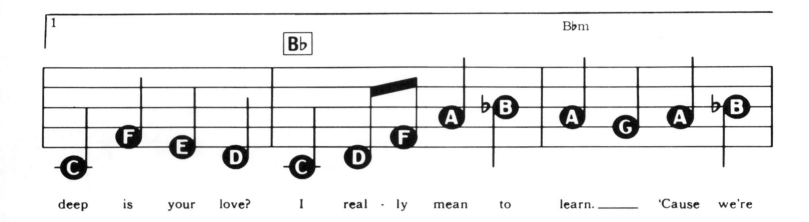

deep is your love? I real · ly mean to learn. _____ 'Cause we're

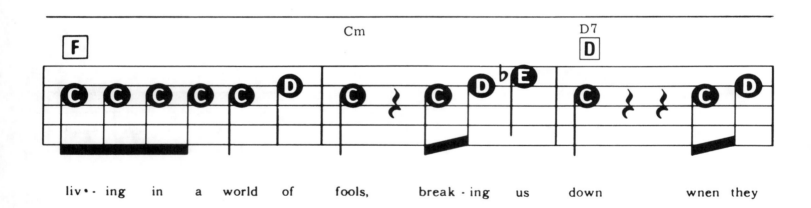

liv · · ing in a world of fools, break · ing us down wnen they

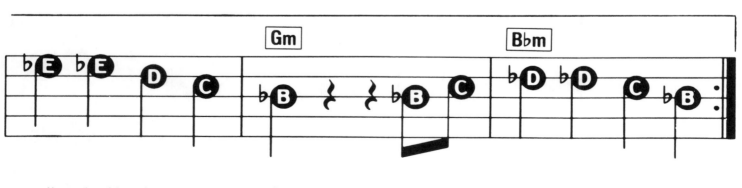

all should let us be. We be · long to you and

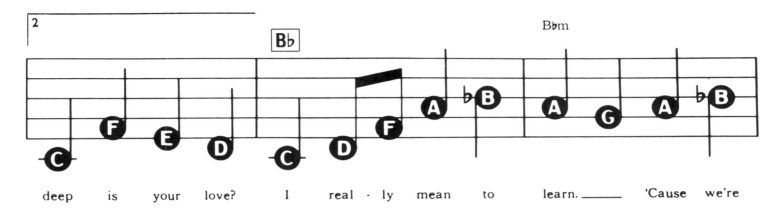

deep   is   your   love?   I   real · ly   mean   to   learn._____ 'Cause we're

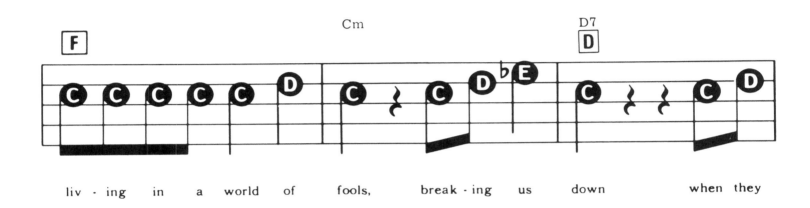

liv - ing   in   a   world   of   fools,   break - ing   us   down   when they

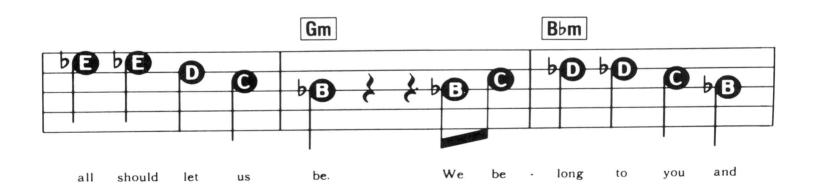

all   should   let   us   be.   We   be - long   to   you   and

D.S. and Fade
(Return to 𝄋
and fade)

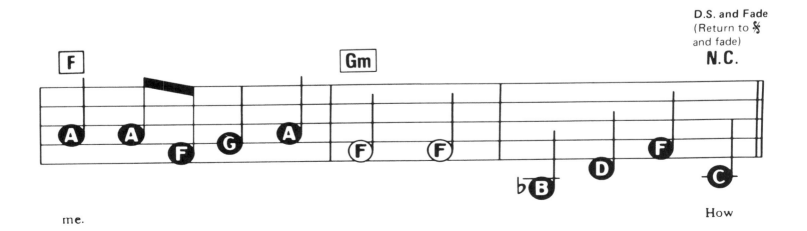

me.   How

1978
Dust in the Wind

Registration 10
Rhythm: Rock

Words and Music by
Kerry Livgren

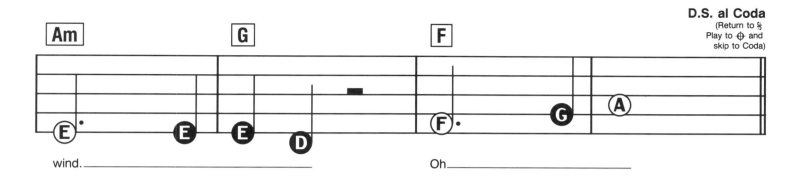

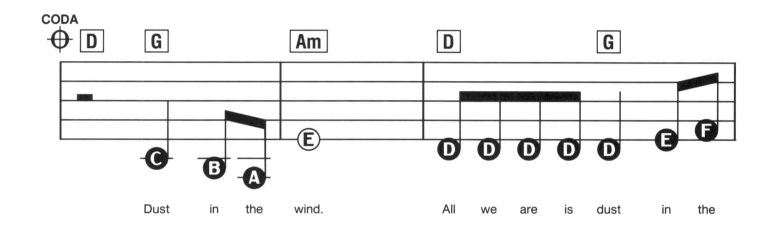

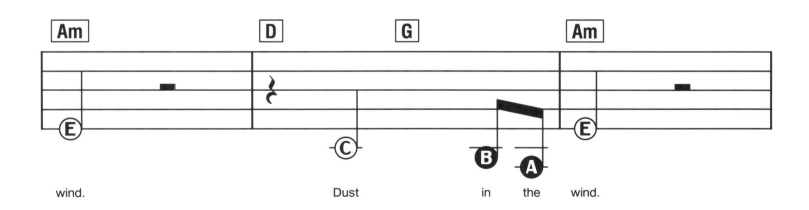

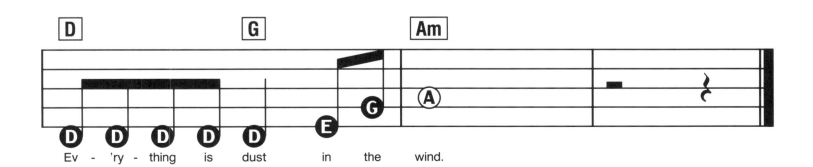

1979
Y.M.C.A.

Registration 9
Rhythm: Disco

Words and Music by Jacques Morali,
Henri Belolo and Victor Willis

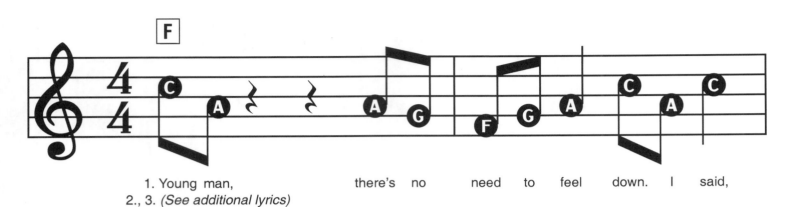

1. Young man, there's no need to feel down. I said,
2., 3. *(See additional lyrics)*

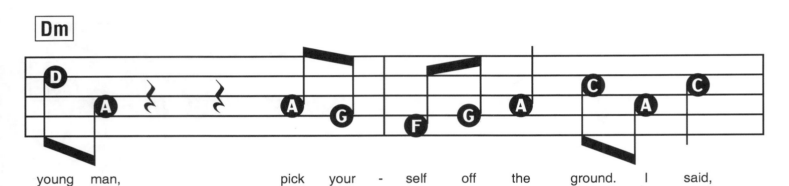

young man, pick your - self off the ground. I said,

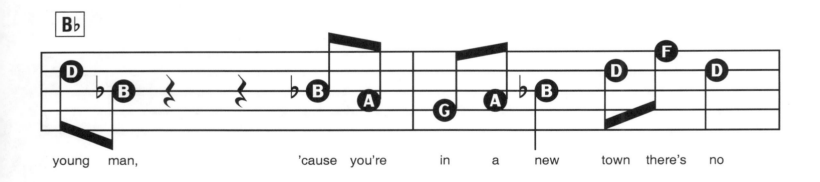

young man, 'cause you're in a new town there's no

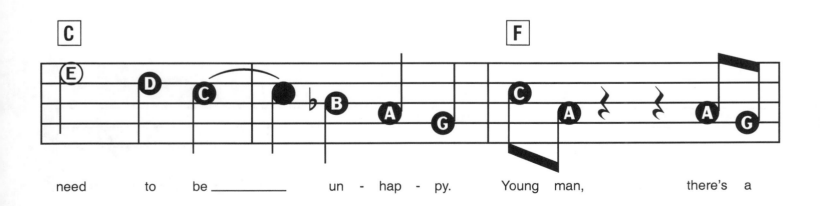

need to be _____ un - hap - py. Young man, there's a

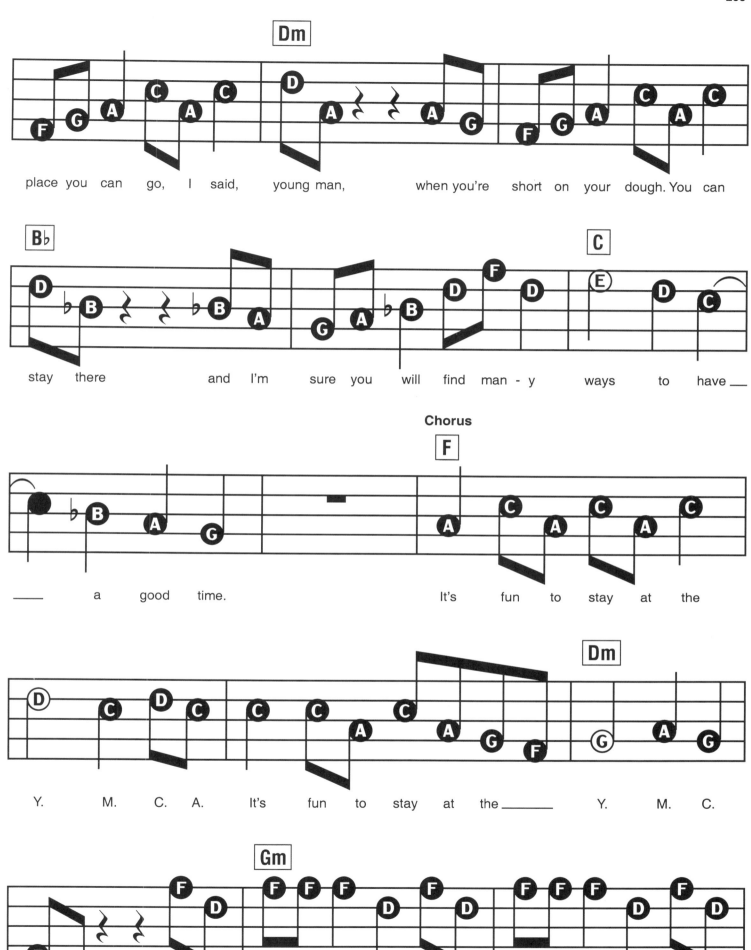

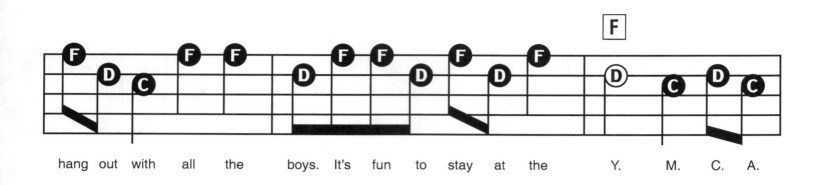

hang out with all the boys. It's fun to stay at the Y. M. C. A.

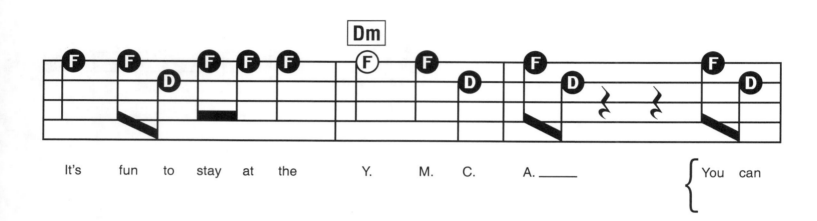

It's fun to stay at the Y. M. C. A. _____ You can

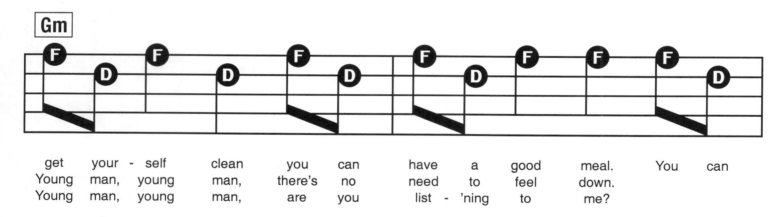

get your - self clean you can have a good meal. You can
Young man, young man, there's no need to feel down. You can
Young man, young man, are you list - 'ning to me?

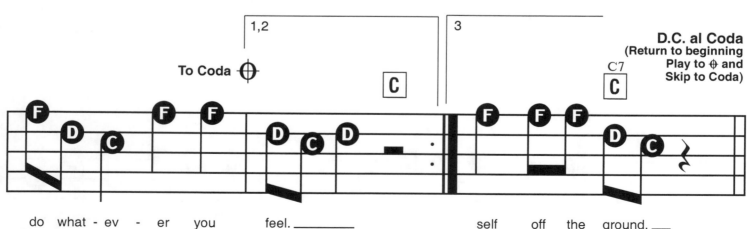

do what - ev - er you feel. _____ self off the ground. ___
Young man, young man, pick your-
Young man, young man, what do

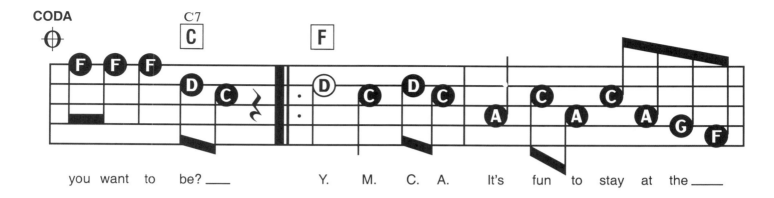

you want to be? ___   Y.   M.   C.   A.   It's   fun   to   stay   at   the ___

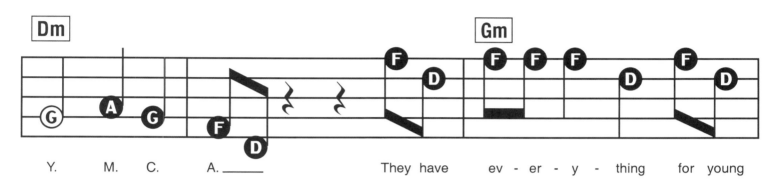

Y.   M.   C.   A. ___   They   have   ev - er - y - thing   for   young

Repeat and Fade

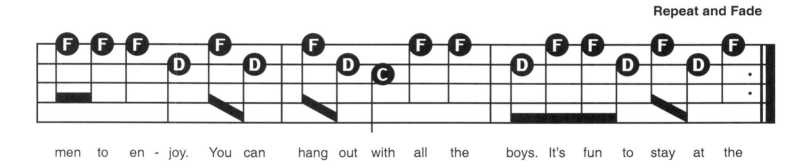

men   to   en - joy.   You   can   hang   out   with   all   the   boys.   It's   fun   to   stay   at   the

Additional Lyrics

2. Young man, are you listening to me?
   I said, young man what do you want to be?
   I said, young man you can make real your dreams
   But you've got to know this one thing.

   No man does it all by himself.
   I said, young man put your pride on the shelf.
   And just go there to the Y.M.C.A.
   I'm sure they can help you today.
   To Chorus:

3. Young man, I was once in your shoes
   I said, I was down and out and with the blues.
   I felt no man cared if I were alive.
   I felt the whole world was so jive.

   That's when someone came up to me
   And said, "Young man, take a walk up the street.
   It's a place there called the Y.M.C.A.
   They can start you back on your way."
   To Chorus:

1980
Sailing

Registration 2
Rhythm: Pops or 8 Beat

Words and Music by
Christopher Cross

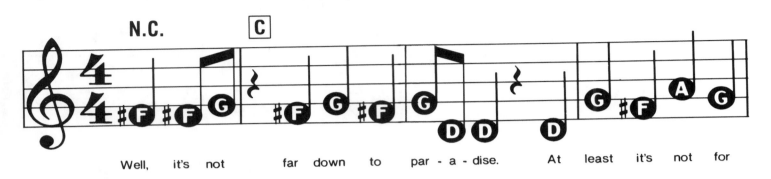

Well, it's not far down to par-a-dise. At least it's not for

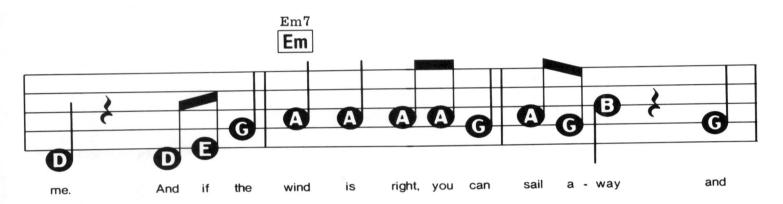

me. And if the wind is right, you can sail a-way and

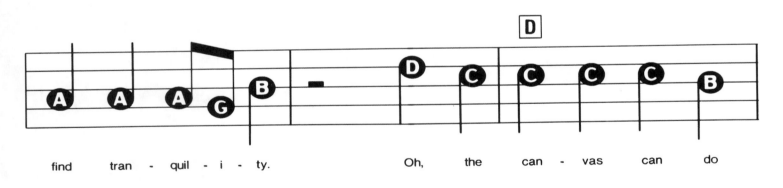

find tran-quil-i-ty. Oh, the can-vas can do

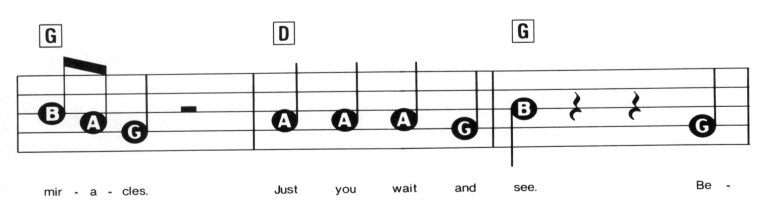

mir-a-cles. Just you wait and see. Be-

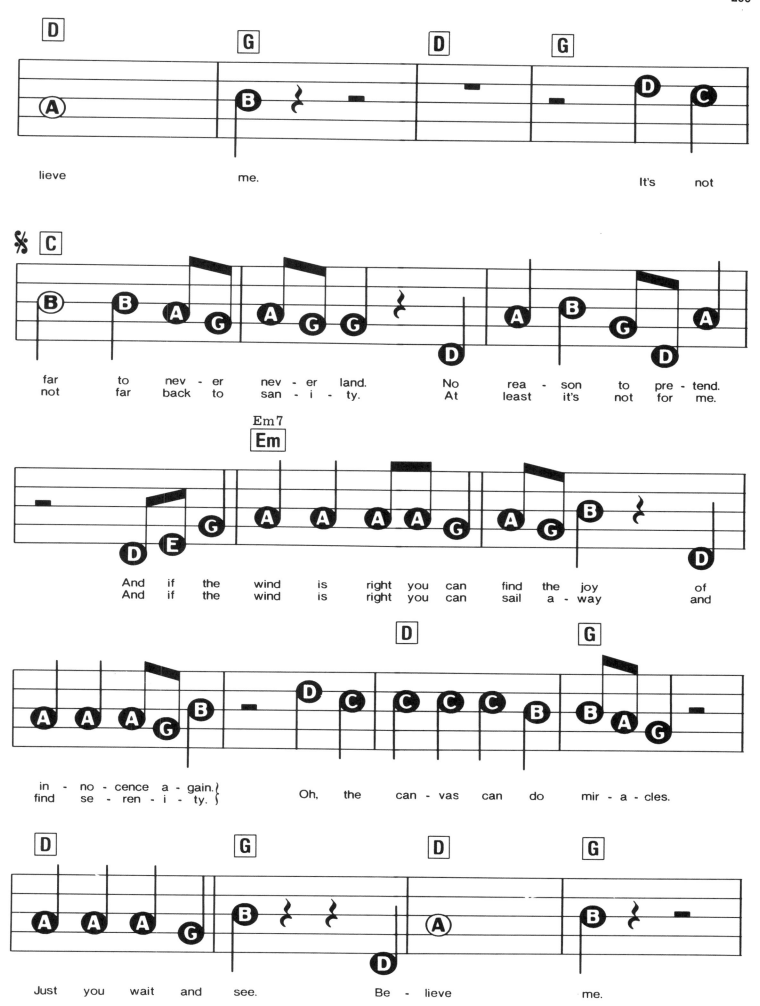

210

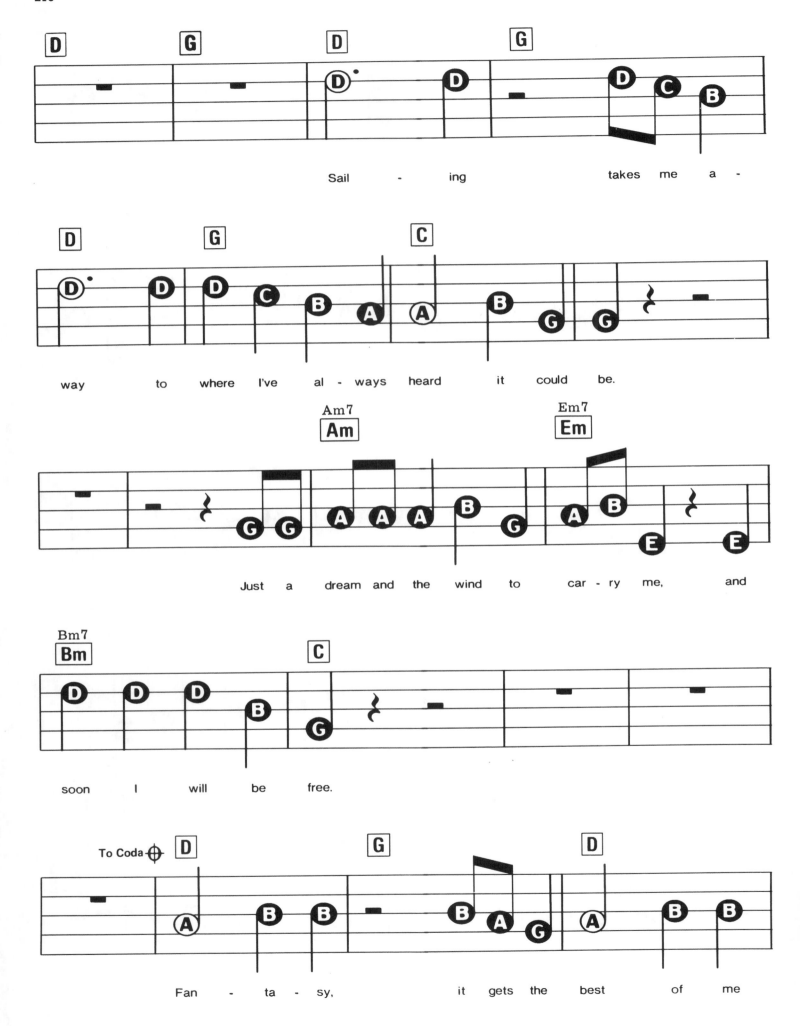

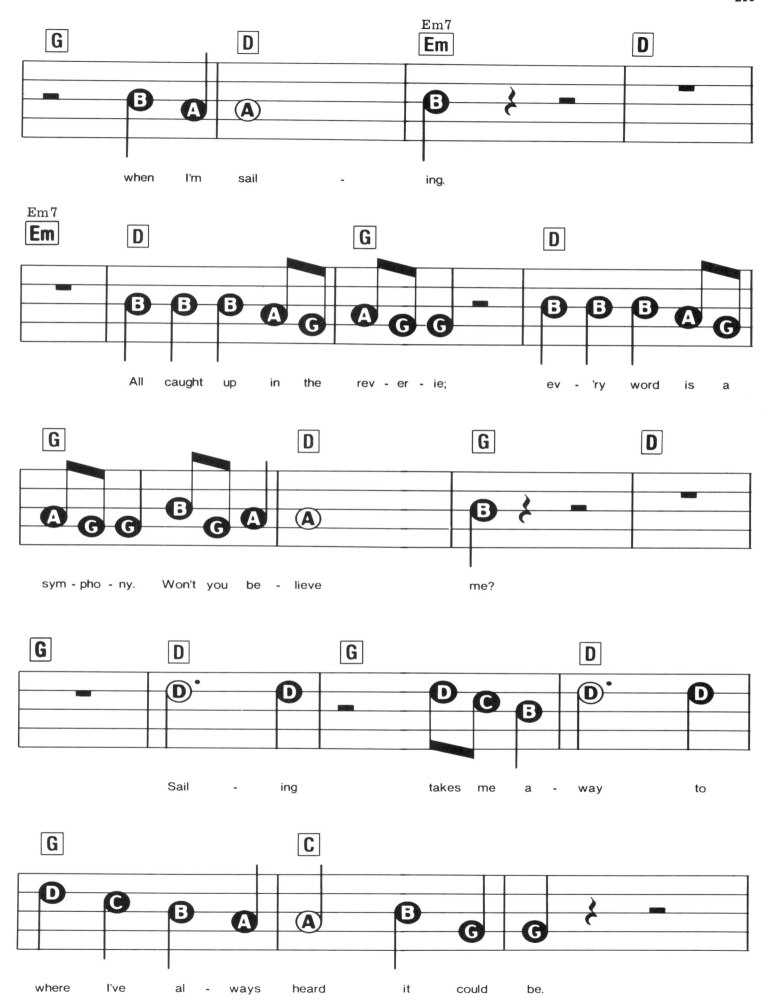

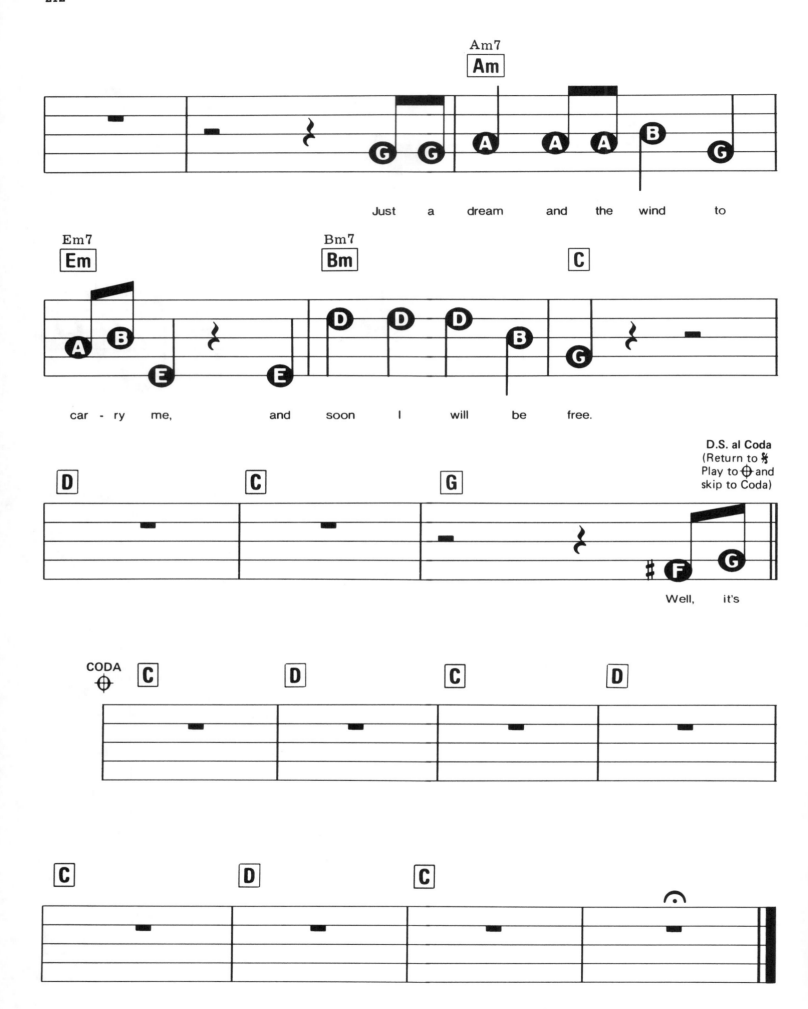

1981
Physical

Registration 2
Rhythm: Rock or Disco

Words and Music by Stephen A. Kipner
and Terry Shaddick

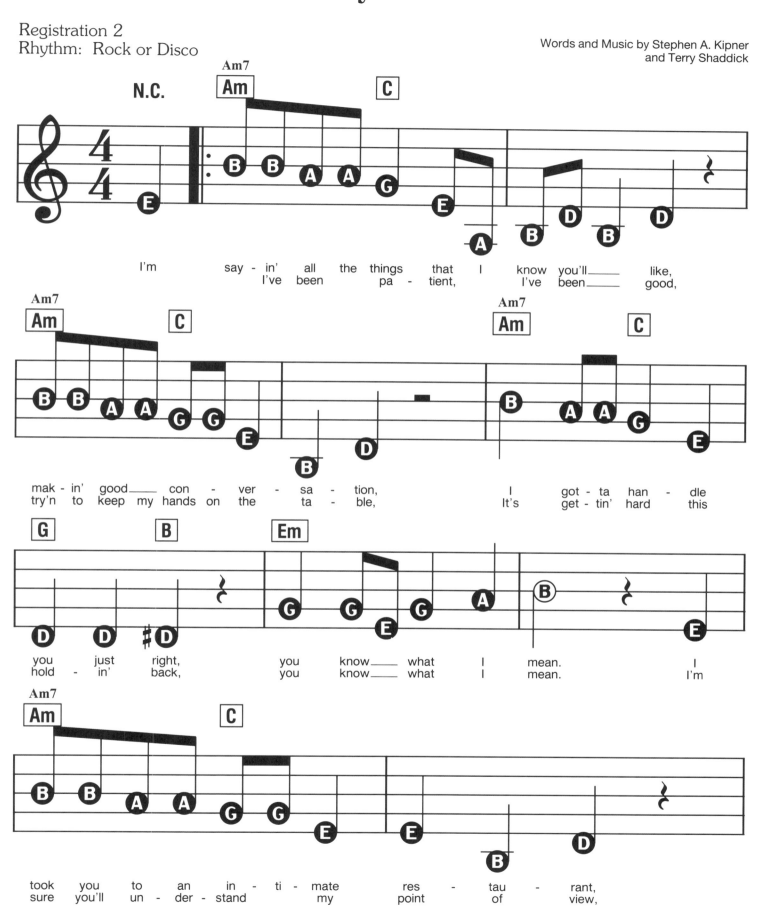

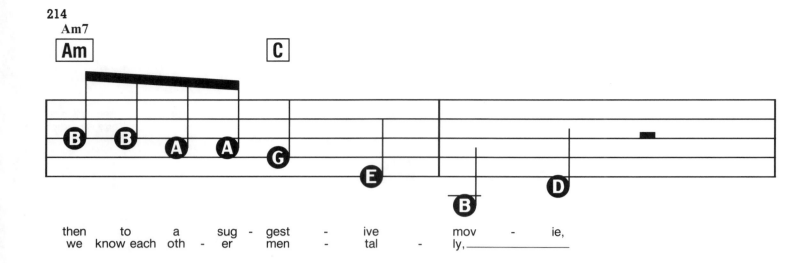

then to a sug - gest - ive mov - ie,
we know each oth - er men - tal - ly, _____

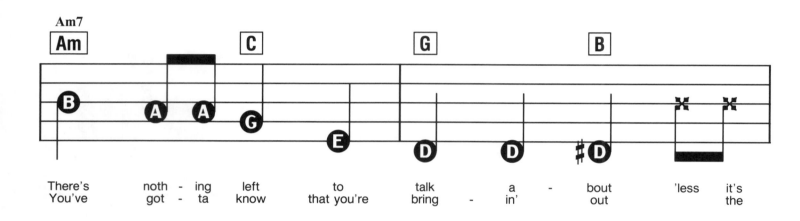

There's noth - ing left to talk a - bout 'less it's
You've got - ta know to that you're bring - in' out the

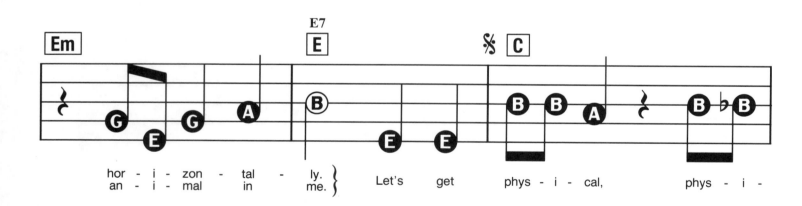

hor - i - zon - tal - ly.
an - i - mal in me. } Let's get phys - i - cal, phys - i -

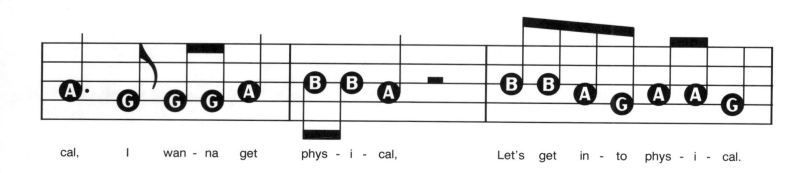

cal, I wan - na get phys - i - cal, Let's get in - to phys - i - cal.

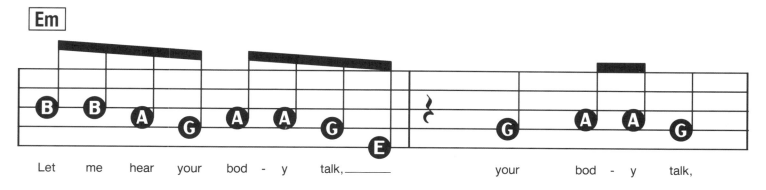

Let me hear your bod - y talk,_____ your bod - y talk,

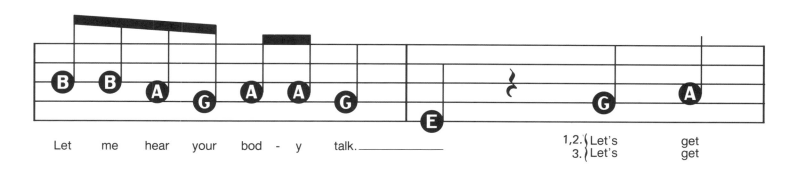

Let me hear your bod - y talk._____
1,2. {Let's get
3. {Let's get

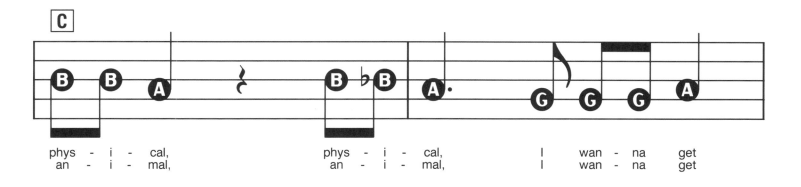

phys - i - cal, phys - i - cal, I wan - na get
an - i - mal, an - i - mal, I wan - na get

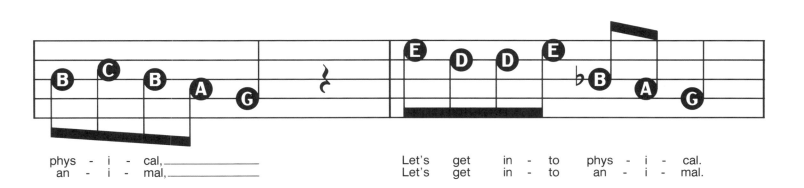

phys - i - cal,_____ Let's get in - to phys - i - cal.
an - i - mal,_____ Let's get in - to an - i - mal.

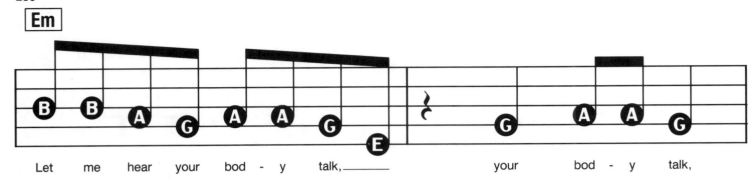

Let me hear your bod - y talk, _____ your bod - y talk,

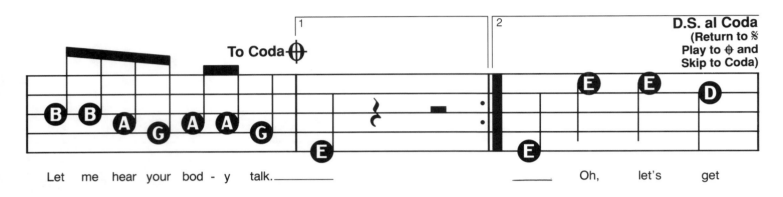

Let me hear your bod - y talk. _____ _____ Oh, let's get

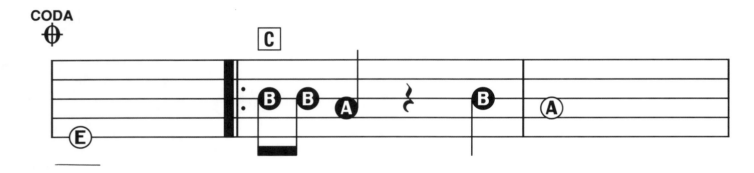

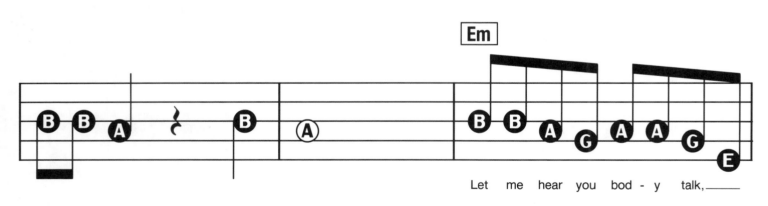

Let me hear you bod - y talk, _____

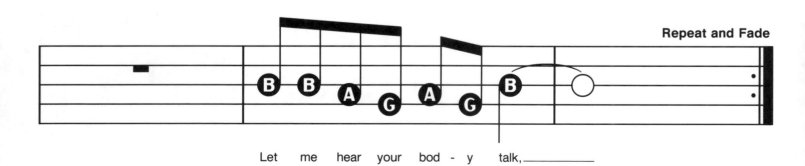

Let me hear your bod - y talk, _____

1982
Chariots of Fire
from CHARIOTS OF FIRE

Registration 5
Rhythm: Rock or Disco

Music by Vangelis

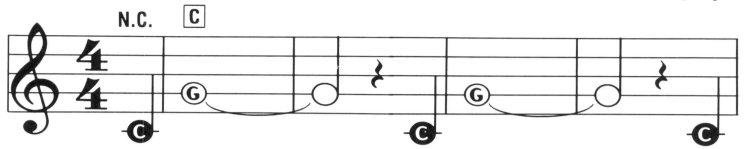

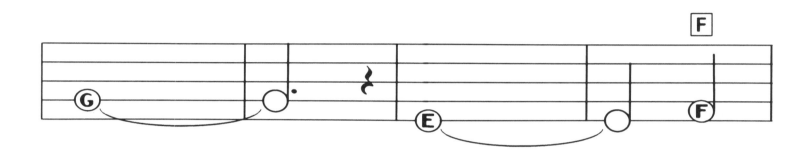

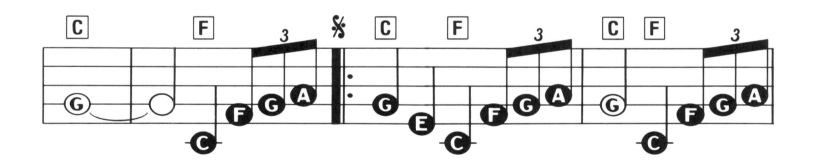

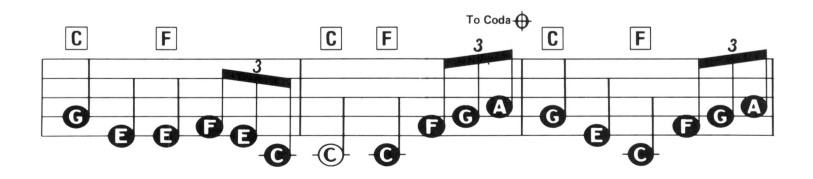

218

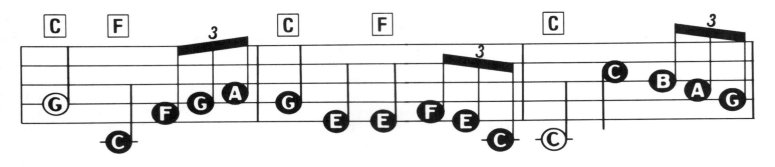

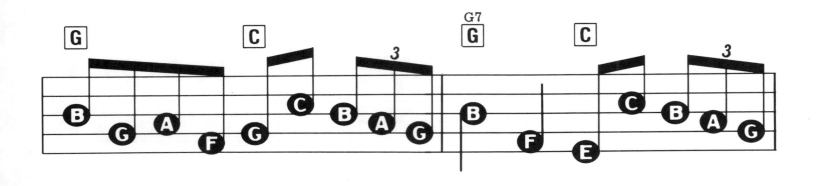

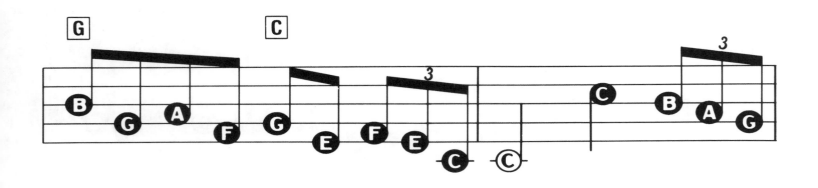

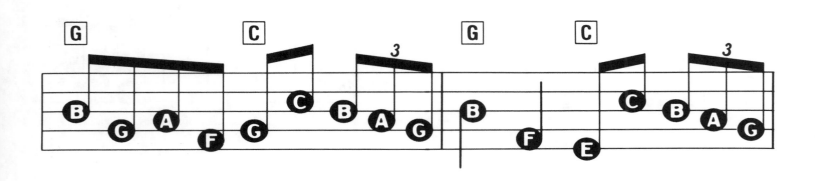

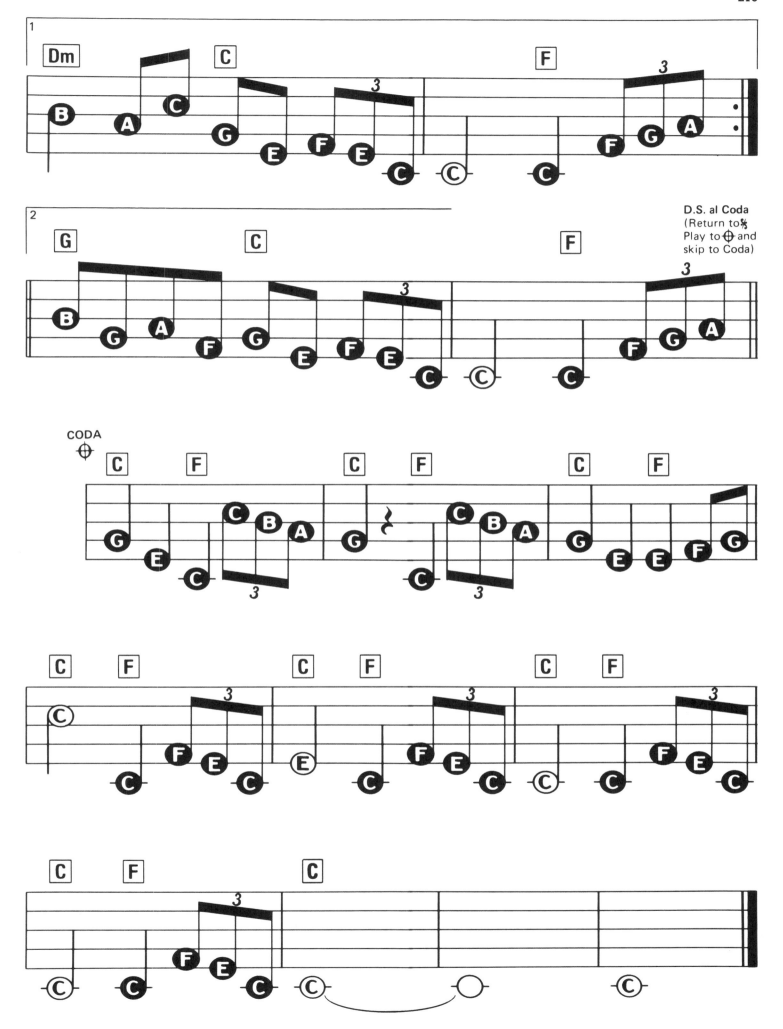

1983
Time After Time

Registration 3
Rhythm: Rock or Jazz Rock

Words and Music by Cyndi Lauper
and Rob Hyman

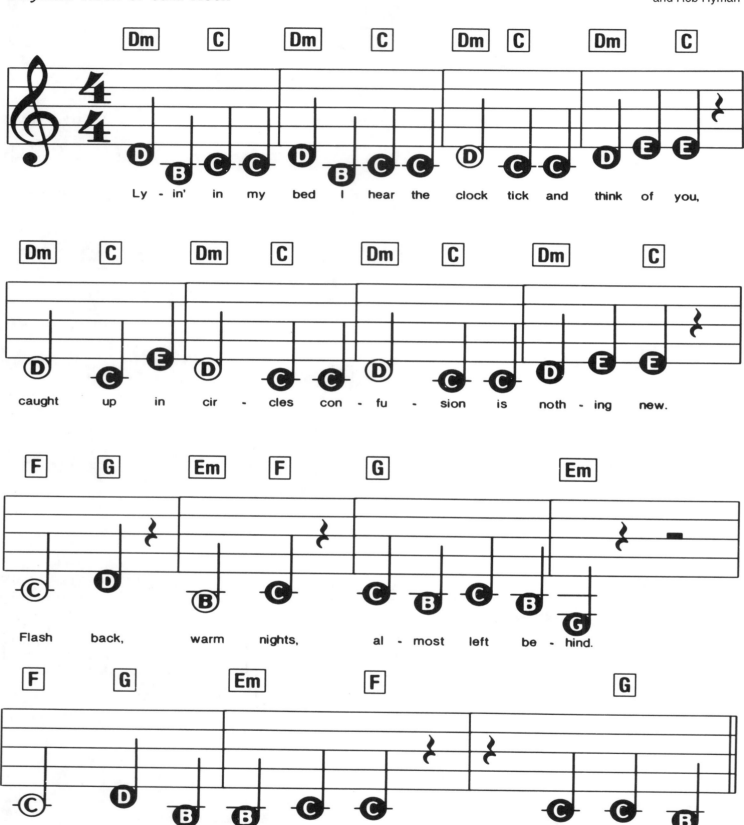

221

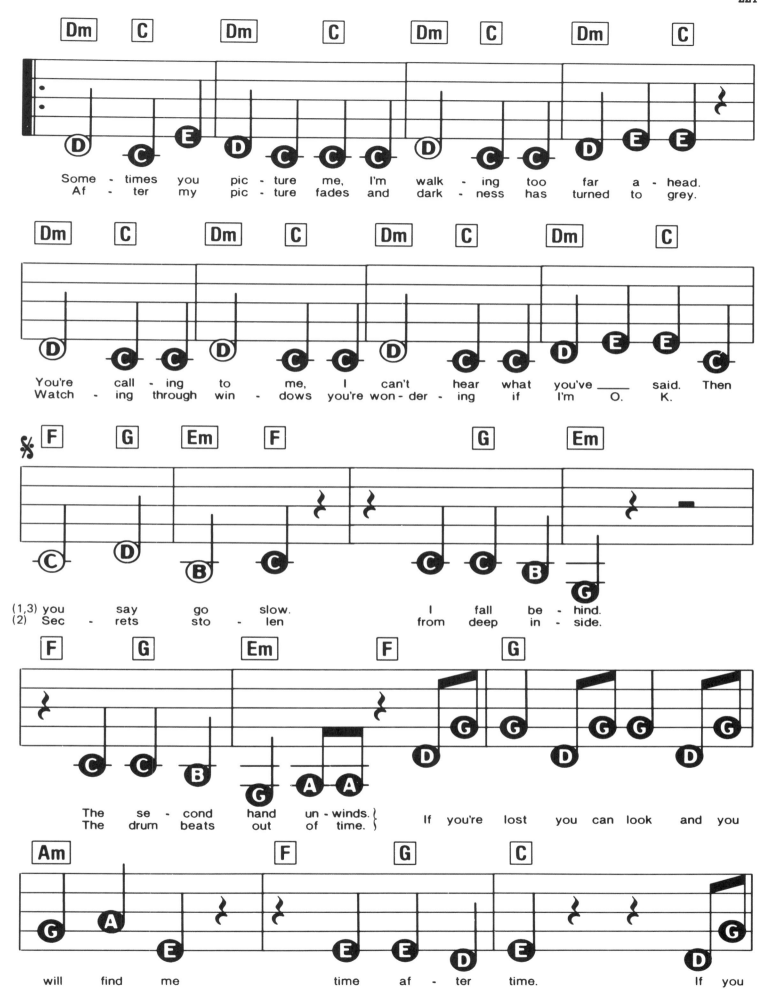

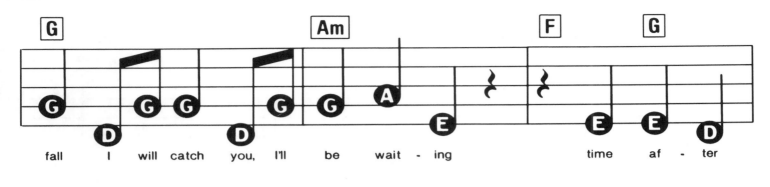

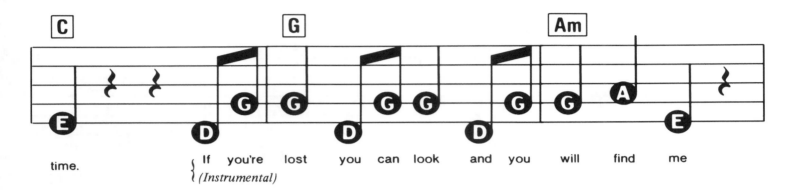

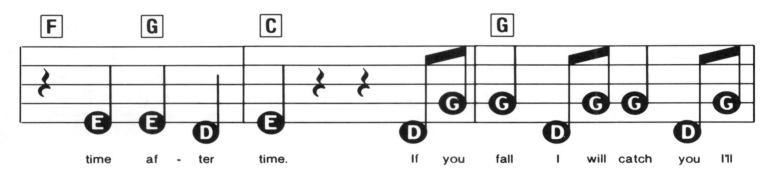

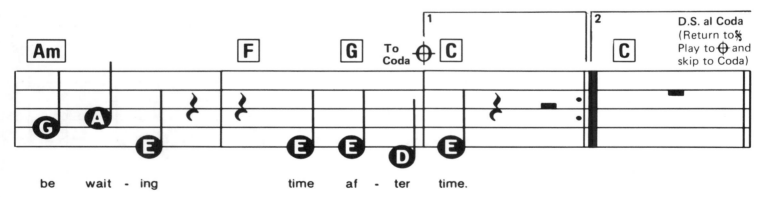

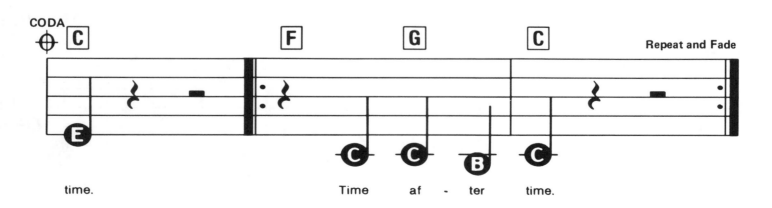

1984
I Just Called to Say I Love You

Registration 2
Rhythm: Rock

Words and Music by
Stevie Wonder

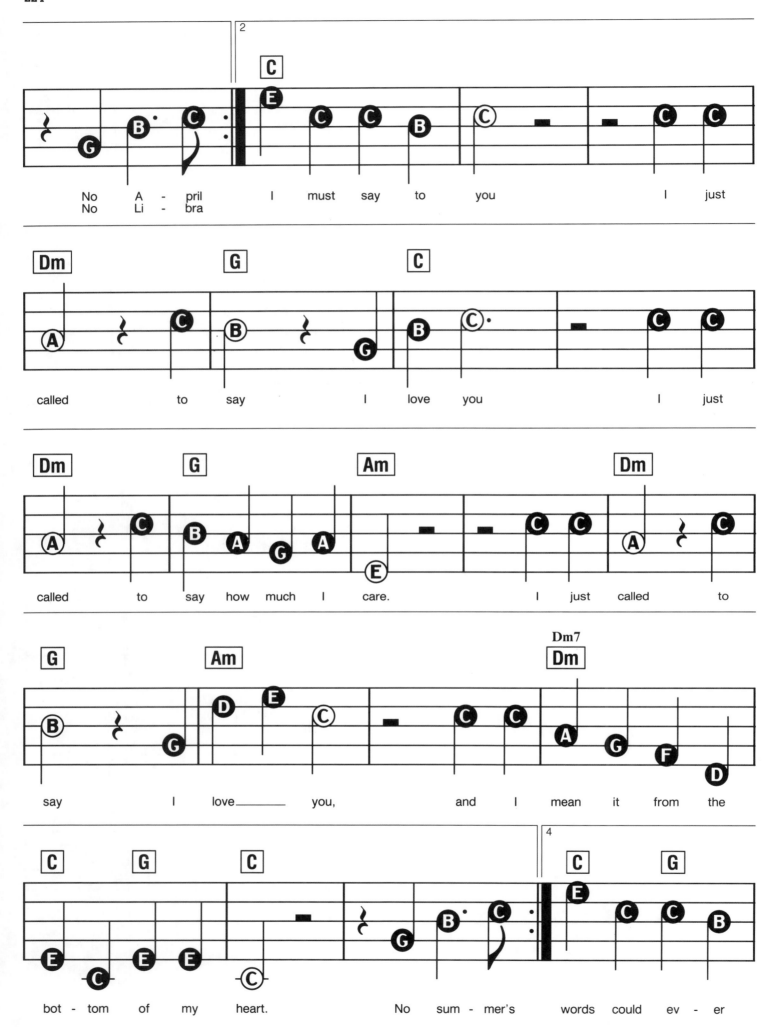

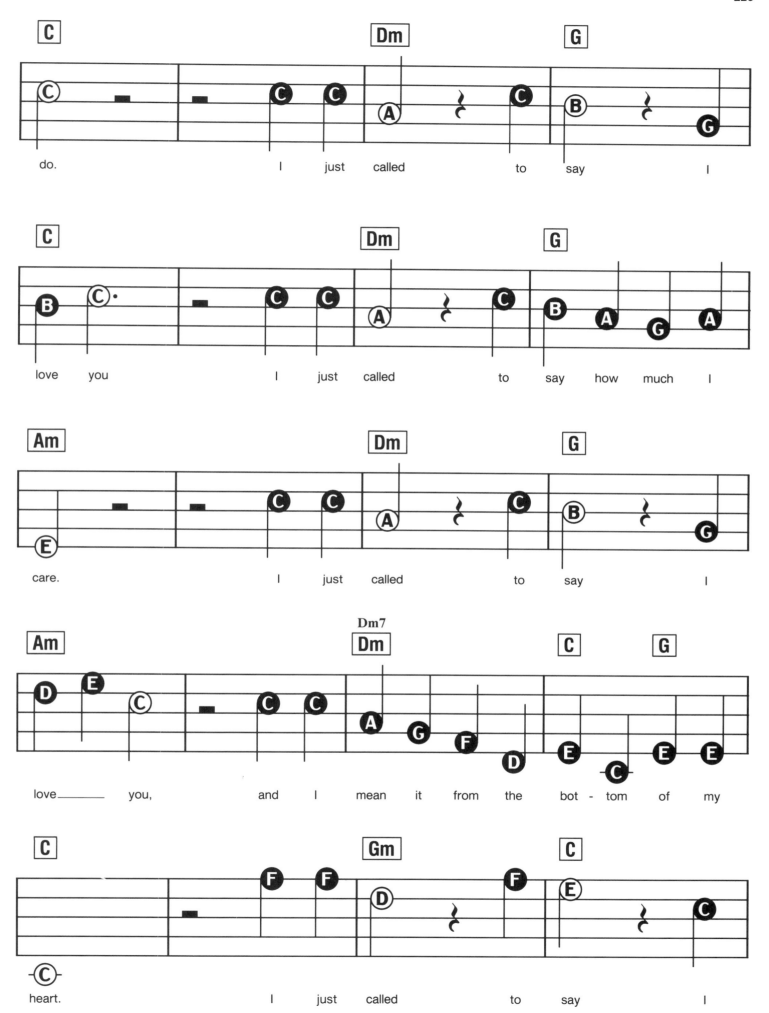

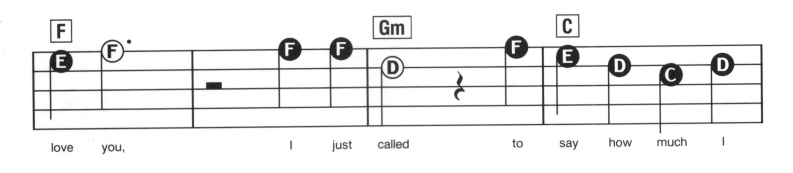

love   you,   I   just called   to   say   how   much   I

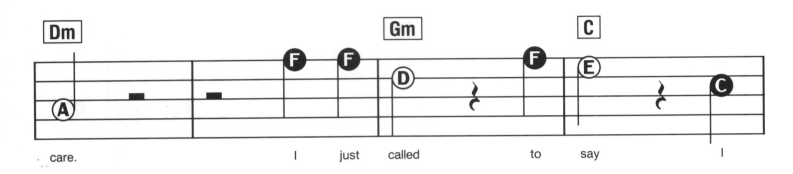

care.   I   just called   to   say   I

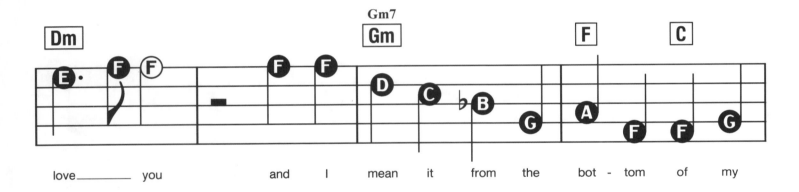

love_____ you   and   I   mean   it from   the   bot - tom   of   my

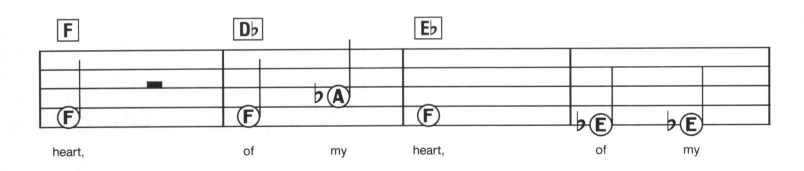

heart,   of   my   heart,   of   my

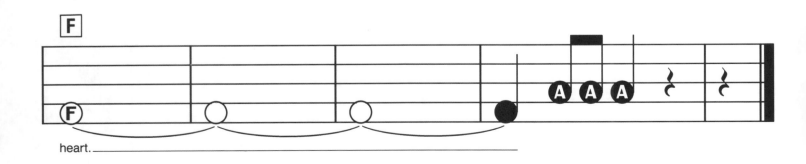

heart._____

1985
We Built This City

Registration 4
Rhythm: Rock or 8 Beat

Words and Music by Bernie Taupin, Martin Page,
Dennis Lambert and Peter Wolf

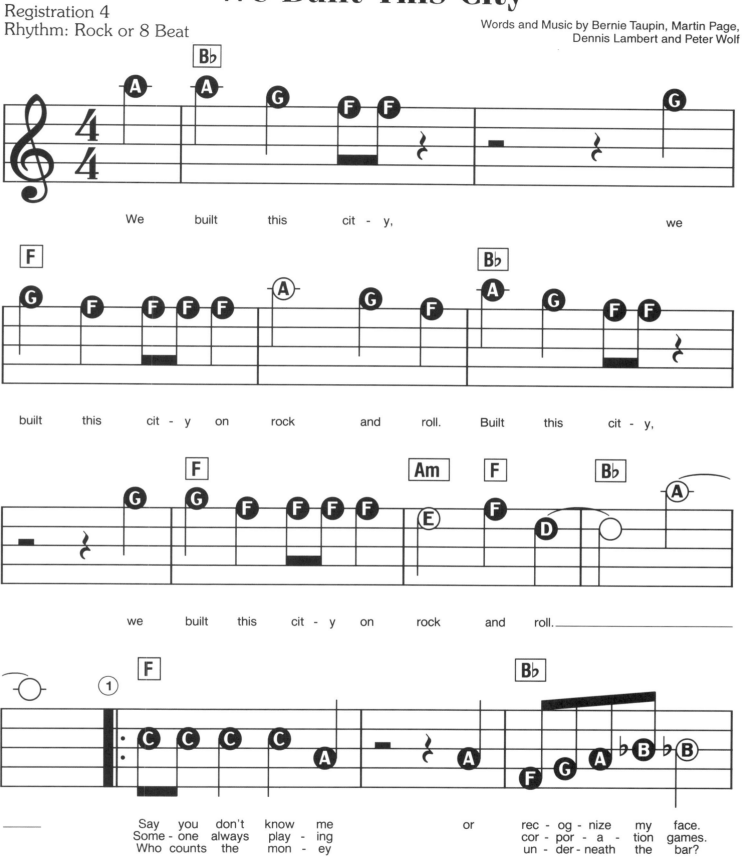

228

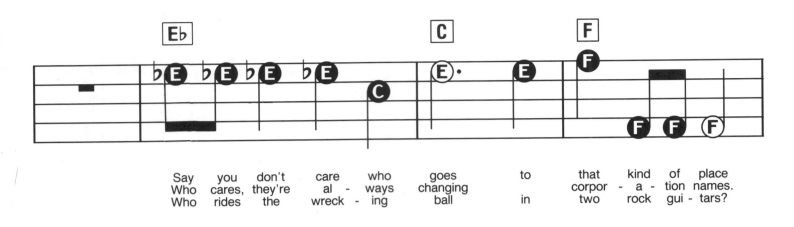

Say you don't care who goes to that kind of place
Who cares, they're al - ways changing corpor - a - tion names.
Who rides the wreck - ing ball in two rock gui - tars?

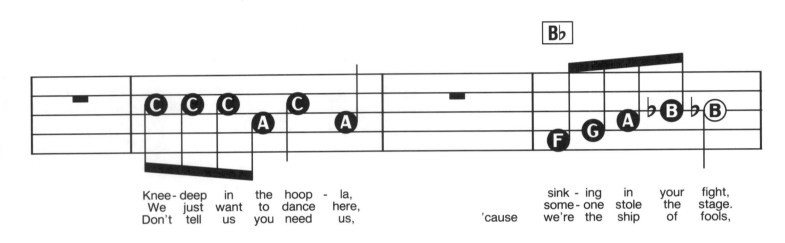

Knee - deep in the hoop - la, sink - ing in your fight,
We just want to dance here, some - one stole the stage.
Don't tell us you need us, 'cause we're the ship of fools,

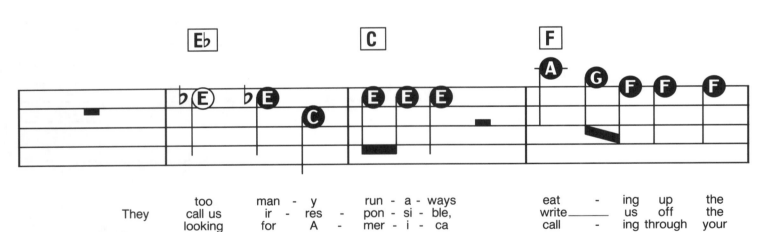

They too man - y run - a - ways eat - ing up the
call us ir - res - pon - si - ble, write___ us off the
looking for A - mer - i - ca call - ing through your

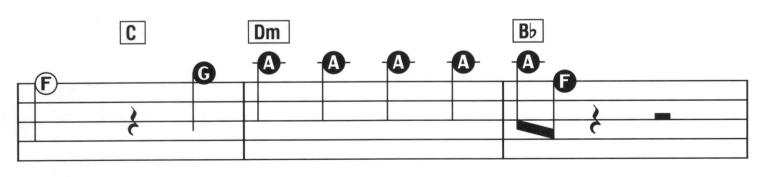

night. }
page. } Mar - co - ni plays the mam - ba,
schools. }

229

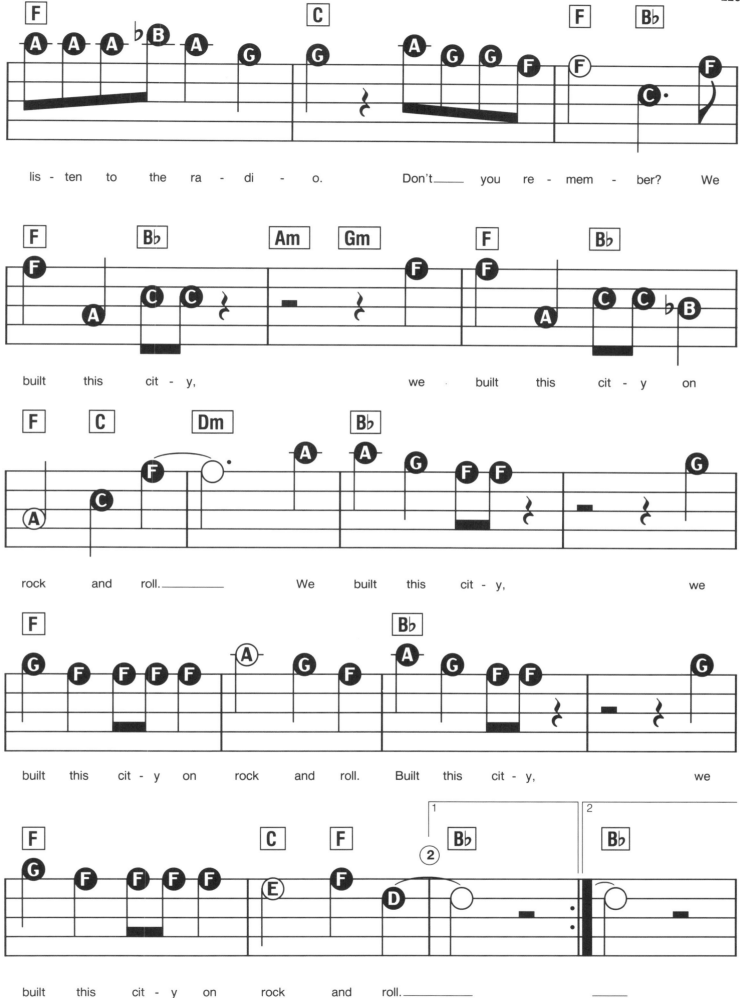

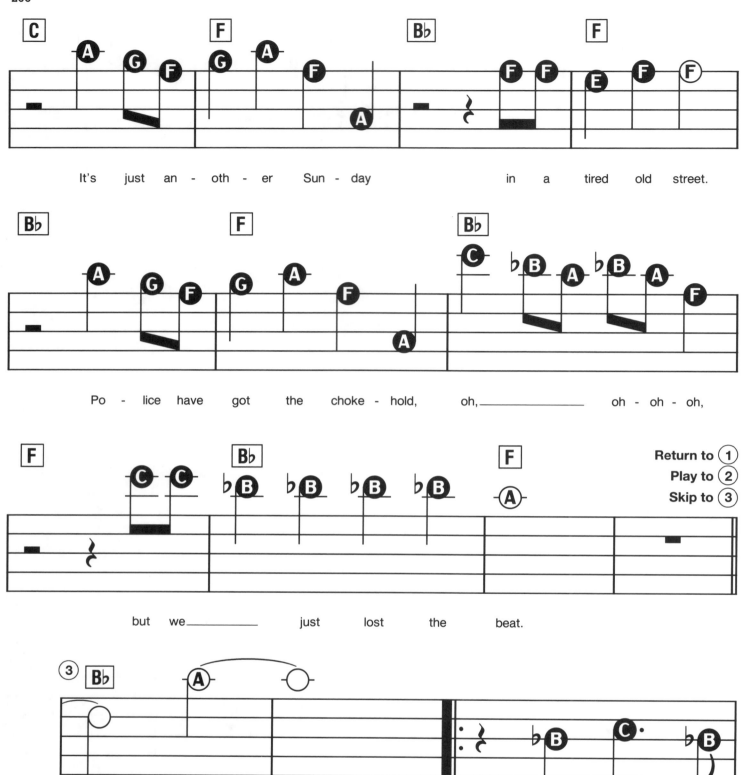

It's just an - oth - er Sun - day   in a tired old street.

Po - lice have got the choke - hold, oh,_____ oh - oh - oh,

Return to ①
Play to ②
Skip to ③

but we_____ just lost the beat.

③ We built, we

Repeat and Fade

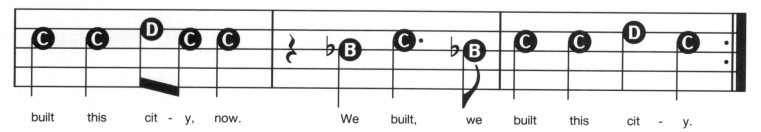

built this cit - y, now.   We built, we built this cit - y.

1986
Glory of Love
Theme from KARATE KID PART II

Registration 1
Rhythm: Rock

Words and Music by David Foster,
Peter Cetera and Diane Nini

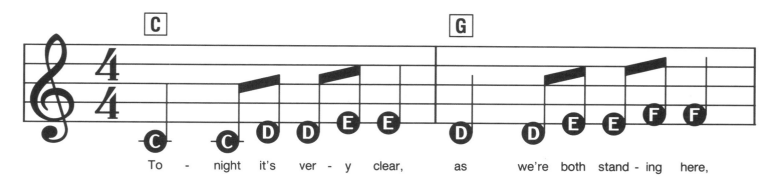

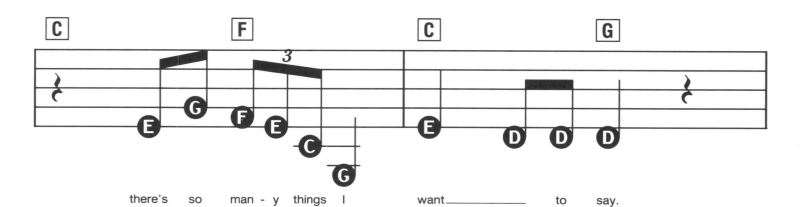

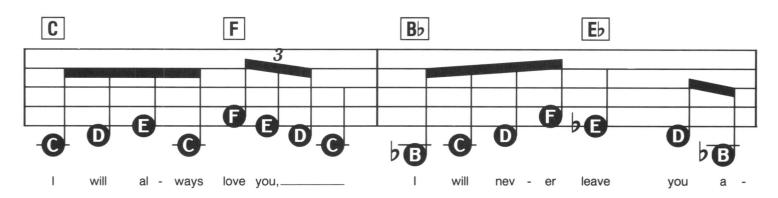

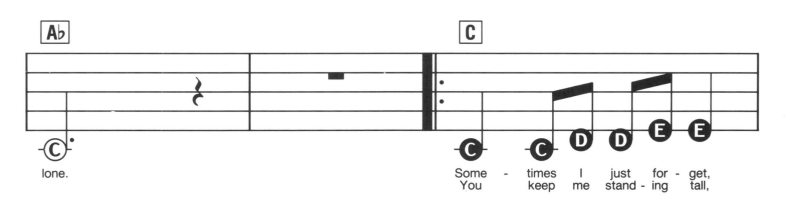

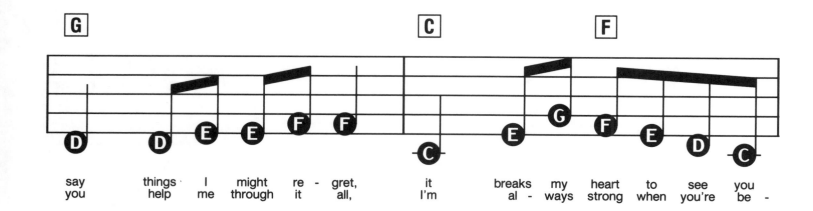

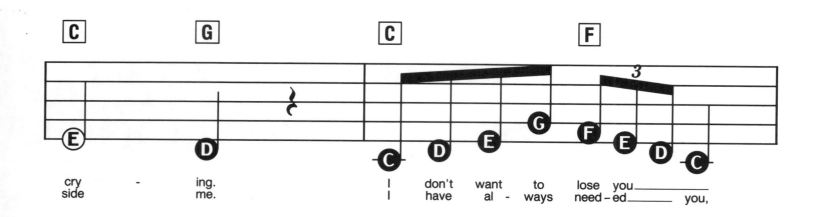

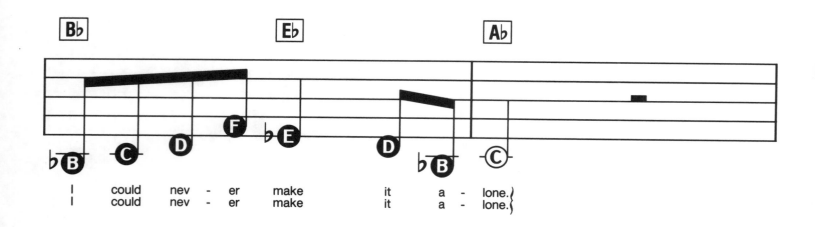

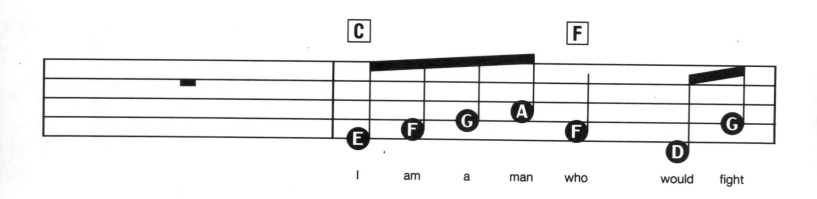

233

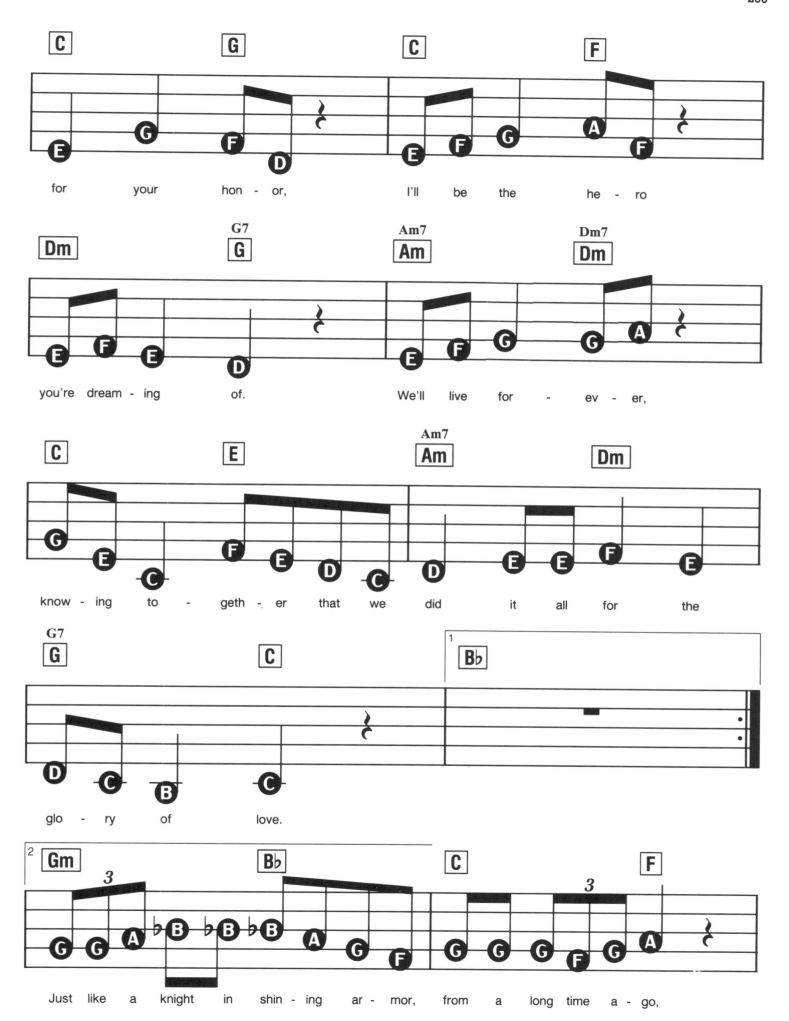

235

1987
I Still Haven't Found
What I'm Looking For

Registration 3
Rhythm: Rock or Disco

Words by Bono
Music by U2

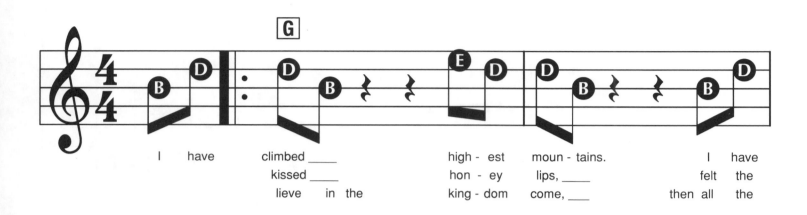

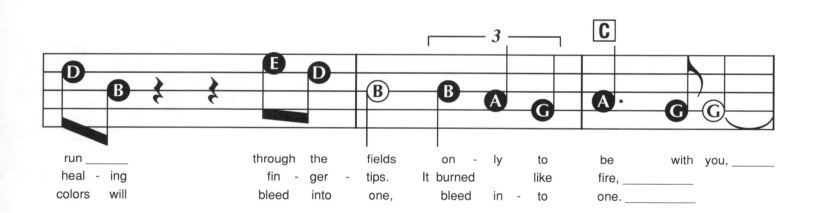

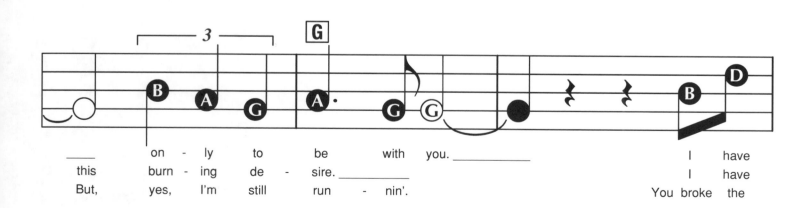

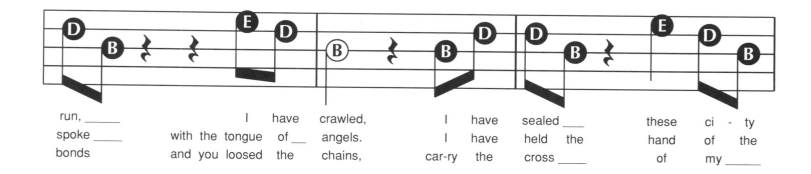

run, _____ I have crawled, I have sealed ___ these ci - ty
spoke _____ with the tongue of ___ angels. I have held the hand of the
bonds and you loosed the chains, car-ry the cross ___ of my _____

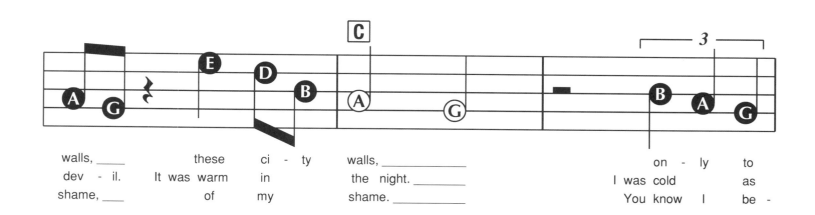

walls, _____ these ci - ty walls, _____ on - ly to
dev - il. It was warm in the night. _____ I was cold as
shame, ___ of my shame. _____ You know I be -

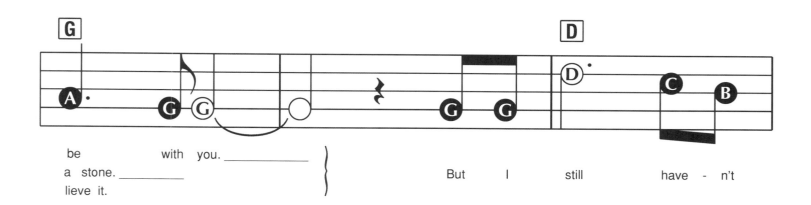

be with you. _____ But I still have - n't
a stone. _____
lieve it.

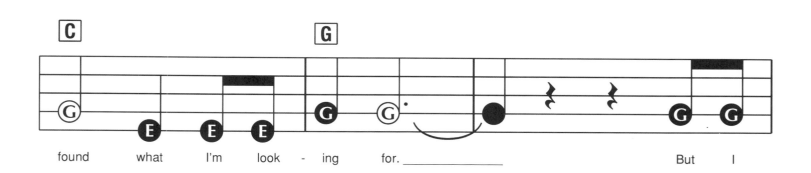

found what I'm look - ing for. _____ But I

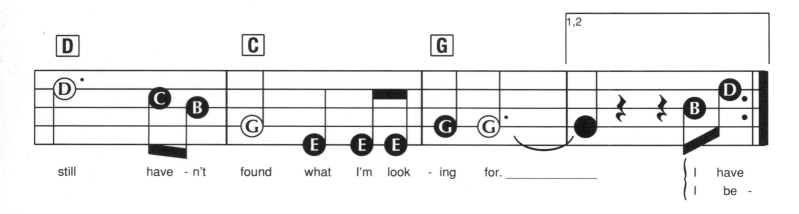

still   have - n't   found   what   I'm   look - ing   for. _____   I have / I be -

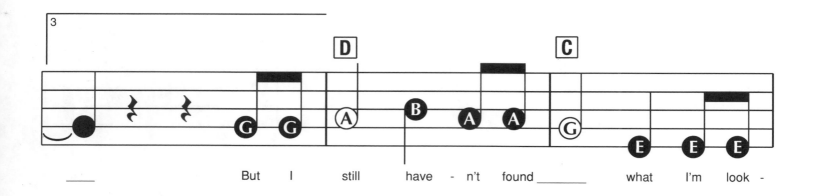

_____   But   I   still   have - n't   found _____   what   I'm   look -

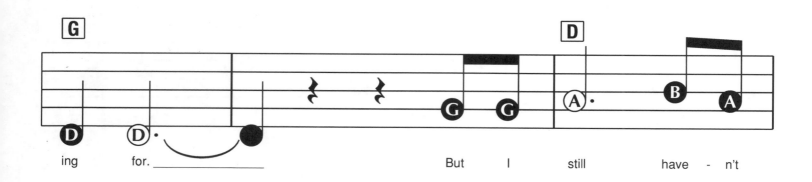

ing   for. _____   But   I   still   have - n't

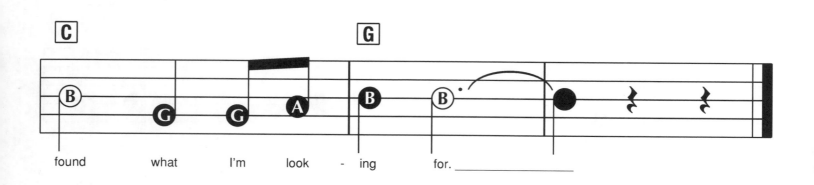

found   what   I'm   look - ing   for. _____

1988
Kokomo
from the Motion Picture COCKTAIL

Registration 7
Rhythm: Bossa Nova or Latin

Words and Music by Mike Love, Terry Melcher,
John Phillips, and Scott McKenzie

A - ru - ba, Ja - mai - ca, Oo_____ I wan - na take ya. Ber -

mu - da, Ba - ha - ma, come_____ on, pret - ty ma - ma. Key

Lar - go, Mon - te - go, Ba - by, why don't we go, Ja -

mai - ca. Off the Flor - i - da Keys_____

There's a place called Ko - ko - mo. That's where you

240

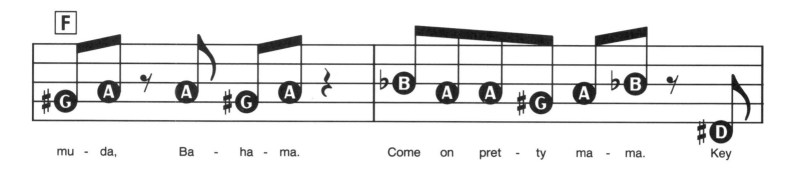

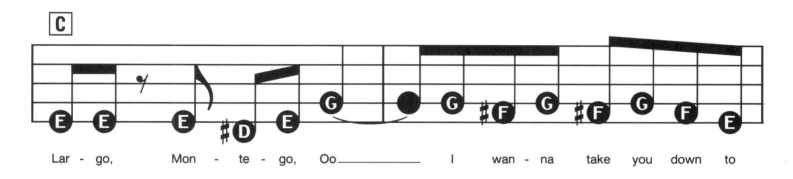

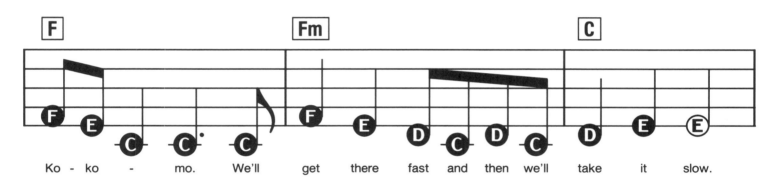

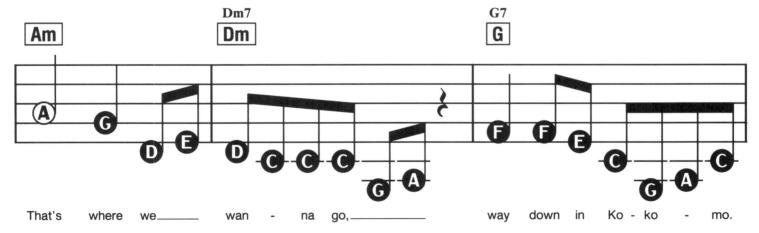

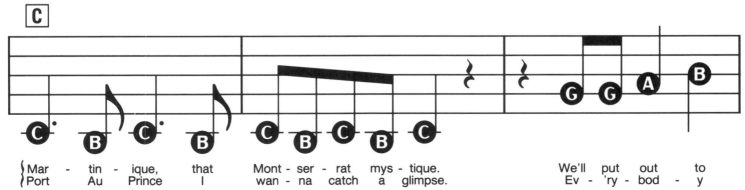

242

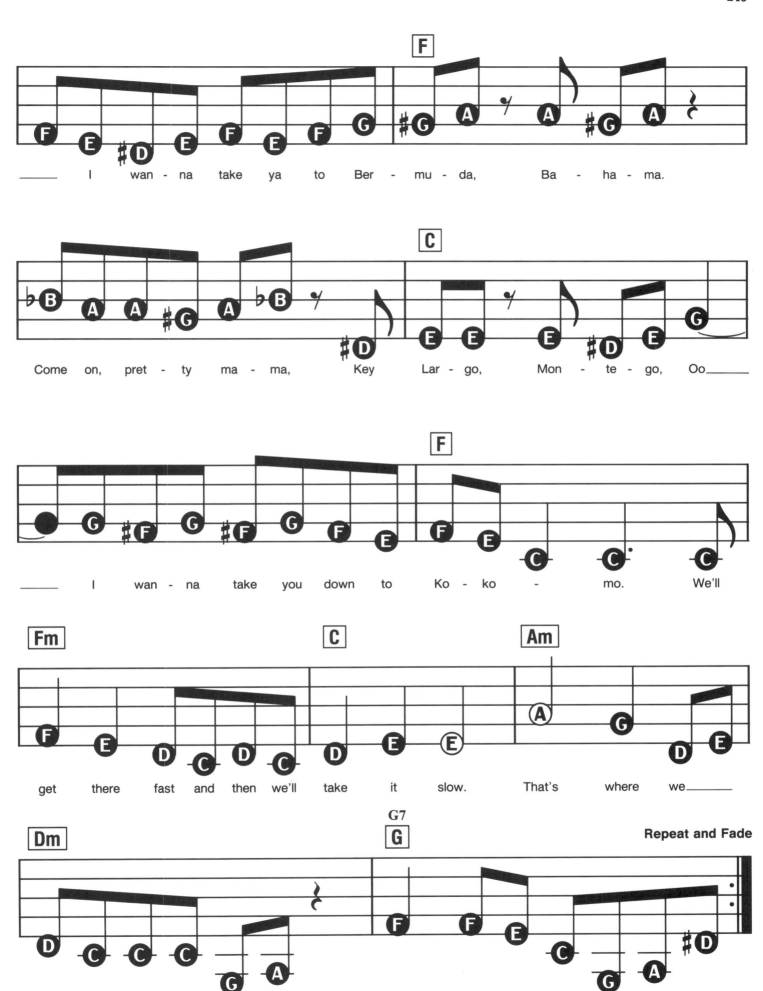

1989
Under the Sea
from Walt Disney's THE LITTLE MERMAID

Registration 7
Rhythm: Bossa Nova or Latin

Lyrics by Howard Ashman
Music by Alan Menken

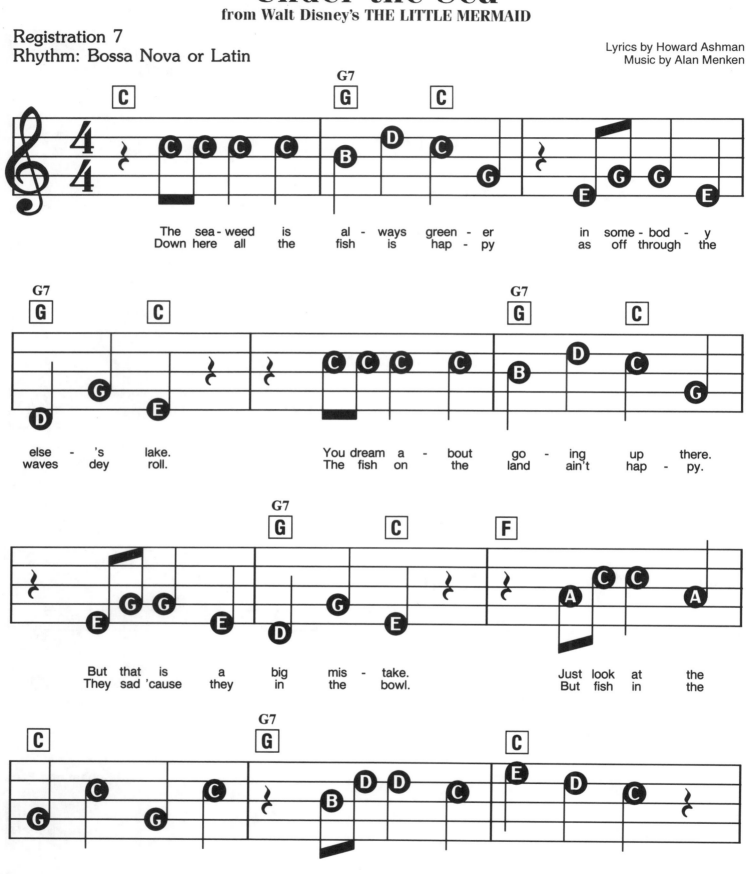

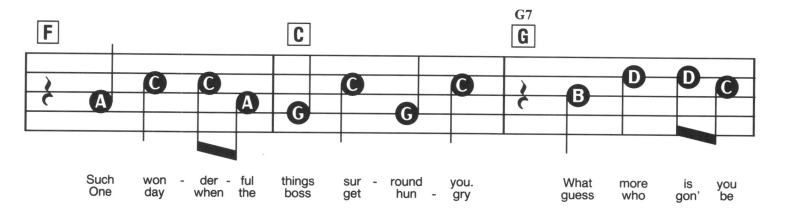

Such won - der - ful things sur - round you.
One day when the boss get hun - gry

What more is you
guess who is gon' be

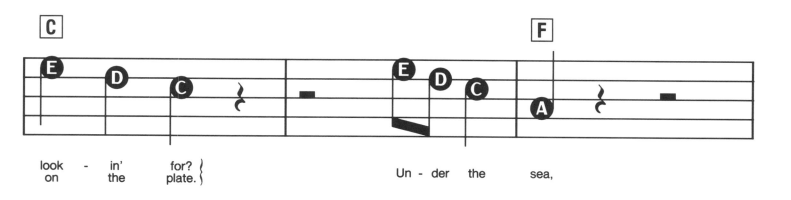

look - in' for?
on the plate.

Un - der the sea,

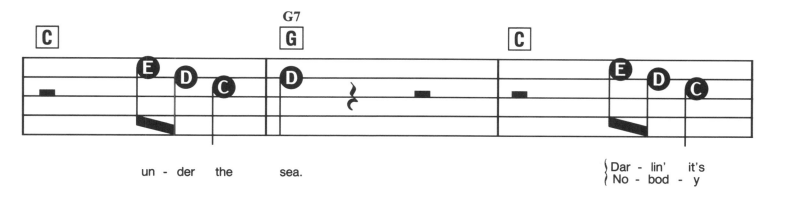

un - der the sea.

Dar - lin' it's
No - bod - y

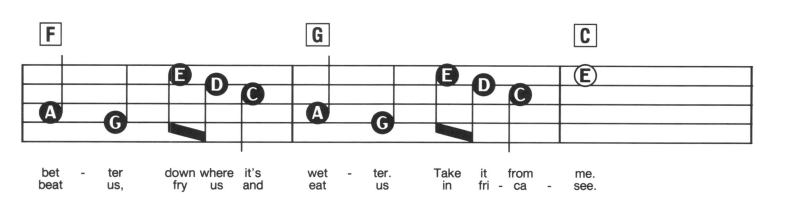

bet - ter, down where it's wet - ter. Take it from me.
beat us, fry us and eat us in fri - ca - see.

246

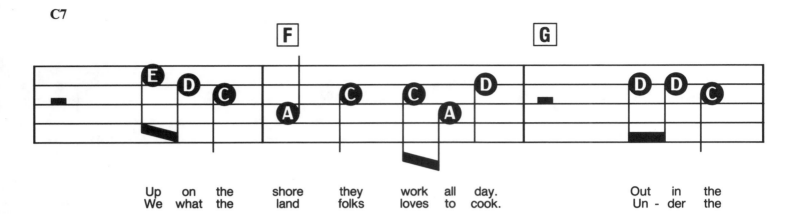

Up on the shore they work all day.
We what the land folks loves to cook.
Out in the
Un - der the

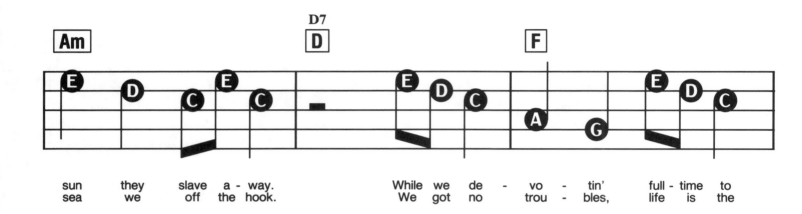

sun they slave a - way.
sea we off the hook.
While we de - vo - tin' full - time to
We got no trou - bles, life is the

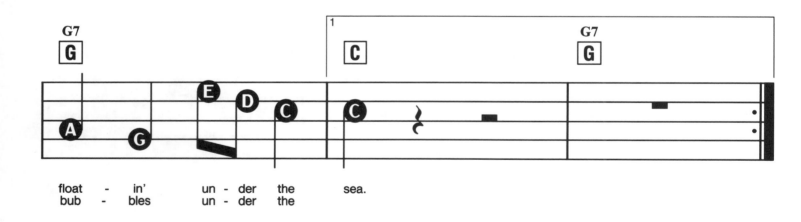

float - in' un - der the sea.
bub - bles un - der the

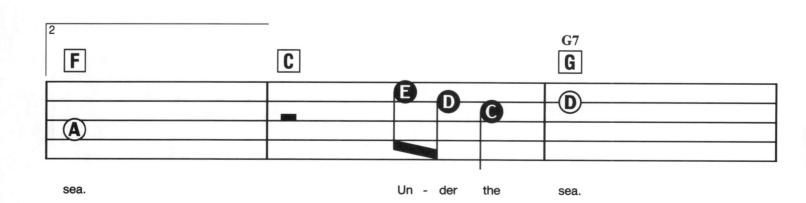

sea.
Un - der the sea.

247

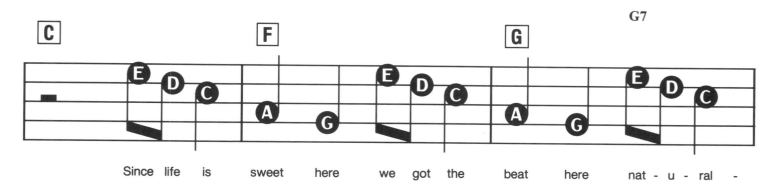

Since life is sweet here we got the beat here nat - u - ral -

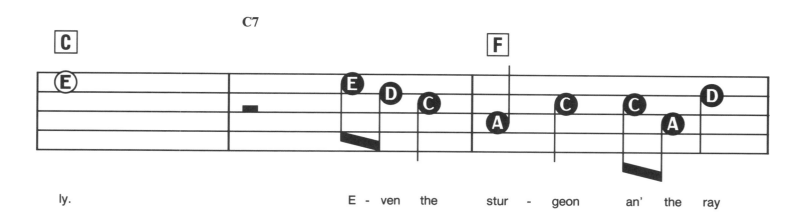

ly. E - ven the stur - geon an' the ray

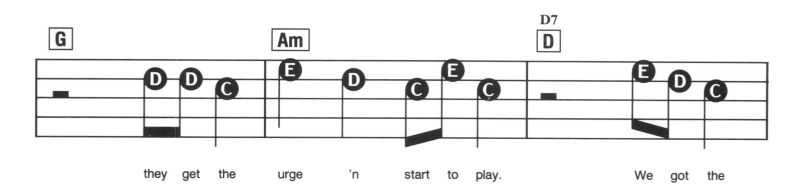

they get the urge 'n start to play. We got the

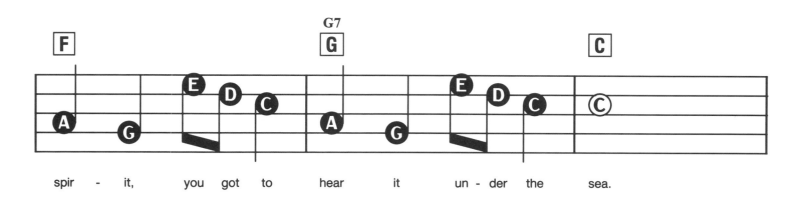

spir - it, you got to hear it un - der the sea.

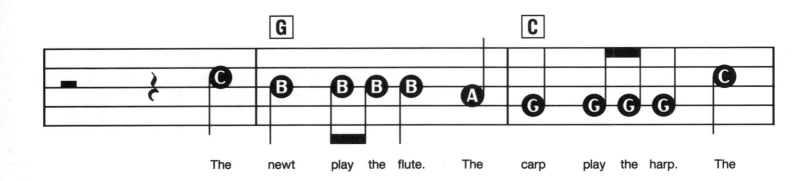

The newt play the flute. The carp play the harp. The

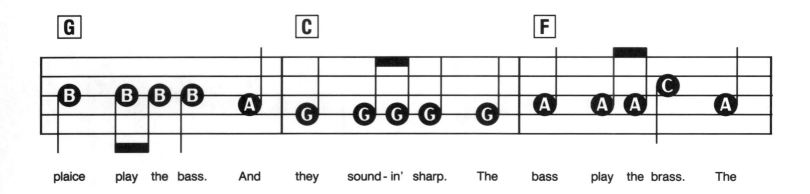

plaice play the bass. And they sound-in' sharp. The bass play the brass. The

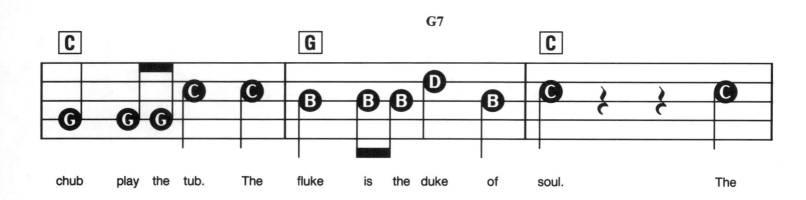

chub play the tub. The fluke is the duke of soul. The

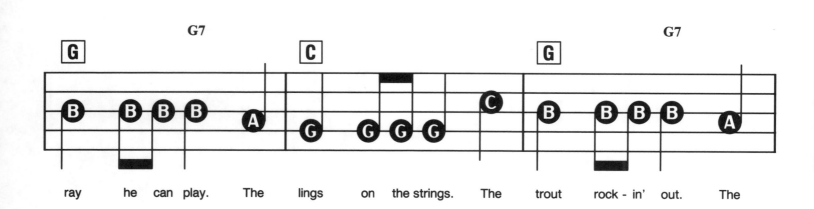

ray he can play. The lings on the strings. The trout rock-in' out. The

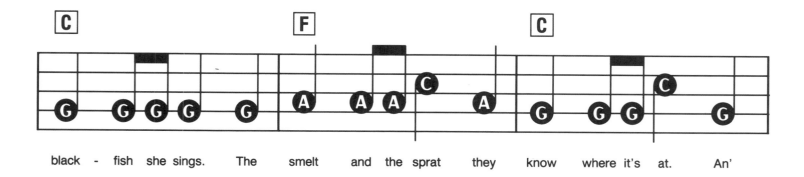

black - fish she sings. The smelt and the sprat they know where it's at. An'

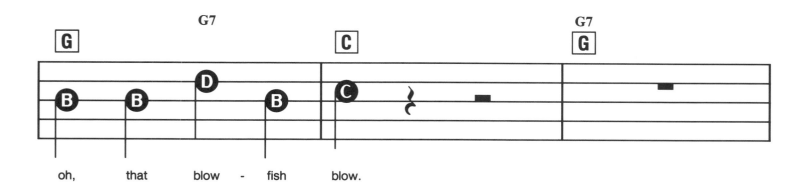

oh, that blow - fish blow.

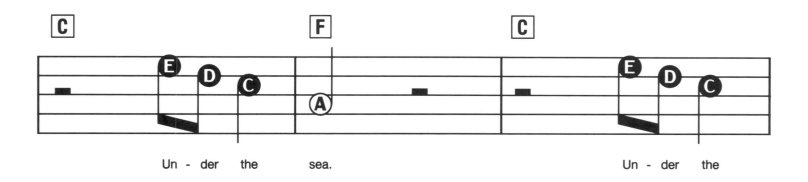

Un - der the sea. Un - der the

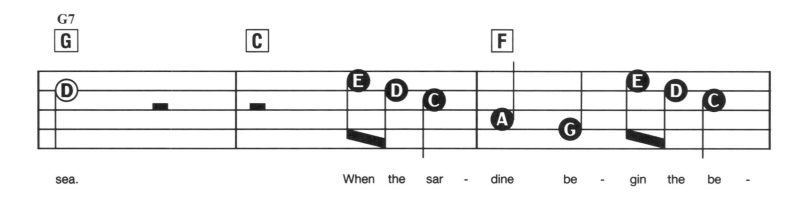

sea. When the sar - dine be - gin the be -

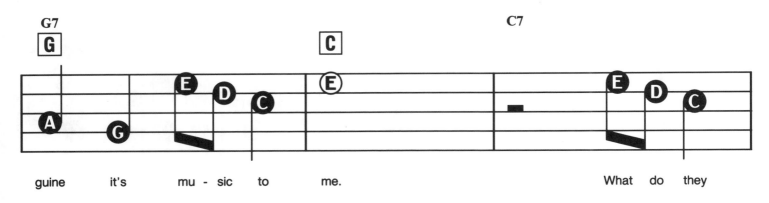

guine it's mu - sic to me. What do they

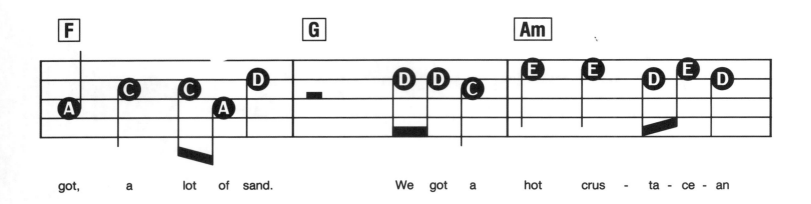

got, a lot of sand. We got a hot crus - ta - ce - an

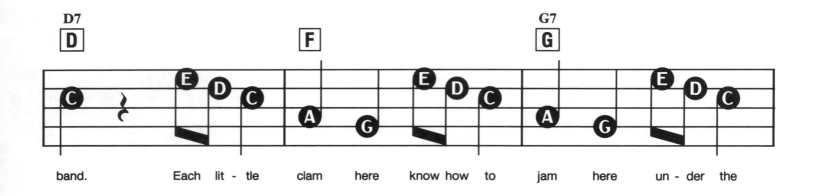

band. Each lit - tle clam here know how to jam here un - der the

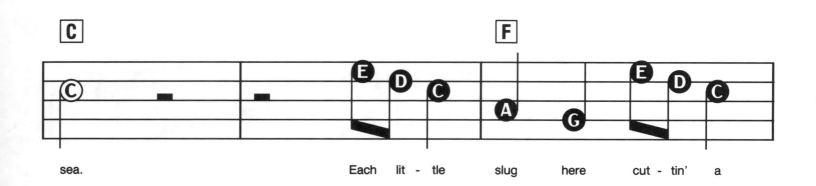

sea. Each lit - tle slug here cut - tin' a

251

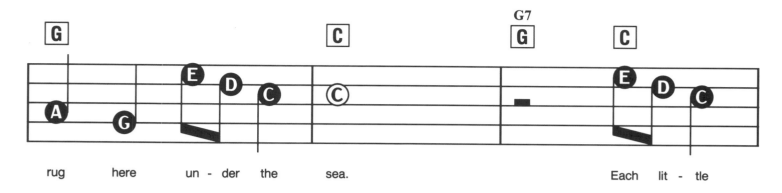

rug here un - der the sea. Each lit - tle

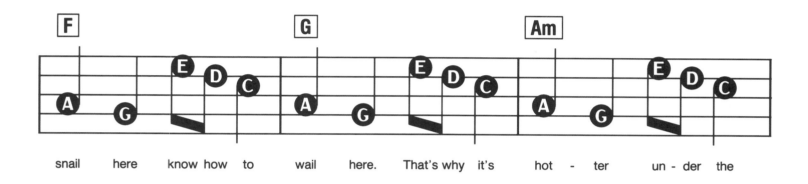

snail here know how to wail here. That's why it's hot - ter un - der the

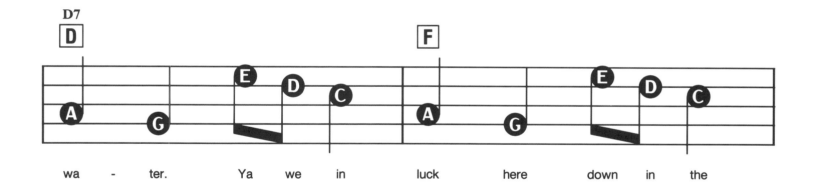

wa - ter. Ya we in luck here down in the

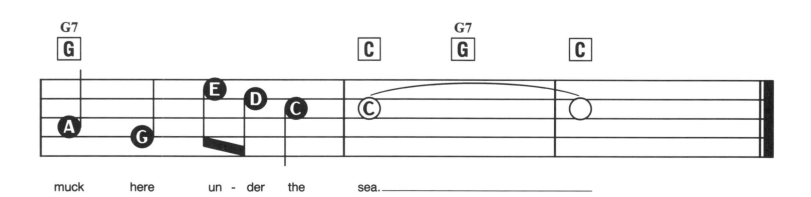

muck here un - der the sea.

1990
How Am I Supposed to Live Without You

Registration 3
Rhythm: Rock or Pops

Words and Music by Michael Bolton
and Doug James

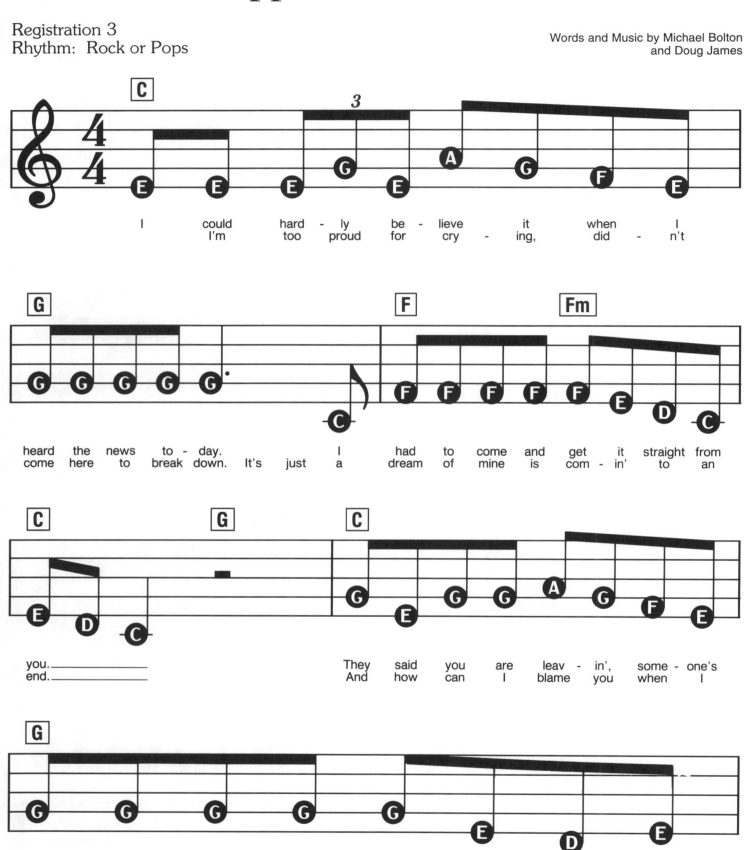

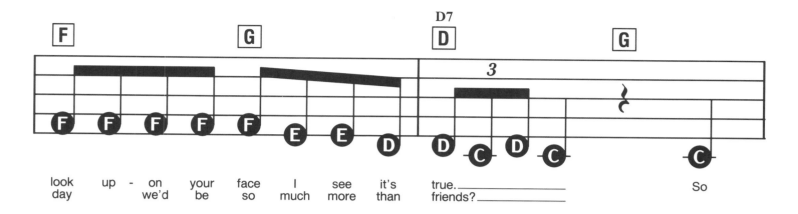

look up - on your face I see it's true. So
day we'd be so much more than friends?

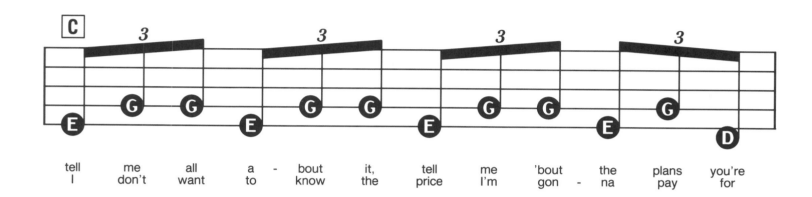

tell me all a - bout it, tell me 'bout the plans you're
I don't want to know the price I'm gon - na pay for

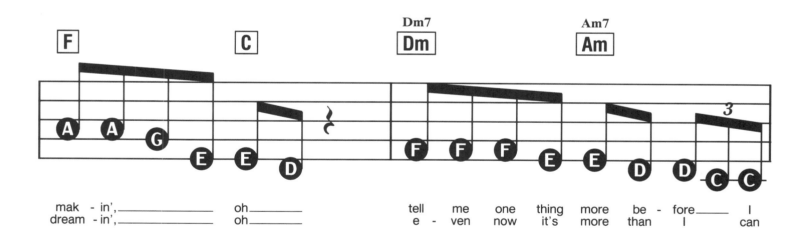

mak - in', oh
dream - in', oh

tell me one thing more be - fore I
e - ven now it's more than I can

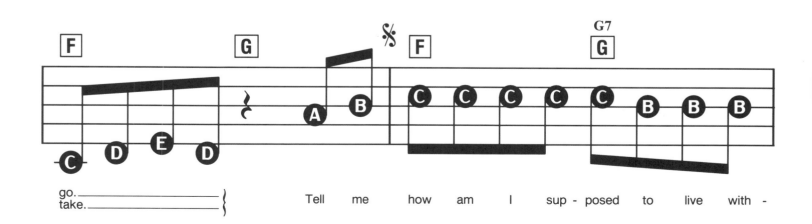

go.
take.

Tell me how am I sup - posed to live with -

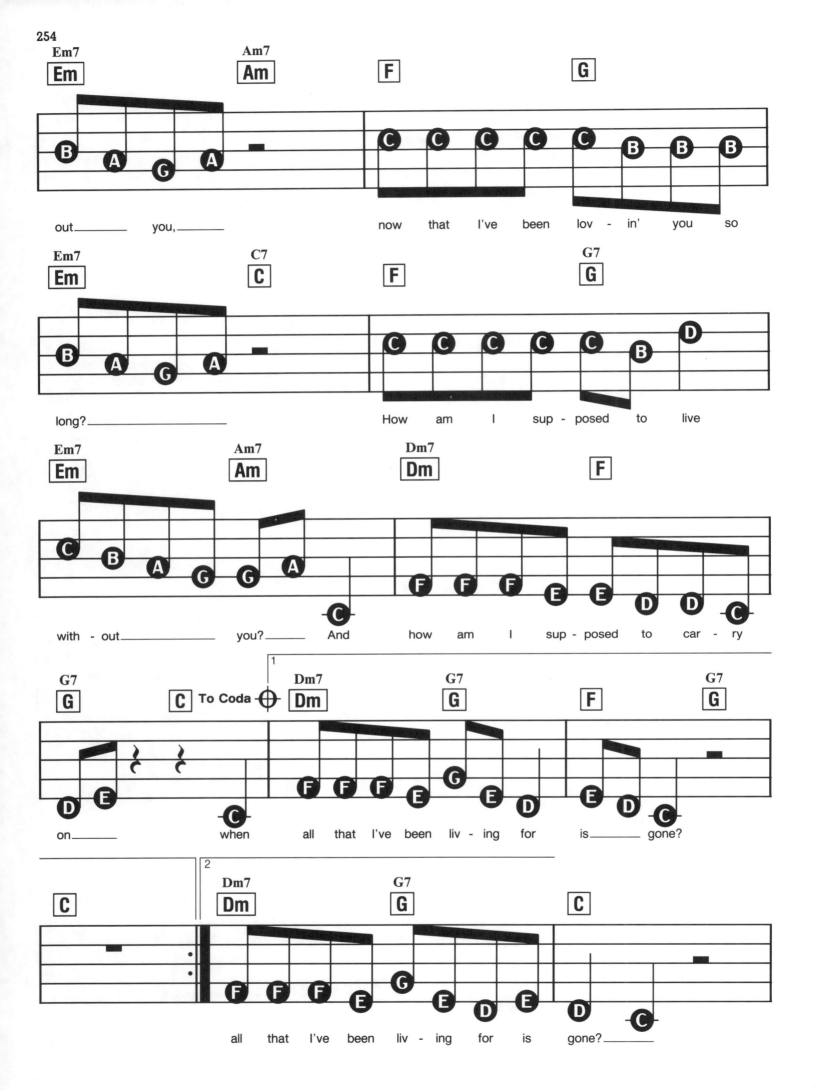

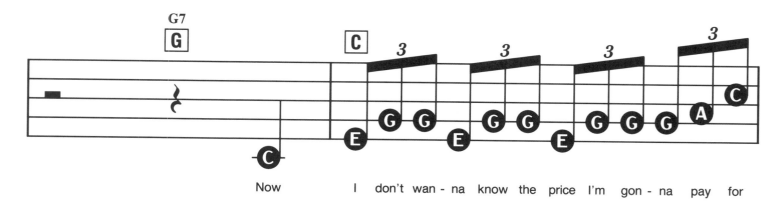

Now   I don't wan - na know the price I'm gon - na pay for

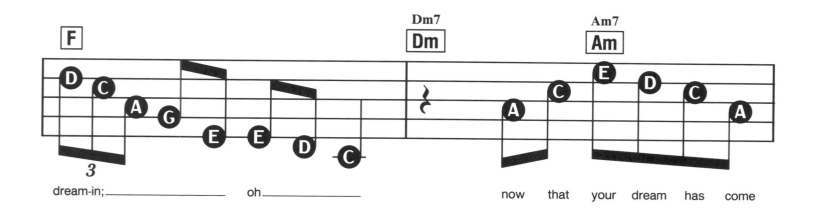

dream-in;_____   oh_____   now   that   your   dream   has   come

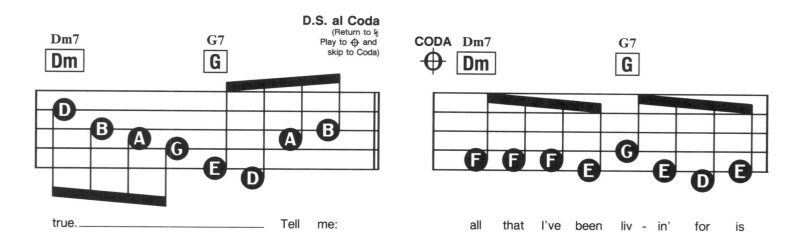

true._____ Tell me: all   that   I've   been   liv - in'   for   is

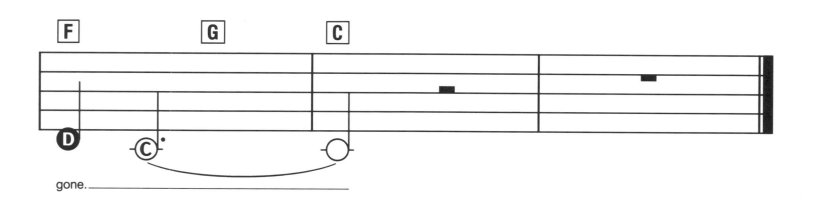

gone._____

1991

Someday

Registration 9
Rhythm: Rock or 8 Beat

Words and Music by Mariah Carey
and Ben Margulies

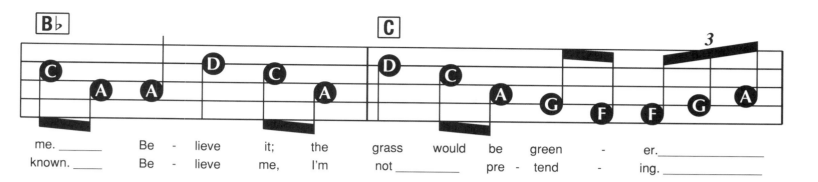

me. _____ Be - lieve it; the grass would be green - er._____
known. _____ Be - lieve me, I'm not _____ pre - tend - ing. _____

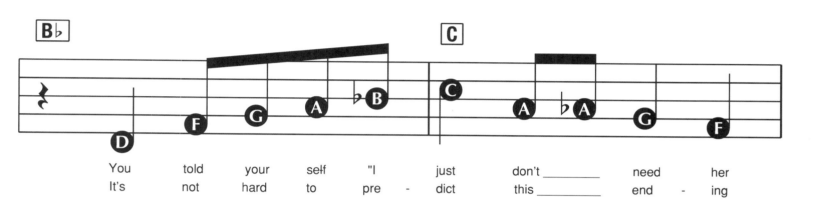

You told your self "I just don't _____ need her
It's not hard to pre - dict this _____ end - ing

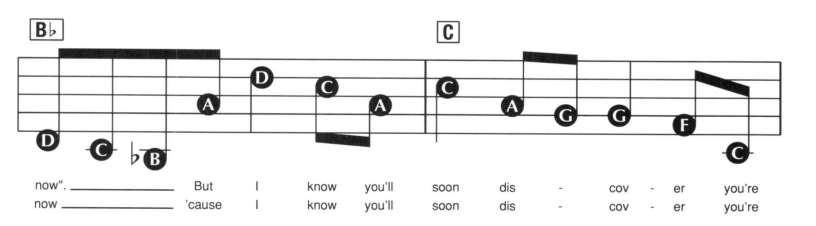

now". _____ But I know you'll soon dis - cov - er you're
now _____ 'cause I know you'll soon dis - cov - er you're

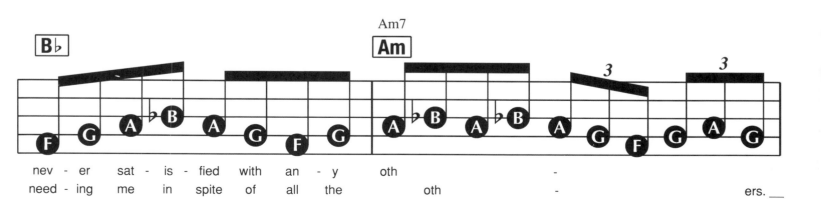

nev - er sat - is - fied with an - y oth -
need - ing me in spite of all the oth - ers. __

258

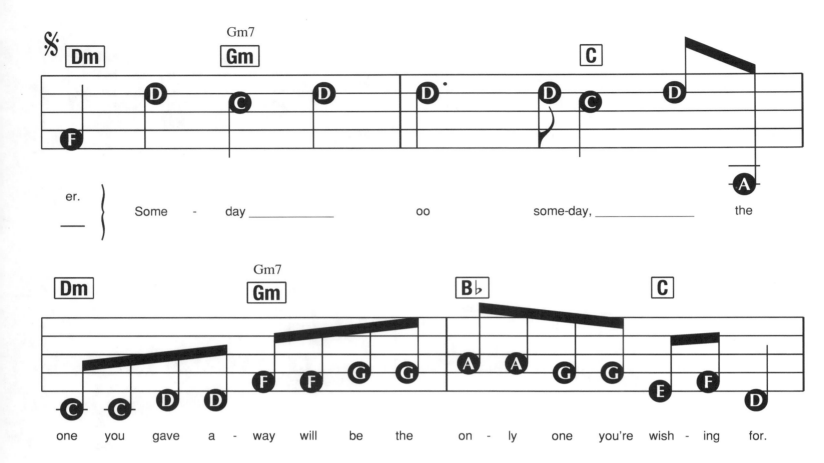

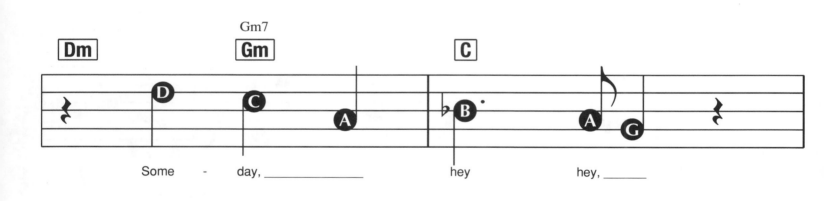

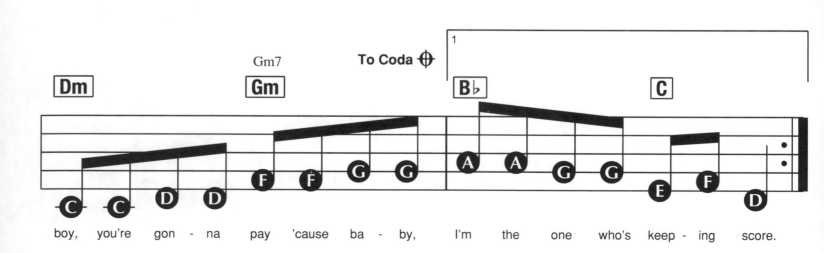

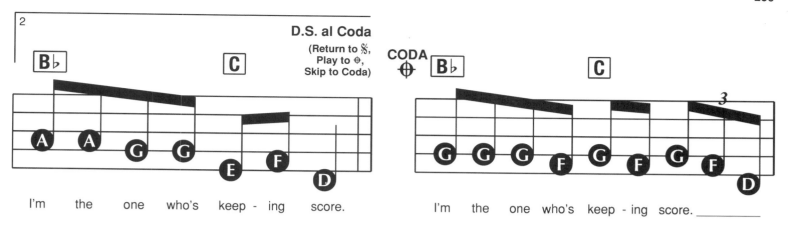

D.S. al Coda
(Return to %,
Play to ⊕,
Skip to Coda)

I'm the one who's keep-ing score.

I'm the one who's keep-ing score. _____

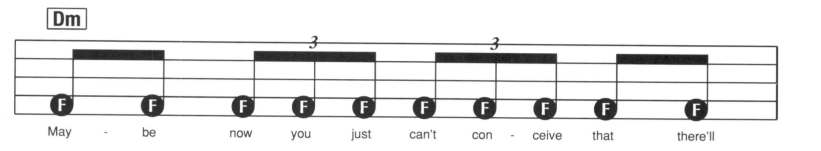

May - be now you just can't con - ceive that there'll

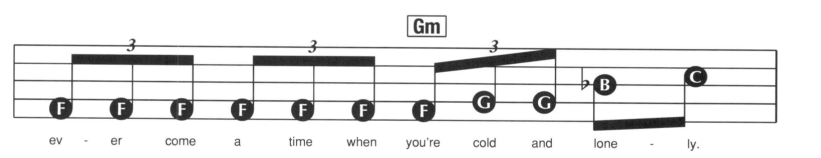

ev - er come a time when you're cold and lone - ly.

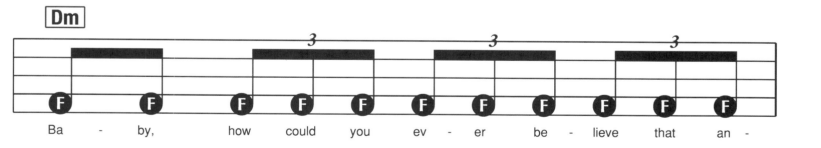

Ba - by, how could you ev - er be - lieve that an -

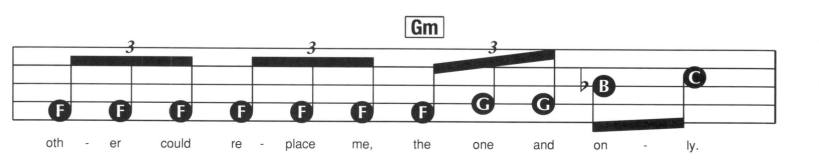

oth - er could re - place me, the one and on - ly.

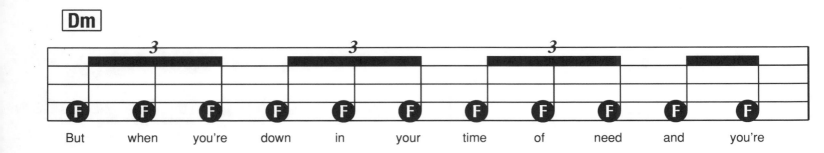

But when you're down in your time of need and you're

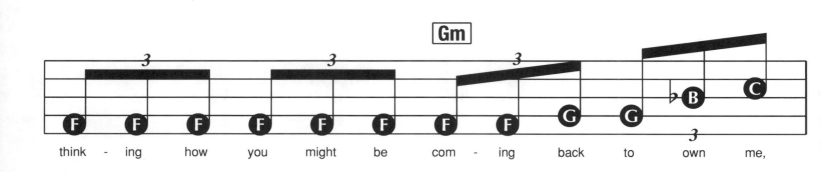

think - ing how you might be com - ing back to own me,

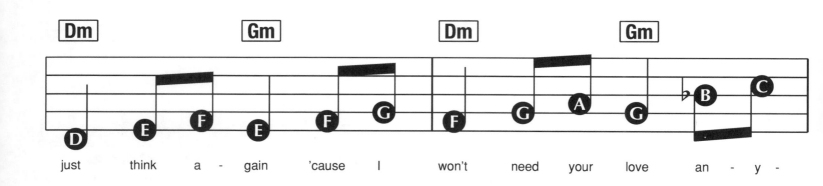

just think a - gain 'cause I won't need your love an - y -

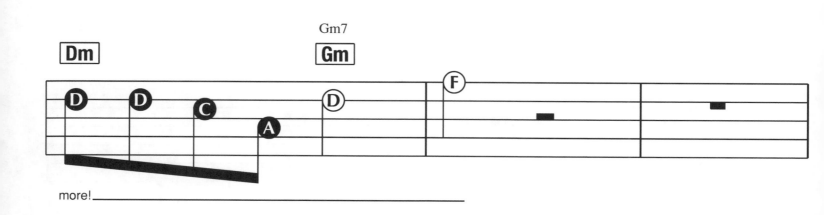

more!

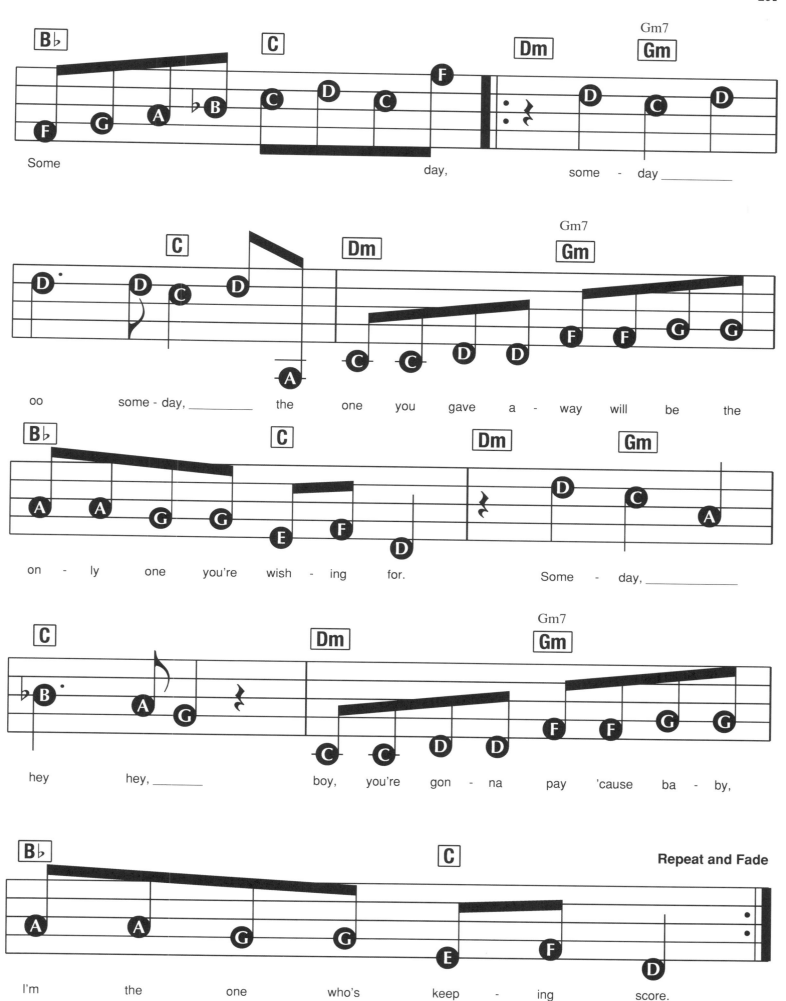

1992

End of the Road
from the Paramount Motion Picture BOOMERANG

Registration 2
Rhythm: Waltz

Words and Music by Babyface,
L.A. Reid and Daryl Simmons

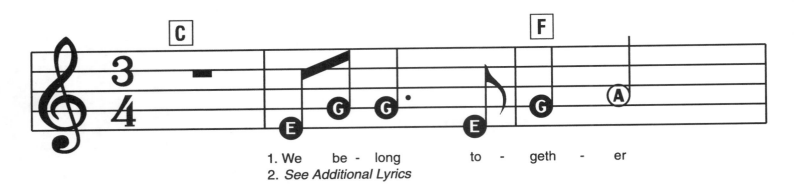

1. We be-long to-geth-er
2. *See Additional Lyrics*

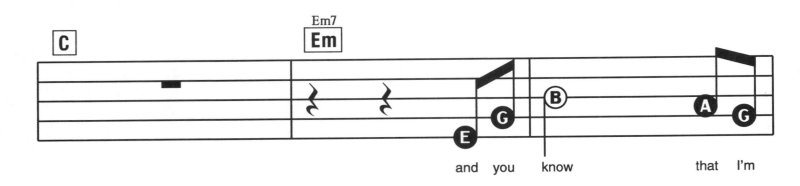

and you know that I'm

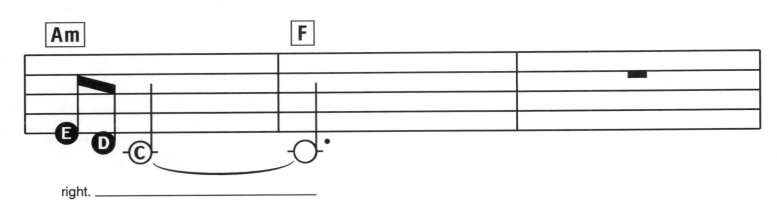

right. _____

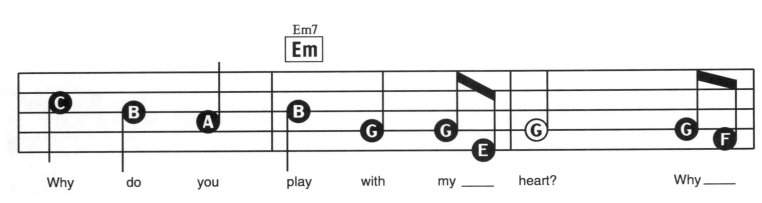

Why do you play with my ____ heart? Why ____

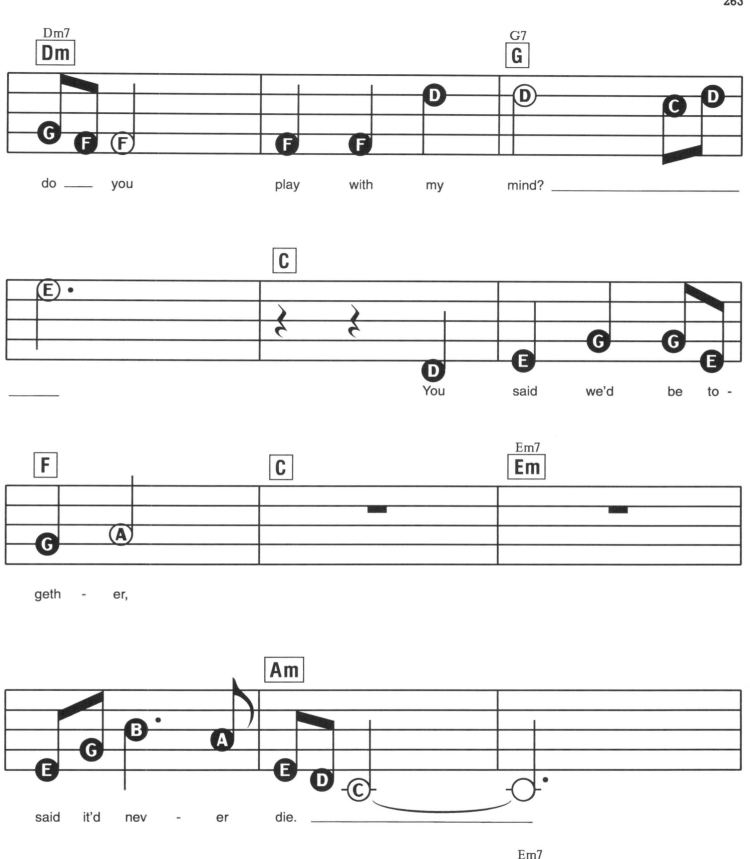

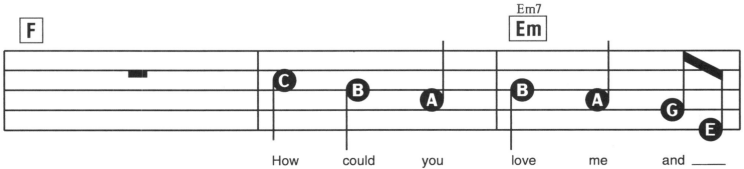

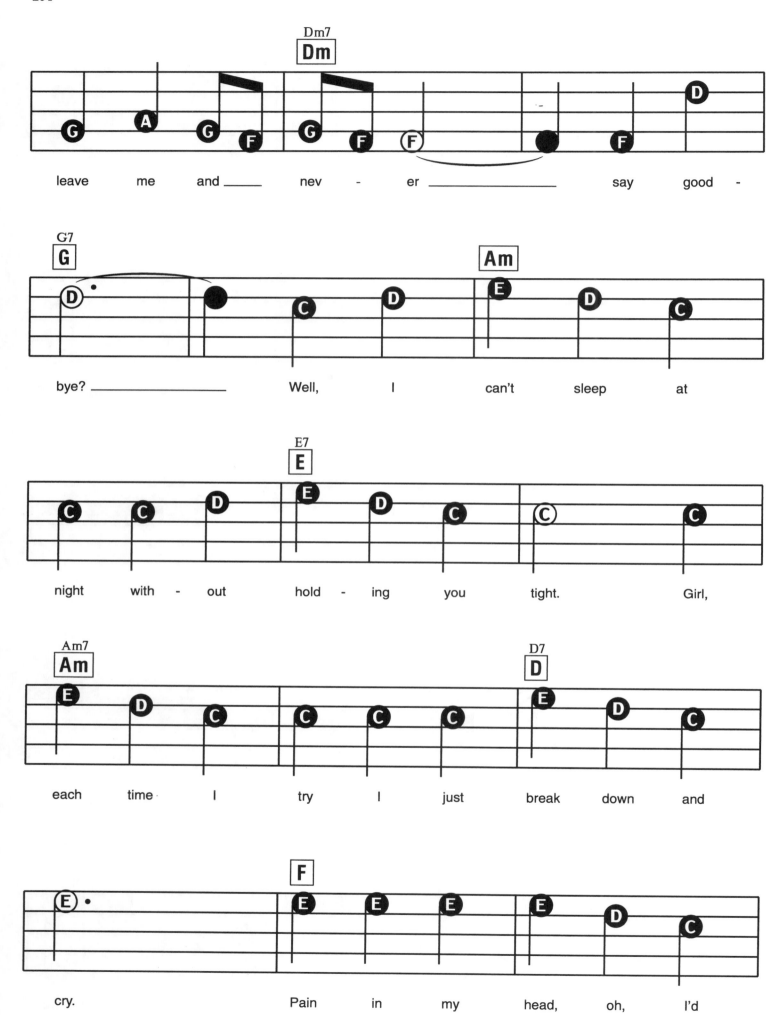

leave   me   and _____   nev - er _____   say   good -

bye? _____   Well,   I   can't   sleep   at

night   with - out   hold - ing   you   tight.   Girl,

each   time   I   try   I   just   break   down   and

cry.   Pain   in   my   head,   oh,   I'd

265

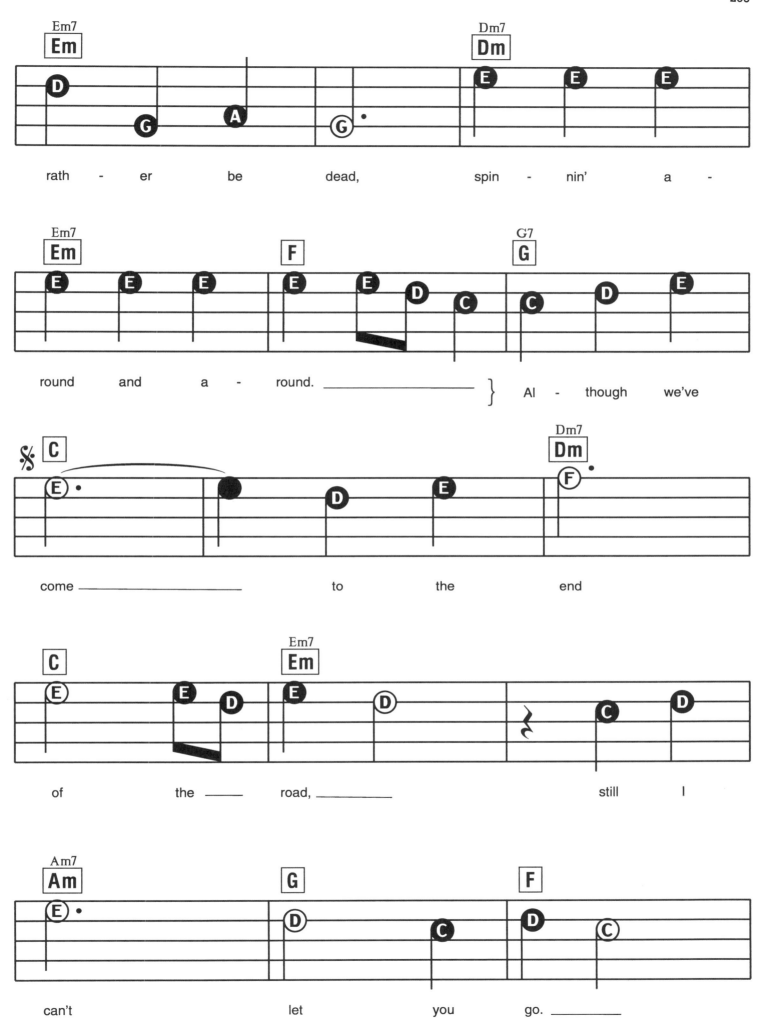

266

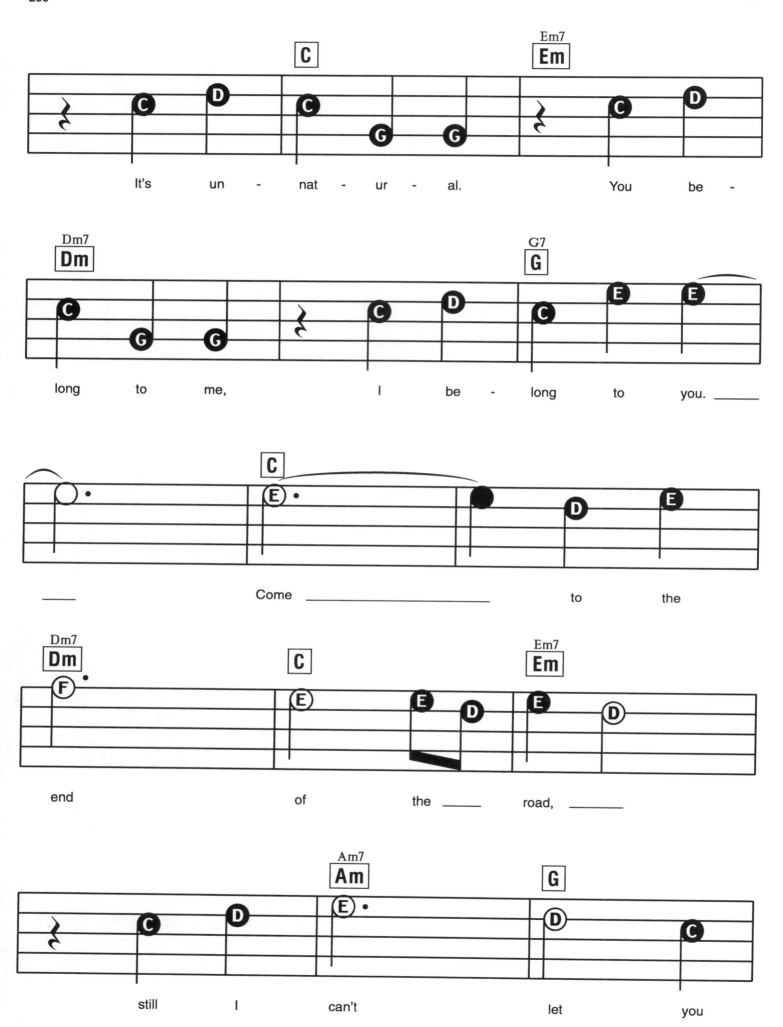

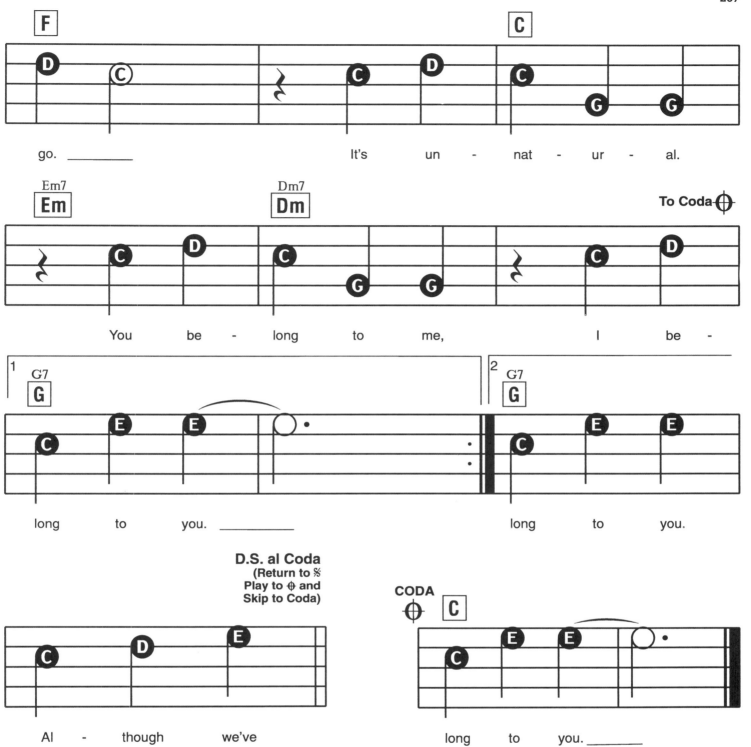

go. _____ It's un - nat - ur - al.

You be - long to me, I be -

long to you. _____ long to you.

D.S. al Coda
(Return to ℅
Play to ⊕ and
Skip to Coda)

Al - though we've

CODA

long to you. _____

Additional Lyrics

2. Girl, I know you really love me, you just don't realize.
   You've never been there before, it's only your first time.
   Maybe I'll forgive you, mmm... maybe you'll try.
   We should be happy together, forever, you and I.

   Could you love me again like you loved me before?
   This time, I want you to love me much more.
   This time, instead just come back to my bed.
   And baby, just don't let me down.

   (Chorus)

1993
Fields of Gold

Registration 4
Rhythm: Rock or 8-Beat

Written and Composed by
Sting

You'll re - mem - ber me, when the west wind moves up -
stay with me, when will you be my love a -

on the fields of bar - ley.
mong the fields of bar - ley?

You'll for - get the sun in his
We'll for - get the sun in his

jeal - ous sky as we walk in fields of gold.
jeal - ous sky as we lie in fields of gold.

So she
See the

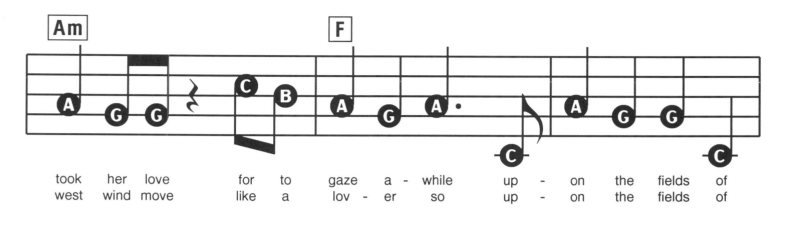

took her love   for to gaze a - while up - on the fields of
west wind move   like a lov - er so up - on the fields of

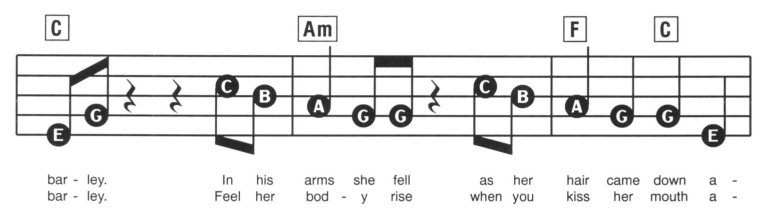

bar - ley.   In his arms she fell as her hair came down a -
bar - ley.   Feel her bod - y rise when you kiss her mouth a -

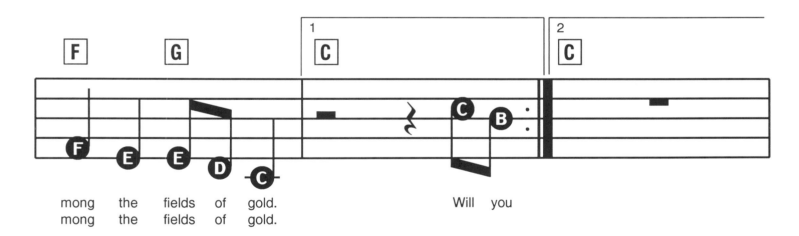

mong the fields of gold.   Will you
mong the fields of gold.

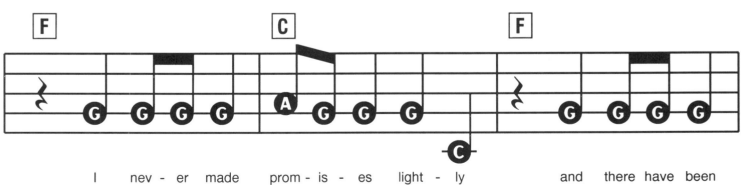

I nev - er made prom - is - es light - ly   and there have been

270

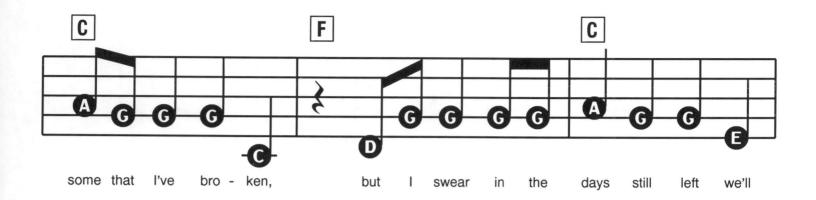

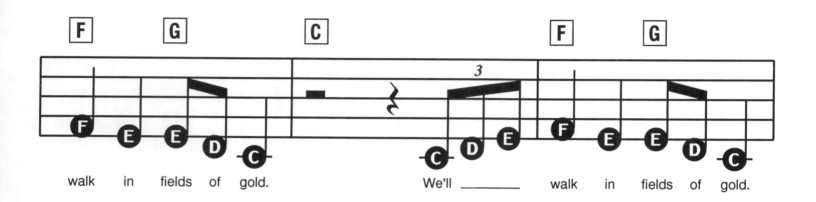

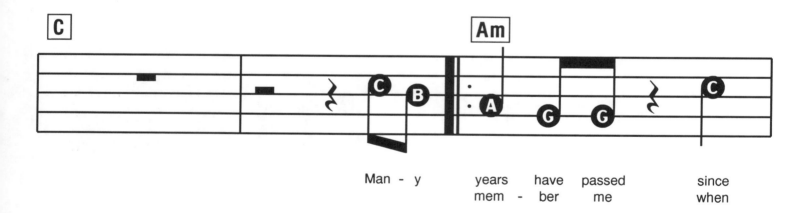

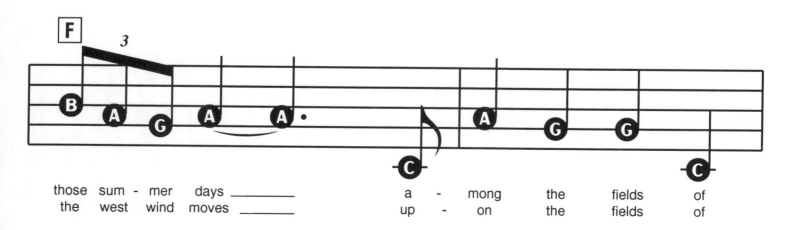

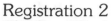

1994

Can You Feel the Love Tonight

from Walt Disney Pictures' THE LION KING

Registration 2
Rhythm: Rock or 8 Beat

Music by Elton John
Lyrics by Tim Rice

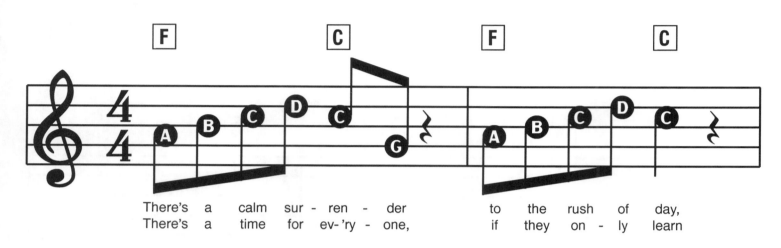

There's a calm sur - ren - der   to the rush of day,
There's a time for ev - 'ry - one,   if they on - ly learn

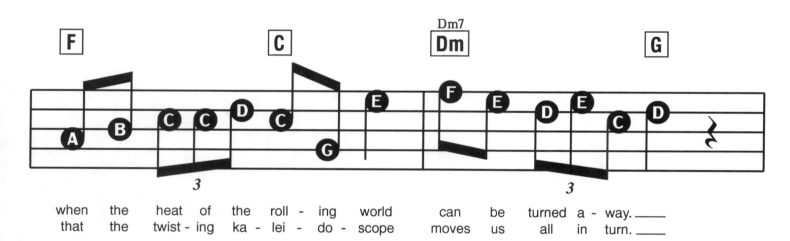

when the heat of the roll - ing world   can be turned a - way.___
that the twist - ing ka - lei - do - scope   moves us all in turn.___

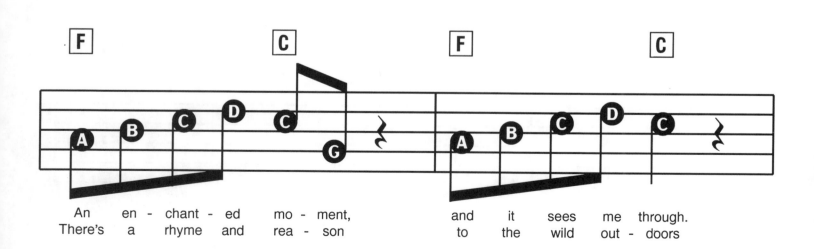

An en - chant - ed mo - ment,   and it sees me through.
There's a rhyme and rea - son   to the wild out - doors

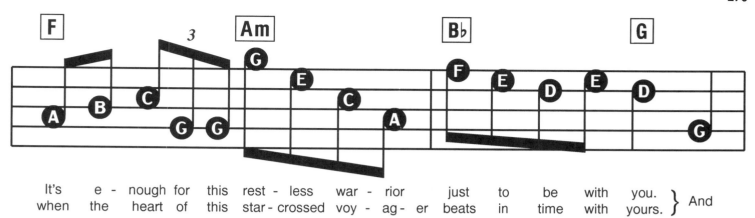

It's e - nough for this rest - less war - rior just to be with you.
when the heart of this star - crossed voy - ag - er beats in time with yours. } And

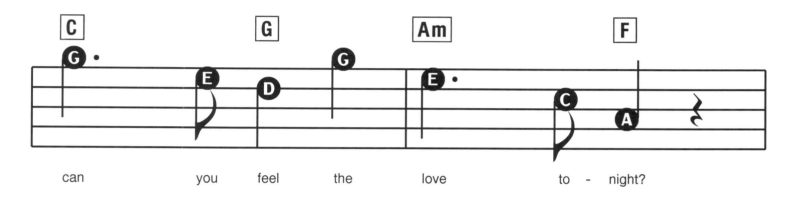

can you feel the love to - night?

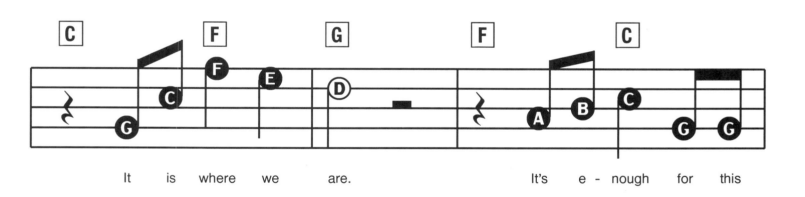

It is where we are. It's e - nough for this

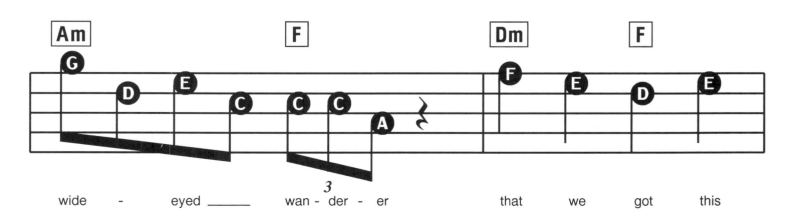

wide - eyed _____ wan - der - er that we got this

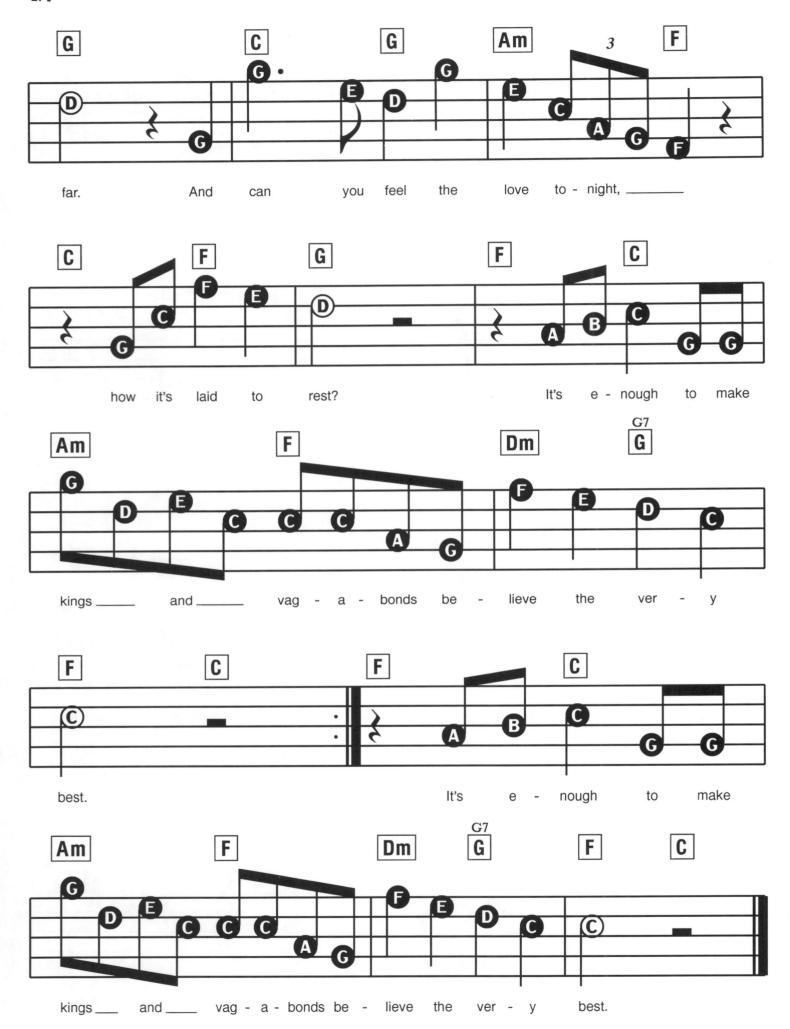

1995

Exhale

(Shoop Shoop)
from the Original Soundtrack Album WAITING TO EXHALE

Registration 2
Rhythm: Ballad or 8 Beat

Words and Music by
Babyface

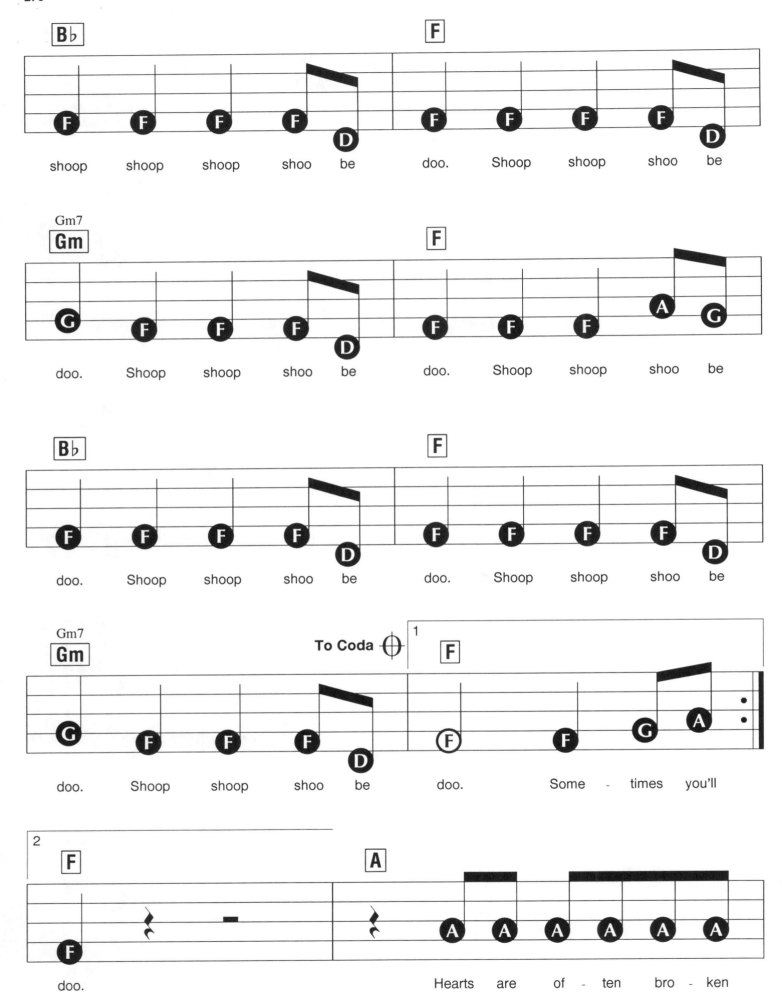

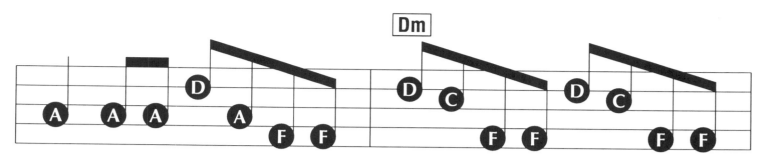

when there are words un - spo - ken. In your soul there's an - swers to your

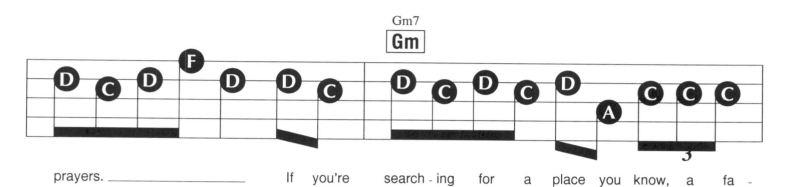

prayers. _____ If you're search - ing for a place you know, a fa -

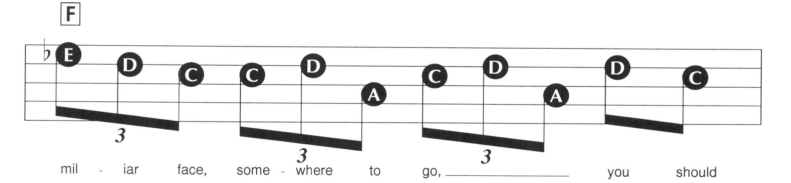

mil - iar face, some - where to go, _____ you should

D.S. al Coda
(Return to 𝄋
Play to ⊕ and
Skip to Coda)

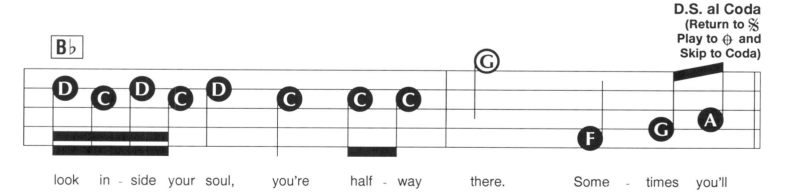

look in - side your soul, you're half - way there. Some - times you'll

CODA

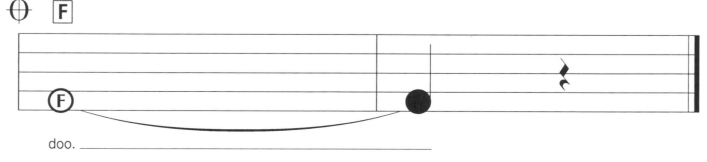

doo. _____

1996
I Finally Found Someone
from THE MIRROR HAS TWO FACES

Registration 2
Rhythm: Rock or 8 Beat

Words and Music by Barbra Streisand, Marvin Hamlisch,
R.J. Lange and Bryan Adams

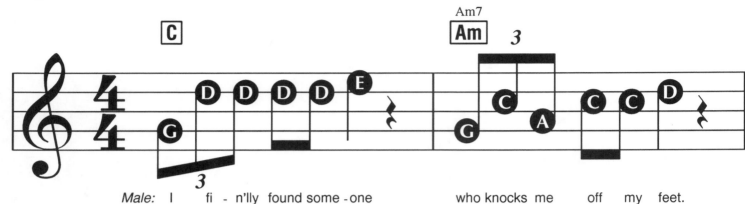

Male: I fi - n'lly found some - one who knocks me off my feet.

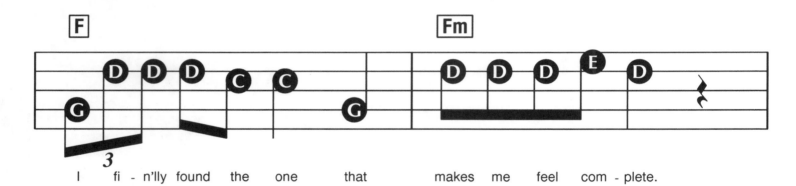

I fi - n'lly found the one that makes me feel com - plete.

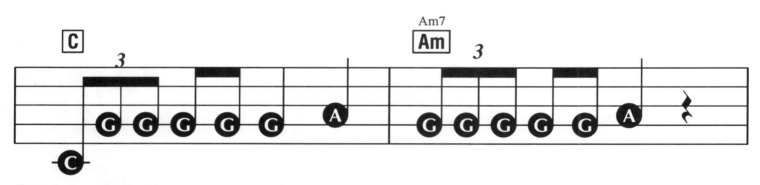

Female: It start - ed o - ver cof - fee. We start - ed out as friends.

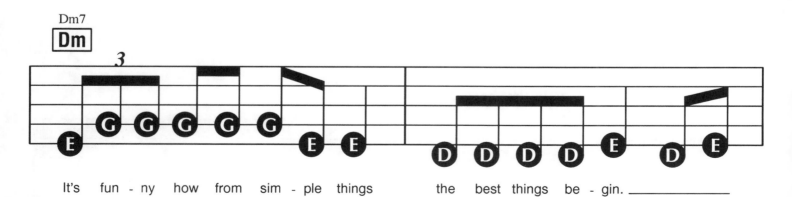

It's fun - ny how from sim - ple things the best things be - gin. _____

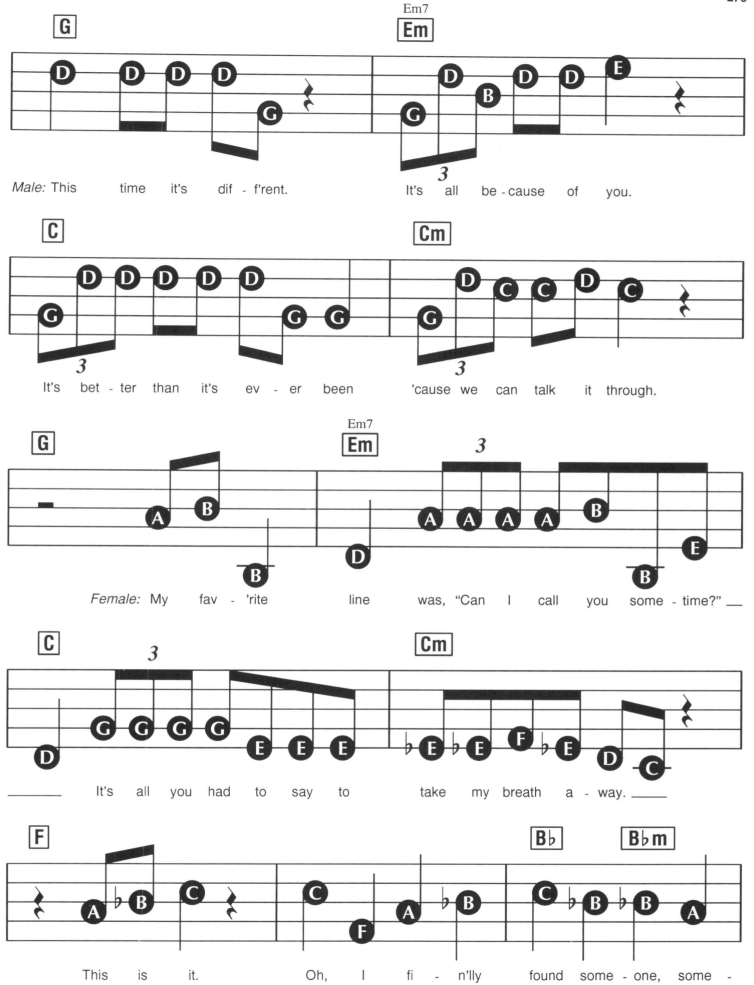

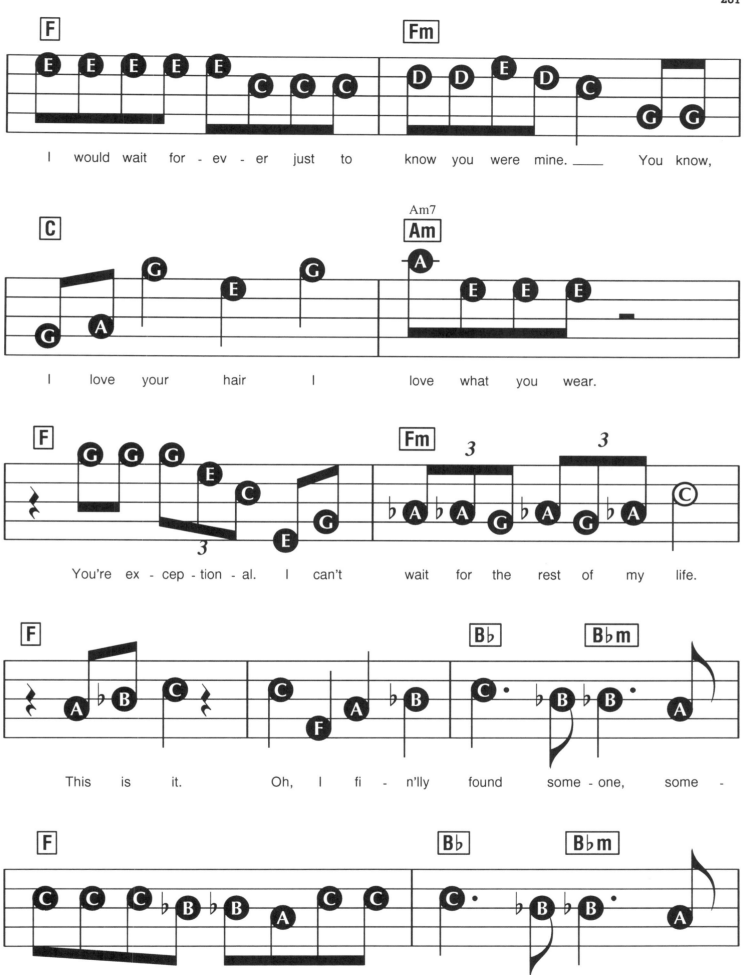

282

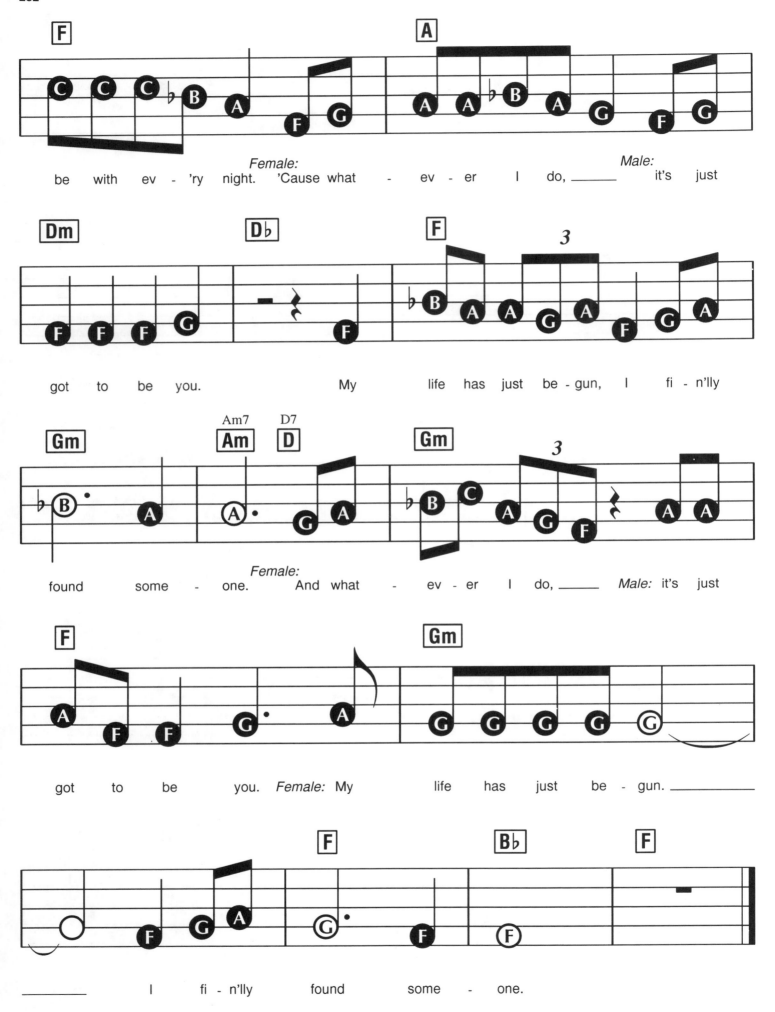

1997
Butterfly Kisses

Registration 8
Rhythm: Ballad

Words and Music by Randy Thomas
and Bob Carlisle

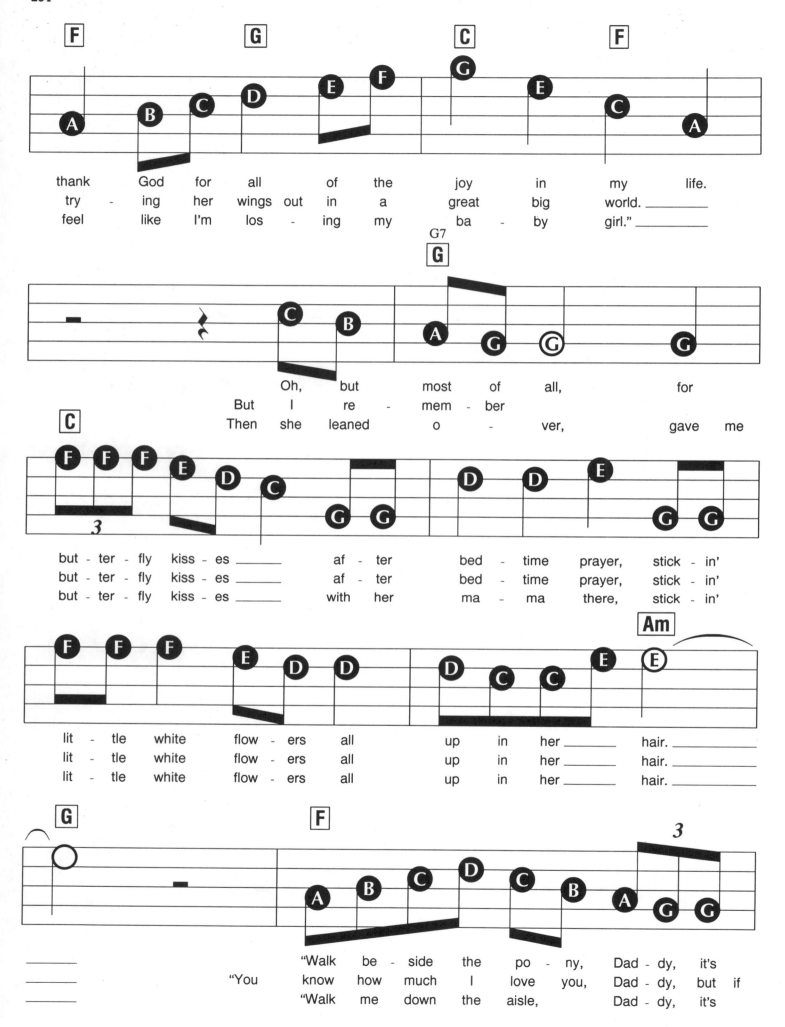

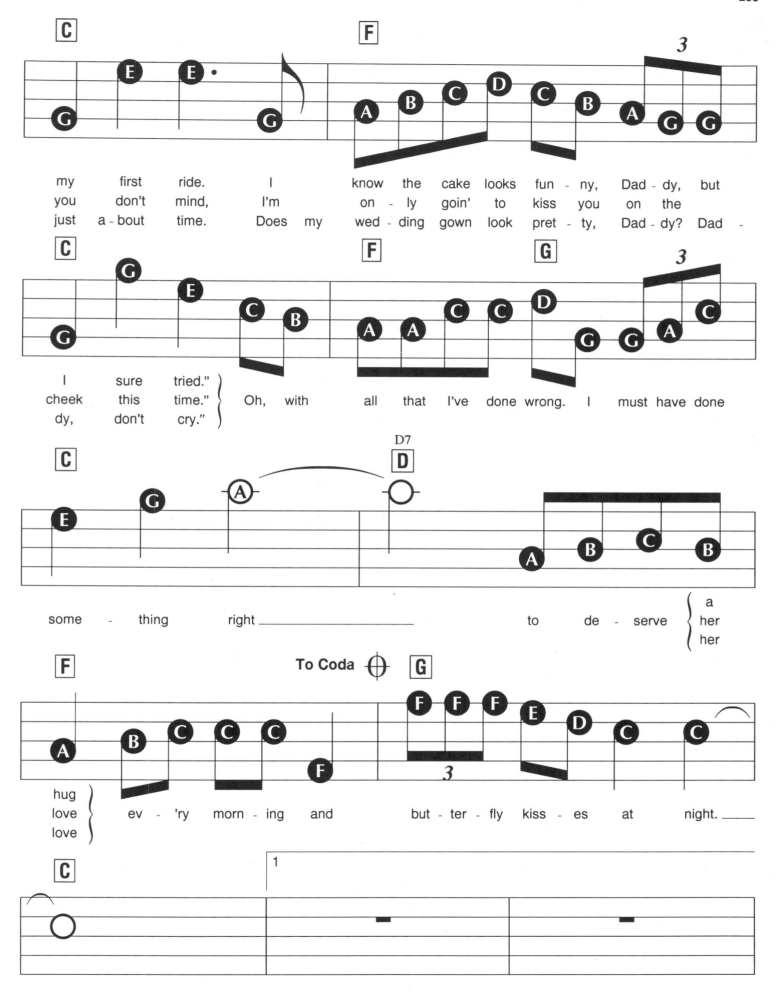

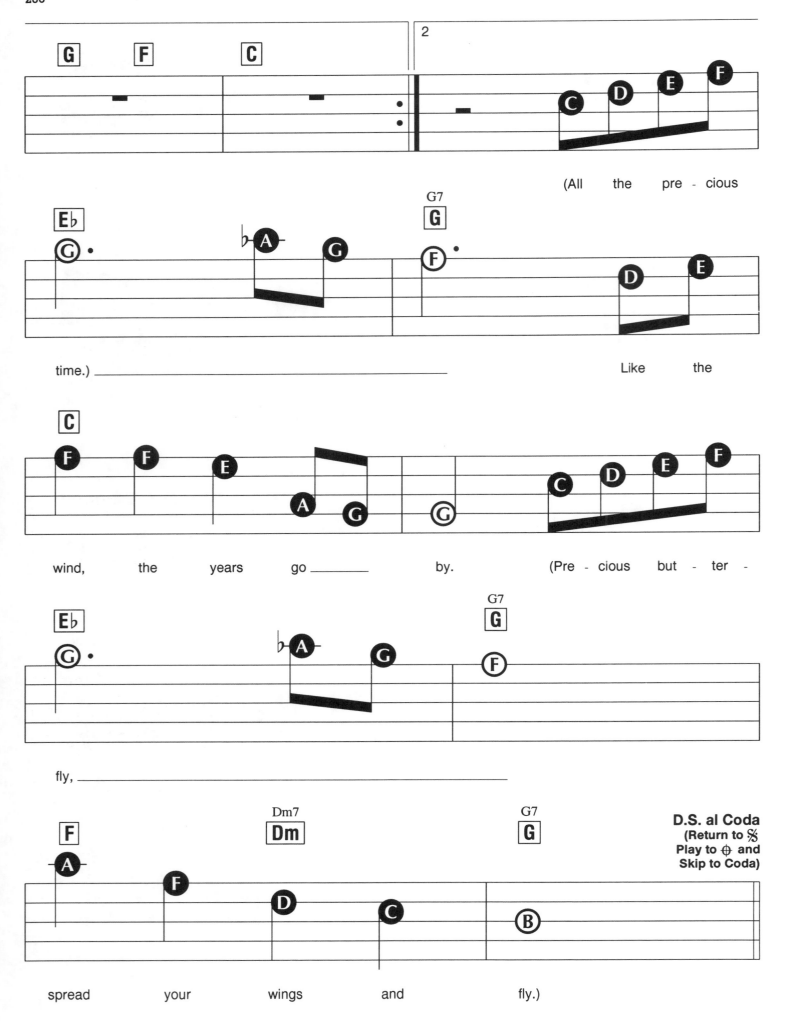

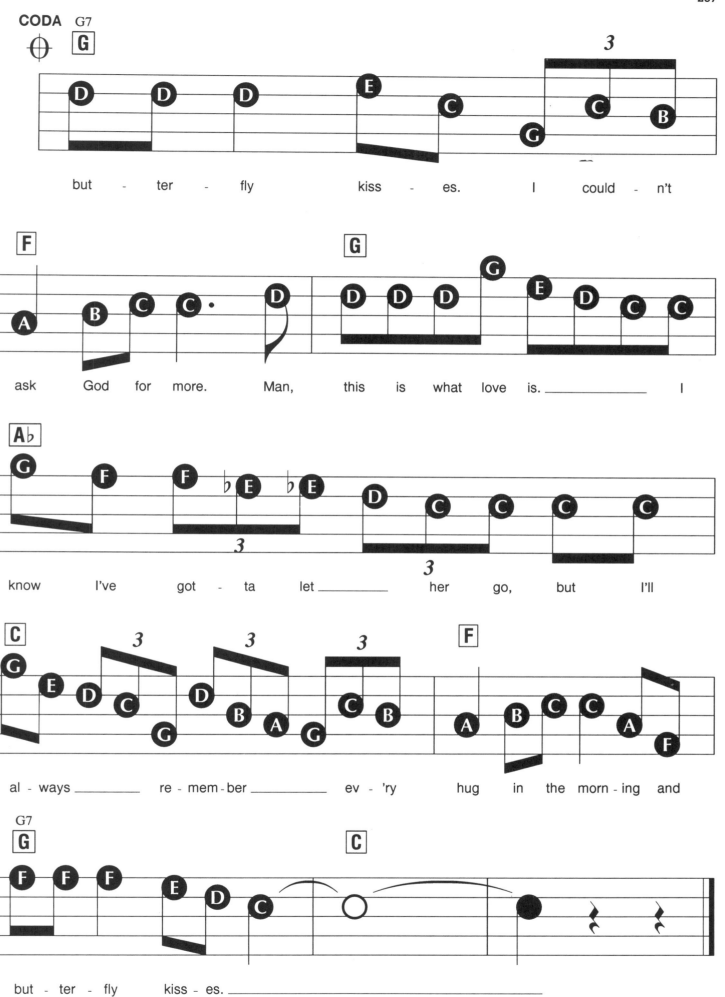

1998
You're Still the One

Registration 9
Rhythm: Rock or 8 Beat

Words and Music by
Shania Twain and R.J. Lange

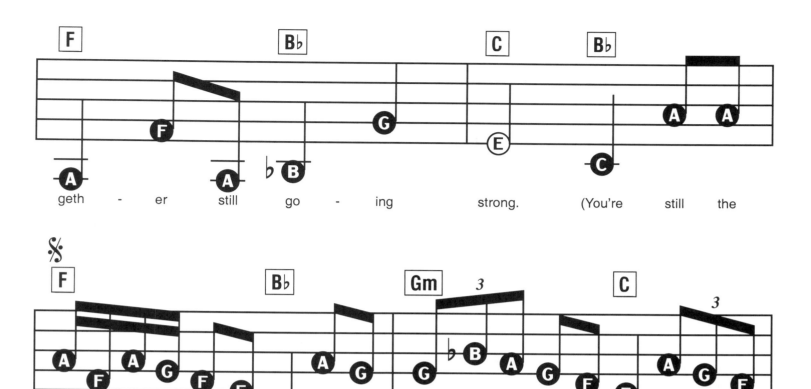

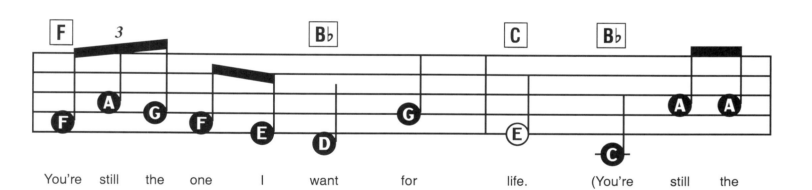

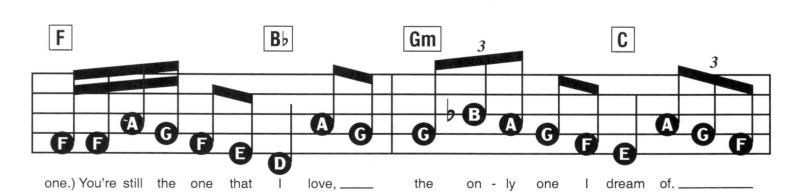

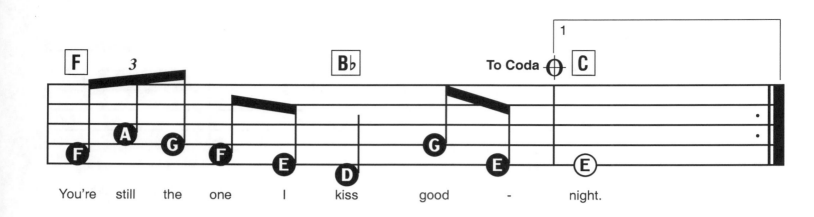

You're still the one I kiss good - night.

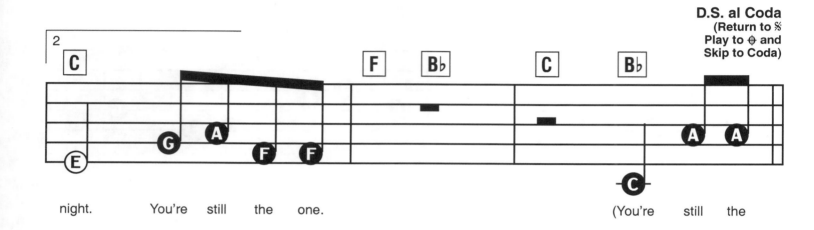

night. You're still the one. (You're still the

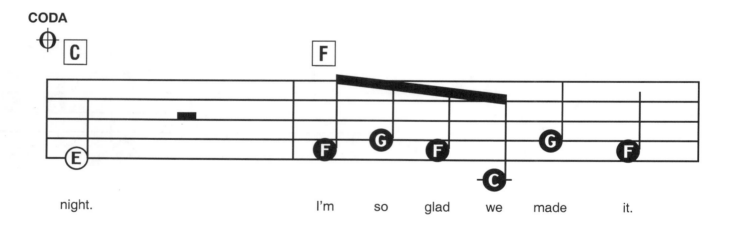

night. I'm so glad we made it.

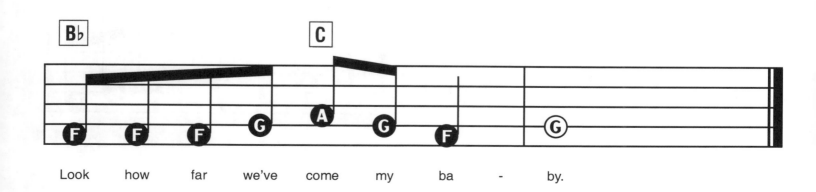

Look how far we've come my ba - by.

1999
You'll Be in My Heart
(Pop Version)
from Walt Disney Pictures' TARZAN™

Registration 1
Rhythm: Rock or Pops

Words and Music by
Phil Collins

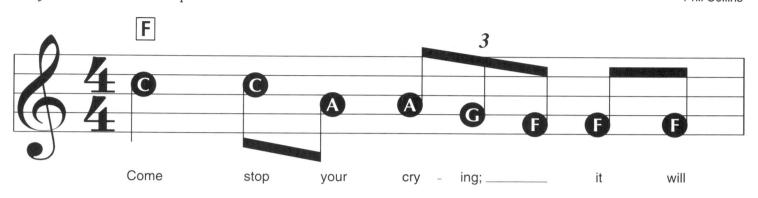

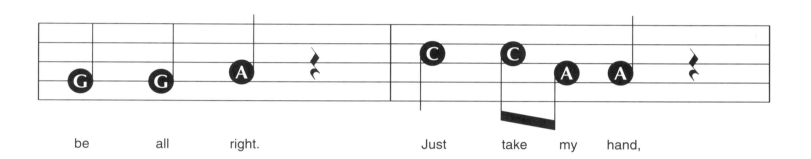

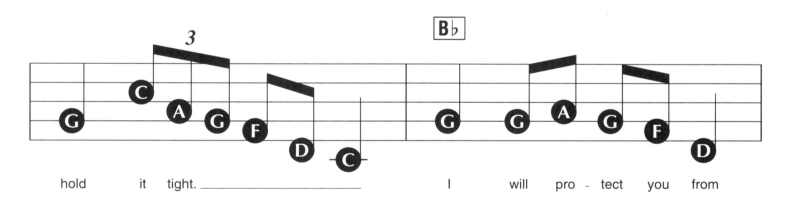

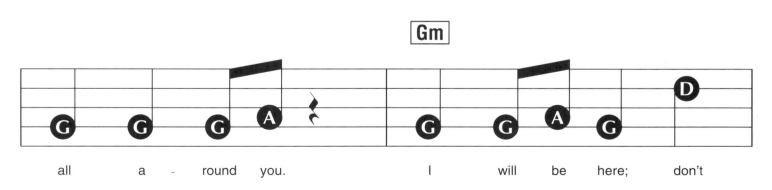

292

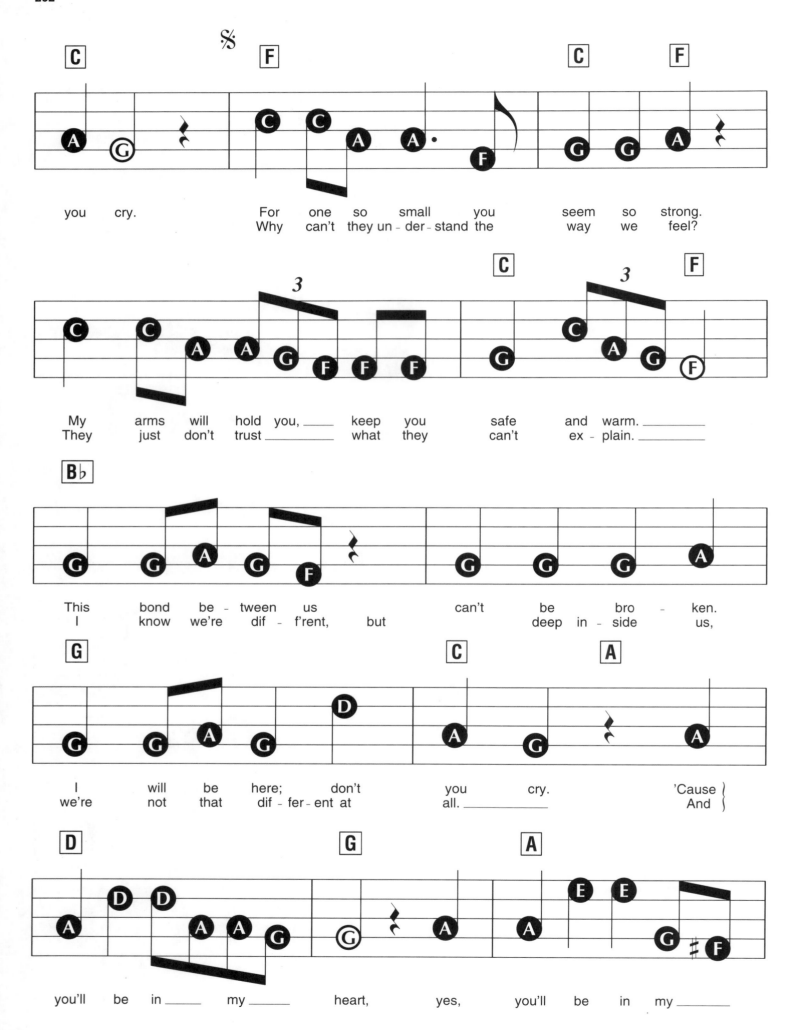

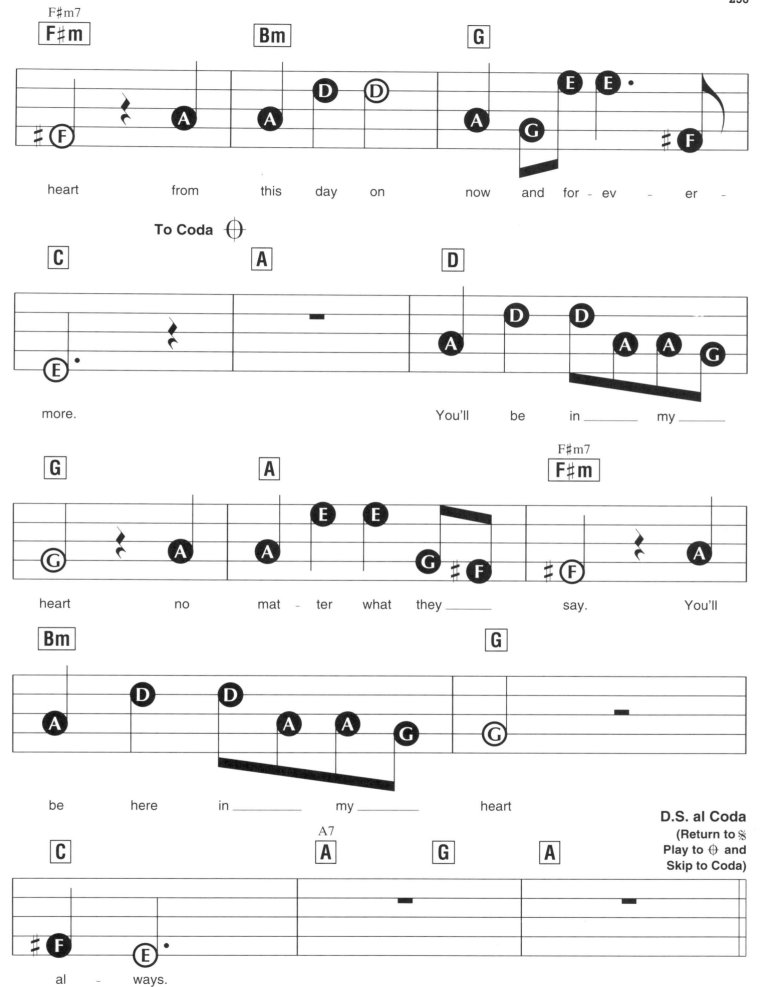

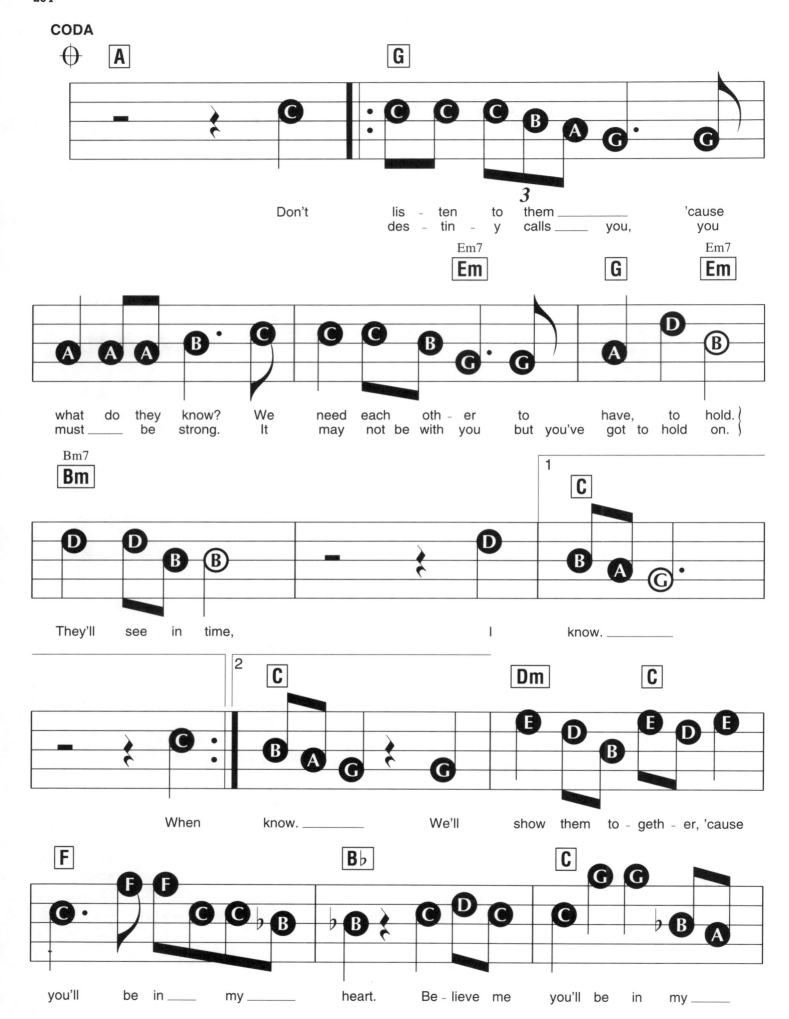

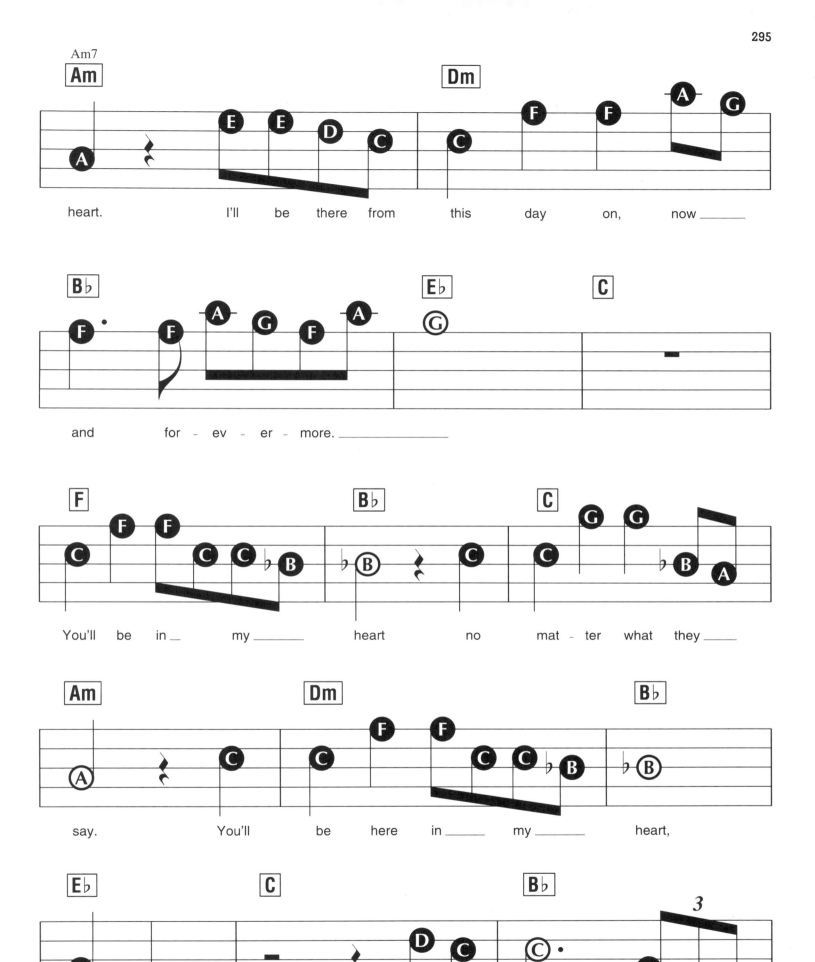

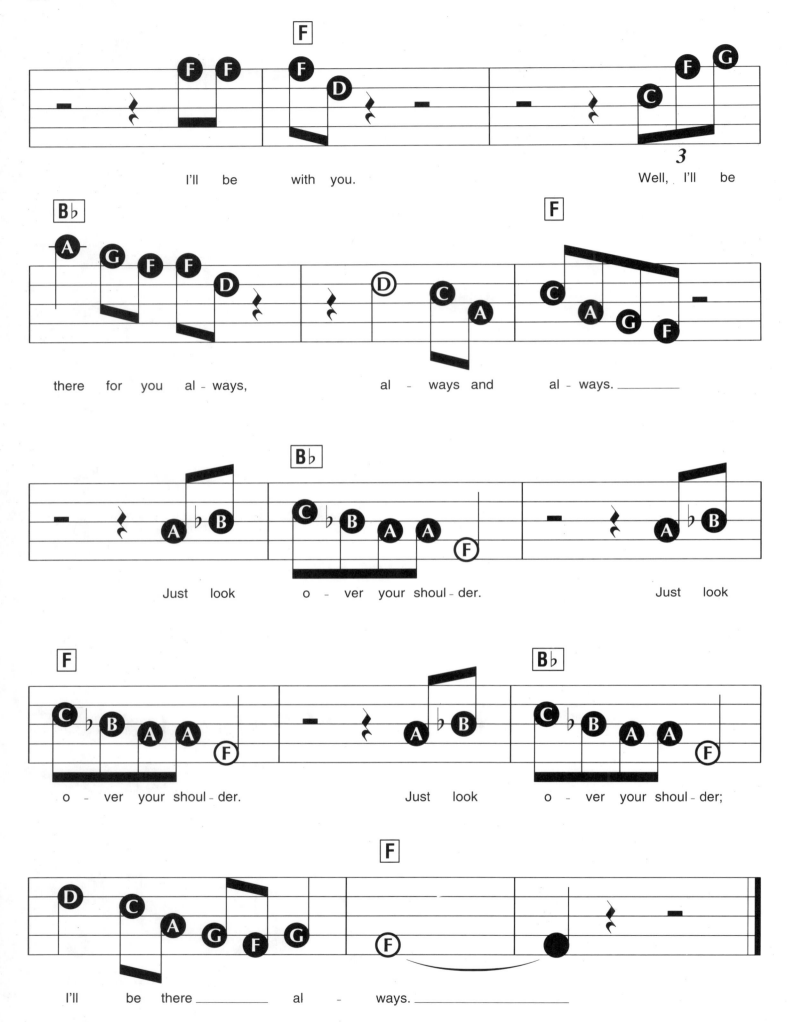